# RATING
# SCALE
# ANALYSIS

# RATING SCALE ANALYSIS

**Benjamin D. Wright**
**Geofferey N. Masters**

*University of Chicago*

MESA PRESS
Chicago
1982

MESA PRESS
5835 Kimbark Ave.
Chicago, IL
60637

Printed in the United States of America
Library of Congress Catalog Card Number 81-84992
ISBN 0-941938-01-8
Cover Design: Andrew W. Wright
Composition: Christopher S. Cott

# PREFACE

This is a book about constructing variables and making measures. We begin by outlining the requirements that a number must meet before it qualifies as a "measure" of something. Our requirements for measurement may seem stringent, but they are not new. They characterize all the instances of useful scientific measurement that we have been able to find. We suspect that their neglect by social scientists has stemmed from the belief that such requirements can never be met in social science research. We do not share this belief. When the basic requirements of the method we describe are approximated in practice, they open the way to measuring systems which enable objective comparisons, useful predictions and the construction of firm bases for the study of psychological development.

The first requirement for making good measures is good raw material. When you construct a variable for yourself, you will have some control over the data you collect. Sometimes, however, the data you work with will be brought to you by someone else, and you will have to do your best with whatever you get. In either case, the materials you work with will have been gathered with a particular purpose in mind. At the heart of this purpose will be the intention to make comparisons along a particular line of inquiry. To achieve this the data must contain the possibility of a single variable along which persons can be measured.

We recommend beginning with a careful examination of the data. In Chapter 2 we show you a set of data which was sent to us. We lay it out and examine it from a variety of angles. Useful questions to ask at this stage are: Does the researcher have a clear idea of what he wants? Is this reflected in the data he has collected? Do these data seem to add up to something? Can we imagine constructing a single variable from them? An experienced eye is helpful: common sense is essential.

We will show you some techniques that we have developed for inspecting data. What we look for are warps and flaws which could make the construction of a variable difficult, and knot holes which may make some data useless. Sometimes data is too extensive to permit the detailed examination we carry out in Chapter 2, but it is always preferable to pinpoint potential problems at the beginning rather than stumbling over them later. No matter how good our tools, or how experienced we are in building variables and making measures, if our data are inadequate, then we will be unable to make useful measures from them.

In Chapter 3 we describe some models for measuring. These are the tools we use to build variables and make measures. We will show you five different measurement models, each of which has been developed for a particular type of data. The model you use will depend on how the data you are working with have been collected and what they are intended to convey. The five models are members of a family of models which share the same basic structure. There are other models in the literature, but in our work we insist on using members of this particular family because only these models are capable of meeting our standards for measurement.

Chapter 4 shows you how to use these models to get results.   We describe four different estimation procedures.   The one you use will depend on your purpose, the nature of the data you are working with and how you do your computing.   The first procedure *PROX* is simple and convenient and does not require a computer.   While *PROX* does not take full advantage of the capabilities of these models, the results it gives are good enough for many applications.   The second procedure *PAIR* is convenient if your data are incomplete.   It can help you to make the best use of the fragments of data you do have.   The third procedure *CON* makes full use of the capabilities of these models but incurs the heaviest computational load and can incur computational problems when attempted with large numbers of items.   The fourth procedure *UCON* is the one we use routinely.   Its results are indistinguishable from those of *CON*, and we have found it fully effective with the variety of data we have examined.

The last and perhaps most important phase in the construction of a variable is its quality control.   We take this up in Chapter 5.   The first question we ask of our analysis is:   Have we succeeded in defining a direction? The "separation" index we describe in Chapter 5 can be used to assess the extent to which items and persons have been separated along a common line.   Only if items are well separated will we be able to tell whether we have succeeded in defining a variable.   Only if persons are well separated will we be able to identify and study individual differences along the variable which the items define.

Once we have established that we have built something of potential utility, the next question is: Does the variable we have built make sense?   You will want to inspect the finished product to see if it makes sense to you.   If you are building a variable for somebody else, the real test will come when you present them with the results of your efforts.   Do they recognize the variable you have constructed as the variable which they hoped would emerge from the data they collected?   Have the pieces come together in a way that makes sense to them?

It is essential at this stage to identify flaws which could limit the utility of the variable or the validity of the measures made with it.   We will describe some procedures for identifying and summarizing misfit.   What we are looking for are weak spots in the construction—items which do not contribute to the definition of a coherent and useful variable, and persons who have not used these items in the way that was intended.   We will analyze the response patterns of some persons with unusual or inconsistent responses, and discuss some frequently encountered problems, like differences in "response set", which you may need to watch for in your work.

Finally, it is important to investigate the extent to which the tentative variable is useful in general: the extent to which its utility can be maintained over time and in other contexts.   We outline some techniques for comparing and monitoring the performances of items over time and from group to group.

In Chapters 6, 7, 8 and 9 we illustrate the use of these techniques by applying them to four quite different data sets.   The data we analyze were collected to measure attitudes towards drug use, fear of crime, knowledge of elementary physics and the development of prekindergarten children.   We offer these four examples to help you see how our methods might be used.

This book has its roots in the measurement philosophy of Georg Rasch, our foundation and guiding star.   It was born in David Andrich's pioneering work on the analysis of rating scales, and nourished in Geoff Masters' doctoral dissertation. The analysis of partial credit data was original with Geoff.

The kind of work we discuss leans heavily on computing. We are deeply indebted to Larry Ludlow for his many valuable contributions to our main computer program, CREDIT.

The companionship, constructive criticism and creative participation of able colleagues has played an especially important part in our work. We are particularly grateful to our MESA colleagues Richard Smith, Tony Kalinowski, Kathy Sloane and Nick Bezruczko. Bruce Choppin and Graham Douglas helped us to make the writing clearer and the algebra more correct. The beautiful graphs were constructed by Mark Wilson. Our opportunity to do this work was greatly enlarged by generous financial support from the Spencer Foundation and the National Institute of Justice.

Benjamin D. Wright
Geofferey N. Masters

*The University of Chicago*
*January 31, 1982*

# CONTENTS

PREFACE                                                                    v

## 1. ESSENTIALS FOR MEASUREMENT                                          1

1.1 Inventing Variables                                                    1
1.2 Constructing Observations                                              3
1.3 Modelling Observations                                                 3
1.4 Building Generality                                                    5
    1.4.1 Frames of Reference                          5
    1.4.2 Continuity                                    6
    1.4.3 Objectivity, Sufficiency and Additivity      6
1.5 Quantifying Comparisons                                                8
    1.5.1 Arithmetic and Linearity                     8
    1.5.2 Origins and Zero Differences                 9
    1.5.3 Units and Least Observable Differences        9

## 2. EXAMINING DATA                                                       11

2.1 An Attitude to Science Variable                                        11
2.2 The Science Questionnaire                                              12
2.3 How Judges Order the Science Activities                                12
2.4 How Children Respond to the Science Activities                         15
    2.4.1 Choosing a Response Format                    15
    2.4.2 The Science Data Matrix                       17
    2.4.3 Scoring Responses Dichotomously              23
2.5 Problems with Scores                                                   32
    2.5.1 The Need for Linearity                        33
    2.5.2 The Need for Sample-free Item Calibrations and
        Test-free Children Measures  34
    2.5.3 The Need for a Common Scale for Children and Activities   34

## 3. MODELS FOR MEASURING                                                 38

3.1 The Family of Models                                                   38
    3.1.1 Dichotomous                                   38
    3.1.2 Partial Credit                                40
    3.1.3 Rating Scale                                  48
    3.1.4 Binomial Trials                               50
    3.1.5 Poisson Counts                                52
3.2 Distinguishing Properties of Rasch Models                              54
    3.2.1 Operating Curves are Logistic Ogives with the Same Slope   54
    3.2.2 Date are Counts of Events                     56
    3.2.3 Parameters are Separable                      57
    3.2.4 Raw Scores are Sufficient Statistics          59
3.3 Summary                                                                59

## 4. ESTIMATION PROCEDURES                                          60

4.1  Introduction                                                    60
4.2  A Simple Procedure: *PROX*                                      61
    4.2.1  Removing Perfect Scores               61
    4.2.2  Linearizing Activity Scores           62
    4.2.3  Removing Sample Level                  63
    4.2.4  Linearizing Children Scores           64
    4.2.5  Removing Sample Dispersion            64
    4.2.6  Calculating Errors of Calibration     66
    4.2.7  Removing Activity Dispersion          66
    4.2.8  Calculating Errors of Measurement     67
4.3  A Pairwise Procedure: *PAIR*                                    67
    4.3.1  Motivation for *PAIR*                  67
    4.3.2  The *PAIR* Procedure                   69
    4.3.3  Comparing *PAIR* and *PROX* Calibrations  72
4.4  An Unconditional Procedure: *UCON*                              72
    4.4.1  The *UCON* Procedure                  73
    4.4.2  *UCON* Estimates for the Science Data  77
4.5  Estimation Procedures for the Partial Credit Model             80
    4.5.1  *PROX*                                80
    4.5.2  *PAIR*                                82
    4.5.3  *CON*                                 85
    4.5.4  *UCON*                                86

## 5. VERIFYING VARIABLES AND SUPERVISING MEASURES                   90

5.1  Introduction                                                    90
5.2  Defining a Variable by Separating Items                         91
5.3  Developing Construct Validity                                   93
5.4  Analyzing Item Fit                                              94
    5.4.1  Identifying Surprising Responses      94
    5.4.2  Accumulating Item Residuals           99
    5.4.3  Standardizing Mean Squares            101
    5.4.4  Estimating Modelled Expectations      101
    5.4.5  Examining Item Misfit                 101
5.5  Identifying Individual Differences by Separating Persons        105
5.6  Developing Concurrent Validity                                  106
5.7  Analyzing Person Fit                                            108
    5.7.1  Accumulating Person Residuals         108
5.8  ''Reliability'' and ''Validity''                               111
    5.8.1  Test ''Reliability''                  113
    5.8.2  Test ''Validity''                    114
5.9  Maintaining Variables by Comparing Estimates                   114
    5.9.1  Plotting Estimates from Different Occasions  115
    5.9.2  Analyzing Standardized Differences    115
    5.9.3  Analyzing Correlations Between Estimates  115

**6. ATTITUDE TO DRUGS**                                          **118**

    6.1 Data *For* Drugs                                    119
    6.2 Data *Against* Drugs                                123
    6.3 *For* Drugs Variable                                123
    6.4 *Against* Drugs Variable                            125
    6.5 Results of the Analyses                             125
    6.6 Comparing *For* and *Against* Statements            129
    6.7 Person Diagnosis                                    132
    6.8 Discussion                                          135

**7. FEAR OF CRIME**                                             **137**

    7.1 A Fear of Crime Variable                            137
    7.2 Results of Rating Scale Analysis                     138
    7.3 Results of Partial Credit Analysis                   142
    7.4 Comparing SCALE and CREDIT Analyses                  145
        7.4.1 Comparing Step Estimates                145
        7.4.2 Comparing Item Fit Statistics           147
    7.5 Discussion                                          151

**8. KNOWLEDGE OF PHYSICS**                                      **152**

    8.1 Answer-Until-Correct Scoring                        153
    8.2 Analyzing Performances Dichotomously                 153
        8.2.1 Right First Try (001)                   155
        8.2.2 Right in Two Tries (011)                161
        8.2.3 Comparing Dichotomous Analyses          164
    8.3 Analyzing Performances Trichotomously (012)          168
        8.3.1 Estimating Item Difficulties            168
        8.3.2 Analyzing Item Fit                      171
        8.3.3 Estimating Abilities                    176
        8.3.4 Diagnosing Person Fit                   177
    8.4 Discussion                                          179

**9. PERFORMANCE OF INFANTS**                                    **180**

    9.1 Defining the Ability Variable                       180
        9.1.1 Examining Item Subtasks                 184
    9.2 Analyzing Item Fit                                  190
    9.3 Diagnosing Misfitting Records                       197

REFERENCES                                                       199

INDEX                                                            203

# 1  ESSENTIALS FOR MEASUREMENT

## 1.1  INVENTING VARIABLES

Science marches on the invention of useful schemes for thinking about experience. The transformation of experience into useful plans for action is facilitated by the collection of relevant observations and their successful accumulation and condensation into objective measures. Measurement begins with the idea of a variable or line along which objects can be positioned, and the intention to mark off this line in equal units so that distances between points on the line can be compared.

The *objects* of measurement in this book are persons, and we call the numbers we derive for them "measures". A person's measure is his estimated position on the line of the variable. The *instruments* of observation are questionnaire and test items, and we call the numbers we derive for them "calibrations" to signify their instrumental role in the measuring process. An item's calibration is its estimated position on the line of the variable along which persons are measured. Persons are measured and items are calibrated on the variable which they work together to define.

The construction of a variable requires a systematic and reproducible relation between items and persons. Because items are accessible to invention and manipulation in a way that persons are not, it is useful to think of a variable as being brought out by its items and, in that sense, defined by them. This book is about how to construct variables and how to use them for measuring. While we confine ourselves to persons answering items, the methods we develop to calibrate and measure are quite general and can be applied to any occasion for measurement.

Variables are the basic tools of science. We use variables to focus, gather and organize experience so that objective comparisons and useful predictions can be made. Because we are born into a world full of well-established variables it can seem that they have always existed as part of an external reality which our ancestors have somehow discovered. This idea of science as the discovery of reality is popular. But science is more than discovery. It is also an expanding and ever-changing network of practical inventions. Progress in science depends on the creation of new variables constructed out of imaginative selections and organizations of experience.

The invention of a variable begins when we notice a pattern of related experiences and have an *idea* about these experiences which helps us to remember their pattern. If the idea orients us to more successful action, we take it as an "explanation" of the pattern and call it a theory. The particular pattern which first intrigued us becomes incidental, and the idea becomes a formula for an idealized pattern embodying our theory. Variables are constructed by a step-by-step process, from casual noticing through directed experience and orderly thinking to quantification. This book describes a method for constructing variables and making measures.

Many of the criticisms and questions that have appeared about attitude [as well as mental and psychological] measurement concern the nature of the fundamental concepts involved and the logic by which measurements are made. . . One of the most frequent questions is that a score on an attitude scale, let us say the scale of attitude toward God, does not truly describe the person's attitude. There are so many complex factors involved in a person's attitude on any social issue that it cannot be adequately described by a simple number such as a score on some sort of test or scale. This is quite true, but it is also equally true of all measurement.

The measurement of any object or entity describes only one attribute of the object measured. *This is a universal characteristic of all measurement.* When the height of a table is measured, the whole table has not been described but only that attribute which has been measured. Similarly, in the measurement of attitudes, only one characteristic of the attitude is described by a measurement of it.

Further, only those characteristics of an object can be measured which can be described in terms of "more" or "less". Examples of such description are: one object is longer than another, one object is hotter than another, one is heavier than another, one person is more intelligent than another, more educated than another, more strongly favorable to prohibition, more religious, more strongly favorable to birth control than another person. These are all traits [i.e., variables] by which two objects or two persons may be compared in terms of "more" or "less".

Only those characteristics can be described by measurement which can be thought of as *linear magnitudes*. In this context, linear magnitudes are weight, length, volume, temperature, amount of education, intelligence, and strength of feeling favorable to an object. Another way of saying the same thing is to note that the measurement of an object is, in effect, to allocate the object to a point on an *abstract continuum*. If the continuum is weight, then individuals [the objects of measurement] may be allocated to an abstract continuum of weight, one direction of which represents small [less] weight while the opposite direction represents large [more] weight. Each person might be allocated to a point on this continuum with any suitable scale which requires some point at which counting begins, called the *origin*, and some *unit of measurement* in terms of which the counting is done.

The linear continuum which is implied in all measurement is always an abstraction. For example, when several people are described as to their weight, each person is in effect allocated to a point on an abstract continuum of weight. All measurement implies the reduction or restatement of the attribute measured to an abstract linear form. There is a popular fallacy that a unit of measurement is a thing—such as a piece of yardstick. This is not so. *A unit of measurement is always a process of some kind which can be repeated without modification in the different parts of the measurement continuum.*

Not all of the characteristics which are conversationally described in terms of "more" or "less" can actually be measured. But any characteristic which lends itself to such description has the possibility of being reduced to measurement. (Thurstone 1931, *257*)

The basic requirements for measuring are:
1) the reduction of experience to a *one dimensional* abstraction,
2) *more or less* comparisons among persons and items,
3) the idea of *linear magnitude* inherent in positioning objects along a line, and
4) a unit determined by a *process* which can be repeated without modification over the range of the variable.

The essence of the process "which can be repeated without modification" is a theory or model for how persons and items must interact to produce useful observations. This model for measuring is fundamental to the construction of measures. It not only specifies how a unit might be defined, but also contains the means for maintaining this unit.

## 1.2  CONSTRUCTING OBSERVATIONS

The idea of a variable implies some *one kind of thing* which we are able to imagine in various amounts. Underlying the idea of a variable is the intention to think in terms of "more" and "less", that is, the intention of *order*. Before we can measure we must first identify events which we believe are indicative of "more" of the variable. These events are then interpreted as steps in the intended direction and are looked for, noted and counted.

Measurement begins with a search for the possibility of order and an attempt to inject this order into organized experiences. Experiments are devised and carefully implemented to bring out how well the capacity, strength or "amount" in a person fares against the resistance, strength or "amount" in an item. The observational procedure operationalizes the idea of order and provides the basic ingredients from which measures are made.

If the observation format treats each item as one step in the intended direction, as in examination questions marked right or wrong, then we look to see whether the person has completed (or failed) that one step. For a series of one-step items we ask: How often have indicative events occurred? If the observation format identifies several possible levels of performance on an item, as in rating scales and examination questions which allow partial credit, then we ask: Which of these ordered performance levels has been reached? How many steps have been taken in the intended direction? In either case, we count the completed steps as independent indications of the relative strengths of (amounts in) the persons and items.

The steps within an item, being perfectly ordered by definition, are completely dependent. To have reached the third step means to have reached and passed through the first and second steps. But the items themselves are usually designed and deployed so that they can function independently of one another and responses to them are expected to be independent in most item analyses. Whether this is approximated in practice, of course, depends on the circumstances and on the success of our efforts to obtain and maintain an approximately uniform level of independence.

## 1.3  MODELLING OBSERVATIONS

For observations to be combined into measures they must be brought together and connected to the idea of measurement which they are intended to imply. The recipe for bringing them together is a mathematical formulation or *measurement model* in which observations and our ideas about the relative strengths of persons and items are connected to one another in a way that

1)   absorbs the inevitable irregularities and uncertainties of experience systematically by specifying the occurrence of an event as a *probability* rather than a certainty,

2)   preserves the idea of *order* in the structure of the observations by requiring these probabilities to be ordered by persons and items simultaneously, as in the cancellation axiom of conjoint measurement, and

3)   enables the independent estimation of distances between pairs of items and pairs of persons by keeping item and person parameters accessible to sufficient estimation and inferential *separation*.

The uncertainties of experience are handled by expressing the model of how person and item parameters combine to produce observable events as a probability.   In formulating the connection between idea and experience we do not attempt to specify exactly what will happen.   Instead, we specify the probability of an indicative event occurring.   This leaves room for the uncertainty of experience without abandoning the construction of order.

The idea of order is maintained by formulating measurement models so that the probabilities of success define a joint order of persons and items.   The stronger of any pair of persons is *always* expected to do better on *any* item, and the weaker of any pair of items is *always* expected to be better done by *any* person.

This is the probabilistic version of

> If a person endorses a more extreme statement, he should endorse *all* less extreme statements if the statements are to be considered a scale. . . .We shall call a set of items of common content a scale if a person with a higher rank than another person is just as high or higher on *every* item than the other person.   (Guttman 1950, *62*)

> A person having a greater ability than another should have the greater probability of solving *any* item of the type in question, and similarly, one item being more difficult than another one means that for *any* person the probability of solving the second item correctly is the greater one.   (Rasch 1960, *117*)

If our expectations for "more" and "less" do not fulfill this basic requirement of order, and hence do not satisfy the cancellation axiom of additive conjoint measurement, they lose their meaning, and the intended variable loses its quantitative basis.   This basic principle of orderliness is the fundamental requirement for measurement.

The appearance of person and item parameters in a measurement model in a way which allows them to be factored is essential if measures are to have any generality.   The measurement model must connect the observations and the parameters they are supposed to indicate in a way which permits the use of any selection of relevant observations to estimate useful values for the parameters.   This can be done effectively only when the formulation relates the parameters so that person parameters can be conditioned out of the model when items are calibrated to obtain sample-free item calibrations, and item parameters can be conditioned out when persons are measured to construct test-free person measures.

## 1.4  BUILDING GENERALITY

For a quantitative comparison to be general, it must be possible to maintain its quantitative basis beyond the moment and context of its realization. It must be possible to compare measures from time to time and place to place without doubting the status of their values and without wondering whether the numbers have lost their meaning. The method by which observations are turned into calibrations and measures must contain the possibility of *invariance* over a useful range of time and place. It must also provide the means for verifying that a useful approximation to this invariance is maintained in practice.

Measures of persons must have meaning extending beyond the items used to obtain them. Their "meaning" must include not only the items used, but also other items of the same sort. If this is not so, the numbers intended as measures are merely arbitrary labels of a temporary description.

The idea of a variable implies a potential innumerability of relevant examples which stand for its generality. These examples must specify an expected order which defines "more" and "less" along one common line and, so, gives the variable its operational definition. The implementation of a variable requires the construction and observation of enough actual examples to confirm the expected order and document the basis for inference.

> One of the first requirements of a solution [to the problem of constructing a rational method of assigning values for the base line of a scale of opinion] is that the scale values of the statements of opinion must be as free as possible, and preferably entirely free, from the actual opinions of individuals or groups. If the scale value of one of the statements should be affected by the opinion of any individual person or group, then it would be impossible to compare the opinion distributions of two groups on the same base. (Thurstone 1928b, *416*)

The invariance of measures must be such that we expect to obtain about the same values for a particular measure no matter which items we use, so long as they define the same variable, and, no matter whom else we happen to have measured. The measures must be "test-free" in the sense that it must not matter which selection of items is used to estimate them. They must be "sample-free" in the sense that it must not matter which sample of persons is used to calibrate these items. The usefulness of person measures, and the item calibrations which enable them, depends on the extent to which persons and items can be worked together to approximate this kind of invariance.

### 1.4.1  Frames of Reference

Scientific ideas are intended to be useful. For ideas to be useful, they must apply over some range of time and place; that is, over some frame of reference. The way we think things are must seem to stay the same within some useful context. We must be able to think that a person's ability remains fixed long enough for us to observe it. We must be able to imagine that we can observe some items attempted, count the steps successfully taken, estimate a measure from this score, and have this estimate relevant to the person for a useful span of time. The difficulties of the items must also remain fixed enough for us to use them to define a variable, compare abilities with it, measure differences and quantify changes.

### 1.4.2 Continuity

In our thoughts about variables and measures on them we are counting on being able to approximate a limited but reproducible continuity. We know that this continuity is not real. We know that we can easily obtain experiences which falsify any continuity we might think up. But we also know that we only need to approximate continuity and be able to supervise its approximation to make good use of it.

All our thinking about variables and measures on them depends on the experienced utility of assuming that a semblance of continuity can be constructed and maintained. The practice of science relies on demonstrations that specified measures and the calibrations on which they are based can be reproduced whenever necessary and shown to be invariant enough to approximate the continuity we count on to make our thoughts about amounts useful. Reproduction is the way continuity is verified. Reproducibility depends on the possibility of replication.

### 1.4.3 Objectivity, Sufficiency and Additivity

The verification of continuity through reproduction depends on being able to estimate differences in item and person strengths independently of one another. The best we can do is to estimate differences in strengths between pairs of items, pairs of persons, or between an item and a person. But inferential separation among these estimations of differences is enough to support independent calibrations of items and measures of persons. The set of differences need only be anchored at a convenient origin in order to free the separate estimates from everything except their differences from that origin.

The separation of item and person parameters must be provided by the mathematical form of the measurement model. This means that the way person and item parameters are modelled to influence observations must be factorable so that conditional probabilities for the differences between any pair of parameters can be written in terms of observations. This is the only structure which supports the use of non-identically distributed observations to estimate distances between pairs of parameters.

> Generally, only part of the statistical information contained in the model and the data is pertinent to a given question, and one is then faced with the problem of separating out that part. The key procedures for such separations are margining to a sufficient statistic and conditioning on an ancillary statistic. (Barndorff-Nielsen 1978, 2)

> The work by G. Rasch on what he has called measurement models and specific objectivity should also be mentioned as a very considerable impetus in the field of inferential separation. (Barndorff-Nielsen 1978, 69)

R.A. Fisher (1934) shows that separability is the necessary and sufficient condition for "sufficient" statistics. Rasch identifies *separability* as the basis for the *specific objectivity* essential for scientific inference. In order that the concepts of person ability and item difficulty could be at all considered meaningful, there must exist a function of the probability of a correct answer which forms an *additive* system in the parameters for persons and items such that the logit correct equals the difference between person ability and item difficulty (Rasch 1960, *118-120*).

Rasch measurement models are based on the nuclear element

$$P\{x;\beta,\delta\} = \exp(\beta - \delta) / [1 + \exp(\beta - \delta)]$$

with statistics $r$ for $\beta$ and $S$ for $\delta$. The appearance of $\beta$ and $\delta$ in linear form enables $P\{x;\delta|r\}$ to be non-informative concerning $\beta$ and $P\{x;\beta|S\}$ to be non-informative concerning $\delta$. It follows that $r$ is sufficient for $x$ concerning $\beta$ but ancillary concerning $\delta$, while $S$ is sufficient for $x$ concerning $\delta$ but ancillary concerning $\beta$. As a result, margining to $r$ and $S$ estimates $\beta$ and $\delta$ sufficiently while conditioning on $S$ or $r$ enables their inferential separation (Barndorff-Nielsen 1978, *50*).

Luce and Tukey (1964) call this relationship between parameters and observations "additivity" and identify it as the *sine qua non* of measurement:

> The essential character of what is classically considered . . . the fundamental measurement of extensive quantities is described by an axiomatization for the comparison of effects of (or responses to) arbitrary combinations of "quantities" of a *single specified kind* . . . Measurement on a ratio scale follows from such axioms. . . The essential character of simultaneous conjoint measurement is described by an axiomatization for the comparison of effects of (or responses to) *pairs* formed from two specified kinds of "quantities". . . Measurement on interval scales which have a common unit follows from these axioms; usually these scales can be converted in a natural way into ratio scales.

> A close relation exists between conjoint measurement and the establishment of response measures in a two-way table, or other analysis-of-variance situations, for which the "effects of columns" and the "effects of rows" are additive. Indeed, the discovery of such measures, which are well known to have important practical advantages, may be viewed as the discovery, via conjoint measurement, of fundamental measures of the row and column variables. (Luce and Tukey 1964, *1*)

> Seeking response measures which make the effects of columns and the effects of rows additive in an analysis-of-variance situation has become increasingly popular as the advantages of such parsimonious descriptions, whether exact or approximate, have become more appreciated. In spite of the practical advantages of such response measures, objections have been raised to their quest, the primary ones being (*a*) that such "tampering" with data is somehow unethical, and (*b*) that one should be interested in fundamental results, not merely empirical ones.

> For those who grant the fundamental character of measurement axiomatized in terms of concatenation, the axioms of simultaneous conjoint measurement overcome both of these objections since their existence shows that qualitatively described "additivity" over pairs of factors of responses or effects is just as axiomatizable as concatenation. Indeed, the additivity is axiomatizable in terms of axioms that lead to scales of the highest repute: interval and ratio scales.

> Moreover, the axioms of conjoint measurement apply naturally to problems of classical physics and permit the measurement of conventional physical quantities on ratio scales.

In the various fields, including the behavioral and biological sciences, where factors producing orderable effects and responses deserve both more useful and more fundamental measurement, the moral seems clear: *when no natural concatenation operation exists, one should try to discover a way to measure factors and responses such that the "effects" of different factors are additive.*    (Luce and Tukey 1964, *4*)

*Additivity* means that the way the person and item parameters enter into the modelled production of the observed behavior can be *linear* as in $\beta_n - \delta_i - \tau_j$ and $\sum_{j=0}^{x} (\beta_n - \delta_{ij})$ or even $\alpha_i \beta_n$, since $\log \alpha_i \beta_n = \log \alpha_i + \log \beta_n$, but *not* as in $\alpha_i(\beta_n - \delta_i)$ or $(\beta_n - \delta_i - \gamma_{ni})$. This is because the estimates of person ability $\beta_n$ or item difficulty $\delta_i$ in these latter expressions cannot be separated from the variable scaling factor $\alpha_i$ (as is the case when item discriminations are parameterized) or the interaction term $\gamma_{ni}$.

*Separability* means that the connection between observations and parameters in the measurement model can be factored so that each parameter and its associated statistics appear as a separate multiplicative component in the modelled likelihood of a suitable set of data.

*Specific objectivity* means that the model can be written in a form in which its parameters are linear in the argument of an exponential expression so that they can be sufficiently estimated and conditioned out of the estimation of other parameters.

The Rasch model is a special case of additive conjoint measurement, a form of fundamental measurement. . . A fit of the Rasch model implies that the cancellation axiom will be satisfied. . . It then follows that items and persons are measured on an interval scale with a common unit.    (Brogden 1977, *633*)

## 1.5   QUANTIFYING COMPARISONS

The purpose of measuring is to derive numbers for objects which enable quantitative comparisons that can be maintained over a useful range of generality.    The idea of measurement contains the image of a single line of inquiry, one dimension, along which objects can be positioned on the basis of observations which add up.    It is taken for granted that the observations are relevant encounters which elicit symptoms of the variable intended and can be accumulated into reproducible indications of the objects' positions.

### 1.5.1   Arithmetic and Linearity

In order for numbers to represent amounts and enable quantitative comparisons, we must construct and maintain a linear scale on which the difference between persons *A* and *B* appears approximately the same whether seen through hard, medium or easy items.    And, also, on which the distance between items *I* and *J* appears approximately the same whether revealed by able, average or unable persons.    Otherwise differences cannot be compared, because subtraction does not hold, rates of development cannot be determined, and the quantitative study of psychological growth and change is impossible.

Linearity requires that the way observations are used to obtain numbers preserve not only the order of the objects and instruments, but also the order of their differences.    If the pairwise differences of three pairs of objects (or instruments) are *AB*, *CD* and *EF*, and if *AB>CD* and *CD>EF*, then it must be reasonable to expect *AB>EF*.    The linearity we count on when we use measures and calibrations depends on a method for transforming observations into numbers which preserves this order of differences.

### 1.5.2  Origins and Zero Differences

The idea of a true origin or "beginning", the place on a line before which the variable does not exist, is beyond experience by definition.    Experienced origins are inevitably arbitrary because the empirical identifications of such points are always circumscribed by time and place, are always temporary and are always improved by experience.    As the search for an "absolute zero" temperature illustrates, new demonstrations inevitably displace "origins" thought to be absolute.    In practice, origins are convenient reference points.    The west counts time in *anno domini*.    Others count from other "beginnings".    Origins are often chosen to avoid negative numbers or for dramatic emphasis as in above ground and *below* freezing.

If origins are arbitrary, what about zero differences?    Could a zero difference provide a non-arbitrary zero-point?    When we observe an identity have we defined a zero?    We might define "identity" as the observation of the "same" performance pattern.    But this would not hold.    We can always imagine more observations which contradict us.    If we maintain contact with the persons or items concerned we will always encounter new observations which document their difference.    Additional observations will eventually falsify every identity thus destroying any origin based on a zero-difference.    We can approximate a zero difference, but we can never demonstrate a perfect one.    The absolute zero of "no difference" is just as beyond experience as the absolute zero of "beginning".

Yet the idea of continuity contains a point where, as ability increases past difficulty, the difference $\beta - \delta$ passes through zero.    By increasing the number of observations we can approximate this idea of a zero difference to any desired degree.    While its observation can only be approximate, the idea of a zero difference is an irresistable consequence of the idea of continuity, and it is the foundation for obtaining a "measure" of an object from calibrated instruments.    The way we obtain an object's measure is by calculating the "calibration" of an imaginary instrument which would have a zero difference from the object.    In practice, of course, we set an origin somewhere convenient and stick to it so that we have a place from which to start counting.

### 1.5.3  Units and Least Observable Differences

To measure off distances, to compare differences and to determine rates of change we need to be able to do arithmetic with the results of our observations.    To be able to do arithmetic we need to be able to count, and to count we need units.    But there are no natural units.    There are only the arbitrary units we construct and decide to use for our counting.

Rasch models define response probabilities from combinations of

$$\pi = \exp\lambda /(1 + \exp\lambda)$$

The *logit* $\log[\pi/(1-\pi)] = \lambda$ is the *probability unit* for $\lambda$ defined by the modelled *process*.   This is the unit which the Rasch process keeps uniform over the range of observations.

The decimal system gives us freedom as to what a *one* count shall be.   But we use integers to count with.   We speak of distances as so many of this or that *unit*.   For this it is natural to choose integers which can represent by convention either the least amount we can observe conveniently e.g., ''one red cent'' (a choice which depends on our observational technique), or the least amount we are interested in knowing about e.g., ''keep the change'' (a choice which depends on our intentions).

This ends our discussion of the essentials of measurement.   The measurement models we use in this book are constructed from ''the Rasch model'' for dichotomous observations and belong to the family of models with separable person and item parameters.   These are the only models known to us which meet the basic requirements for measurement.

# 2   EXAMINING DATA

In this chapter we examine the data that will be used to illustrate our measurement method in Chapters 4 and 5.   Our purpose is to introduce some general techniques for inspecting data, and to set the stage for our subsequent statistical analysis.   The data were collected by the Cleveland Museum of Natural History to measure the attitudes of school children toward science.*   We will use these data to try to build a liking-for-science variable along which children's attitudes to science can be measured, and then we will attempt to measure the attitudes of seventy-five school children.

The questions that will guide us are: Can we build a liking-for-science variable from these data?   Do some of the data appear unsuitable for this task?   Do the questionnaire items seem to define a useful range of attitudes toward science?   Are the responses of the seventy-five children consistent with the ordering of these items?   Have any children given unexpected or erratic responses?   Our examination of the liking-for-science data is detailed and elementary because we intend to use the observations that we make in this chapter as background for the statistical analyses in Chapters 4 and 5.

## 2.1 AN ATTITUDE TO SCIENCE VARIABLE

One goal of science classes and museum programs is to develop a liking for science.   These programs hope to cultivate children's curiosity and to encourage their eagerness to explore in ever more organized and constructive ways.   If we are willing to think of each child as having some level of liking for science at any given time, and of children as varying in their amount of this liking, then each child's liking for science can be thought of as a point on a line of increasingly positive attitudes as in Figure 2.1.   Children who don't like science are located to the left on this line, and children who like science a lot are located to the right.   The growth or decay of a child's liking for science is followed by charting his movement along this line.

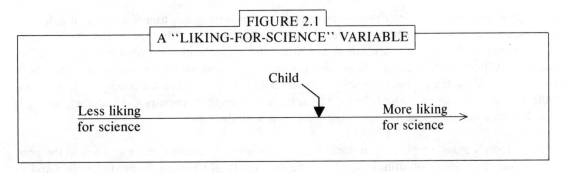

FIGURE 2.1
A "LIKING-FOR-SCIENCE" VARIABLE

* We are grateful to Julian Mingus for making these data available to us.

Like all variables, this "liking-for-science" line is an abstraction.   Whether it is useful to think of children as having positions on a single liking-for-science variable depends first on our ability to collect observations which support such an idea, and second on the utility of the attitude measures we then make.   Our "liking-for-science" line will be justified if the measures it leads to are useful for following changes in liking for science, identifying the kinds of science-related activities individual children are ready to enjoy, selecting appropriate classroom activities, or evaluating the effectiveness of programs intended to develop children's liking for science.

To build such a line we must find a way to collect data that could reflect children's liking for science.   One possibility is to think up a range of activities which represent various degrees of interest in science, and then to ask children which of these activities they like.   An activity which should be easy to like is "Watching monkeys". Slightly harder to like might be "Observing a monkey to see what it eats", and harder still, "Consulting an encyclopedia to find out where monkeys come from".   If we can develop a range of activities which seem to represent increasing levels of interest in science, then we may be able to mark out a line of increasingly positive attitude.   Once activities are ordered along such a line, each child's position on the line can be interpreted in terms of the kinds of activities that child can be expected to like and dislike.

## 2.2 THE SCIENCE QUESTIONNAIRE

The Cleveland Museum of Natural History assembled twenty-five science-related activities for its study of children's liking for science.   Some of these, like Activity *19* "Going to the zoo", are easy to like.   Others, like Activity *6* "Looking up a strange animal or plant in an encyclopedia", require more effort and should be liked only by children who are motivated by a general liking for science.   A list of these activities in the order in which they were administered appears in Figure 2.2.

## 2.3 HOW JUDGES ORDER THE SCIENCE ACTIVITIES

When the items in an attitude questionnaire are examined for their intention, it should be possible to anticipate their ordering along the variable they are supposed to define, and in this ordering it should be possible to "see" a line of increasing attitude.   If we can order the twenty-five science activities from easiest-to-like to hardest-to-like, then we should be able to recognize in this ordering the liking-for-science variable that they are intended to specify.

One approach to laying out a variable of increasing attitude is to ask a group of judges to arrange the questionnaire items in order of increasing intensity.   F.H. Allport developed scales in this way in 1925 to measure attitudes toward the prohibition of alcohol and the Ku Klux Klan.   Allport wrote a set of statements for each scale and asked six judges to order these statements along the attitude variable they seemed to define.   Then he attempted to measure the attitudes of college students toward each issue by having them mark the statement on each scale which came closest to expressing their own attitude.

Allport's study sparked Thurstone's interest in attitude measurement and led to the construction of a variety of attitude scales at the University of Chicago during the 1920's and to a series of Thurstone papers on the possibility of measuring attitudes.   Thurstone asked judges

FIGURE 2.2
THE SCIENCE QUESTIONNAIRE

1. Watching birds
2. Reading books on animals
3. Reading books on plants
4. Watching the grass change from season to season
5. Finding old bottles and cans
6. Looking up a strange animal or plant in a dictionary or encyclopedia
7. Watching the same animal move many days
8. Looking in the cracks in the sidewalks for small animals
9. Learning the names of weeds
10. Listening to a bird sing
11. Finding out where an animal lives
12. Going to a museum
13. Growing a garden
14. Looking at pictures of plants
15. Reading stories of animals
16. Making a map
17. Watching animals to see what plants they eat
18. Going on a picnic
19. Going to the zoo
20. Watching bugs
21. Watching a bird make a nest
22. Finding out what different animals eat
23. Watching a rat
24. Finding out what flowers live on
25. Talking with friends about plants

not only to order statements, but also to sort them into piles which appeared to be equally different in intensity. Thurstone recognized the importance of being able to express attitude measures on a scale with a "defensible unit of measurement", and hoped that "equal appearing intervals" would provide a rational unit for his scales (Thurstone 1928a, *542*).

To see whether we could establish agreement on the ordering of the twenty-five science activities in Figure 2.2, we asked nine adults to order them from easiest-to-like to hardest-to-like. Then we asked the same nine adults to group the twenty-five ordered activities into eleven "equally spaced" piles, placing the easiest-to-like activities in the first pile, and the hardest-to-like activities in the eleventh. Figure 2.3a shows the results of this sorting for some of the twenty-five activities.

The eight activities upon which there was *most* agreement are listed at the top of Figure 2.3a. The nine judges agreed that Activity *9* "Learning the names of weeds" was very hard to like. Five judges placed this activity in "hardest-to-like" pile 11. The other four judges placed it in piles 9 and 10. The nine judges also agreed that Activity *18* "Going on a picnic" was very easy to like. Eight judges placed this activity in "easiest-to-like" pile 1. The ninth judge placed it in pile 2. Listed between Activities *9* and *18* in Figure 2.3a are six other activities which the judges felt were not as hard to like as learning the names of weeds, but not as easy to like as going on a picnic.

FIGURE 2.3a
HOW NINE JUDGES ORDERED THE SCIENCE ACTIVITIES

| ACTIVITY NUMBER | ACTIVITY | 1 (EASY-TO-LIKE) | 2 | 3 | 4 | 5 | 6 | 7 | 8 | 9 | 10 | 11 (HARD-TO-LIKE) | MEDIAN PLACEMENT | MIDRANGE* OF PLACEMENTS |
|---|---|---|---|---|---|---|---|---|---|---|---|---|---|---|
| *9* | Learning the names of weeds | | | | | | | | | XX | XX | XXXXX | 11 | 2 |
| *7* | Watching the same animal move many days | X | | | | X | X | | X | XXX | XX | | 9 | 5 |
| *4* | Watching the grass change from season to season | | | X | | X | XX | X | XXXX | | | | 7 | 3 |
| *15* | Reading stories of animals | X | | | XX | X | X | X | XX | | X | | 6 | 4 |
| *21* | Watching a bird make a nest | | XX | XX | XX | XX | | X | | | | | 4 | 3 |
| *1* | Watching birds | X | XX | XX | XX | X | X | | | | | | 3 | 3 |
| *19* | Going to the zoo | XXXX | X | XX | | X | X | | | | | | 2 | 4 |
| *18* | Going on a picnic | XXXXXXXX | X | | | | | | | | | | 1 | 0 |
| *5* | Finding old bottles and cans | X | | X | X | | | X | X | | XX | XX | 8 | 8 |
| *16* | Making a map | | XX | | X | X | X | | X | X | XX | | 6 | 8 |
| *23* | Watching a rat | | X | X | | | X | | | | XX | XXXX | 10 | 8 |

* MIDRANGE = Difference between 25th and 75th percentiles

There is less agreement among judges on some of these activities than on others. For example, while most judges placed Activity *7* "Watching the same animal move many days" above pile 5, one judge felt that this was among the easiest activities to like, and placed it in pile 1. At the bottom of Figure 2.3a are the results for the three activities upon which there was *least* agreement.

While some judges felt that these three activities were easy to like, others felt that they were hard to like. Thurstone encountered this problem in 1928 when attempting to use judges' orderings to position statements along a line of increasingly positive attitudes toward the church. He referred to such statements as "ambiguous" and deleted them from his questionnaire.

The medians and midranges of judges' placements are shown on the right of Figure 2.3a. The midranges for the eight activities at the top are relatively small, and so, the median placements for these eight activities provide a useful indication of their ordering along the science variable. But the large midranges for Activities *5*, *16* and *23* at the bottom of Figure 2.3a make the median placements for these three activities meaningless as indications of their locations among the other activities.

The relation between the median placement and midrange is plotted in Figure 2.3b for all twenty-five science activities. The eight least ambiguous activities are connected by a line. The three most ambiguous activities are circled. The fourteen activities not listed in Figure 2.3a are in the middle of the plot.

Our attempt to find a natural order in the twenty-five science activities on which persons examining them would agree has identified Activities *5*, *16* and *23* as more ambiguous than the others. The fact that our nine judges had trouble agreeing on where these three activities stand among the others suggests that they may not belong on the same liking-for-science variable. It is essential that such activities be identified and deleted from the final questionnaire.

> Ideally the scaling method should be designed so that it will automatically throw out of the scale any statements which do not belong in its natural sequence. (Thurstone 1928b, *417*)

Our nine judges have provided us with an ordering of the twenty-five science activities which looks reasonable. But how general is this order? To what extent does this ordering of the activities reflect the idiosyncratic preferences of these nine judges? To construct a useful liking-for-science variable, we must be able to calibrate activities along a single line, and these calibrations must have a generality which extends beyond the particular persons used to obtain them.

> If the scale is to be regarded as valid, the scale values of the statements should not be affected by the opinions of the people who help to construct it. This may turn out to be a severe test in practice, but the scaling method must stand such a test before it can be accepted as being more than a description of the people who construct the scale. At any rate, to the extent that the present method of scale construction is affected by the opinions of the readers who help to sort out the original statements into a scale, to that extent the validity or universality of the scale may be challenged. (Thurstone 1928a, *547–548*)

## 2.4 HOW CHILDREN RESPOND TO THE SCIENCE ACTIVITIES

### 2.4.1 Choosing a Response Format

The first task in the construction of an attitude variable is to assemble a set of items which might work together to define one common line of inquiry. The second task is to choose a

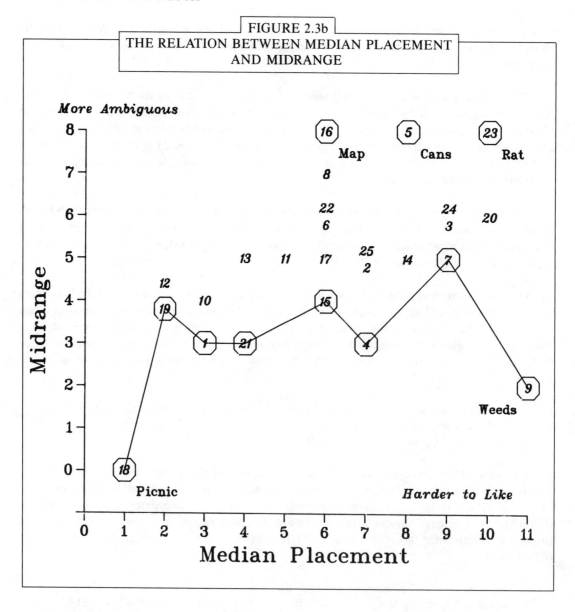

FIGURE 2.3b
THE RELATION BETWEEN MEDIAN PLACEMENT
AND MIDRANGE

format for recording responses to these items. For the science questionnaire, one approach is to ask each child to indicate which of the twenty-five activities he *likes*. If a score of 1 is assigned for liking an activity and 0 for not liking it, then responses resemble scores on an achievement test and can be analyzed accordingly. An alternative, which seems to get at the same thing, is to ask each child which activities he *dislikes*. In general, however, these two approaches do not produce equivalent results. If we give a child a list of the twenty-five activities and ask him to mark the activities he likes, and then give him a second list of the same twenty-five activities and ask him to mark the activities he dislikes, the results will be equivalent only if every activity is marked on one *and only one* of these two lists.. Activities which are not marked on either list will be activities which this child neither likes nor dislikes.

A common practice for dealing with statements which are neither liked nor disliked in attitude questionnaires is to provide a "neutral" alternative. But this practice has not been universally accepted, and there has been extensive discussion of the misuse of the neutral category by respondents who do not wish to participate.

The constructors of the science questionnaire decided to provide a neutral response alternative with the intention that it be used to express an attitude between liking and disliking. Children recorded their responses by drawing a mouth on a blank face alongside each activity. The alternatives offered are shown in Figure 2.4a.

### 2.4.2 The Science Data Matrix

*Ordering Children's Attitudes.* Responses of seventy-five children to the twenty-five science activities are displayed in Figure 2.4b. This "data matrix" is composed of 0's (*Dislike*), 1's (*Not Sure/Don't Care*) and 2's (*Like*). There are seventy-five rows, one for each child, and twenty-five columns, one for each activity. Can we use the entries in this matrix to calibrate the twenty-five activities along a line of increasingly favorable attitudes to science, and to measure the attitudes of these seventy-five children on this line?

Each row of this matrix contains the responses of one child to the twenty-five activities in the science questionnaire. Each child is identified by a number on the left of the matrix. By summing across a child's row of responses a score is obtained for that child. This score appears on the right of the matrix. The seventy-five children have been sorted so that the child with the highest score (Child 2, score = 50) is at the top, and the child with the lowest score (Child 53, score = 12) is at the bottom. From his row of responses at the top of Figure 2.4b we see that Child 2 *liked* all twenty-five activities in this questionnaire. Child 53 at the bottom of the matrix liked only one activity and *disliked* fourteen. Children who like most activities make high scores on the questionnaire and appear at the top of the matrix. Children who dislike many of the activities make low scores and appear at the bottom.

*Ordering the Science Activities.* Each of the twenty-five columns in Figure 2.4b contains the responses of these seventy-five children to one activity. Each activity is identified by its

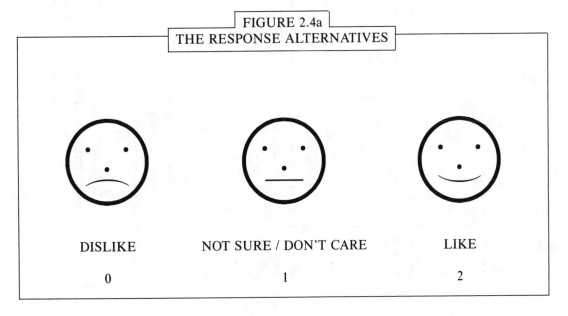

FIGURE 2.4a
THE RESPONSE ALTERNATIVES

DISLIKE    NOT SURE / DON'T CARE    LIKE

0    1    2

# FIGURE 2.4b
# SCIENCE DATA MATRIX

| Child Number | 18 | 19 | 12 | 10 | 13 | 11 | 21 | 2 | 15 | 1 | 24 | 22 | 17 | 6 | 14 | 3★ | 25 | 16 | 9 | 7 | 8 | 4 | 20 | 23 | 5 | Child Score | 0 | 1 | 2 |
|---|---|---|---|---|---|---|---|---|---|---|---|---|---|---|---|---|---|---|---|---|---|---|---|---|---|---|---|---|---|
| 2 | 2 | 2 | 2 | 2 | 2 | 2 | 2 | 2 | 2 | 2 | 2 | 2 | 2 | 2 | 2 | 2 | 2 | 2 | 2 | 2 | 2 | 2 | 2 | 2 | 2 | 50 | 0 | 0 | 25 |
| 41 | 2 | 2 | 2 | 2 | 2 | 2 | 2 | 2 | 2 | 2 | 2 | 2 | 2 | 2 | 2 | 2 | 2 | 2 | 2 | 2 | 2 | 2 | 2 | 1 | 2 | 49 | 0 | 1 | 24 |
| 34 | 2 | 2 | 2 | 2 | 2 | 2 | 2 | 2 | 2 | 2 | 2 | 2 | 2 | 2 | 2 | 2 | 2 | 2 | 2 | 2 | 2 | 2 | 2 | 1 | 1 | 48 | 0 | 2 | 23 |
| 17 | 2 | 2 | 2 | 2 | 2 | 2 | 2 | 2 | 2 | 2 | 2 | 2 | 2 | 2 | 2 | 2 | 2 | 2 | 2 | 2 | 2 | 2 | 2 | 1 | 0 | 47 | 1 | 1 | 23 |
| 50 | 2 | 2 | 2 | 2 | 2 | 2 | 2 | 2 | 2 | 2 | 2 | 2 | 2 | 2 | 2 | 2 | 2 | 2 | 1 | 2 | 2 | 1 | 1 | 1 | 1 | 46 | 0 | 4 | 21 |
| 45 | 2 | 2 | 2 | 2 | 2 | 2 | 2 | 2 | 2 | 2 | 2 | 2 | 2 | 2 | 2 | 2 | 2 | 2 | 2 | 1 | 2 | 1 | 2 | 0 | 0 | 45 | 2 | 1 | 22 |
| 7 | 2 | 2 | 2 | 2 | 2 | 2 | 2 | 2 | 2 | 2 | 2 | 2 | 2 | 2 | 2 | 2 | 2 | 0 | 2 | 2 | 0 | 2 | 2 | 0 | 2 | 44 | 3 | 0 | 22 |
| 48 | 2 | 2 | 2 | 2 | 2 | 2 | 2 | 2 | 2 | 2 | 2 | 2 | 2 | 2 | 2 | 2 | 1 | 2 | 2 | 2 | 1 | 1 | 0 | 0 | 2 | 43 | 2 | 3 | 20 |
| 16 | 2 | 2 | 2 | 2 | 2 | 2 | 2 | 2 | 2 | 2 | 2 | 2 | 2 | 2 | 2 | 2 | 2 | 2 | 1 | 1 | 1 | 1 | 0 | 1 | 2 | 43 | 1 | 5 | 19 |
| 25 | 2 | 2 | 2 | 2 | 2 | 2 | 2 | 2 | 2 | 2 | 2 | 2 | 2 | 2 | 2 | 2 | 1 | 2 | 0 | 2 | 1 | 1 | 0 | 1 | 2 | 42 | 2 | 4 | 19 |
| 59 | 2 | 2 | 2 | 2 | 2 | 2 | 2 | 2 | 2 | 2 | 2 | 2 | 2 | 2 | 2 | 2 | 1 | 2 | 1 | 2 | 1 | 1 | 0 | 2 | 0 | 42 | 2 | 4 | 19 |
| 39 | 2 | 2 | 2 | 2 | 2 | 2 | 2 | 2 | 2 | 2 | 2 | 2 | 2 | 1 | 2 | 2 | 1 | 2 | 1 | 2 | 1 | 1 | 1 | 0 | 0 | 41 | 2 | 5 | 18 |
| 18 | 2 | 2 | 2 | 2 | 2 | 2 | 2 | 2 | 2 | 2 | 2 | 2 | 2 | 2 | 2 | 2 | 1 | 2 | 1 | 0 | 2 | 1 | 0 | 0 | 0 | 41 | 3 | 3 | 19 |
| 56 | 2 | 2 | 2 | 2 | 2 | 2 | 2 | 2 | 2 | 2 | 2 | 2 | 1 | 2 | 2 | 2 | 1 | 2 | 1 | 2 | 0 | 1 | 1 | 0 | 0 | 40 | 3 | 4 | 18 |
| 57 | 2 | 2 | 2 | 2 | 2 | 2 | 2 | 2 | 2 | 2 | 2 | 2 | 2 | 2 | 2 | 2 | 2 | 2 | 0 | 0 | 0 | 0 | 0 | 0 | 0 | 40 | 5 | 0 | 20 |
| 23 | 2 | 2 | 2 | 2 | 2 | 2 | 2 | 2 | 2 | 2 | 2 | 2 | 1 | 1 | 1 | 2 | 1 | 1 | 2 | 1 | 1 | 1 | 1 | 1 | 1 | 40 | 0 | 10 | 15 |
| 40 | 2 | 2 | 2 | 2 | 2 | 2 | 2 | 2 | 2 | 2 | 2 | 2 | 2 | 1 | 2 | 2 | 1 | 2 | 0 | 1 | 1 | 0 | 0 | 0 | 0 | 39 | 3 | 5 | 17 |
| 70 | 2 | 2 | 2 | 2 | 2 | 2 | 2 | 2 | 2 | 2 | 2 | 2 | 2 | 1 | 2 | 1 | 2 | 1 | 2 | 0 | 2 | 0 | 0 | 0 | 0 | 39 | 4 | 3 | 18 |
| 33 | 2 | 2 | 2 | 2 | 2 | 2 | 2 | 2 | 2 | 2 | 2 | 2 | 2 | 1 | 1 | 0 | 1 | 1 | 2 | 2 | 0 | 0 | 0 | 0 | 0 | 38 | 4 | 4 | 17 |
| 38 | 2 | 2 | 2 | 2 | 2 | 2 | 2 | 2 | 2 | 2 | 2 | 1 | 1 | 1 | 1 | 1 | 1 | 1 | 1 | 1 | 2 | 1 | 0 | 0 | 0 | 38 | 1 | 10 | 14 |
| 43 | 2 | 2 | 2 | 2 | 2 | 2 | 2 | 2 | 2 | 2 | 1 | 1 | 2 | 1 | 1 | 2 | 2 | 0 | 0 | 0 | 0 | 0 | 0 | 0 | 1 | 37 | 4 | 5 | 16 |
| 74 | 2 | 2 | 2 | 2 | 2 | 2 | 2 | 2 | 2 | 2 | 1 | 2 | 2 | 2 | 2 | 2 | 2 | 0 | 2 | 0 | 0 | 0 | 0 | 0 | 0 | 37 | 6 | 1 | 18 |
| 60 | 2 | 2 | 2 | 2 | 2 | 2 | 2 | 2 | 1 | 2 | 1 | 1 | 1 | 1 | 1 | 2 | 1 | 1 | 2 | 1 | 1 | 1 | 0 | 0 | 1 | 36 | 0 | 12 | 12 |
| 64 | 2 | 2 | 2 | 2 | 2 | 2 | 2 | 2 | 1 | 2 | 2 | 1 | 2 | 1 | 1 | 1 | 1 | 1 | 2 | 1 | 0 | 1 | 0 | 0 | 0 | 36 | 3 | 8 | 14 |
| 58 | 2 | 2 | 2 | 2 | 2 | 2 | 2 | 2 | 1 | 2 | 1 | 2 | 1 | 2 | 1 | 1 | 2 | 0 | 1 | 1 | 0 | 1 | 0 | 0 | 0 | 35 | 4 | 7 | 14 |
| 11 | 2 | 2 | 2 | 2 | 2 | 2 | 2 | 2 | 2 | 2 | 2 | 1 | 2 | 2 | 2 | 0 | 0 | 1 | 1 | 0 | 0 | 0 | 0 | 0 | 0 | 35 | 6 | 3 | 16 |
| 22 | 2 | 2 | 2 | 2 | 2 | 2 | 2 | 2 | 1 | 2 | 1 | 1 | 1 | 1 | 1 | 1 | 1 | 1 | 1 | 1 | 1 | 1 | 1 | 1 | 1 | 35 | 0 | 15 | 10 |
| 51 | 2 | 2 | 2 | 2 | 2 | 2 | 2 | 2 | 1 | 2 | 1 | 1 | 2 | 2 | 1 | 2 | 1 | 2 | 1 | 0 | 0 | 0 | 0 | 0 | 0 | 34 | 5 | 6 | 14 |
| 3 | 2 | 2 | 2 | 2 | 2 | 2 | 2 | 2 | 1 | 1 | 1 | 1 | 1 | 1 | 1 | 1 | 2 | 1 | 1 | 0 | 1 | 1 | 1 | 0 | 0 | 34 | 2 | 12 | 11 |
| 63 | 2 | 2 | 2 | 2 | 2 | 2 | 2 | 2 | 1 | 1 | 2 | 2 | 1 | 1 | 1 | 0 | 2 | 2 | 0 | 1 | 1 | 1 | 0 | 0 | 0 | 34 | 4 | 8 | 13 |
| ★ 8 | 2 | 2 | 2 | 2 | 2 | 2 | 2 | 2 | 2 | 2 | 2 | 1 | 2 | 0 | 1 | 2 | 0 | 2 | 1 | 0 | 0 | 0 | 0 | 0 | 0 | 33 | 7 | 3 | 15 |
| ★ 71 | 2 | 0 | 2 | 1 | 0 | 2 | 2 | 2 | 2 | 0 | 2 | 2 | 2 | 0 | 0 | 1 | 2 | 0 | 2 | 0 | 1 | 2 | 2 | 2 | 2 | 33 | 7 | 3 | 15 |
| 69 | 2 | 2 | 2 | 2 | 2 | 2 | 2 | 2 | 1 | 2 | 2 | 1 | 2 | 1 | 1 | 1 | 1 | 1 | 2 | 1 | 0 | 1 | 0 | 0 | 0 | 33 | 5 | 7 | 13 |
| 19 | 2 | 2 | 2 | 2 | 2 | 2 | 1 | 1 | 2 | 1 | 2 | 2 | 0 | 1 | 1 | 2 | 2 | 1 | 0 | 1 | 0 | 0 | 0 | 0 | 0 | 32 | 6 | 6 | 13 |
| 42 | 2 | 2 | 2 | 2 | 2 | 1 | 1 | 2 | 2 | 1 | 2 | 1 | 1 | 1 | 2 | 2 | 1 | 1 | 1 | 1 | 0 | 0 | 0 | 0 | 0 | 32 | 3 | 12 | 10 |
| 24 | 2 | 2 | 2 | 2 | 2 | 1 | 2 | 2 | 1 | 1 | 2 | 1 | 1 | 1 | 1 | 2 | 2 | 0 | 0 | 2 | 1 | 1 | 0 | 0 | 0 | 32 | 5 | 8 | 12 |
| 31 | 2 | 2 | 2 | 2 | 1 | 2 | 2 | 2 | 1 | 1 | 2 | 1 | 1 | 1 | 1 | 0 | 1 | 1 | 1 | 1 | 1 | 1 | 1 | 1 | 0 | 31 | 2 | 15 | 8 |
| 65 | 2 | 2 | 2 | 2 | 2 | 2 | 2 | 2 | 1 | 1 | 1 | 0 | 1 | 1 | 1 | 0 | 2 | 0 | 1 | 0 | 1 | 1 | 2 | 2 | 2 | 31 | 5 | 9 | 11 |
| 54 | 2 | 2 | 2 | 1 | 2 | 1 | 2 | 1 | 1 | 1 | 1 | 1 | 1 | 1 | 2 | 1 | 1 | 1 | 2 | 1 | 1 | 0 | 0 | 0 | 0 | 30 | 3 | 14 | 8 |
| 66 | 2 | 2 | 2 | 2 | 2 | 2 | 2 | 2 | 1 | 1 | 2 | 2 | 1 | 1 | 0 | 1 | 0 | 1 | 0 | 1 | 0 | 0 | 0 | 0 | 0 | 30 | 7 | 6 | 12 |
| 1 | 2 | 2 | 2 | 2 | 2 | 2 | 2 | 2 | 1 | 1 | 2 | 1 | 1 | 0 | 0 | 1 | 0 | 1 | 0 | 2 | 0 | 1 | 0 | 0 | 0 | 30 | 6 | 8 | 11 |
| 61 | 2 | 2 | 2 | 2 | 2 | 1 | 1 | 1 | 1 | 1 | 2 | 2 | 1 | 1 | 1 | 1 | 1 | 2 | 1 | 2 | 0 | 0 | 1 | 0 | 0 | 29 | 5 | 11 | 9 |
| 67 | 2 | 2 | 1 | 1 | 2 | 2 | 2 | 2 | 1 | 1 | 1 | 1 | 1 | 2 | 0 | 1 | 1 | 2 | 1 | 0 | 1 | 0 | 1 | 0 | 0 | 29 | 5 | 11 | 9 |
| 28 | 2 | 2 | 2 | 2 | 2 | 1 | 2 | 1 | 2 | 2 | 1 | 2 | 0 | 1 | 1 | 1 | 1 | 0 | 2 | 1 | 0 | 0 | 0 | 0 | 1 | 29 | 6 | 9 | 10 |
| 10 | 2 | 2 | 2 | 2 | 1 | 2 | 1 | 1 | 2 | 2 | 2 | 1 | 1 | 1 | 1 | 0 | 1 | 1 | 2 | 0 | 1 | 0 | 0 | 0 | 0 | 28 | 6 | 10 | 9 |
| 21 | 2 | 2 | 2 | 2 | 2 | 1 | 2 | 1 | 1 | 1 | 1 | 1 | 1 | 1 | 1 | 1 | 1 | 1 | 1 | 1 | 1 | 1 | 0 | 0 | 0 | 28 | 3 | 16 | 6 |
| 62 | 2 | 2 | 2 | 2 | 2 | 2 | 2 | 2 | 2 | 0 | 0 | 2 | 0 | 1 | 1 | 2 | 0 | 0 | 2 | 0 | 0 | 0 | 0 | 0 | 0 | 28 | 11 | 0 | 14 |
| ★ 73 | 0 | 2 | 1 | 2 | 0 | 2 | 0 | 0 | 0 | 2 | 2 | 2 | 1 | 1 | 2 | 1 | 2 | 1 | 2 | 0 | 1 | 2 | 2 | 0 | 0 | 28 | 8 | 6 | 11 |
| 44 | 2 | 2 | 1 | 2 | 2 | 1 | 2 | 1 | 2 | 1 | 2 | 1 | 0 | 2 | 2 | 1 | 1 | 1 | 1 | 0 | 0 | 0 | 0 | 0 | 0 | 28 | 6 | 10 | 9 |
| 27 | 2 | 2 | 2 | 1 | 2 | 1 | 2 | 1 | 1 | 1 | 2 | 1 | 1 | 0 | 1 | 1 | 1 | 0 | 1 | 1 | 0 | 1 | 0 | 2 | 0 | 27 | 5 | 13 | 7 |
| 15 | 1 | 2 | 1 | 1 | 1 | 1 | 1 | 1 | 1 | 1 | 1 | 1 | 1 | 1 | 1 | 1 | 1 | 1 | 1 | 1 | 1 | 2 | 1 | 1 | 1 | 27 | 0 | 23 | 2 |
| 35 | 2 | 2 | 2 | 1 | 1 | 1 | 1 | 2 | 1 | 1 | 2 | 2 | 1 | 1 | 1 | 1 | 1 | 1 | 0 | 0 | 0 | 0 | 1 | 0 | 2 | 27 | 3 | 17 | 5 |
| 37 | 2 | 2 | 2 | 2 | 1 | 1 | 1 | 2 | 1 | 1 | 2 | 2 | 1 | 1 | 1 | 1 | 1 | 0 | 1 | 0 | 0 | 0 | 0 | 0 | 0 | 27 | 6 | 11 | 8 |
| 4 | 2 | 2 | 2 | 2 | 2 | 1 | 2 | 0 | 1 | 1 | 1 | 1 | 1 | 1 | 1 | 2 | 0 | 1 | 0 | 1 | 0 | 0 | 0 | 1 | 0 | 27 | 5 | 13 | 7 |
| 52 | 2 | 2 | 1 | 1 | 1 | 1 | 1 | 1 | 1 | 1 | 1 | 1 | 1 | 1 | 1 | 1 | 1 | 1 | 1 | 1 | 1 | 1 | 1 | 1 | 1 | 27 | 0 | 23 | 2 |
| 32 | 2 | 1 | 2 | 1 | 2 | 2 | 2 | 2 | 1 | 1 | 2 | 1 | 1 | 1 | 1 | 1 | 1 | 0 | 0 | 0 | 0 | 0 | 0 | 0 | 0 | 26 | 7 | 10 | 8 |
| 46 | 2 | 2 | 2 | 2 | 2 | 2 | 2 | 2 | 0 | 2 | 1 | 2 | 2 | 2 | 0 | 0 | 0 | 0 | 0 | 0 | 0 | 0 | 1 | 0 | 0 | 26 | 11 | 2 | 12 |
| 20 | 2 | 2 | 2 | 2 | 2 | 1 | 2 | 1 | 1 | 1 | 2 | 0 | 1 | 2 | 0 | 2 | 2 | 0 | 0 | 0 | 0 | 0 | 0 | 0 | 0 | 26 | 9 | 6 | 10 |
| 75 | 2 | 2 | 2 | 2 | 1 | 2 | 2 | 2 | 1 | 1 | 0 | 0 | 1 | 2 | 0 | 1 | 0 | 1 | 0 | 0 | 1 | 0 | 0 | 0 | 1 | 26 | 8 | 8 | 9 |
| 36 | 2 | 2 | 2 | 1 | 2 | 1 | 1 | 1 | 1 | 1 | 1 | 1 | 1 | 0 | 1 | 1 | 1 | 0 | 1 | 0 | 0 | 0 | 1 | 0 | 2 | 25 | 5 | 15 | 5 |
| 26 | 1 | 1 | 1 | 1 | 1 | 1 | 1 | 1 | 1 | 1 | 1 | 1 | 1 | 1 | 1 | 1 | 1 | 1 | 1 | 1 | 1 | 1 | 1 | 1 | 1 | 25 | 0 | 25 | 0 |
| 55 | 2 | 2 | 2 | 1 | 2 | 1 | 1 | 0 | 1 | 1 | 1 | 2 | 1 | 1 | 1 | 2 | 1 | 0 | 2 | 1 | 0 | 0 | 1 | 1 | 0 | 25 | 6 | 13 | 6 |
| 6 | 2 | 2 | 2 | 1 | 1 | 1 | 0 | 0 | 1 | 1 | 1 | 1 | 1 | 1 | 0 | 1 | 0 | 0 | 1 | 1 | 0 | 1 | 1 | 2 | 2 | 24 | 6 | 14 | 5 |
| 9 | 2 | 1 | 2 | 2 | 2 | 1 | 2 | 1 | 0 | 0 | 1 | 0 | 1 | 1 | 0 | 0 | 1 | 1 | 1 | 0 | 1 | 0 | 0 | 2 | 1 | 24 | 7 | 12 | 6 |
| 13 | 2 | 2 | 2 | 2 | 1 | 1 | 1 | 2 | 2 | 1 | 0 | 1 | 0 | 1 | 0 | 1 | 0 | 1 | 0 | 1 | 1 | 0 | 0 | 0 | 0 | 24 | 7 | 12 | 6 |
| 47 | 2 | 2 | 1 | 2 | 2 | 2 | 1 | 1 | 1 | 1 | 0 | 0 | 0 | 2 | 1 | 1 | 0 | 1 | 0 | 1 | 0 | 0 | 0 | 0 | 2 | 24 | 8 | 10 | 7 |
| 14 | 2 | 2 | 2 | 2 | 2 | 0 | 0 | 1 | 0 | 2 | 2 | 0 | 1 | 1 | 0 | 1 | 0 | 2 | 0 | 0 | 1 | 0 | 0 | 1 | 0 | 23 | 11 | 5 | 9 |
| 49 | 1 | 1 | 1 | 1 | 0 | 1 | 1 | 1 | 1 | 1 | 1 | 1 | 1 | 1 | 1 | 1 | 1 | 0 | 2 | 0 | 1 | 0 | 0 | 2 | 1 | 21 | 6 | 17 | 2 |
| 5 | 2 | 2 | 1 | 1 | 1 | 1 | 1 | 0 | 0 | 1 | 1 | 1 | 0 | 1 | 0 | 0 | 1 | 0 | 1 | 0 | 0 | 1 | 1 | 1 | 1 | 19 | 8 | 15 | 2 |
| 68 | 2 | 2 | 2 | 2 | 0 | 1 | 0 | 2 | 1 | 1 | 1 | 0 | 1 | 0 | 0 | 0 | 0 | 1 | 0 | 0 | 0 | 0 | 0 | 0 | 0 | 19 | 12 | 7 | 6 |
| 12 | 2 | 1 | 1 | 1 | 0 | 2 | 0 | 1 | 1 | 0 | 0 | 0 | 0 | 2 | 0 | 1 | 1 | 0 | 1 | 0 | 0 | 1 | 0 | 1 | 2 | 17 | 12 | 9 | 4 |
| 30 | 2 | 2 | 2 | 2 | 2 | 1 | 1 | 0 | 0 | 1 | 0 | 2 | 0 | 0 | 0 | 0 | 0 | 0 | 0 | 0 | 0 | 0 | 0 | 1 | 0 | 16 | 15 | 4 | 6 |
| 72 | 2 | 1 | 1 | 1 | 0 | 1 | 0 | 0 | 1 | 0 | 0 | 0 | 0 | 0 | 1 | 0 | 0 | 0 | 1 | 1 | 2 | 2 | 0 | 0 | 0 | 14 | 14 | 8 | 3 |
| 29 | 2 | 2 | 1 | 1 | 0 | 1 | 1 | 0 | 0 | 1 | 0 | 0 | 0 | 0 | 0 | 0 | 1 | 0 | 0 | 1 | 0 | 1 | 0 | 2 | 1 | 14 | 14 | 8 | 3 |
| 53 | 2 | 1 | 1 | 0 | 0 | 1 | 1 | 1 | 1 | 0 | 0 | 0 | 0 | 0 | 0 | 0 | 1 | 1 | 0 | 0 | 0 | 0 | 0 | 1 | 0 | 12 | 14 | 10 | 1 |
| **Activity Score** | 145 | 141 | 137 | 130 | 127 | 121 | 119 | 116 | 111 | 109 | 107 | 97 | 95 | 91 | 88 | 88 | 85 | 83 | 80 | 69 | 54 | 52 | 50 | 42 | 37 | | **0** | **1** | **2** |
| Frequency of Response 0 | 1 | 1 | 0 | 2 | 7 | 2 | 6 | 8 | 7 | 3 | 10 | 12 | 12 | 12 | 14 | 13 | 17 | 14 | 21 | 25 | 32 | 32 | 36 | 44 | 47 | | | | |
| Frequency of Response 1 | 3 | 7 | 13 | 16 | 9 | 25 | 19 | 18 | 25 | 35 | 23 | 29 | 31 | 35 | 34 | 36 | 31 | 39 | 28 | 31 | 32 | 34 | 28 | 20 | 19 | | | | |
| Frequency of Response 2 | 71 | 67 | 62 | 57 | 59 | 48 | 50 | 49 | 43 | 37 | 42 | 34 | 32 | 28 | 27 | 26 | 27 | 22 | 26 | 19 | 11 | 9 | 11 | 11 | 9 | | | | |

Child Score column at right; Frequency of Response (0, 1, 2) at far right.

Activity Number across top. Starred activity: 3.

Frequency of Response rows at bottom: 0, 1, 2.

number at the top of the matrix.   The entries in each column are summed down the matrix over the seventy-five children to obtain a score for that activity.   These activity scores appear at the bottom of the matrix.   They too have been sorted so that the easiest-to-like activity with the highest score (Activity *18*, score = 145) is on the left of the matrix, and the hardest-to-like activity with the lowest score (Activity *5*, score = 37) is on the right.

From the column of responses to Activity *18* on the left of the matrix we see that most of these seventy-five children *liked* "Going on a picnic".   But Activity *5* on the right of the matrix, "Finding old bottles and cans", was liked by very few children, and *disliked* by most.

***Investigating Unusual Activities.*** The upper left corner of Figure 2.4b contains the responses of high-scoring children to activities which are easy to like.   These responses are almost all 2's.   This is what we expect.   Children who like most of these twenty-five activities should certainly like the ones that are easy to like.   The lower right corner of Figure 2.4b contains the responses of low-scoring children to activities which are difficult to like.   In this corner of the matrix 2's are rare.

A triangular pattern of 2's is the hallmark of the orderliness we seek.   To bring out the structure in these data the 1's and 0's have been removed and the remaining matrix of 2's displayed in Figure 2.4c.   Now the pattern of 2's is obvious.   The few activities that high-scoring children at the top of the matrix do not like are on the far right of the matrix, while the few activities that low-scoring children at the bottom do like tend to be on the far left.   The triangular shape of this pattern is an indication that in general the activities are functioning together to define a single line of inquiry.

A closer examination of the pattern, however, reveals a few puzzles.   If a particular activity defines the same dimension as the majority of activities, then there should be agreement between the responses children make to this activity and their scores on the questionnaire as a whole.   Consider, for example, the column of responses given to Activity *3* "Reading books on plants".   Twenty-six children gave a 2 to this activity.   These twenty-six children are almost all at the top of the matrix.   In fact, seventeen of the eighteen children who scored above 38 on the questionnaire gave a 2 to Activity *3*, while none of the twenty-six children who scored below 28 gave it a 2.   This is the type of response pattern we expect when a particular activity follows the same line of inquiry as the majority of activities.

Consider now responses to Activities *23* "Watching a rat" and *5* "Finding old bottles and cans" on the far right of the matrix.   Eleven children gave a 2 to Activity *23*.   But they were not all high-scoring children.   In fact, only three of these eleven children scored above 38 on the questionnaire, while six scored below 28.   Low-scoring children appear to like watching a rat more than high-scoring children.   Similarly, only two of the nine children who gave a 2 to Activity *5* scored above 38, while five scored below 28.   Low-scoring children also appear to like finding old bottles and cans more than high-scoring children.

The aim of our work with these data is to calibrate a sequence of activities along a line of increasing liking for science.   But first, we must establish whether these activities work together to define a single variable.   If they do not, then our efforts to position all twenty-five activities along a line in a useful way will be in vain.

The 2's in the lower right corner of Figure 2.4c are unexpected responses.   While we might not be surprised to find a few unlikely responses in this corner of the matrix, when they

# FIGURE 2.4c
## "LIKING" SCIENCE ACTIVITIES

Child Number ... Activity Number ... Child Score

| Child No. | 18 | 19 | 12 | 10 | 13 | 11 | 21 | 2 | 15 | 1 | 24 | 22 | 17 | 6 | 14 | 3 | 25 | 16 | 9 | 7 | 8 | 4 | 20 | 23 | 5 | Child Score |
|---|---|---|---|---|---|---|---|---|---|---|---|---|---|---|---|---|---|---|---|---|---|---|---|---|---|---|
| 2 | 2 | 2 | 2 | 2 | 2 | 2 | 2 | 2 | 2 | 2 | 2 | 2 | 2 | 2 | 2 | 2 | 2 | 2 | 2 | 2 | 2 | 2 | 2 | 2 | 2 | 50 |
| 41 | 2 | 2 | 2 | 2 | 2 | 2 | 2 | 2 | 2 | 2 | 2 | 2 | 2 | 2 | 2 | 2 | 2 | 2 | 2 | 2 | 2 | 2 | | 2 | 2 | 49 |
| 34 | 2 | 2 | 2 | 2 | 2 | 2 | 2 | 2 | 2 | 2 | 2 | 2 | 2 | 2 | 2 | 2 | 2 | 2 | 2 | 2 | 2 | 2 | | | | 48 |
| 17 | 2 | 2 | 2 | 2 | 2 | 2 | 2 | 2 | 2 | 2 | 2 | 2 | 2 | 2 | 2 | 2 | 2 | 2 | 2 | 2 | 2 | 2 | 2 | | | 47 |
| 50 | 2 | 2 | 2 | 2 | 2 | 2 | 2 | 2 | 2 | 2 | 2 | 2 | 2 | 2 | 2 | 2 | 2 | 2 | 2 | 2 | 2 | 2 | | | | 46 |
| 45 | 2 | 2 | 2 | 2 | 2 | 2 | 2 | 2 | 2 | 2 | 2 | 2 | 2 | 2 | 2 | 2 | 2 | 2 | 2 | 2 | 2 | | 2 | | | 45 |
| 7 | 2 | 2 | 2 | 2 | 2 | 2 | 2 | 2 | 2 | 2 | 2 | 2 | 2 | 2 | 2 | 2 | 2 | 2 | 2 | | 2 | 2 | | 2 | | 44 |
| 48 | 2 | 2 | 2 | 2 | 2 | 2 | 2 | 2 | 2 | 2 | 2 | 2 | 2 | 2 | 2 | 2 | 2 | 2 | 2 | | 2 | 2 | | | | 43 |
| 16 | 2 | 2 | 2 | 2 | 2 | 2 | 2 | 2 | 2 | 2 | 2 | 2 | 2 | 2 | 2 | 2 | 2 | 2 | 2 | | | | | | | 43 |
| 25 | 2 | 2 | 2 | 2 | 2 | 2 | 2 | 2 | 2 | 2 | 2 | 2 | 2 | 2 | 2 | 2 | 2 | 2 | 2 | | 2 | | | | | 42 |
| 59 | 2 | 2 | 2 | 2 | 2 | 2 | 2 | 2 | 2 | 2 | 2 | 2 | 2 | 2 | 2 | 2 | 2 | 2 | 2 | | | | | 2 | | 42 |
| 39 | 2 | 2 | 2 | 2 | 2 | 2 | 2 | 2 | 2 | 2 | 2 | 2 | 2 | 2 | 2 | 2 | 2 | 2 | | 2 | | | | | | 41 |
| 18 | 2 | 2 | 2 | 2 | 2 | 2 | 2 | 2 | 2 | 2 | 2 | 2 | 2 | 2 | | 2 | 2 | 2 | | 2 | | | 2 | | | 41 |
| 56 | 2 | 2 | 2 | 2 | 2 | 2 | 2 | 2 | 2 | 2 | 2 | 2 | 2 | | 2 | 2 | 2 | 2 | | 2 | | | | | | 40 |
| 57 | 2 | 2 | 2 | 2 | 2 | 2 | 2 | 2 | 2 | 2 | 2 | 2 | | 2 | 2 | 2 | 2 | 2 | 2 | 2 | | | | | | 40 |
| 23 | 2 | 2 | 2 | 2 | 2 | 2 | 2 | 2 | 2 | 2 | 2 | 2 | | | | | | 2 | | 2 | | | | | | 40 |
| 40 | 2 | 2 | 2 | 2 | 2 | 2 | 2 | 2 | 2 | 2 | 2 | 2 | | | | 2 | 2 | 2 | | | | | | | | 39 |
| 70 | 2 | 2 | 2 | 2 | 2 | 2 | 2 | 2 | 2 | 2 | 2 | 2 | 2 | 2 | | | | 2 | | 2 | | 2 | | | | 39 |
| 33 | 2 | 2 | 2 | 2 | 2 | 2 | 2 | 2 | 2 | 2 | 2 | 2 | 2 | 2 | | | | | | | 2 | 2 | | | | 38 |
| 38 | 2 | 2 | 2 | 2 | 2 | 2 | 2 | 2 | 2 | 2 | 2 | 2 | 2 | 2 | | | | | | | | | 2 | | | 38 |
| 43 | 2 | 2 | 2 | 2 | 2 | 2 | 2 | 2 | 2 | 2 | 2 | | 2 | | | 2 | | | 2 | 2 | | | | | | 37 |
| 74 | 2 | 2 | 2 | 2 | 2 | 2 | 2 | 2 | 2 | 2 | | 2 | 2 | 2 | | 2 | 2 | 2 | | 2 | | | | | | 37 |
| 60 | 2 | 2 | 2 | 2 | 2 | 2 | 2 | 2 | 2 | | 2 | | | | | 2 | | | | 2 | | | | | | 36 |
| 64 | 2 | 2 | 2 | 2 | 2 | 2 | 2 | 2 | | 2 | | 2 | 2 | 2 | | | | | | 2 | | | | | | 36 |
| 58 | 2 | 2 | 2 | 2 | 2 | 2 | 2 | 2 | 2 | | | 2 | | 2 | | 2 | 2 | | | 2 | | | | | | 35 |
| 11 | 2 | 2 | 2 | 2 | 2 | 2 | 2 | 2 | 2 | 2 | | 2 | 2 | 2 | | 2 | 2 | 2 | | | | | | | | 35 |
| 22 | 2 | 2 | 2 | 2 | 2 | 2 | 2 | 2 | 2 | | | 2 | | | | | | | | | | | | | | 35 |
| 51 | 2 | 2 | 2 | 2 | 2 | 2 | 2 | 2 | 2 | | | 2 | | | | 2 | 2 | | 2 | 2 | | | | | | 34 |
| 3 | 2 | 2 | 2 | 2 | 2 | 2 | 2 | 2 | 2 | | | | | | | | | 2 | | | | | | | | 34 |
| 63 | 2 | 2 | 2 | 2 | 2 | 2 | 2 | 2 | | | | 2 | 2 | | | | | | 2 | 2 | | | | | | 34 |
| 8 | 2 | 2 | 2 | 2 | 2 | 2 | 2 | 2 | 2 | 2 | | 2 | | 2 | | | | 2 | | 2 | | | | | | 33 |
| ★ 71 | 2 | | 2 | | | 2 | 2 | 2 | 2 | 2 | | 2 | 2 | 2 | | | | 2 | | 2 | | | 2 | 2 | 2 | 33 |
| 69 | 2 | 2 | 2 | 2 | 2 | 2 | 2 | 2 | | | 2 | 2 | | 2 | | | | 2 | | 2 | | | | | | 33 |
| 19 | 2 | 2 | 2 | 2 | 2 | 2 | 2 | 2 | | | 2 | 2 | | | 2 | 2 | 2 | | | | | | | | | 32 |
| 42 | 2 | 2 | 2 | 2 | 2 | | 2 | 2 | 2 | | 2 | 2 | | | 2 | 2 | | | | | | | | | | 32 |
| 24 | 2 | 2 | 2 | 2 | 2 | | 2 | 2 | | 2 | | 2 | | | | 2 | 2 | | | 2 | | | | | | 32 |
| 31 | 2 | 2 | 2 | 2 | | 2 | 2 | 2 | | 2 | | | | | | | | | | | | | | | | 31 |
| 65 | 2 | 2 | 2 | 2 | | 2 | 2 | 2 | | | | | | | | | | 2 | | | | | | 2 | 2 | 31 |
| 54 | 2 | 2 | 2 | | 2 | | 2 | | | | | | | 2 | | | | 2 | 2 | | | | | | | 30 |
| 66 | 2 | 2 | 2 | 2 | 2 | 2 | 2 | 2 | 2 | | 2 | 2 | 2 | | | | | | | | | | | | | 30 |
| 1 | 2 | 2 | 2 | 2 | 2 | 2 | 2 | 2 | 2 | | 2 | 2 | | | | | | | | 2 | | | | | | 30 |
| 61 | 2 | 2 | 2 | 2 | 2 | | | | | 2 | 2 | | | | | | | 2 | | 2 | | | | | | 29 |
| 67 | 2 | 2 | | 2 | 2 | 2 | 2 | 2 | | | | | | 2 | | | | 2 | | | | | | | | 29 |
| 28 | 2 | 2 | 2 | 2 | | 2 | | 2 | 2 | | 2 | | | | | | | | | 2 | | | | | | 29 |
| 10 | 2 | 2 | 2 | 2 | | 2 | | 2 | 2 | 2 | | | | | | | | | 2 | | | | | | | 28 |
| 21 | 2 | 2 | 2 | 2 | 2 | | 2 | | | | | | | | | | | | | | | | | | | 28 |
| 62 | 2 | 2 | 2 | 2 | 2 | 2 | | 2 | | 2 | | | | 2 | | 2 | 2 | | 2 | 2 | | | | | | 28 |
| ★ 73 | | 2 | 2 | | 2 | | 2 | | | | 2 | 2 | 2 | | | 2 | | 2 | | 2 | | | 2 | 2 | | 28 |
| 44 | 2 | 2 | | 2 | 2 | 2 | | 2 | | | 2 | | 2 | 2 | | | | | | | | | | 2 | | 28 |
| 27 | 2 | 2 | 2 | | 2 | | 2 | | | | 2 | | | | | | | | | | | | | | | 27 |
| 15 | | 2 | | | | | | | | | | | | | | | | | | | | | | 2 | | 27 |
| 35 | 2 | 2 | 2 | | 2 | | | | | | | | | | | | | | | | | | | | 2 | 27 |
| 37 | 2 | 2 | 2 | 2 | 2 | | 2 | | 2 | 2 | | | | | | | | | | | | | | | | 27 |
| 4 | 2 | 2 | 2 | 2 | 2 | | 2 | | | | | | | | | | | | | | 2 | | | | | 27 |
| 52 | 2 | 2 | | | | | | | | | | | | | | | | | | | | | | | | 27 |
| 32 | 2 | | 2 | | 2 | 2 | 2 | 2 | | | 2 | 2 | 2 | | | | | | | | | | | | | 26 |
| 46 | 2 | 2 | 2 | 2 | 2 | 2 | 2 | 2 | | 2 | | 2 | 2 | 2 | | | | | | | | | | | | 26 |
| 20 | 2 | 2 | 2 | 2 | 2 | | 2 | | | | 2 | | | | | 2 | | 2 | 2 | | | | | | | 26 |
| 75 | 2 | 2 | 2 | 2 | 2 | | 2 | 2 | 2 | | | | | | | 2 | | | | | | | | | | 26 |
| 36 | 2 | 2 | 2 | | 2 | | | | | | | | | | | | | | | | | | | | 2 | 25 |
| 26 | | | | | | | | | | | | | | | | | | | | | | | | | | 25 |
| 55 | 2 | 2 | 2 | | 2 | | | | | | | | 2 | | | | | 2 | | | | | | | | 25 |
| 6 | 2 | 2 | 2 | | | | | | | | | | | | | | | | | | | | | 2 | 2 | 24 |
| 9 | | | 2 | 2 | 2 | | 2 | | | | | | | | | | | | | | | | | 2 | | 24 |
| 13 | 2 | 2 | 2 | 2 | | | | 2 | 2 | | | | | | | | | | | | | | | | | 24 |
| 47 | 2 | 2 | | 2 | 2 | 2 | | | | | | | | 2 | | | | | | | | | | | 2 | 24 |
| 14 | 2 | 2 | 2 | 2 | 2 | | | | | 2 | 2 | | | 2 | | | | | | | 2 | | | | | 23 |
| 49 | | | | | | | | | | | | | | | | | | | 2 | | | | | 2 | | 21 |
| 5 | 2 | 2 | | | | | | | | | | | | | | | | | | | | | | | | 19 |
| 68 | 2 | 2 | 2 | 2 | | | | 2 | 2 | | | | | | | | | | | | | | | | | 19 |
| 12 | 2 | | | | | 2 | | | | | | | | 2 | | | | | | | | | | | 2 | 17 |
| 30 | 2 | 2 | 2 | 2 | 2 | | | | | | 2 | | | | | | | | | | | | | | | 16 |
| 72 | 2 | | | | | | | | | | | | | | | | | | | | | | | 2 | 2 | 14 |
| 29 | 2 | 2 | | | | | | | | | | | | | | | | | | | | | | 2 | | 14 |
| 53 | 2 | | | | | | | | | | | | | | | | | | | | | | | | | 12 |
| **Activity Score** | 145 | 141 | 137 | 130 | 127 | 121 | 119 | 116 | 111 | 109 | 107 | 97 | 95 | 91 | 88 | 88 | 85 | 83 | 80 | 69 | 54 | 52 | 50 | 42 | 37 | |

pile up to form a column or a row of misplaced 2's, that is a sign of trouble. A column of misplaced 2's is an indication that an activity is not functioning as intended, that it is not collaborating with the other activities to define a single variable.

It seems clear from Figure 2.4c that Activities *5* and *23* do not fit with the other activities. There appears to be almost no relationship between liking these activities and liking the others. When we look back at Figures 2.3a and 2.3b we see that Activities *5* and *23* are two of the three activities which our judges had most trouble positioning among the other activities. The responses of these seventy-five children to Activities *5* and *23* add to our suspicion that they do not belong on the same liking-for-science line as the majority of these activities.

The third activity upon which the judges showed poor agreement was *16*, "Making a map". We see in Figure 2.4c that three low-scoring children liked this relatively difficult activity, and a few high-scoring children did not like it. While the responses to this activity are not as disorderly as the responses to Activities *5* and *23*, neither are they as orderly as the responses to Activity *3*. Does this activity belong on the line defined by the majority of the science activities? To make a decision on Activity *16* it would be helpful if we could estimate *how* unlikely the unexpected responses to Activity *16* are. In particular, it would be helpful to know how unlikely this pattern of responses would be if Activity *16* were assumed to define the same attitude variable as the other activities. In Chapter 5 we develop a statistic which tells how well each activity fits with the other activities in a questionnaire.

***Identifying Children with Unusual Responses.*** A column of misplaced 2's in Figure 2.4c is a sign that an activity is not functioning to define the science variable as intended. A row of misplaced 2's is a sign that a child has responded in an unusual way. Consider the responses of Child *8*. This child liked the twelve activities which were easiest to like and, as Figure 2.4b shows, disliked the five hardest-to-like activities. His responses are consistent with the ordering of the activities by activity score, and we should be able to use his score of 33 to tell us where he stands among these activities without having to refer to the particulars of his responses.

Now consider the responses made by Child *71* in the next row of Figure 2.4b. This child also made a score of 33 on the questionnaire, but the way in which he did so is puzzling. He did not like three of the easy-to-like activities on the left of the matrix, but liked the three activities which were hardest to like. If we reorder the twenty-five activities on the basis of this child's responses we obtain a very different difficulty ordering from the one at the bottom of the matrix. Not only does the 33 of Child *71* not tell the same story as the 33 of Child *8*, but we cannot use the summary ordering of the twenty-five activities at the bottom of the matrix to tell us what the 33 of Child *71* means in terms of liked and disliked activities. The same problem arises for Child *73* further down the matrix.

We can learn still more about the science data matrix by removing the 1's and 2's to show the pattern of 0's. This pattern is displayed in Figure 2.4d. As expected, the 0's are concentrated in the lower right corner of the matrix (low-scoring children responding to activities which are hard to like). Two strings of unexpected 0's spoil this picture. These strings are in the response records of Children *71* and *73*—the same children identified for their surprising patterns of likes. We see that these two children like a surprising number of hard-to-like activities, and dislike a surprising number of easy-to-like activities.

# FIGURE 2.4d
## "DISLIKING" SCIENCE ACTIVITIES

Child Number — Activity Number — Child Score

Activity Number (column headers, left to right):
18  19  12  10  13  11  21  2  15  1  24  22  17  6  14  3  25  16  9  7  8  4  20  23  5

| Child | 18 | 19 | 12 | 10 | 13 | 11 | 21 | 2 | 15 | 1 | 24 | 22 | 17 | 6 | 14 | 3 | 25 | 16 | 9 | 7 | 8 | 4 | 20 | 23 | 5 | Score |
|---|---|---|---|---|---|---|---|---|---|---|---|---|---|---|---|---|---|---|---|---|---|---|---|---|---|---|
| 2 | | | | | | | | | | | | | | | | | | | | | | | | | | 50 |
| 41 | | | | | | | | | | | | | | | | | | | | | | | | | | 49 |
| 34 | | | | | | | | | | | | | | | | | | | | | | | | | | 48 |
| 17 | | | | | | | | | | | | | | | | | | | | | | | | 0 | | 47 |
| 50 | | | | | | | | | | | | | | | | | | | | | | | | | | 46 |
| 45 | | | | | | | | | | | | | | | | | | | | | | | | 0 | 0 | 45 |
| 7 | | | | | | | | | | | | | | | | | | | 0 | | | 0 | | | 0 | 44 |
| 48 | | | | | | | | | | | | | | | | | | | | | | | | 0 | 0 | 43 |
| 16 | | | | | | | | | | | | | | | | | | | | | | | | 0 | | 43 |
| 25 | | | | | | | | | | | | | | | | | | | | | 0 | | | 0 | | 42 |
| 59 | | | | | | | | | | | | | | | | | | | | | | | 0 | | 0 | 42 |
| 39 | | | | | | | | | | | | | | | | | | | | | | | | 0 | 0 | 41 |
| 18 | | | | | | | | | | | | | | | | | | | | | 0 | | | 0 | 0 | 41 |
| 56 | | | | | | | | | | | | | | | | | | | | | 0 | | | 0 | 0 | 40 |
| 57 | | | | | | | | | | | | | | | | | | | | | 0 | 0 | 0 | 0 | 0 | 40 |
| 23 | | | | | | | | | | | | | | | | | | | | | | | | | | 40 |
| 40 | | | | | | | | | | | | | | | | | | | | | 0 | | | 0 | 0 | 39 |
| 70 | | | | | | | | | | | | | | | | | | | | | 0 | | 0 | 0 | 0 | 39 |
| 33 | | | | | | | | | | | | | | | | | | 0 | | | | | 0 | 0 | 0 | 38 |
| 38 | | | | | | | | | | | | | | | | | | | | | | | | | 0 | 38 |
| 43 | | | | | | | | | | | | | | | | | | | | | 0 | 0 | 0 | 0 | | 37 |
| 74 | | | | | | | | | | | | | | | | | | | | 0 | 0 | 0 | 0 | 0 | | 37 |
| 60 | | | | | | | | | | | | | | | | | | | | | | | | 0 | | 36 |
| 64 | | | | | | | | | | | | | | | | | | | | | | 0 | | 0 | | 36 |
| 58 | | | | | | | | | | | | | | | | | | | | 0 | | 0 | | 0 | 0 | 35 |
| 11 | | | | | | | | | | | | | | | | | | | 0 | 0 | | 0 | | 0 | 0 | 35 |
| 22 | | | | | | | | | | | | | | | | | | | | | | | | | | 35 |
| 51 | | | | | | | | | | | | | | | | | | | | | 0 | 0 | | 0 | 0 | 34 |
| 3 | | | | | | | | | | | | | | | | | | | | | 0 | | | | 0 | 34 |
| 63 | | | | | | | | | | | | | | | | | 0 | | | 0 | | | | 0 | 0 | 34 |
| 8 | | | | | | | | | | | | | | | 0 | | | 0 | | | 0 | 0 | 0 | 0 | 0 | 33 |
| ★ 71 | | 0 | | | 0 | | | | | | 0 | | | | 0 | 0 | | | | | 0 | 0 | | | | 33 |
| 69 | | | | | | | | | | | | | | | | | | | | | | 0 | 0 | 0 | 0 | 33 |
| 19 | | | | | | | | | | | | 0 | | | | | | | | | 0 | 0 | | 0 | 0 | 32 |
| 42 | | | | | | | | | | | | | | | | | | | | | | | | 0 | 0 | 32 |
| 24 | | | | | | | | | | | | | | | | 0 | 0 | | | | | | | 0 | 0 | 32 |
| 31 | | | | | | | | | | | | | | | 0 | | | | | | | | | | | 31 |
| 65 | | | | | | | | | | | 0 | | | | | 0 | | 0 | | | 0 | | | | | 31 |
| 54 | | | | | | | | | | | | | | | | | | | | | | | | 0 | 0 | 30 |
| 66 | | | | | | | | | | | | | | | | 0 | | 0 | | | 0 | | | 0 | 0 | 30 |
| 1 | | | | | | | | | | | | | 0 | 0 | | 0 | | | | | 0 | | | 0 | 0 | 30 |
| 61 | | | | | | | | | | | | | | | | | | 0 | | | 0 | | | 0 | 0 | 29 |
| 67 | | | | | | | | | | | | | 0 | 0 | | | | | | | 0 | | | 0 | 0 | 29 |
| 28 | | | | | | | | | | | | | 0 | 0 | | | | | | | 0 | | | 0 | 0 | 29 |
| 10 | | | | | | | | | | | | | | | | 0 | | | | | 0 | | 0 | 0 | 0 | 28 |
| 21 | | | | | | | | | | | | | | | | | | | | | | | | 0 | 0 | 28 |
| 62 | | | | | | | | | | | | 0 | 0 | | | 0 | | | | | 0 | | 0 | 0 | 0 | 28 |
| ★ 73 | 0 | | | | 0 | | 0 | 0 | 0 | | | | | | | | | | | | 0 | | | 0 | 0 | 28 |
| 44 | | | | | | | | | | | | | | 0 | | | | | | | 0 | | 0 | 0 | 0 | 28 |
| 27 | | | | | | | | | | | | 0 | 0 | | | | | | | | 0 | | | 0 | | 27 |
| 15 | | | | | | | | | | | | | | | | | | | | | | | | | | 27 |
| 35 | | | | | | | | | | | | | | | | | | | | | 0 | 0 | 0 | | | 27 |
| 37 | | | | | | | | | | | | | | | | | | | | | 0 | 0 | 0 | 0 | 0 | 27 |
| 4 | | | | | | | | 0 | | | | | | | | | | | | | 0 | 0 | 0 | | 0 | 27 |
| 52 | | | | | | | | | | | | | | | | | | | | | | | | | | 27 |
| 32 | | | | | | | | | | | | | | | | | 0 | | | | 0 | 0 | 0 | 0 | 0 | 26 |
| 46 | | | | | | | | | 0 | | | | | | 0 | 0 | 0 | 0 | 0 | | 0 | 0 | 0 | 0 | 0 | 26 |
| 20 | | | | | | | | | | | 0 | | | | | 0 | | | | | 0 | 0 | 0 | 0 | 0 | 26 |
| 75 | | | | | | | | | | | 0 | 0 | | | | 0 | 0 | | | | 0 | 0 | 0 | 0 | | 26 |
| 36 | | | | | | | | | | | | | | 0 | | | | | | | 0 | 0 | 0 | | | 25 |
| 26 | | | | | | | | | | | | | | | | | | | | | | | | | | 25 |
| 55 | | | | | | 0 | | | | | | | | | | | 0 | | | | 0 | 0 | | | 0 | 25 |
| 6 | | | | | | 0 | 0 | | | | | | | | | | 0 | 0 | | | 0 | 0 | | | | 24 |
| 9 | | | | | | | | | | 0 | 0 | | 0 | 0 | 0 | | | | | | 0 | | 0 | | | 24 |
| 13 | | | | | | | | | | | 0 | | | | 0 | | | | | 0 | | 0 | | 0 | 0 | 24 |
| 47 | | | | | | | | | | | 0 | 0 | 0 | | | 0 | | | | | 0 | | 0 | 0 | | 24 |
| 14 | | | | | | 0 | 0 | | | | 0 | 0 | | | | 0 | | 0 | | | 0 | | 0 | | 0 | 23 |
| 49 | | | | | 0 | | | | | | | | | | | | 0 | 0 | | | 0 | 0 | 0 | | | 21 |
| 5 | | | | | | | | 0 | 0 | | | | | | | 0 | 0 | | | | 0 | 0 | 0 | | | 19 |
| 68 | | | | | 0 | | 0 | | | | | | | 0 | | 0 | 0 | 0 | | | 0 | 0 | | 0 | 0 | 19 |
| 12 | | | | | 0 | | 0 | | | 0 | 0 | | 0 | | | 0 | 0 | | | | 0 | 0 | 0 | 0 | | 17 |
| 30 | | | | | | | 0 | 0 | | 0 | 0 | | 0 | 0 | 0 | 0 | 0 | 0 | | | 0 | 0 | 0 | | 0 | 16 |
| 72 | | 0 | 0 | 0 | 0 | | | | | | 0 | 0 | 0 | 0 | 0 | 0 | 0 | 0 | | | 0 | 0 | | | 0 | 14 |
| 29 | | 0 | | 0 | 0 | | | | | | 0 | 0 | 0 | 0 | 0 | 0 | 0 | 0 | | | 0 | 0 | 0 | 0 | | 14 |
| 53 | | 0 | 0 | | | | | | | 0 | 0 | 0 | 0 | 0 | 0 | 0 | 0 | | | | | 0 | 0 | 0 | 0 | 12 |

Activity Score: 145 141 137 130 127 121 119 116 111 109 107 97 95 91 88 88 85 83 80 69 54 52 50 42 37

The responses of Children *71* and *73* leave us puzzled about their liking for science. The only other children who dislike the activities on the far left of the matrix are the very low-scoring children at the bottom. Does this mean that Children *71* and *73* have attitudes like children at the bottom of the matrix? On the other hand, from the number of hard-to-like activities they like (Figure 2.4c), we might conclude that their attitudes are more like the attitudes of children near the top of the matrix. Apart from Child *71*, the only other child who likes all three of the hardest-to-like activities is Child *2* at the top of the matrix with a perfect score of 50. The responses of Children *71* and *73* do not tell us where they are on the attitude variable defined by the rest of these children.

Just as we need a way to decide how unlikely the responses to an activity are, given the activity's score, we also need a way to decide *how* unlikely a child's row of responses are, given his score. In Chapter 5 we develop a statistic which can be used to assess how well any particular child's responses fit with the score ordering of the activities.

***Identifying Differences in Response Style.*** While Children *8* and *71* differ in the activities they prefer, they do not differ in the way they use these response categories. The frequencies with which each category of response was used by each child are shown on the right of Figure 2.4b. Children *8* and *71* made their score of 33 by disliking (0) seven activities, being unsure (1) about three activities, and liking (2) the remaining fifteen. But this pattern of category use is not followed by Child *69* who also has a score of 33.

The response frequencies on the right of Figure 2.4b reveal some interesting differences among these children. Consider the seven children whose frequencies are reproduced in Table 2.4a. The third row of Table 2.4a contains the orderly responses of Child *62*. This child liked easy-to-like activities on the left of the matrix and disliked hard-to-like activities on the right. But Child *62* did not respond "not sure/don't care" to *any* activity. For this child there appears to be only one decision for each activity—a choice between liking and disliking. Child *46* has a similar set of frequencies. He responds "not sure/don't care" to only two of the twenty-five activities.

Contrast this with the responses of Child *26* who made a score of 25. This child gave a 1 to all twenty-five activities. Perhaps Child *26* was simply uncooperative, but there are other children like *15* and *52* who express some preferences yet respond "not sure/don't care" to most activities. Child *52*, for example, said he liked Activities *18* "Going on a picnic" and *19* "Going to the zoo", but neither liked nor disliked any of the other twenty-three.

Children *46* and *26*, with their very different use of the response alternatives, have almost the same scores on the questionnaire. Do we believe that their attitudes are almost identical? We will certainly want individual differences like these drawn to our attention. Before accepting the scores of Children *26*, *15* and *52* as indications of their attitudes, we may wish to investigate the reasons for their apparent hesitancy to commit themselves.

### 2.4.3 Scoring Responses Dichotomously

One approach to analyzing the science data in Figure 2.4b is to rescore children's responses into *two* response categories and to calibrate the twenty-five science activities and measure the attitudes of these seventy-five children from these dichotomously-scored responses. The two

## TABLE 2.4a
## SOME RESPONSE PATTERNS

| CHILD NUMBER | ACTIVITIES ORDERED BY ACTIVITY SCORE | CHILD SCORE | FREQUENCY OF RESPONSE 0 | 1 | 2 |
|---|---|---|---|---|---|
| 8 | 2 2 2 2 2 2 2 2 2 2 2 2 1 2 0 1 2 0 2 1 0 0 0 0 0 | 33 | 7 | 3 | 15 |
| 71 | 2 0 2 1 0 2 2 2 2 2 0 2 2 2 0 0 1 2 0 2 0 1 2 2 2 | 33 | 7 | 3 | 15 |
| 62 | 2 2 2 2 2 2 2 2 2 2 0 0 2 0 2 2 0 0 2 0 0 0 0 0 0 | 28 | 11 | 0 | 14 |
| 46 | 2 2 2 2 2 2 2 2 0 2 1 2 2 2 0 0 0 0 0 0 0 0 1 0 0 | 26 | 11 | 2 | 12 |
| 26 | 1 1 1 1 1 1 1 1 1 1 1 1 1 1 1 1 1 1 1 1 1 1 1 1 1 | 25 | 0 | 25 | 0 |
| 15 | 1 2 1 1 1 1 1 1 1 1 1 1 1 1 1 1 1 1 1 1 1 1 2 1 1 | 27 | 0 | 23 | 2 |
| 52 | 2 2 1 1 1 1 1 1 1 1 1 1 1 1 1 1 1 1 1 1 1 1 1 1 1 | 27 | 0 | 23 | 2 |

## FIGURE 2.4e
## SCORING RESPONSES DICHOTOMOUSLY

| | DISLIKE | NOT SURE / DON'T CARE | LIKE |
|---|---|---|---|
| | 0 | 1 | 2 |
| Only a smile counts "for" | 0 | 0 | 1 |
| Only a frown counts "against" | 0 | 1 | 1 |

ways to rescore the science data are shown in Figure 2.4e. The first counts only smiles. The second counts only frowns.

We will explore these possible rescorings of the science data for two reasons. First, a well-established method already exists for the analysis of dichotomously-scored responses (see Wright and Stone 1979). If we can show that the science variable can be defined as well from dichotomously scored responses as from the original three-category responses, and, if children can be measured equally well from their rescored responses, then we can use the simpler, more familiar procedure for analyzing dichotomous responses. Second, rescoring response alternatives to a smaller number of categories is a widespread and rarely questioned procedure. But how objective is this procedure? It would be interesting to know what loss of information occurs when responses are rescored, and whether rescoring can be misleading.

The responses of the seventy-five children have been rescored using the (001) "only smiles" scheme. The rescored data matrix is shown in Figure 2.4f. This matrix is not identical to the matrix in Figure 2.4c because new row and column sums have been obtained based on the rescored responses, and the rows and columns have been resorted accordingly. The responses of the seventy-five children have also been rescored using the (011) "only frowns" scheme. This matrix appears in Figure 2.4g. New row and column sums have been obtained, and the rows and columns resorted.

***Calibrating Activities.*** We are trying to find a natural ordering in the twenty-five science activities, one which we can use to mark out a line of increasing liking for science, and thus provide an operational definition of a liking-for-science variable. Since the alternative rescorings (001) and (011) both preserve the order of the original response alternatives, we do not expect them to lead to different orderings of the science activities. In fact, if we are to use

# FIGURE 2.4f
## ONLY A SMILE COUNTS "FOR"
## SCORING (001)

Child Number / Activity Number / Child Score

| Child Number | 18 | 19 | 12 | 13 | 10 | 21 | 2 | 11 | 15 | 24 | 1 | 22 | 17 | 6 | 14 | 25 | 9 | 3 | 16 | 7 | 23 | 8 | 20 | 4 | 5 | Child Score |
|---|---|---|---|---|---|---|---|---|---|---|---|---|---|---|---|---|---|---|---|---|---|---|---|---|---|---|
| 2 | 1 | 1 | 1 | 1 | 1 | 1 | 1 | 1 | 1 | 1 | 1 | 1 | 1 | 1 | 1 | 1 | 1 | 1 | 1 | 1 | 1 | 1 | 1 | 1 | 1 | 25 |
| 41 | 1 | 1 | 1 | 1 | 1 | 1 | 1 | 1 | 1 | 1 | 1 | 1 | 1 | 1 | 1 | 1 | 1 | 1 | 1 | 1 | 1 | 1 | 1 | 1 |  | 24 |
| 34 | 1 | 1 | 1 | 1 | 1 | 1 | 1 | 1 | 1 | 1 | 1 | 1 | 1 | 1 | 1 | 1 | 1 | 1 | 1 | 1 | 1 | 1 | 1 | 1 |  | 23 |
| 17 | 1 | 1 | 1 | 1 | 1 | 1 | 1 | 1 | 1 | 1 | 1 | 1 | 1 | 1 | 1 | 1 | 1 | 1 | 1 | 1 | 1 | 1 | 1 | 1 |  | 23 |
| 7 | 1 | 1 | 1 | 1 | 1 | 1 | 1 | 1 | 1 | 1 | 1 | 1 | 1 | 1 | 1 | 1 | 1 | 1 | 1 | 1 | 1 |  | 1 | 1 | 1 | 22 |
| 45 | 1 | 1 | 1 | 1 | 1 | 1 | 1 | 1 | 1 | 1 | 1 | 1 | 1 | 1 | 1 | 1 | 1 | 1 | 1 | 1 |  |  | 1 | 1 |  | 22 |
| 50 | 1 | 1 | 1 | 1 | 1 | 1 | 1 | 1 | 1 | 1 | 1 | 1 | 1 | 1 | 1 | 1 | 1 | 1 | 1 | 1 |  |  | 1 |  |  | 21 |
| 48 | 1 | 1 | 1 | 1 | 1 | 1 | 1 | 1 | 1 | 1 | 1 | 1 | 1 | 1 | 1 | 1 | 1 | 1 | 1 |  | 1 |  | 1 |  |  | 20 |
| 57 | 1 | 1 | 1 | 1 | 1 | 1 | 1 | 1 | 1 | 1 | 1 | 1 | 1 | 1 | 1 | 1 | 1 | 1 | 1 | 1 | 1 |  |  |  |  | 20 |
| 16 | 1 | 1 | 1 | 1 | 1 | 1 | 1 | 1 | 1 | 1 | 1 | 1 | 1 | 1 | 1 | 1 | 1 | 1 | 1 |  |  |  |  |  |  | 19 |
| 18 | 1 | 1 | 1 | 1 | 1 | 1 | 1 | 1 | 1 | 1 | 1 | 1 | 1 | 1 | 1 | 1 | 1 | 1 |  |  |  |  |  | 1 |  | 19 |
| 25 | 1 | 1 | 1 | 1 | 1 | 1 | 1 | 1 | 1 | 1 | 1 | 1 | 1 | 1 | 1 | 1 | 1 | 1 |  |  |  | 1 |  |  |  | 19 |
| 59 | 1 | 1 | 1 | 1 | 1 | 1 | 1 | 1 | 1 | 1 | 1 | 1 | 1 | 1 | 1 | 1 | 1 | 1 |  |  | 1 |  |  |  |  | 19 |
| 39 | 1 | 1 | 1 | 1 | 1 | 1 | 1 | 1 | 1 | 1 | 1 | 1 | 1 | 1 | 1 | 1 | 1 |  | 1 | 1 |  |  |  |  |  | 18 |
| 56 | 1 | 1 | 1 | 1 | 1 | 1 | 1 | 1 | 1 | 1 | 1 | 1 | 1 | 1 | 1 | 1 | 1 |  | 1 |  |  |  |  |  |  | 18 |
| 70 | 1 | 1 | 1 | 1 | 1 | 1 | 1 | 1 | 1 | 1 | 1 | 1 | 1 | 1 |  | 1 |  |  | 1 | 1 |  |  | 1 |  |  | 18 |
| 74 | 1 | 1 | 1 | 1 | 1 | 1 | 1 | 1 | 1 | 1 | 1 | 1 | 1 | 1 |  | 1 |  |  | 1 | 1 | 1 |  |  |  |  | 18 |
| 40 | 1 | 1 | 1 | 1 | 1 | 1 | 1 | 1 | 1 | 1 | 1 | 1 | 1 | 1 | 1 | 1 |  | 1 |  |  |  |  |  |  |  | 17 |
| 33 | 1 | 1 | 1 | 1 | 1 | 1 | 1 | 1 | 1 | 1 | 1 | 1 | 1 | 1 |  | 1 |  |  |  |  |  | 1 |  | 1 |  | 17 |
| 11 | 1 | 1 | 1 | 1 | 1 | 1 | 1 | 1 | 1 | 1 | 1 | 1 | 1 | 1 |  | 1 | 1 |  | 1 |  |  |  |  |  |  | 16 |
| 43 | 1 | 1 | 1 | 1 | 1 | 1 | 1 | 1 | 1 | 1 | 1 | 1 | 1 | 1 |  |  | 1 | 1 |  | 1 |  |  |  |  |  | 16 |
| 23 | 1 | 1 | 1 | 1 | 1 | 1 | 1 | 1 | 1 | 1 | 1 | 1 | 1 | 1 |  |  | 1 |  |  | 1 |  |  |  |  |  | 15 |
| 71 | 1 |  | 1 |  |  | 1 | 1 | 1 | 1 |  | 1 | 1 | 1 | 1 |  |  |  |  | 1 | 1 | 1 |  | 1 |  | 1 | 15 |
| 8 | 1 | 1 | 1 | 1 | 1 | 1 | 1 | 1 | 1 | 1 | 1 | 1 | 1 |  | 1 |  | 1 |  | 1 |  |  |  |  |  |  | 15 |
| 62 | 1 | 1 | 1 | 1 | 1 | 1 | 1 | 1 | 1 | 1 | 1 | 1 |  | 1 |  |  | 1 |  | 1 |  |  |  |  |  |  | 14 |
| 64 | 1 | 1 | 1 | 1 | 1 | 1 | 1 | 1 | 1 |  | 1 | 1 | 1 |  | 1 |  |  |  | 1 |  |  |  |  |  |  | 14 |
| 51 | 1 | 1 | 1 | 1 | 1 | 1 | 1 | 1 | 1 | 1 |  |  | 1 | 1 | 1 | 1 |  | 1 |  |  |  |  |  |  |  | 14 |
| 58 | 1 | 1 | 1 | 1 | 1 | 1 | 1 | 1 | 1 | 1 | 1 |  | 1 | 1 |  |  | 1 |  |  |  |  |  |  |  |  | 14 |
| 38 | 1 | 1 | 1 | 1 | 1 | 1 | 1 | 1 | 1 | 1 | 1 | 1 | 1 |  | 1 |  |  |  |  |  |  |  | 1 |  |  | 14 |
| 63 | 1 | 1 | 1 | 1 | 1 | 1 | 1 | 1 | 1 | 1 | 1 | 1 |  |  |  |  | 1 |  | 1 |  |  |  |  |  |  | 13 |
| 19 | 1 | 1 | 1 | 1 | 1 | 1 | 1 | 1 | 1 |  | 1 | 1 |  |  | 1 |  | 1 |  | 1 |  |  |  |  |  |  | 13 |
| 69 | 1 | 1 | 1 | 1 | 1 | 1 | 1 | 1 |  | 1 | 1 |  |  |  |  |  | 1 |  | 1 |  |  |  |  |  |  | 13 |
| 46 | 1 | 1 | 1 | 1 | 1 | 1 | 1 | 1 |  | 1 | 1 | 1 |  | 1 |  |  |  |  |  |  |  |  |  |  |  | 12 |
| 24 | 1 | 1 | 1 | 1 | 1 | 1 | 1 | 1 |  |  |  |  |  |  |  | 1 |  | 1 |  | 1 |  |  |  |  |  | 12 |
| 60 | 1 | 1 | 1 | 1 | 1 | 1 |  | 1 | 1 |  | 1 |  |  |  |  | 1 |  | 1 |  |  |  |  |  |  |  | 12 |
| 66 | 1 | 1 | 1 | 1 | 1 | 1 |  | 1 | 1 | 1 | 1 |  |  |  |  |  |  |  |  |  |  |  |  |  |  | 12 |
| 65 | 1 | 1 | 1 | 1 | 1 | 1 | 1 | 1 |  |  |  |  |  |  |  |  |  |  | 1 |  | 1 |  |  |  | 1 | 11 |
| 3 | 1 | 1 | 1 | 1 | 1 | 1 | 1 |  | 1 |  | 1 |  |  |  |  |  |  |  | 1 |  |  |  |  |  |  | 11 |
| 73 |  |  |  |  | 1 |  |  | 1 | 1 |  | 1 | 1 |  |  | 1 | 1 | 1 |  |  |  |  |  | 1 | 1 |  | 11 |
| 1 | 1 | 1 | 1 | 1 | 1 |  | 1 |  | 1 | 1 | 1 |  |  |  |  |  |  |  |  | 1 |  |  |  |  |  | 11 |
| 20 | 1 | 1 | 1 | 1 | 1 | 1 |  |  |  | 1 |  |  |  | 1 | 1 |  |  |  |  | 1 |  |  |  |  |  | 10 |
| 28 | 1 | 1 | 1 | 1 | 1 |  |  | 1 | 1 |  | 1 |  |  |  |  | 1 |  |  |  | 1 |  |  |  |  |  | 10 |
| 42 | 1 | 1 | 1 |  | 1 |  |  | 1 | 1 | 1 | 1 |  |  |  |  |  |  | 1 |  |  |  |  |  |  |  | 10 |
| 22 | 1 | 1 | 1 |  | 1 | 1 | 1 | 1 | 1 | 1 |  |  |  |  |  |  |  |  |  |  |  |  |  |  |  | 10 |
| 44 | 1 | 1 |  | 1 |  |  | 1 | 1 | 1 |  |  |  |  | 1 | 1 |  |  |  |  |  |  |  |  |  |  | 9 |
| 10 | 1 | 1 | 1 |  | 1 |  |  | 1 | 1 | 1 |  | 1 |  |  |  |  | 1 |  |  |  |  |  |  |  |  | 9 |
| 61 | 1 | 1 | 1 | 1 | 1 |  |  |  | 1 | 1 |  |  |  |  |  | 1 | 1 |  |  |  |  |  |  |  |  | 9 |
| 14 | 1 | 1 | 1 | 1 | 1 |  |  |  | 1 | 1 |  |  |  |  |  |  |  |  |  |  |  | 1 |  |  |  | 9 |
| 67 | 1 | 1 |  |  | 1 | 1 | 1 | 1 | 1 |  |  |  | 1 |  |  |  | 1 |  |  |  |  |  |  |  |  | 9 |
| 75 | 1 | 1 | 1 | 1 | 1 | 1 | 1 | 1 | 1 |  |  |  |  |  |  |  | 1 |  |  |  |  |  |  |  |  | 9 |
| 37 | 1 | 1 | 1 | 1 |  |  |  |  |  | 1 |  | 1 |  |  |  |  |  |  |  |  |  |  |  |  |  | 8 |
| 54 | 1 | 1 | 1 |  |  | 1 |  |  |  |  |  |  | 1 |  |  |  |  | 1 |  | 1 |  |  |  |  |  | 8 |
| 31 | 1 | 1 | 1 |  | 1 | 1 | 1 | 1 |  | 1 |  |  |  |  |  |  |  |  |  |  |  |  |  |  |  | 8 |
| 32 | 1 | 1 | 1 | 1 | 1 |  |  | 1 |  |  |  |  |  |  |  |  |  | 1 |  |  |  |  |  |  |  | 8 |
| 4 | 1 | 1 | 1 | 1 | 1 | 1 | 1 |  |  |  |  |  |  |  |  |  |  |  | 1 |  |  |  |  |  |  | 7 |
| 47 | 1 | 1 |  | 1 |  |  | 1 |  |  |  |  |  | 1 |  |  |  |  |  |  |  |  |  |  | 1 |  | 7 |
| 27 | 1 | 1 | 1 | 1 | 1 |  |  | 1 |  | 1 |  |  |  |  |  |  |  |  |  |  | 1 |  |  |  |  | 7 |
| 13 | 1 | 1 | 1 |  | 1 |  | 1 |  | 1 |  |  |  |  |  |  |  |  |  |  |  |  |  |  |  |  | 6 |
| 21 | 1 | 1 | 1 | 1 | 1 | 1 |  |  |  |  |  |  |  |  |  |  |  |  |  |  |  |  |  |  |  | 6 |
| 55 | 1 | 1 | 1 | 1 |  |  |  | 1 |  |  |  |  |  |  |  |  |  |  | 1 |  |  |  |  |  |  | 6 |
| 30 | 1 | 1 | 1 | 1 | 1 |  |  |  |  |  |  | 1 |  |  |  |  |  |  |  |  |  |  |  |  |  | 6 |
| 9 | 1 |  | 1 | 1 | 1 | 1 |  |  |  |  |  |  |  |  |  |  |  |  |  |  | 1 |  |  |  |  | 6 |
| 68 | 1 | 1 | 1 |  | 1 |  | 1 |  | 1 |  |  |  |  |  |  |  |  |  |  |  |  |  |  |  |  | 6 |
| 36 | 1 | 1 | 1 | 1 |  |  |  |  |  |  |  |  |  |  |  |  |  |  |  |  |  |  |  |  | 1 | 5 |
| 6 | 1 | 1 | 1 |  |  |  |  |  |  |  |  |  |  |  |  |  |  |  |  |  | 1 |  |  |  | 1 | 5 |
| 35 | 1 | 1 | 1 | 1 |  |  |  |  |  |  |  |  |  |  |  |  |  |  |  |  |  |  |  |  | 1 | 5 |
| 12 | 1 |  |  |  |  |  |  | 1 |  |  |  | 1 |  |  |  |  |  |  |  |  | 1 |  |  |  |  | 4 |
| 72 | 1 |  |  |  |  |  |  |  |  |  |  |  |  |  |  |  |  |  |  |  | 1 |  | 1 |  |  | 3 |
| 29 |  | 1 |  |  |  |  |  |  |  |  |  |  |  |  |  |  |  |  |  |  | 1 |  |  |  |  | 3 |
| 5 | 1 | 1 |  |  |  |  |  |  |  |  |  |  |  |  |  |  |  |  |  |  |  |  |  |  |  | 2 |
| 52 | 1 | 1 |  |  |  |  |  |  |  |  |  |  |  |  |  |  |  |  |  |  |  |  |  |  |  | 2 |
| 49 |  |  |  |  |  |  |  |  |  |  |  |  |  |  |  |  |  |  | 1 |  | 1 |  |  |  |  | 2 |
| 15 |  | 1 |  |  |  |  |  |  |  |  |  |  |  |  |  |  |  |  |  |  |  |  | 1 |  |  | 2 |
| 53 | 1 |  |  |  |  |  |  |  |  |  |  |  |  |  |  |  |  |  |  |  |  |  |  |  |  | 1 |
| 26 |  |  |  |  |  |  |  |  |  |  |  |  |  |  |  |  |  |  |  |  |  |  |  |  |  | 0 |
| **Activity Score** | 71 | 67 | 62 | 59 | 57 | 50 | 49 | 48 | 43 | 42 | 37 | 34 | 32 | 28 | 27 | 27 | 26 | 26 | 22 | 19 | 11 | 11 | 11 | 9 | 9 | |

## FIGURE 2.4g
## ONLY A FROWN COUNTS "AGAINST" SCORING (011)

Child Number — Activity Number — Child Score

| Child Number | 12 | 18 | 19 | 11 | 10 | 1 | 21 | 15 | 13 | 2 | 24 | 6 | 22 | 17 | 3 | 14 | 16 | 25 | 9 | 7 | 8 | 4 | 20 | 23 | 5 | Child Score |
|---|---|---|---|---|---|---|---|---|---|---|---|---|---|---|---|---|---|---|---|---|---|---|---|---|---|---|
| 2 | 1 | 1 | 1 | 1 | 1 | 1 | 1 | 1 | 1 | 1 | 1 | 1 | 1 | 1 | 1 | 1 | 1 | 1 | 1 | 1 | 1 | 1 | 1 | 1 | 1 | 25 |
| 15 | 1 | 1 | 1 | 1 | 1 | 1 | 1 | 1 | 1 | 1 | 1 | 1 | 1 | 1 | 1 | 1 | 1 | 1 | 1 | 1 | 1 | 1 | 1 | 1 | 1 | 25 |
| 22 | 1 | 1 | 1 | 1 | 1 | 1 | 1 | 1 | 1 | 1 | 1 | 1 | 1 | 1 | 1 | 1 | 1 | 1 | 1 | 1 | 1 | 1 | 1 | 1 | 1 | 25 |
| 23 | 1 | 1 | 1 | 1 | 1 | 1 | 1 | 1 | 1 | 1 | 1 | 1 | 1 | 1 | 1 | 1 | 1 | 1 | 1 | 1 | 1 | 1 | 1 | 1 | 1 | 25 |
| 26 | 1 | 1 | 1 | 1 | 1 | 1 | 1 1 | 1 | 1 | 1 | 1 | 1 | 1 | 1 | 1 | 1 | 1 | 1 | 1 | 1 | 1 | 1 | 1 | 1 | 1 | 25 |
| 34 | 1 | 1 | 1 | 1 | 1 | 1 | 1 | 1 | 1 | 1 | 1 | 1 | 1 | 1 | 1 | 1 | 1 | 1 | 1 | 1 | 1 | 1 | 1 | 1 | 1 | 25 |
| 41 | 1 | 1 | 1 | 1 | 1 | 1 | 1 | 1 | 1 | 1 | 1 | 1 | 1 | 1 | 1 | 1 | 1 | 1 | 1 | 1 | 1 | 1 | 1 | 1 | 1 | 25 |
| 50 | 1 | 1 | 1 | 1 | 1 | 1 | 1 | 1 | 1 | 1 | 1 | 1 | 1 | 1 | 1 | 1 | 1 | 1 | 1 | 1 | 1 | 1 | 1 | 1 | 1 | 25 |
| 52 | 1 | 1 | 1 | 1 | 1 | 1 | 1 | 1 | 1 | 1 | 1 | 1 | 1 | 1 | 1 | 1 | 1 | 1 | 1 | 1 | 1 | 1 | 1 | 1 | 1 | 25 |
| 16 | 1 | 1 | 1 | 1 | 1 | 1 | 1 | 1 | 1 | 1 | 1 | 1 | 1 | 1 | 1 | 1 | 1 | 1 | 1 | 1 | 1 | 1 | 1 |  | 1 | 24 |
| 17 | 1 | 1 | 1 | 1 | 1 | 1 | 1 | 1 | 1 | 1 | 1 | 1 | 1 | 1 | 1 | 1 | 1 | 1 | 1 | 1 | 1 | 1 | 1 | 1 |  | 24 |
| 38 | 1 | 1 | 1 | 1 | 1 | 1 | 1 | 1 | 1 | 1 | 1 | 1 | 1 | 1 | 1 | 1 | 1 | 1 | 1 | 1 | 1 | 1 | 1 | 1 |  | 24 |
| 60 | 1 | 1 | 1 | 1 | 1 | 1 | 1 | 1 | 1 | 1 | 1 | 1 | 1 | 1 | 1 | 1 | 1 | 1 | 1 | 1 | 1 | 1 | 1 | 1 |  | 24 |
| 31 | 1 | 1 | 1 | 1 | 1 | 1 | 1 | 1 | 1 | 1 | 1 | 1 | 1 | 1 | 1 | 1 | 1 | 1 | 1 | 1 | 1 | 1 | 1 |  |  | 23 |
| 45 | 1 | 1 | 1 | 1 | 1 | 1 | 1 | 1 | 1 | 1 | 1 | 1 | 1 | 1 | 1 | 1 | 1 | 1 | 1 | 1 | 1 | 1 | 1 |  |  | 23 |
| 48 | 1 | 1 | 1 | 1 | 1 | 1 | 1 | 1 | 1 | 1 | 1 | 1 | 1 | 1 | 1 | 1 | 1 | 1 | 1 | 1 | 1 | 1 | 1 |  |  | 23 |
| 25 | 1 | 1 | 1 | 1 | 1 | 1 | 1 | 1 | 1 | 1 | 1 | 1 | 1 | 1 | 1 | 1 | 1 | 1 |  | 1 | 1 | 1 | 1 |  | 1 | 23 |
| 3 | 1 | 1 | 1 | 1 | 1 | 1 | 1 | 1 | 1 | 1 | 1 | 1 | 1 | 1 | 1 | 1 | 1 | 1 | 1 | 1 |  | 1 | 1 | 1 |  | 23 |
| 59 | 1 | 1 | 1 | 1 | 1 | 1 | 1 | 1 | 1 | 1 | 1 | 1 | 1 | 1 | 1 | 1 | 1 | 1 | 1 | 1 |  | 1 | 1 | 1 |  | 23 |
| 39 | 1 | 1 | 1 | 1 | 1 | 1 | 1 | 1 | 1 | 1 | 1 | 1 | 1 | 1 | 1 | 1 | 1 | 1 | 1 | 1 | 1 | 1 |  |  |  | 23 |
| 35 | 1 | 1 | 1 | 1 | 1 | 1 | 1 | 1 | 1 | 1 | 1 | 1 | 1 | 1 | 1 | 1 | 1 | 1 | 1 | 1 |  |  |  | 1 | 1 | 22 |
| 7 | 1 | 1 | 1 | 1 | 1 | 1 | 1 | 1 | 1 | 1 | 1 | 1 | 1 | 1 | 1 | 1 | 1 | 1 | 1 |  | 1 |  | 1 | 1 |  | 22 |
| 18 | 1 | 1 | 1 | 1 | 1 | 1 | 1 | 1 | 1 | 1 | 1 | 1 | 1 | 1 | 1 | 1 | 1 | 1 | 1 |  | 1 |  | 1 | 1 |  | 22 |
| 40 | 1 | 1 | 1 | 1 | 1 | 1 | 1 | 1 | 1 | 1 | 1 | 1 | 1 | 1 | 1 | 1 | 1 | 1 | 1 |  | 1 |  | 1 | 1 |  | 22 |
| 54 | 1 | 1 | 1 | 1 | 1 | 1 | 1 | 1 | 1 | 1 | 1 | 1 | 1 | 1 | 1 | 1 | 1 | 1 | 1 |  | 1 | 1 | 1 |  |  | 22 |
| 56 | 1 | 1 | 1 | 1 | 1 | 1 | 1 | 1 | 1 | 1 | 1 | 1 | 1 | 1 | 1 | 1 | 1 | 1 | 1 |  | 1 | 1 | 1 |  |  | 22 |
| 21 | 1 | 1 | 1 | 1 | 1 | 1 | 1 | 1 | 1 | 1 | 1 | 1 | 1 | 1 | 1 | 1 | 1 | 1 | 1 |  | 1 | 1 | 1 |  |  | 22 |
| 42 | 1 | 1 | 1 | 1 | 1 | 1 | 1 | 1 | 1 | 1 | 1 | 1 | 1 | 1 | 1 | 1 | 1 | 1 | 1 |  | 1 | 1 | 1 |  |  | 22 |
| 64 | 1 | 1 | 1 | 1 | 1 | 1 | 1 | 1 | 1 | 1 | 1 | 1 | 1 | 1 | 1 | 1 | 1 | 1 | 1 |  | 1 | 1 |  |  |  | 22 |
| 33 | 1 | 1 | 1 | 1 | 1 | 1 | 1 | 1 | 1 | 1 | 1 | 1 | 1 | 1 | 1 | 1 | 1 | 1 | 1 |  | 1 | 1 |  |  |  | 21 |
| 43 | 1 | 1 | 1 | 1 | 1 | 1 | 1 | 1 | 1 | 1 | 1 | 1 | 1 | 1 | 1 | 1 | 1 | 1 | 1 |  |  |  |  |  | 1 | 21 |
| 63 | 1 | 1 | 1 | 1 | 1 | 1 | 1 | 1 | 1 | 1 | 1 | 1 | 1 | 1 | 1 | 1 | 1 | 1 |  |  | 1 | 1 | 1 |  |  | 21 |
| 58 | 1 | 1 | 1 | 1 | 1 | 1 | 1 | 1 | 1 | 1 | 1 | 1 | 1 | 1 | 1 | 1 | 1 | 1 |  |  | 1 | 1 | 1 |  |  | 21 |
| 70 | 1 | 1 | 1 | 1 | 1 | 1 | 1 | 1 | 1 | 1 | 1 | 1 | 1 | 1 | 1 | 1 | 1 | 1 | 1 | 1 |  |  |  |  |  | 21 |
| 24 | 1 | 1 | 1 | 1 | 1 | 1 | 1 | 1 | 1 | 1 | 1 | 1 | 1 | 1 | 1 | 1 | 1 | 1 | 1 | 1 | 1 |  |  |  |  | 20 |
| 51 | 1 | 1 | 1 | 1 | 1 | 1 | 1 | 1 | 1 | 1 | 1 | 1 | 1 | 1 | 1 | 1 | 1 | 1 | 1 | 1 | 1 |  |  |  |  | 20 |
| 27 | 1 | 1 | 1 | 1 | 1 | 1 | 1 | 1 | 1 | 1 | 1 | 1 | 1 | 1 | 1 | 1 | 1 | 1 |  | 1 |  | 1 |  | 1 | 1 | 20 |
| 61 | 1 | 1 | 1 | 1 | 1 | 1 | 1 | 1 | 1 | 1 | 1 | 1 | 1 | 1 | 1 | 1 | 1 | 1 | 1 |  | 1 |  |  | 1 |  | 20 |
| 4 | 1 | 1 | 1 | 1 | 1 | 1 | 1 | 1 | 1 | 1 | 1 | 1 | 1 | 1 | 1 | 1 | 1 | 1 | 1 |  | 1 |  | 1 |  |  | 20 |
| 36 | 1 | 1 | 1 | 1 | 1 | 1 | 1 | 1 | 1 | 1 | 1 | 1 | 1 | 1 | 1 | 1 | 1 |  |  | 1 |  |  |  | 1 | 1 | 20 |
| 65 | 1 | 1 | 1 | 1 | 1 | 1 | 1 | 1 | 1 | 1 | 1 | 1 | 1 | 1 | 1 | 1 |  |  |  | 1 |  | 1 | 1 | 1 | 1 | 20 |
| 67 | 1 | 1 | 1 | 1 | 1 | 1 | 1 | 1 | 1 | 1 | 1 | 1 | 1 | 1 | 1 | 1 | 1 |  |  | 1 |  | 1 | 1 | 1 |  | 20 |
| 69 | 1 | 1 | 1 | 1 | 1 | 1 | 1 | 1 | 1 | 1 | 1 | 1 | 1 | 1 | 1 | 1 | 1 |  | 1 |  | 1 |  |  |  |  | 20 |
| 57 | 1 | 1 | 1 | 1 | 1 | 1 | 1 | 1 | 1 | 1 | 1 | 1 | 1 | 1 | 1 | 1 | 1 | 1 | 1 | 1 |  |  |  |  |  | 20 |
| 37 | 1 | 1 | 1 | 1 | 1 | 1 | 1 | 1 | 1 | 1 | 1 | 1 | 1 | 1 | 1 | 1 | 1 | 1 | 1 | 1 |  |  |  |  |  | 19 |
| 28 | 1 | 1 | 1 | 1 | 1 | 1 | 1 | 1 | 1 | 1 |  | 1 | 1 | 1 | 1 |  | 1 | 1 | 1 | 1 |  | 1 |  |  | 1 | 19 |
| 49 | 1 | 1 | 1 | 1 | 1 | 1 | 1 | 1 |  | 1 | 1 | 1 | 1 | 1 | 1 |  | 1 | 1 | 1 |  |  | 1 |  | 1 | 1 | 19 |
| 10 | 1 | 1 | 1 | 1 | 1 | 1 | 1 | 1 | 1 | 1 | 1 | 1 |  | 1 | 1 | 1 | 1 | 1 | 1 | 1 |  | 1 |  |  |  | 19 |
| 11 | 1 | 1 | 1 | 1 | 1 | 1 | 1 | 1 | 1 | 1 | 1 | 1 | 1 | 1 | 1 | 1 |  | 1 | 1 |  | 1 | 1 |  |  |  | 19 |
| 19 | 1 | 1 | 1 | 1 | 1 | 1 | 1 | 1 | 1 | 1 |  | 1 | 1 | 1 | 1 |  | 1 | 1 |  | 1 | 1 |  | 1 |  |  | 19 |
| 6 | 1 | 1 | 1 | 1 | 1 | 1 | 1 | 1 | 1 |  | 1 | 1 | 1 | 1 | 1 |  |  |  | 1 | 1 |  | 1 | 1 | 1 | 1 | 19 |
| 55 | 1 | 1 | 1 | 1 | 1 |  | 1 | 1 | 1 |  | 1 | 1 | 1 | 1 | 1 | 1 | 1 |  | 1 |  |  |  | 1 | 1 |  | 19 |
| 1 | 1 | 1 | 1 | 1 | 1 | 1 | 1 | 1 | 1 |  | 1 | 1 | 1 | 1 | 1 |  | 1 |  | 1 | 1 |  | 1 |  |  | 1 | 19 |
| 44 | 1 | 1 | 1 | 1 | 1 | 1 | 1 | 1 | 1 | 1 | 1 | 1 | 1 | 1 | 1 | 1 | 1 | 1 | 1 | 1 |  |  |  |  |  | 19 |
| 74 | 1 | 1 | 1 | 1 | 1 | 1 | 1 | 1 | 1 | 1 | 1 | 1 | 1 | 1 | 1 |  | 1 | 1 | 1 | 1 |  |  |  |  |  | 19 |
| 66 | 1 | 1 | 1 | 1 | 1 | 1 | 1 | 1 | 1 | 1 | 1 | 1 | 1 | 1 |  | 1 |  | 1 | 1 |  | 1 |  |  |  |  | 18 |
| 8 | 1 | 1 | 1 | 1 | 1 | 1 | 1 | 1 | 1 | 1 | 1 | 1 | 1 | 1 | 1 |  |  | 1 | 1 |  | 1 |  |  |  |  | 18 |
| 9 | 1 | 1 | 1 | 1 | 1 | 1 | 1 | 1 | 1 | 1 |  |  | 1 | 1 | 1 |  | 1 | 1 | 1 | 1 |  | 1 |  | 1 | 1 | 18 |
| 32 | 1 | 1 | 1 | 1 | 1 | 1 | 1 | 1 | 1 | 1 |  | 1 | 1 | 1 | 1 |  | 1 | 1 | 1 | 1 |  |  |  |  |  | 18 |
| 71 | 1 | 1 | 1 | 1 | 1 | 1 | 1 | 1 | 1 |  | 1 |  | 1 | 1 | 1 |  | 1 | 1 |  | 1 |  | 1 |  | 1 | 1 | 18 |
| 13 | 1 | 1 |  | 1 | 1 | 1 | 1 | 1 | 1 | 1 |  |  | 1 | 1 | 1 | 1 | 1 | 1 |  |  | 1 | 1 | 1 |  |  | 18 |
| 5 | 1 | 1 | 1 | 1 | 1 | 1 | 1 |  | 1 |  |  | 1 | 1 | 1 | 1 |  | 1 |  |  | 1 |  |  | 1 | 1 | 1 | 17 |
| 73 | 1 | 1 | 1 | 1 | 1 |  |  |  |  |  | 1 | 1 | 1 | 1 | 1 |  | 1 | 1 | 1 |  | 1 | 1 | 1 |  |  | 17 |
| 47 | 1 | 1 | 1 | 1 | 1 |  | 1 | 1 | 1 | 1 |  |  |  | 1 | 1 | 1 | 1 |  | 1 |  | 1 |  |  |  | 1 | 17 |
| 75 | 1 | 1 | 1 | 1 | 1 | 1 | 1 | 1 | 1 | 1 |  |  |  | 1 | 1 | 1 |  | 1 |  | 1 |  |  |  |  | 1 | 16 |
| 20 | 1 | 1 | 1 | 1 | 1 | 1 | 1 | 1 | 1 | 1 | 1 | 1 |  | 1 | 1 |  | 1 | 1 |  |  |  |  |  |  |  | 16 |
| 62 | 1 | 1 | 1 | 1 | 1 | 1 | 1 | 1 | 1 | 1 |  | 1 | 1 | 1 |  | 1 |  |  |  |  |  |  |  |  |  | 14 |
| 14 | 1 | 1 | 1 | 1 | 1 | 1 |  |  | 1 | 1 | 1 | 1 | 1 |  | 1 |  |  |  | 1 |  | 1 |  |  | 1 |  | 14 |
| 46 | 1 | 1 | 1 | 1 | 1 | 1 |  | 1 |  | 1 | 1 | 1 | 1 | 1 |  |  |  |  |  |  |  |  | 1 |  |  | 14 |
| 12 | 1 | 1 | 1 | 1 | 1 |  |  |  | 1 |  |  | 1 |  | 1 |  |  | 1 | 1 |  |  | 1 |  | 1 | 1 | 1 | 13 |
| 68 | 1 | 1 | 1 | 1 | 1 | 1 |  | 1 |  | 1 | 1 | 1 | 1 |  |  | 1 |  |  |  | 1 |  |  |  |  |  | 13 |
| 29 | 1 | 1 | 1 | 1 | 1 |  | 1 |  |  |  |  |  |  |  |  |  |  |  |  | 1 |  |  | 1 | 1 | 1 | 11 |
| 53 | 1 | 1 | 1 | 1 |  |  | 1 | 1 |  | 1 |  |  |  |  | 1 |  |  | 1 | 1 | 1 |  |  |  |  | 1 | 11 |
| 72 | 1 | 1 | 1 |  |  | 1 |  | 1 | 1 |  |  |  |  |  |  |  | 1 |  |  | 1 | 1 | 1 | 1 |  | 11 |
| 30 | 1 | 1 | 1 | 1 | 1 | 1 | 1 |  | 1 |  |  |  | 1 |  |  |  |  |  |  |  |  |  |  | 1 |  | 10 |
| Activity Score | 75 | 74 | 74 | 73 | 73 | 72 | 69 | 68 | 68 | 67 | 65 | 63 | 63 | 63 | 62 | 61 | 61 | 58 | 54 | 50 | 43 | 43 | 39 | 31 | 28 | |

rescored responses to lay out a variable, it is essential that alternative rescorings like (001) and (011) do not lead to different operational definitions of the variable.

The activity serial numbers at the top of Figures 2.4f and 2.4g, however, show that the twenty-five science activities are ordered *differently* by these alternative rescorings.  Activity *12*, for example, is to the right of Activities *18* and *19* under the (001) scoring, but to the left of these two activities under the (011) scoring.  To investigate just how different these two orderings of the activities are, we have plotted the activity scores at the bottom of Figure 2.4f against the activity scores at the bottom of Figure 2.4g in Figure 2.4h.

Our motive for making Figure 2.4h was to study the reordering of activities caused by the alternative rescorings.  But a glance at Figure 2.4h reveals a more striking feature.  The activity scores when plotted against each other do not follow the straight line we may have expected.  Instead, they are scattered about a curve which we have drawn in by eye.  Before

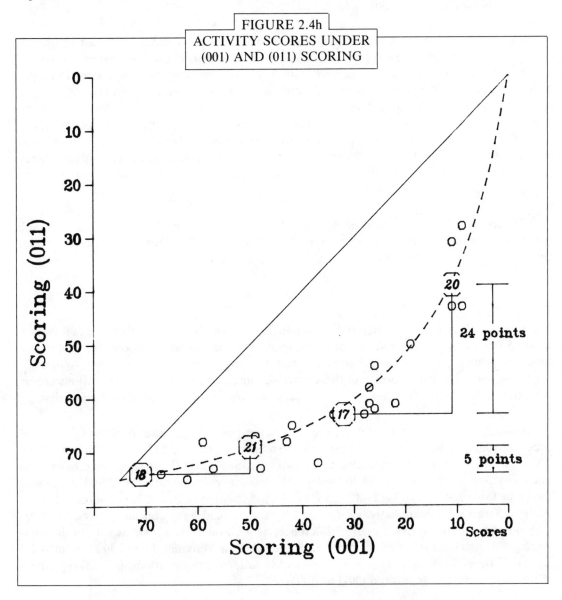

FIGURE 2.4h
ACTIVITY SCORES UNDER
(001) AND (011) SCORING

we investigate our original question—How different are the orderings of the activities under these alternative rescorings?—we need to understand what this curve tells us about activity scores.

We will begin by looking at four activities which lie close to the curve (Activities *18*, *21*, *17* and *20*). On the horizontal axis, under the (001) scoring, Activities *18* and *21* are *twenty-one* score points apart. So are Activities *17* and *20*. This means that if we were to use the (001) activity scores to position these four activities along an attitude-to-science continuum, we would position Activities *18* and *21* the same distance apart as Activities *17* and *20*.

If we consider scores on the vertical (011) axis, however, we find that Activities *18* and *21* are now only *five* score points apart, while Activities *17* and *20* have become *twenty-four* score points apart. This means that if we were to use the 011 scores to position these four activities along an attitude-to-science continuum, we would position Activities *17* and *20* about five times as far apart as Activities *18* and *21*!

What we have stumbled across is a problem inherent in any scores obtained by simply summing the columns or rows of a data matrix. This problem is that *raw scores are not on an interval scale which can be generalized*. A difference of one score point on the left of Figure 2.4h does not have the same meaning as a difference of one score point on the right. One score point at the top of Figure 2.4h does not have the same meaning as one score point at the bottom. Raw activity scores cannot provide a clear picture of the attitude to science variable. The conclusions we reach about the relative positions of Activities *18*, *21*, *17* and *20* on this variable, for example, are different under the alternative rescorings. This inconsistency threatens to interfere with our attempt to construct a general attitude to science variable with a defensible unit of measurement.

Fortunately, these non-linear activity scores can be transformed to a new metric which can maintain a constant unit from one end of the continuum to the other. This transformation changes each activity score $S$ into a "logit" score $d$ through

$$d = \log[(N - S)/S]$$

where $N$ is the number of children in the sample (in this case $N = 75$). This changes *high* raw scores $S$ into *low* logit scores $d$, so that on the logit scale the activities which are easiest to like have lowest logit scores. Table 2.4b shows how this transformation works for Activities *18*, *21*, *17* and *20*. The raw scores $S$ of these activities under the (001) and (011) scorings are on the left of Table 2.4b. On the right, these scores are transformed to their logit equivalents.

Table 2.4b shows that the twenty-one raw score points separating Activities *18* and *21* under the (001) scoring have been transformed to a difference of $-2.23$ logits on the new scale, while the five score points separating these two activities under the (011) scoring have been transformed to a difference of $-2.16$ logits. The logit scores for Activities *17* and *20* are also shown in Table 2.4b. The logit difference between Activities *17* and *20* is not about the same as the difference between Activities *18* and *21*, as we would have concluded from the (001) scoring; nor is it almost five times the difference, as we would have concluded from the (011) scoring. Instead, on the logit scale, the distance between Activities *17* and *20* is about $-1.5$ logits or .7 times the distance between Activities *18* and *21*, and this relationship holds regardless of whether responses are scored (001) or (011).

| | TABLE 2.4b | | | |
| TRANSFORMING ACTIVITY SCORES INTO LOGITS | | | | |

| ACTIVITY NUMBER | RAW ACTIVITY SCORE $S$ | | TRANSFORMED LOGIT SCORE $d = \log[(N-S)/S]$ | |
| | (001) | (011) | (001) | (011) |
| 18 | 71 | 74 | $-2.94$ | $-4.60$ |
| 21 | 50 | 69 | $-0.71$ | $-2.44$ |
| **Difference** | **21** | **5** | **$-2.23$** | **$-2.16$** |
| 17 | 32 | 63 | 0.28 | $-1.66$ |
| 20 | 11 | 39 | 1.73 | $-0.08$ |
| **Difference** | **21** | **24** | **$-1.45$** | **$-1.58$** |

Having encountered and dealt with the non-linearity of activity raw scores, we return to the question that led us to draw Figure 2.4h in the first place, and we plot the activity scores from the alternative rescorings again.  This time, because they are expressed in logits, they appear without the confounding of non-linearity. This new plot is shown in Figure 2.4i.  Now Activities *18*, *21*, *17* and *20* which followed the curve in Figure 2.4h follow a straight line which runs parallel to the identity line.  The reason the activities are distributed about this line rather than about the identity line is that each of the twenty-five activities is more difficult when scored (001) than when it is scored (011).  To bring these activities on to the same scale it is necessary to subtract 1.8 logits (the difference between the two diagonal lines in Figure 2.4i) from the difficulty of every activity under the (001) scoring.

With the confounding of non-linearity removed, we are ready to consider the distribution of activities about the straight line we have drawn through them.  The activities which lie furthest from this line are Activities *13* and *1*.  Under the (001) scoring, Activity *13* is the fourth easiest activity to like.  But under the (011) scoring, it is the ninth.  Under the (001) scoring, Activity *1* is the eleventh easiest activity to like.  But under the (011) scoring, it is the sixth.  These activities change their relative standing among the other activities as we change from one scoring scheme to the other.  But if a change in scoring alters the activity definition of the liking-for-science variable, then how will we decide which arrangement of activities is best for defining a general variable?

To investigate Activities *13* and *1* further, we have taken their category frequencies from the bottom of Figure 2.4b and displayed them in Table 2.4c.  Under the (001) scoring, the raw activity scores for Activities *13* and *1* are 59 and 37.  Under the (011) scoring, they are $59 + 9 = 68$ and $37 + 35 = 72$.  Thus under the (001) scoring Activity *13* has the higher score and appears easier to like, while under the (011) scoring, Activity *1* has the higher score and appears easier to like.  How shall we decide which activity is more likable?

Although fewer children *disliked* Activity *1* than Activity *13*, it is also true that fewer children *liked* this activity than Activity *13*.  It is the tendency of these children to make greater use of the neutral response on Activity *1* than on Activity *13* that causes the different orderings of these two activities under the alternative rescorings.

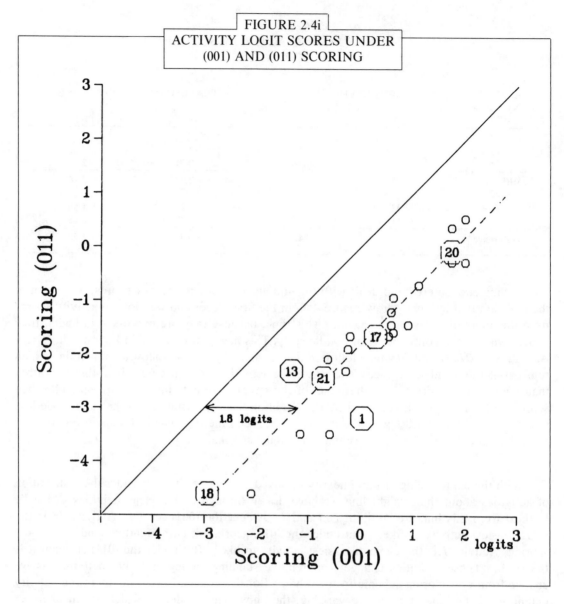

FIGURE 2.4i
ACTIVITY LOGIT SCORES UNDER
(001) AND (011) SCORING

TABLE 2.4c
RESCORING ACTIVITIES *13* AND *1*

| ACTIVITY NUMBER | CATEGORY FREQUENCIES | | | (001) | | (011) | |
|---|---|---|---|---|---|---|---|
| | 0 | 1 | 2 | RAW SCORE | LOGIT SCORE | RAW SCORE | LOGIT SCORE |
| *13* | 7 | 9 | 59 | 59 | −1.32 | 68 | −2.31 |
| *1* | 3 | 35 | 37 | 37 | 0.04 | 72 | −3.18 |
| | | | Difference | 22 | −1.36 | −4 | 0.87 |

This inconsistency in the ordering of Activities *1* and *13* would have gone undetected if we had used only one of the two scoring schemes.   It was only by trying both rescorings and plotting the resulting activity scores against one another that we noticed that Activities *1* and

*13* shifted their positions among the other activities as we changed from one scoring scheme to the other.

***Measuring Attitudes.*** In addition to seeking an objective ordering of the twenty-five science activities, we also seek an objective ordering of the seventy-five children along this liking-for-science variable.  For this we investigate the ordering of the seventy-five children under the (001) and (011) scorings.  On the right of Figures 2.4f and 2.4g are the scores for each child under the alternative rescorings.  These children scores have been plotted against one another in Figure 2.4j.  Now we see a scattering of points in the upper left corner of the picture.  The three points in the extreme corner are of particular interest.  Child *26* is the child who made twenty-five 1's on the questionnaire.  This gives him a score of 0 under the (001) scoring, but a perfect score of 25 under the (011) scoring. Depending on how his responses are rescored, Child *26* is estimated to be either the child with the *most* positive attitude to science, or the child with the *least* positive attitude to science! Similarly, Children *15* and *52* made perfect scores of 25 under the (011) scoring, but scores of only 2 under the (001) scoring.

In the middle of the picture, along the identity line, are Children *62, 57, 7* and *2*.  These are children who did not respond "not sure/don't care" to any item and, as a result, made the same raw score under both rescorings.

The child scores plotted in Figure 2.4j suffer from the same problem as the activity scores in Figure 2.4h.  They are not on the same interval scale.  The curve we have drawn in Figure 2.4j is the mirror image of the curve in Figure 2.4h.  It connects a zero score with a perfect score under each rescoring.  Five children positioned close to this curve have been circled for reference.

Each score *r* can be transformed to a common interval scale using the logit transformation

$$b = \log[r/(L-r)]$$

where *L* is the number of activities (in this case $L = 25$). This transformation changes *high* raw scores *r* into *high* logit scores *b*, so that on the logit scale the children with the most positive attitudes to science have the highest logit scores.

The logit scores for the seventy-five children are plotted against each other in Figure 2.4k.  Now the children located along the curve in Figure 2.4j are located along a straight line which runs parallel to the identity line, but 1.8 logits to its left.  Children *26, 15* and *52* do not appear in Figure 2.4k.  These children did not "dislike" any activity, and so made perfect scores of 25 and logit scores of plus infinity under the 011 scoring.  The spread of children around this line is an indication that the alternative rescorings do not produce identical orderings of children.  What we conclude about the relative attitudes of the children in this sample will depend upon which of the two rescorings we choose to use.

These contradictions would not have been exposed had we used only one rescoring of the original responses.  The discrepancies were exposed when we used both rescorings and then performed secondary analyses in which the results of the alternative rescorings were compared.  In general, if we ignore the original observation format and look at only one rescoring of responses, we risk missing such contradictions.  As the number of response alternatives increases beyond three, the number of alternative rescorings of the data, and hence the number of secondary analyses needed to compare these rescorings, increases rapidly.  These obser-

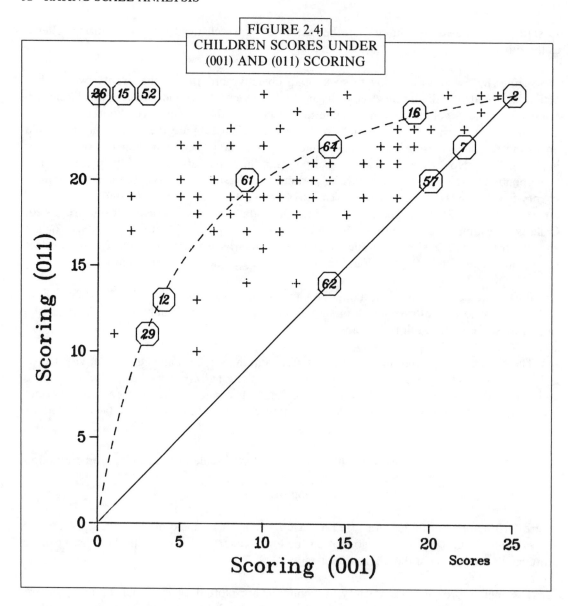

FIGURE 2.4j
CHILDREN SCORES UNDER
(001) AND (011) SCORING

vations lead us to recommend *against* rescoring multiple response category data. The method we develop in the chapters to follow has the advantage of being able to expose contradictions like those discovered here by means of a *single* analysis based on the original observation format.

## 2.5 PROBLEMS WITH SCORES

Before leaving our inspection of the science data, let us review some of the problems that arise when we try to build variables and measure persons using raw scores from the margins of a data matrix.

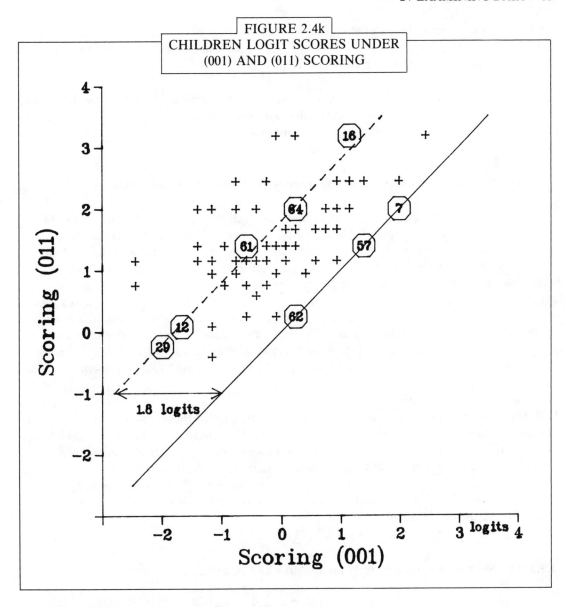

FIGURE 2.4k
CHILDREN LOGIT SCORES UNDER
(001) AND (011) SCORING

### 2.5.1 The Need for Linearity

The first problem with both activity scores and children scores is that they are not expressed on a linear scale. Trying to see the science variable in the raw activity scores is like trying to see oneself in a warped mirror—while the parts may be in order, they are not in proportion. Raw activity scores distort both ends of the variable, making distances between children at the extremes look shorter than they would look if the activities were centered on these extreme children. To rectify this, the activity scores can be transformed to a "logit" metric. This straightening process removes the distortions at both extremes and shows the variable in a form which does not depend on how activities are targeted on children.

The non-linearity of raw scores may not be obvious in any single set of item or person scores—just as the distortions produced by a warped mirror may not be obvious unless you have seen your image in other mirrors. But it becomes obvious when item scores are obtained from samples at different levels of ability or attitude, or when person scores are obtained from subsets of items at different levels of difficulty. As we have just seen, it also becomes obvious when scores are constructed from different rescorings of the same data.

The activity scores and children scores must be re-expressed on a linear scale if we want to do arithmetic with them. Even the simplest statistics like means and standard deviations assume linearity. Raw scores do not provide linearity.

### 2.5.2 The Need for Sample-free Item Calibrations and Test-free Children Measures

A second problem with raw scores is that their values depend on the particulars of the questionnaire and of the sample of children being measured. The children scores on the right of Figure 2.4b reflect both the number of activities in the questionnaire and the likability of these activities. If we were to delete some activities from the questionnaire, then these children would make lower scores. Or, if we replaced some of the hardest-to-like activities with an equal number of easy-to-like activities, then we would expect these children to make higher scores. Because children scores depend on the number of activities in the questionnaire and on their likability, it is not possible to compare scores made on different questionnaires directly. Before such comparisons can be made, raw children scores must be transformed into "measures" which are freed of the particulars of the activities used to obtain them.

The same is true of the activity scores at the bottom of Figure 2.4b. These scores reflect both the number of children in the sample and the attitudes of these children to science. If we were to remove some children from the analysis, then these activities would have lower scores. If we replaced some of the children with less positive attitudes with an equal number of children with more positive attitudes, then we would expect the twenty-five activities to have higher activity scores. Before the likability of activities on different questionnaires can be compared, raw activity scores must be transformed into "calibrations" which are freed of the particulars of the children used to obtain them.

### 2.5.3 The Need for a Common Scale for Children and Activities

We hope to use the observations in Figure 2.4b to estimate a position on a liking-for-science variable for each of the twenty-five science activities and each of the seventy-five children. We expect hard-to-like activities to define high levels of liking for science, and easy-to-like activities to define low levels of liking for science. But when the children scores on the right of Figure 2.4b and the activity scores at the bottom of Figure 2.4b are examined, it is seen that these two sets of scores run in different directions and in different units. The activities hardest to like on the right of the matrix have the lowest activity scores, while the children with the most positive attitudes at the top of the matrix have the highest children scores. This makes it difficult to interpret a child's score in terms of activity scores and, so, makes it difficult to position children and activities on the same line.

The logit transformation can help to overcome this problem. We can transform the children scores on the right of Figure 2.4b into logit scores by

$$b = \log[r/(50-r)]$$

where $r$ is the child's score and $2 \times 25 = 50$ is the highest score a child can make on this science questionnaire. The way in which this transformation works is shown in Figure 2.5a. The curve in Figure 2.5a describes the relationship between children's raw scores $r$ and their transformed logit scores $b$.

Figure 2.5a shows that equal differences in the raw score metric do not represent equal differences in the logit metric. In the raw score metric the difference between a score of 40 and a score of 45 is the same as the difference between a score of 25 and a score of 30. But when these scores are transformed, the difference of five score points between 40 and 45 represents twice as much difference in attitude (.8 logits) as a difference of five score points between 25 and 30 (.4 logits). This is because 25 and 30 are near the middle of the set of possible scores, while 40 and 45 are near the upper limit of 50. Under this transformation a child with a high raw score ends up with a high logit score.

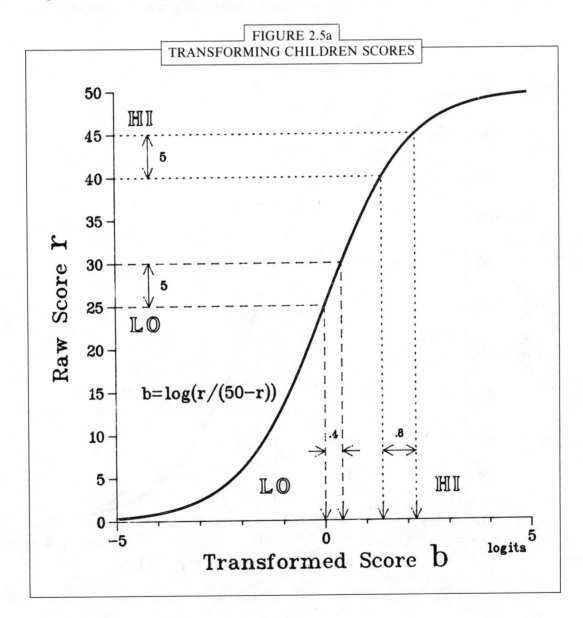

FIGURE 2.5a
TRANSFORMING CHILDREN SCORES

The activity scores at the bottom of Figure 2.4b can also be transformed into logit scores by

$$d = \log[(150-S)/S]$$

where $S$ is the activity score, and $2 \times 75 = 150$ is the highest value this score can take. The way this works can be seen in Figure 2.5b. This curve is the mirror image of the curve in Figure 2.5a and describes the relationship between raw activity scores $S$ and their transformed logit scores $d$.

Once again, equal differences in the raw score metric do not represent equal differences in the logit metric. A difference of one score point at the extremes of the raw score range represents a larger difference in difficulty than a difference of one score point in the middle of the range. Figure 2.5b also shows that when high-scoring activities are transformed to the

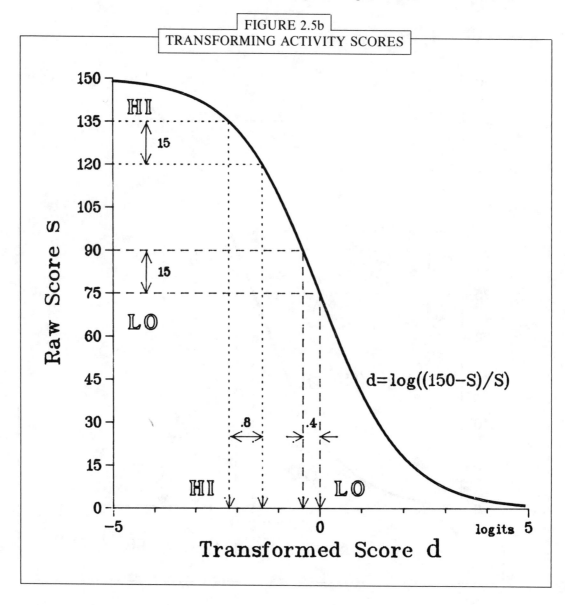

FIGURE 2.5b
TRANSFORMING ACTIVITY SCORES

logit scale, they take on *low* logit scores, while low-scoring activities take on *high* logit scores.    Thus, the direction of the activity scores is reversed so that now they run in the same direction as the children scores.

The logit transformations yield children and activity scores which run in the same direction.    But before we can make direct comparisons between them, they must also be expressed on a scale with the same unit and origin.    Chapter 4 describes how to make these further adjustments so that children logits and activity logits can be compared directly.

# 3 MODELS FOR MEASURING

In this chapter we describe five measurement models. These are the tools we use to construct variables and make measures from data. They are the heart of our psychometric method. All five are members of a family of measurement models which share the possibility of sample-free item calibration and test-free person measurement.

The five models we describe have been developed for use with five different response formats. They are Rasch's *Dichotomous* model (Rasch 1960), the *Poisson Counts* model (Rasch 1960), the *Binomial Trials* model (Rasch 1972; Andrich 1978a, 1978b), the *Rating Scale* model (Andrich 1978c, 1978d, 1979; Masters 1980) and the *Partial Credit* model (Masters, in press; Masters and Wright 1981).

We will develop each of these models and show how they share a common algebraic form. We will see that the Poisson, Binomial, Rating Scale and Partial Credit models can be thought of as simple extensions of Rasch's Dichotomous model to other response formats. Finally, we will summarize the distinguishing properties of this family of models.

## 3.1 THE FAMILY OF MODELS

### 3.1.1 Dichotomous

The simplest response format records only two levels of performance on an item. These are usually "Fail" and "Pass", but they could be any pair of exhaustive and mutually exclusive response alternatives. We can think of items scored in this way as "one-step" items. If this one step is completed, then the person scores 1 on the item. If it is not completed, then the person scores 0. This all-or-nothing format gives no credit for responses which are almost correct or for partially completed solutions to problems. It is the most frequently used format for scoring performances on educational tests.

In the 1950's Georg Rasch introduced and used a measurement model for dichotomously-scored performances. This model, which is often referred to as "the Rasch model", has been widely applied to the analysis of educational test data and to the construction and maintenance of item banks. A detailed introduction to this Dichotomous model, a description of estimation procedures and tests of person and item fit and a worked example are available in *Best Test Design* (Wright and Stone 1979).

To expedite our discussion we will write Rasch's Dichotomous model as

**Dichotomous**
**Model**
$$\phi_{nil} = \frac{\exp(\beta_n - \delta_{il})}{1 + \exp(\beta_n - \delta_{il})} \qquad (3.1.1)$$

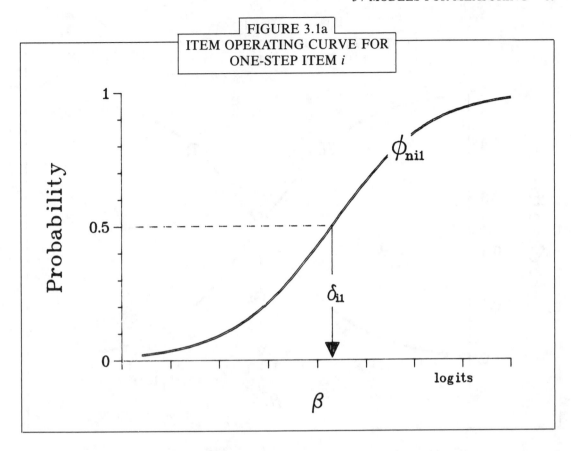

FIGURE 3.1a
ITEM OPERATING CURVE FOR
ONE-STEP ITEM $i$

where $\phi_{nil}$ is person $n$'s probability of scoring 1 rather than 0 on item $i$, $\beta_n$ is the ability of person $n$, and $\delta_{il}$ is the difficulty of the one step in item $i$.

Equation (3.1.1) specifies the way in which the probability of success on item $i$ is supposed to be governed by person ability and item difficulty. This relationship is pictured in Figure 3.1a. The curve in Figure 3.1a describes the modelled probability $\phi_{nil}$ of passing item $i$—the probability of scoring 1 *rather than* 0 on item $i$.

For the development that follows it is useful to introduce $\pi_{ni0}$ as person $n$'s probability of scoring 0 on item $i$, and $\pi_{nil}$ as their probability of scoring 1. In the dichotomous case, this additional notation is redundant since $\pi_{nil}$ is simply the probability $\phi_{nil}$ of completing the first and only step in item $i$, and $\pi_{ni0} = 1 - \phi_{nil}$. However, this notation will be convenient when we consider more than two ordered response alternatives. For now, we note that (3.1.1) can be rewritten

$$\phi_{nil} \;=\; \frac{\pi_{nil}}{\pi_{ni0} + \pi_{nil}} \;=\; \frac{\exp(\beta_n - \delta_{il})}{1 + \exp(\beta_n - \delta_{il})} \qquad (3.1.2)$$

which makes explicit that $\phi_{nil}$ is person n's probability of scoring 1 *rather than* 0 on item $i$. Of course, when only two responses are possible, $\pi_{ni0} + \pi_{nil} = 1$ and $\phi_{nil} = \pi_{nil}$.

Figure 3.1b shows the model "category probability curves" for this one-step item $i$. These curves show the way in which the probability $\pi_{ni0}$ of scoring 0 and the probability $\pi_{nil}$ of

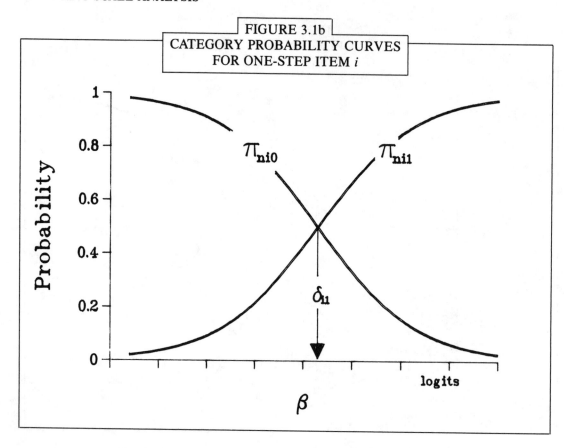

FIGURE 3.1b
CATEGORY PROBABILITY CURVES
FOR ONE-STEP ITEM $i$

scoring 1 on a one-step item vary with ability.   The item parameter $\delta_{il}$ is at the intersection of the probability curves for categories 0 and 1.

### 3.1.2 Partial Credit

A simple extension of right/wrong scoring is to identify one or more intermediate levels of performance on an item and to award partial credit for reaching these intermediate levels.   Three items for which a partial credit format might be used are shown in Figure 3.1c.   Four ordered levels of performance are identified in each item.   These levels are labelled 0, 1, 2 and 3, with 3 being the highest level of performance possible.

When four ordered performance levels are identified in an item, the item can be thought of as a "three-step" item.   The three steps in the mathematics item are shown in Figure 3.1d.   The first step is to solve the division $9.0/0.3 = ?$ to make a 1 rather than a 0.   The second step, which can be taken only if the first step has been completed, is to solve the subtraction $30 - 5 = ?$ to make a 2 rather than a 1, and the third step, which can be taken only if the first two steps have been completed, is to solve $\sqrt{25} = ?$   to make a score of 3 rather than 2.

To develop a Partial Credit model for this sort of item we will consider a two-step item $i$ with performance levels 0, 1 and 2.   We begin with an expression for the probability of person $n$ scoring 1 rather than 0 on this item which is identical to the Dichotomous model (3.1.2)

FIGURE 3.1c

## THREE ITEMS FOR WHICH PARTIAL CREDIT MIGHT BE AWARDED

**Mathematics item**

$$\sqrt{9.0/0.3 - 5} = ?$$

No steps taken .................... 0
9.0/0.3 = 30 ...................... 1
30 − 5 = 25 ..................... 2
$\sqrt{25}$ = 5 ....................... 3

**Screening test item** *

Draw a circle

| 0 | 1 | 2 | 3 |
|---|---|---|---|
| No response | Scribble, no resemblance to circle | Lack of closure, much overlap, more than ⅓ of figure distorted | Closure, no more than ⅔″ overlap, 2/3 figure round |

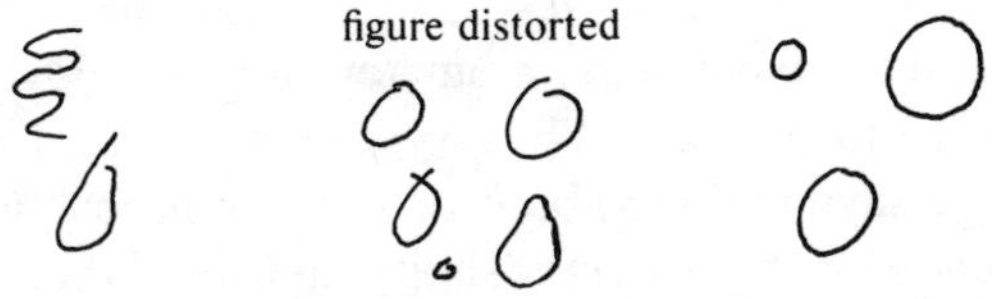

**Geography item**

The capital city of Australia is

a. Wellington ...................... 1
b. Canberra ...................... 3
c. Montreal ...................... 0
d. Sydney ........................ 2

* From: Mardell, C. and Goldenberg, D., DIAL, Developmental Indicators for the Assessment of Learning, 1972.

FIGURE 3.1d

## A THREE-STEP MATHEMATICS ITEM

PERFORMANCE LEVELS

| | 0 | 1 | 2 | 3 |
|---|---|---|---|---|
| 9.0/0.3 = ? | First Step 0 ⟶ 1 | | | |
| 30 − 5 = ? | | Second Step 1 ⟶ 2 | | |
| $\sqrt{25}$ = ? | | | Third Step 2 ⟶ 3 | |

$$\phi_{nil} \quad = \quad \frac{\pi_{nil}}{\pi_{ni0} + \pi_{nil}} \quad = \quad \frac{\exp(\beta_n - \delta_{il})}{1 + \exp(\beta_n - \delta_{il})} \qquad\qquad (3.1.3)$$

The only differences are that now, since we are considering more than two ordered performance levels, $\pi_{ni0} + \pi_{nil} < 1$, and, while $\delta_{il}$ still governs the probability of completing the first step to score 1 rather than 0, the first step is not the *only* step in item $i$.

The second step from level 1 to level 2 can be taken *only* if the first step from level 0 to level 1 has been completed. A parallel expression for the probability of completing this second step in item $i$ is

$$\phi_{ni2} \quad = \quad \frac{\pi_{ni2}}{\pi_{nil} + \pi_{ni2}} \quad = \quad \frac{\exp(\beta_n - \delta_{i2})}{1 + \exp(\beta_n - \delta_{i2})} \qquad\qquad (3.1.4)$$

This gives the probability of person $n$ scoring 2 rather than 1 on item $i$ as a function of the same person ability $\beta_n$ and a second item parameter $\delta_{i2}$ which governs the probability of making the transition from level 1 to level 2. While $\delta_{i2}$ governs the probability of completing the step from level 1 to level 2, it says nothing about person $n$'s probability of reaching level 1 in the first place. That depends on the person's ability and the difficulty of the first step in the item.

For items with more than two steps, additional probability expressions of the same form as (3.1.3) and (3.1.4) can be introduced to describe the probability of scoring 3 rather than 2, 4 rather than 3, and so on, in terms of item step parameters $\delta_{i3}$, $\delta_{i4}$, . . . , $\delta_{im}$. This leads to a general Partial Credit model

$$\phi_{nik} \quad = \quad \frac{\pi_{nik}}{\pi_{nik-1} + \pi_{nik}} \quad = \quad \frac{\exp(\beta_n - \delta_{ik})}{1 + \exp(\beta_n - \delta_{ik})} \qquad k = 1, 2, \ldots, m_i \qquad (3.1.5)$$

which can be used to describe any ordered sequence of dichotomous steps.

For a one-step item ($m = 1$) we model just *one* operating curve which describes the probability of scoring 1 rather than 0 on the item (Figure 3.1a). For a two-step item ($m = 2$) we model *two* operating curves—one for each step. The first describes the probability of scoring 1 rather than 0 on the item. The second describes the probability of scoring 2 rather than 1 (Figure 3.1e). These operating curves are simple logistic ogives of the same slope which differ only in their location on the ability continuum. While we have drawn the curve for the second step in item $i$ to the right of the curve for the first, so that the second step is more difficult, this difficulty order is not necessary. The second step in item $i$ could be easier to complete than the first, even though it can only be attempted after the first has been completed. In that case, the curves in Figure 3.1e would be in the opposite order.

From (3.1.5), and with the requirement that person $n$ must make one of the $m_i + 1$ possible scores on item $i$ (i.e., $\sum_{k=0}^{m_i} \pi_{nik} = 1$), a general expression for the probability of person $n$ scoring $x$ on item $i$ follows

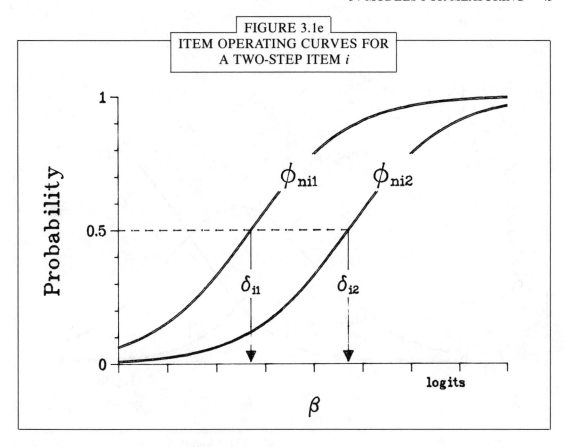

FIGURE 3.1e
ITEM OPERATING CURVES FOR
A TWO-STEP ITEM $i$

**Partial Credit Model**

$$\pi_{nix} = \frac{\exp\sum_{j=0}^{x}(\beta_n - \delta_{ij})}{\sum_{k=0}^{m_i}\exp\sum_{j=0}^{k}(\beta_n - \delta_{ij})} \qquad x = 0, 1, \ldots, m_i \qquad (3.1.6)$$

where $\delta_{i0} \equiv 0$ so that $\sum_{j=0}^{0}(\beta_n - \delta_{ij}) = 0$ and $\exp\sum_{j=0}^{0}(\beta_n - \delta_{ij}) = 1$. The observation $x$ in (3.1.6) is the *count* of the completed item steps. The numerator $\exp\sum_{j=0}^{x}(\beta_n - \delta_{ij})$ contains only the difficulties of these $x$ completed steps, $\delta_{i1}, \delta_{i2}, \ldots, \delta_{ix}$. The denominator is the sum of all $m_i + 1$ possible numerators.

Figure 3.1f shows the category probability curves for the two-step item $i$ in Figure 3.1e. Now there are three probability curves, one for each response category. As in the dichotomous case (Figure 3.1b), $\delta_{i1}$ is at the intersection of the model probability curves for categories 0 and 1. The second item parameter $\delta_{i2}$ is at the intersection of the model probability curves for categories 1 and 2.

If the first step in item $i$ were easier ($\delta_{i1}$ further to the left in Figure 3.1f), and the second step were harder ($\delta_{i2}$ further to the right), then the probability curve for the middle response category $\pi_{ni1}$ would be more prominent, meaning that the probability of completing *only the first step* would be greater at every value of $\beta_n$.

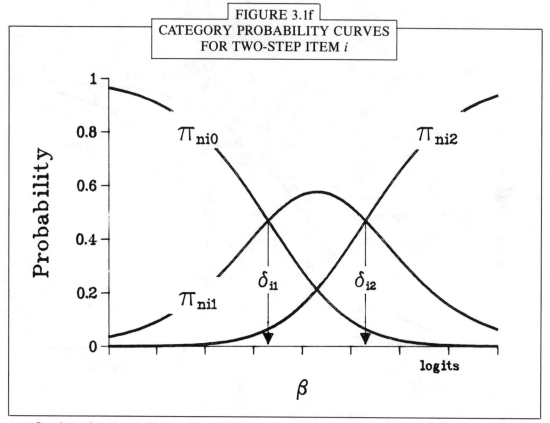

FIGURE 3.1f
CATEGORY PROBABILITY CURVES
FOR TWO-STEP ITEM $i$

On the other hand, if $\delta_{i1}$ and $\delta_{i2}$ were brought closer together in Figure 3.1f, then every person's probability of completing only the first step in item $i$ (i.e., every person's probability of scoring 1) would decrease. When the second step is made *easier* than the first ($\delta_{i2} < \delta_{i1}$), the probability curve for the middle response category drops still further, and every person becomes even less likely to complete only the first step. This is illustrated in Figure 3.1g. Notice that $\delta_{i1}$ is still the point on the ability continuum where the probability curves for categories 0 and 1 intersect, and $\delta_{i2}$ is still at the intersection of the probability curves for categories 1 and 2. Even though the second step in Figure 3.1g is easier than the first, the defined order of the response categories requires that this easier second step be undertaken only after the harder first step has been successfully completed.

***Item "Steps" vs Item "Levels".*** The item "step" parameters $\delta_{i1}$, $\delta_{i2}$, . . . , $\delta_{im}$ in (3.1.5) and (3.1.6) can be contrasted with an alternative set of parameters which are sometimes used to represent ordered response categories (Edwards and Thurstone 1952; Samejima 1969). To see the difference between the two sets of parameters consider the data displayed in Table 3.1a.

Table 3.1a shows the responses of ten persons to a three-step item $i$. Each person's score on this item is shown on the far right of the table. This score $x_{ni}$ can be interpreted as the number of steps completed by person $n$ taking item $i$ or, if the ordered performance levels are labelled 0, 1, 2 and 3, as the highest performance level in item $i$ reached by person $n$. The alternative dichotomous variable $y_{nik}$ in Table 3.1a is assigned the value 1 if person $n$ reaches the $k$'th performance level and 0 otherwise. Seven persons in Table 3.1a completed the first step in item $i$ and reached level 1 ($y_{ni1} = 1$). Of these, five also completed the second step and reached level 2 ($y_{ni2} = 1$), and of these, three went on to complete the third step and reached

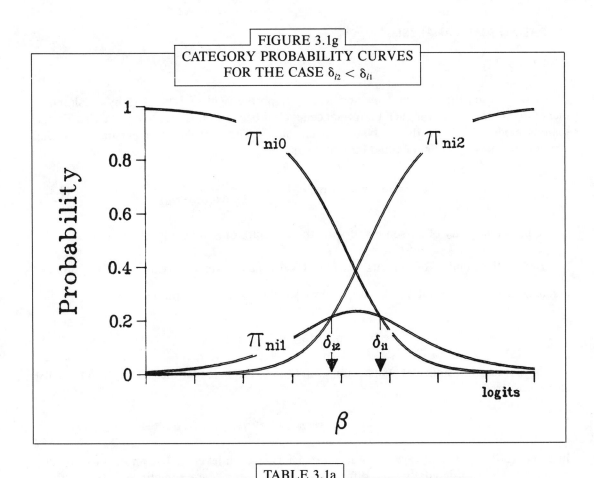

# FIGURE 3.1g
## CATEGORY PROBABILITY CURVES
### FOR THE CASE $\delta_{i2} < \delta_{i1}$

# TABLE 3.1a
## SOME PERFORMANCES ON A THREE-STEP ITEM $i$

| PERSON NUMBER $n$ | PERFORMANCE LEVELS | | | | PERSON SCORE |
|---|---|---|---|---|---|
| | 0 $y_{ni0}$ | 1 $y_{ni1}$ | 2 $y_{ni2}$ | 3 $y_{ni3}$ | $x_{ni}$ |
| *1* | 1 | 1 | 1 | 1 | **3** |
| *2* | 1 | | | | **0** |
| *3* | 1 | 1 | 1 | | **2** |
| *4* | 1 | 1 | | | **1** |
| *5* | 1 | | | | **0** |
| *6* | 1 $\xrightarrow{\text{First Step}}$ 1 | $\xrightarrow{\text{Second Step}}$ 1 | $\xrightarrow{\text{Third Step}}$ 1 | | **3** |
| *7* | 1 | 1 | | | **1** |
| *8* | 1 | 1 | 1 | | **2** |
| *9* | 1 | | | | **0** |
| *10* | 1 | 1 | 1 | 1 | **3** |
| Count | $S_{i0} = 10$ | $S_{i1} = 7$ | $S_{i2} = 5$ | $S_{i3} = 3$ | |

level 3 ($y_{ni3} = 1$).

If we replace the column of person scores $x_{ni}$ on the right of Table 3.1a by a column of dichotomous scores $y_{nik}$ for each performance level, it becomes possible to try Rasch's Dichotomous model (3.1.1) on the analysis of these data.   The probability of person $n$ reaching performance level $k$ in item $i$ could be written as

$$\pi^{*}_{nik} \quad = \quad P\{y_{nik} = 1; \beta_n, \gamma_{ik}\} \quad = \quad \frac{\exp(\beta_n - \gamma_{ik})}{1 + \exp(\beta_n - \gamma_{ik})} \tag{3.1.7}$$

where $\beta_n$ is the ability of person $n$ and $\gamma_{ik}$ is the difficulty of *reaching* level $k$ in item $i$.

But as the number of persons reaching level $k$ can never be greater than the number reaching level $k-1$ in an item, the item scores $S_{ik} = \sum_{n}^{N} y_{nik}$ must be ordered

$$S_{i1} \geqslant S_{i2} \geqslant S_{i3} \ldots \geqslant S_{im}$$

and, because $S_{ik}$ is a sufficient statistic for $\gamma_{ik}$ in (3.1.7), estimates for these item "levels" must also be ordered

$$\hat{\gamma}_{i1} \leqslant \hat{\gamma}_{i2} \leqslant \hat{\gamma}_{i3} \ldots \leqslant \hat{\gamma}_{im}$$

In other words, it must always be as easy or easier to reach level $k-1$ in an item as to reach level $k$.   These ordered "level" difficulties $\gamma_{i1}, \gamma_{i2}, \ldots \gamma_{im}$ are sometimes referred to as "category boundaries".   They invite three observations.

**First**, the intention of Rasch's Dichotomous model is that each dichotomously scored observation $y_{nik}$ be governed by only one person parameter and only one item parameter, and that it be independent of all other influences.   But it is impossible for a person in Table 3.1a to reach level 3 ($y_{ni3} = 1$) if they have not first reached level 1 ($y_{ni1} = 1$), and then level 2 ($y_{ni2} = 1$).   There are two ways a person may fail to reach level 3 in item $i$ ($y_{ni3} = 0$).   The first is that they reach level 2, but then fail step 3.   The second is that they fail either step 1 or step 2, and so never attempt step 3.   Whether or not a person reaches performance level 3 depends not only on the difficulty of the third step, but also on the difficulties of the two preceding steps.   This hierarchical dependence among levels contradicts the intention that $P\{y_{ni3} = 1\}$ be governed by $\beta_n$ and $\gamma_{i3}$ only.

**Second**, we can calculate person $n$'s probability of scoring $x$ on item $i$ from (3.1.7) by subtracting cumulative probabilities.   In the three-category case, these category probabilities are

$$\pi_{ni0} \quad = \quad 1 - \pi^{*}_{ni1} \quad = \quad \frac{1 + \exp(\beta_n - \gamma_{i2})}{\Psi}$$

$$\pi_{ni1} \quad = \quad \pi^{*}_{ni1} - \pi^{*}_{ni2} \quad = \quad \frac{\exp(\beta_n - \gamma_{i1}) - \exp(\beta_n - \gamma_{i2})}{\Psi} \tag{3.1.8}$$

$$\pi_{ni2} \quad = \quad \pi^{*}_{ni2} \quad = \quad \frac{\exp(\beta_n - \gamma_{i2}) + \exp(2\beta_n - \gamma_{i1} - \gamma_{i2})}{\Psi}$$

where $\Psi$ is the sum of the three numerators.

Formulation (3.1.7) has been proposed as a latent trait model in which the probability of person $n$ scoring $x$ on item $i$ is expressed as a function of the person's ability $\beta_n$ and the "level" difficulties $\gamma_{i1}$ and $\gamma_{i2}$ (Samejima 1969). Equations (3.1.8), however, show that no simple expression for $\pi_{nix}$, the probability of person $n$ scoring $x$ on item $i$, follows from (3.1.7). Further, there is no way to condition the person parameter $\beta_n$ out of the estimation equations for $\gamma_{i1}$ and $\gamma_{i2}$ except by treating item $i$ as though it were *two* independent dichotomous items with difficulties $\gamma_{i1}$ and $\gamma_{i2}$, which by definition it is not. When ordered item "levels" are parameterized, the latent trait model that results does not permit the separation of person and item parameters and, so, lacks the conditions necessary for objective comparisons of persons and items.

**Third**, by substituting values of $\gamma_{i1}$ and $\gamma_{i2}$ into (3.1.8), values of the model probabilities $\pi_{ni0}$, $\pi_{ni1}$ and $\pi_{ni2}$ can be calculated for any value of $\beta_n$. Figure 3.1h shows the category probability curves for the case $\gamma_{i1} = -1$, $\gamma_{i2} = +1$. From Figure 3.1h it can be seen that the "level" difficulties $\gamma_{i1}$ and $\gamma_{i2}$ are the points on the ability continuum at which $\pi_{ni0} = 0.5$ and $\pi_{ni2} = 0.5$. The "step" difficulties $\delta_{i1}$ and $\delta_{i2}$ in Figure 3.1f, in contrast, correspond to the intersections of the category probability curves.

Our approach to item $i$ in Table 3.1a does not involve ordered "level" difficulties (i.e., $\gamma_{i1}$, the difficulty of reaching level 1; $\gamma_{i2}$, the difficulty of reaching level 2, and $\gamma_{i3}$, the difficulty of reaching level 3), but is based instead on the difficulties $\delta_{i1}$, $\delta_{i2}$ and $\delta_{i3}$ of each successive "step" in the item. The third step in item $i$, for example, is from level 2 to

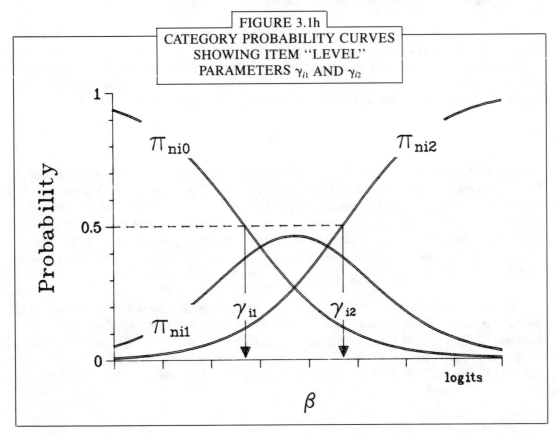

FIGURE 3.1h
CATEGORY PROBABILITY CURVES
SHOWING ITEM "LEVEL"
PARAMETERS $\gamma_{i1}$ AND $\gamma_{i2}$

level 3.   The difficulty of this third step governs how likely it is that a person completing the first two steps will also complete the third (i.e., how likely it is that he will make a 3 *rather than* a 2 on item *i*).   Unlike the item levels $\gamma_{i1}, \gamma_{i2}, \ldots, \gamma_{im}$ in (3.1.7) and (3.1.8), each of which represents the difficulty of reaching a performance level, the difficulties $\delta_{i1}, \delta_{i2}, \ldots, \delta_{im}$ of taking steps can be separated from and estimated independently of the person parameters in the model.

### 3.1.3 Rating Scale

The structure of the mathematics item in Figure 3.1c invites a "step" interpretation.   But this idea can be applied to any item with ordered response alternatives.   For an item on an attitude questionnaire, "completing the *k*'th step" can be thought of as choosing the *k*'th alternative over the $(k-1)$'th in response to the item.   Thus a person who chooses to *Agree* with a statement on an attitude questionnaire when given the ordered categories

| Strongly Disagree | Disagree | Agree | Strongly Agree |
|:---:|:---:|:---:|:---:|
| 0 | 1 | 2 | 3 |

to choose among, can be considered to have chosen *Disagree* over *Strongly Disagree* (first step taken) and also *Agree* over *Disagree* (second step taken), but to have failed to choose *Strongly Agree* over *Agree* (third step *not* taken).

The relative difficulties of the "steps" in a rating scale item are usually intended to be governed by the fixed set of rating points accompanying the items.   As the same set of rating points is used with every item, it is usually thought that the relative difficulties of the steps in each item should not vary from item to item.   This expectation can be incorporated into the Partial Credit model by resolving each item step into two components so that

$$\delta_{ik} = \delta_i + \tau_k$$

where $\delta_i$ is the location or "scale value" of item *i* on the variable and $\tau_k$ is the location of the *k*'th step in each item relative to that item's scale value.   Under this simplification, which is depicted for two items *i* and *j* in Figure 3.1i, the only difference remaining between items is the difference in their location on the variable.   The pattern of item steps around this location, which is supposed to be determined by the fixed set of rating points used with the items, is described by the "threshold" parameters $\tau_1, \tau_2, \ldots, \tau_m$, and is estimated *once* for the entire item set.

The item parameters $\delta_i$ and $\delta_j$ in Figure 3.1i describe the locations on the variable of the pair of operating curves for each item.   To estimate $\tau_1$ and $\tau_2$ some arbitrary constraint is necessary.   Here, $\tau_1$ and $\tau_2$ are constrained by setting $\tau_. = 0$ (i.e., $\tau_1 = -\tau_2$).   This locates $\delta$ at the center of each ogive pair.   In practice, it may be more useful to think of each item's scale value as the location of the *k*'th step in each item, in which case the alternative constraint $\tau_k = 0$ would be used.

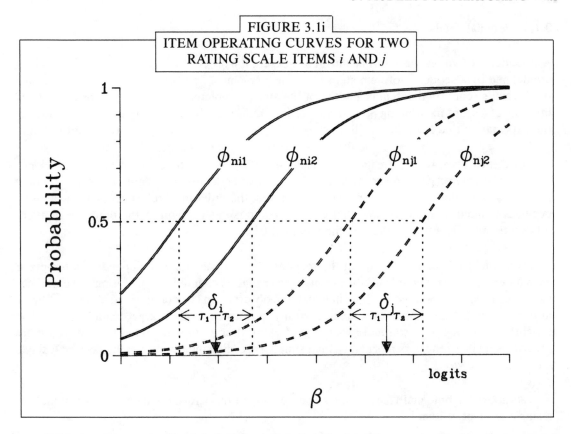

FIGURE 3.1i
ITEM OPERATING CURVES FOR TWO
RATING SCALE ITEMS $i$ AND $j$

With $\delta_{ik} = \delta_i + \tau_k$ the Partial Credit model (3.1.5) simplifies to the Rating Scale model (Andrich 1978c, 1978d, 1979)

$$\phi_{nik} = \frac{\pi_{nik}}{\pi_{nik-1} + \pi_{nik}} = \frac{\exp[\beta_n - (\delta_i + \tau_k)]}{1 + \exp[\beta_n - (\delta_i + \tau_k)]} \qquad k = 1, 2, \ldots, m \qquad (3.1.9)$$

which, like the Partial Credit model, can be written as the probability of person $n$ responding in category $x$ to item $i$

**Rating Scale Model**
$$\pi_{nix} = \frac{\exp\sum_{j=0}^{x}[\beta_n - (\delta_i + \tau_j)]}{\sum_{k=0}^{m}\exp\sum_{j=0}^{k}[\beta_n - (\delta_i + \tau_j)]} \qquad x = 0, 1, \ldots, m \qquad (3.1.10)$$

where $\tau_0 \equiv 0$ so that $\exp\sum_{j=0}^{0}[\beta_n - (\delta_i + \tau_j)] = 1$.

When this model is applied to the analysis of a rating scale, a position on the variable $\beta_n$ is estimated for each person $n$, a scale value $\delta_i$ is estimated for each item $i$, and $m$ response "thresholds" $\tau_1, \tau_2, \ldots, \tau_m$ are estimated for the $m+1$ rating categories. We will use this model in Chapters 4 and 5 to analyze the science data from Chapter 2.

### 3.1.4 Binomial Trials

Under the two response formats just considered, the ordered performance levels in an item are defined by a sequence of item steps.   These steps must be taken in a specified order, and the person's score on the item is a count of the steps completed.   When the steps are defined in terms of a set of fixed rating points, the Partial Credit model can be simplified by introducing the expectation that the relative difficulties of the item steps will not vary from item to item.

In the two response formats we consider next, successes on an item can occur in *any* order.   The ordered performance levels $0, 1, 2 \ldots m$ are defined as the number of independent successes on an item.   These response formats treat the order in which successes (or failures) occur as unimportant and assume that each outcome is independent of the outcome of every other attempt.   The first of these is the binomial trials format.

Binomial trials data result when the response format calls for $m$ independent attempts at each item, and the number of successes $x$ in these $m$ trials is counted.   This format is sometimes useful for tests of psychomotor skills in which the observation is a count of the number of times in $m$ independent attempts a task is successfully performed (e.g., a target is hit or a beanbag caught).   Allowing a person more than one attempt at an item is intended to lead to a more precise estimate of the person's ability than simply recording their failure or success on a single attempt.

A model for binomial trials data can be developed from Rasch's dichotomous model for a single attempt at item i

$$P \;=\; \frac{\exp(\beta_n - \delta_i)}{1 + \exp(\beta_n - \delta_i)}$$

Under the assumption that each attempt is independent of every other attempt, the probability of person $n$ succeeding on $x$ particular attempts (e.g., the first $x$) and failing the other $(m-x)$ attempts is

$$P^x (1-P)^{m-x}$$

As there are $\binom{m}{x}$ ways of succeeding on $x$ of $m$ attempts, person $n$'s probability of succeeding on any $x$ attempts is

$$\pi_{nix} \;=\; \binom{m}{x} P^x (1-P)^{m-x}$$

Substituting for $P$ in this expression produces

$$\pi_{nix} \;=\; \binom{m}{x} \frac{\exp[x(\beta_n - \delta_i)]}{[1 + \exp(\beta_n - \delta_i)]^m}$$

which can be rewritten

**Binomial Trials Model**
$$\pi_{nix} = \frac{\exp\sum\limits_{j=0}^{x}[\beta_n - (\delta_i + c_j)]}{\sum\limits_{k=0}^{m}\exp\sum\limits_{j=0}^{k}[\beta_n - (\delta_i + c_j)]} \qquad x = 0, 1, \ldots, m \qquad (3.1.11)$$

where $c_j = \log[\, j\,/(m-j+1)]$.

In this Binomial Trials model (Rasch, 1972; Andrich, 1978a,1978c), the $c_j$'s, rather than being parameters estimated from data, have fixed values which result from the assumption that the $m$ attempts are independent Bernoulli trials.

Once again, it is possible to think in terms of $m$ "steps" associated with each binomial trials item. The $k$'th step is to succeed on $k$ rather than $k-1$ attempts at the item. From (3.1.11) it follows that the probability of completing this step is

$$\phi_{nik} = \frac{\pi_{nik}}{\pi_{nik-1} + \pi_{nik}} = \frac{\exp[\beta_n - (\delta_i + c_k)]}{1 + \exp[\beta_n - (\delta_i + c_k)]} \qquad k = 1, 2, \ldots, m \qquad (3.1.12)$$

When the Binomial Trials model is written in this form, it is seen to define a series of parallel logistic ogives. Each ogive describes the model probability of succeeding on $k$ rather than $k-1$ attempts at item i. However, rather than estimating a location $\delta_{ik}$ for each of these ogives (Partial Credit model), or fixing the relative difficulties of the steps within each item and estimating this pattern of item steps *once* for all items (Rating Scale model), the Binomial Trials model, through its assumption that the $m$ attempts at item i are independent Bernoulli trials, expects the relative difficulties of the steps within each item to take *particular* values.

Table 3.1b shows values of $c_k$ for $m$ from one through eight. Each row of this table shows the fixed pattern of step difficulties for a given value of $m$. The entries in this table can be thought of either as the difficulties of the steps in an item with scale value $\delta_i = 0$, or as the difficulties of the steps in a binomial trials item relative to the item's scale value $\delta_i$.

The first "step" in a binomial trials item is to succeed on any one of $m$ attempts to make a 1 rather than a 0 on the item. If only one attempt is allowed per item (i.e., $m = 1$), then $c_1 = \log(1/1) = 0$, and the difficulty of succeeding on this one attempt is $\delta_i$. However, if more than one attempt is allowed, then the difficulty of succeeding on any one of these $m$ attempts

| TABLE 3.1b |
| --- |
| VALUES OF $c_k$ FOR THE BINOMIAL TRIALS MODEL |

$(m = 1, 2, \ldots, 8)$

| $m$ | $c_1$ | $c_2$ | $c_3$ | $c_4$ | $c_5$ | $c_6$ | $c_7$ | $c_8$ |
|---|---|---|---|---|---|---|---|---|
| 1 | .00 | | | | | | | |
| 2 | $-.69$ | .69 | | | | | | |
| 3 | $-1.10$ | .00 | 1.10 | | | | | |
| 4 | $-1.39$ | $-.41$ | .41 | 1.39 | | | | |
| 5 | $-1.61$ | $-.69$ | .00 | .69 | 1.61 | | | |
| 6 | $-1.79$ | $-.92$ | $-.29$ | .29 | .92 | 1.79 | | |
| 7 | $-1.95$ | $-1.10$ | $-.51$ | .00 | .51 | 1.10 | 1.95 | |
| 8 | $-2.08$ | $-1.25$ | $-.69$ | $-.22$ | .22 | .69 | 1.25 | 2.08 |

(i.e., the difficulty of the first "step") is $\delta_i + c_I = \delta_i + \log[1/(m-1+1)] = \delta_i - \log m$. It follows that the greater the number of attempts $m$ allowed at item $i$, the easier it is to take the first step and succeed on any *one* of these $m$ attempts.

The second step in item $i$ is to succeed on any one of the other $m-1$ attempts in order to make a 2 rather than a 1 on the item. Because it is always harder to succeed on one of $m-1$ attempts than on one of $m$ attempts, the second step in a binomial trials item is always more difficult than the first. Since the number of attempts remaining decreases with each successfully completed step, the $k$'th step in a repeated trials item is always more difficult than the $(k-1)$'th.

### 3.1.5 Poisson Counts

In binomial trials data the observation $x_{ni}$ counts the number of times person $n$ is successful in $m$ attempts at item $i$. This count takes values between 0 and a finite number of attempts $m$. In some testing situations, however, there is no clear upper limit on the number of events (failures or successes) which might be observed and counted. This is the case, for example, when the observation is a count of the number of times person $n$ successfully completes some task $i$ in a fixed period of time, or when the observation is a count of the errors made by person $n$ reading passage $i$ on a reading test. Under this response format the observation $x_{ni}$ is a count of events which have innumerable opportunities to occur, but little probability of doing so on any particular opportunity. A person reading a passage on an oral reading test, for example, has at least as many opportunities to misread a word as there are words in the passage, but his probability of misreading any particular word is usually rather small.

Rasch (1960) used a Poisson model in 1952 to analyze errors and speed in reading. To develop that model here it is convenient to continue counting successes rather than errors. The Poisson model can be developed by considering an item $i$ which presents a large number of opportunities for success $m$, but for which any person's probability of success $P$ on any particular opportunity is small. The probability of person $n$ succeeding on $x$ of $m$ opportunities is given by the binomial expression

$$\pi_{nix} = \binom{m}{x} P^x (1-P)^{m-x}$$

for which person $n$'s expected number of successes on item $i$ is $\lambda_{ni} = mP$.

If, as $m$ becomes large and $P$ becomes small, the expected number of successes $\lambda_{ni} = mP$ remains constant, then this probability can be replaced by the Poisson expression

$$\pi_{nix} = \frac{\lambda_{ni}^x}{x! \, \exp(\lambda_{ni})} \tag{3.1.13}$$

which gives the probability of person $n$ making $x$ successes on item $i$ when the possible number of successes has no upper limit (i.e., $m$ has become infinite). This probability is a function of person $n$'s expected number of successes $\lambda_{ni}$ on item $i$, which in turn must be a function of the person's ability $\beta_n$ and the item's difficulty $\delta_i$.

If we now think in terms of a series of "steps" associated with item $i$, then the first step is to succeed once on item $i$ rather than not at all, the second is to succeed twice rather than once, and so on.   Since $\pi_{ni0} = 1/(\exp\lambda_{ni})$ and $\pi_{ni1} = \lambda_{ni}/(\exp\lambda_{ni})$, the probability of person $n$ completing the first "step" in item $i$ is

$$\frac{\pi_{ni1}}{\pi_{ni0} + \pi_{ni1}} \;=\; \frac{\lambda_{ni}}{1 + \lambda_{ni}}$$

In the Dichotomous, Partial Credit, Rating Scale and Binomial Trials models the probability of person $n$ completing the first step in item $i$ takes the general form

$$\frac{\pi_{ni1}}{\pi_{ni0} + \pi_{ni1}} \;=\; \frac{\exp(\beta_n - \delta_{i1})}{1 + \exp(\beta_n - \delta_{i1})}$$

The similarity of these expressions suggests a simple interpretation of $\lambda_{ni}$ in terms of the person's ability $\beta_n$ and the difficulty $\delta_{i1}$ of the first step in item $i$.

Substituting $\lambda_{ni} = \exp(\beta_n - \delta_{i1})$   in (3.1.13) yields

$$\pi_{nix} \;=\; \frac{\exp[x(\beta_n - \delta_{i1})]}{x! \; \exp[\exp(\beta_n - \delta_{i1})]} \tag{3.1.14}$$

This Poisson Counts model can be expressed in the Partial Credit form by noting that since $x! = \prod_{j=1}^{x} j = \exp\left(\sum_{j=1}^{x} \log j\right)$,

$$\frac{\exp[x(\beta_n - \delta_{i1})]}{x!} \;=\; \exp\left[ x(\beta_n - \delta_{i1}) - \sum_{j=1}^{x} \log j \right]$$

If $\delta_{i0} \equiv 0$ and $\delta_{ij} \equiv \delta_{i1} + \log j$ for $j > 0$, this simplifies to

$$\frac{\exp[x(\beta_n - \delta_{i1})]}{x!} \;=\; \exp\sum_{j=0}^{x}(\beta_n - \delta_{ij}) \tag{3.1.15}$$

From the definition of the exponential function

$$\exp(\lambda) \;=\; \sum_{k=0}^{\infty} \frac{\lambda^k}{k!}$$

it follows that

$$\exp[\exp(\beta_n - \delta_{i1})] \;=\; \sum_{k=0}^{\infty} \frac{\exp[k(\beta_n - \delta_{i1})]}{k!}$$

which, with (3.1.15), can be written

$$\exp[\exp(\beta_n - \delta_{i1})] \;\; = \;\; \sum_{k=0}^{\infty} \exp[\sum_{j=0}^{k} (\beta_n - \delta_{ij})]$$

These observations enable the Poisson Counts model to be written

**Poisson Counts**
**Model**
$$\pi_{nix} \;\; = \;\; \frac{\exp\sum\limits_{j=0}^{x} (\beta_n - \delta_{ij})}{\sum\limits_{k=0}^{\infty} \exp\sum\limits_{j=0}^{k} (\beta_n - \delta_{ij})} \qquad x = 0, 1, \ldots, \infty \qquad (3.1.16)$$

where $\delta_{i0} \equiv 0$ so that $\exp\sum\limits_{j=0}^{0} (\beta_n - \delta_{ij}) \equiv 1$ and $\delta_{ij} \equiv \delta_{i1} + \log j$ for $j > 0$.

Thus the Poisson Counts model can be thought of as the version of the Partial Credit model in which $m = \infty$ and $\delta_{ij} = \delta_{i1} + \log j$. In this model, as in the Binomial Trials model for finite $m$, the pattern of item steps is fixed by the model and is the same for every item. This fixed pattern of steps results from the assumption that the opportunities are Bernoulli trials and the use of the Poisson distribution to approximate the binomial when the number of opportunities is large and the probability of success on any given opportunity is small.

Figure 3.1j shows the probability curves defined by (3.1.16) for the first seven response categories in a Poisson counts item. This pattern of probability curves continues indefinitely to the right, with the curve for each category being slightly lower than the preceding curve on its left. These curves describe the way in which the probabilities of scoring 0, 1, 2, ..., ∞ on item $i$ vary with ability. The same pattern of curves applies to each item. Only the location of this pattern (specified by $\delta_{i1}$) varies from item to item.

In the Rating Scale and Binomial Trials models, the location of each item on the continuum is summarized in an item "scale value" defined as the mean step difficulty for the item ($\delta_i \equiv \delta_i$.). In the Poisson Counts model, the number of steps is infinite. This prevents the calculation of a mean step difficulty. It is convenient, however, to set $\delta_i = \delta_{i1}$ so that the item "scale value" corresponds to the position of a person who is as likely to make a 1 as a 0 on item $i$. The difficulty of the $j$'th step in item $i$ is then defined as $\delta_{ij} = \delta_i + \log j$.

## 3.2 DISTINGUISHING PROPERTIES OF RASCH MODELS

### 3.2.1 Operating Curves are Logistic Ogives with the Same Slope

The Dichotomous, Partial Credit, Rating Scale, Binomial Trials and Poisson Counts models share a common algebraic form. This shared form is captured in the general expression

$$\phi_{nix} \;\; = \;\; \frac{\pi_{nix}}{\pi_{nix-1} + \pi_{nix}} \;\; = \;\; \frac{\exp(\beta_n - \delta_{ix})}{1 + \exp(\beta_n - \delta_{ix})} \qquad x = 1, 2, \ldots, m_i \qquad (3.2.1)$$

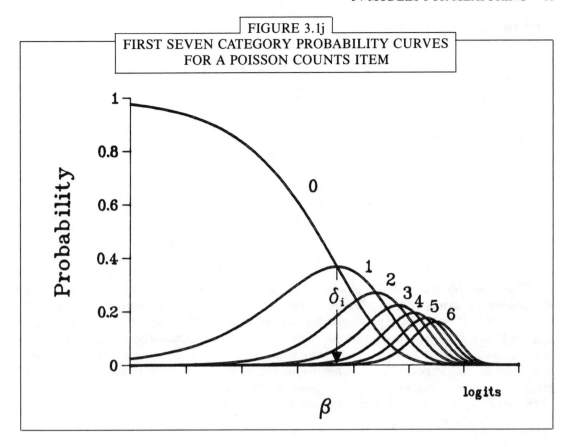

FIGURE 3.1j

FIRST SEVEN CATEGORY PROBABILITY CURVES
FOR A POISSON COUNTS ITEM

which gives the probability of person $n$ scoring $x$ *rather than* $x-1$ on item $i$ as a function of the person parameter $\beta_n$ and an item parameter $\delta_{ix}$ which governs the transition from performance level $x-1$ to performance level $x$ in item $i$.

Equation (3.2.1) defines a series of $m_i$ parallel ogives with locations $\delta_{i1}$, $\delta_{i2}$, . . . ,$\delta_{im_i}$ for each item $i$.   These ogives describe the probability of scoring 1 rather than 0, 2 rather than 1, . . . , $m_i$ rather than $m_i - 1$ on item i.

An important feature of (3.2.1) is that it *does not use a slope parameter.*   The deliberate exclusion of a slope parameter distinguishes Rasch models from other latent trait models which allow the slopes of operating curves to vary from person to person (Lumsden 1976), item to item (Birnbaum 1968; Samejima 1969), or even to vary within the same item (Bock 1972).   The consequence of modelling operating curves to have the *same* slope is that all person parameters ($\beta_n$) and all item parameters (($\delta_{ix}$)) are point locations on a single latent variable, and so, can be expressed in the *same* scale units.

Special cases of (3.2.1) can be developed when the ordered response categories $0, 1, . . . , m$ are defined in special ways.   Table 3.2 shows the structure of $\delta_{ix}$ for the five measurement models described in this chapter.

### 3.2.2 Data are Counts of Events

With the requirement that person $n$ must respond in one of the available $m_i + 1$ response categories, (i.e., $\sum_{k=0}^{m_i} \pi_{nik} = 1$), (3.2.1) can be written as the probability of person $n$ scoring $x$ on item $i$

$$\pi_{nix} = \frac{\exp \sum_{j=0}^{x} (\beta_n - \delta_{ij})}{\sum_{k=0}^{m_i} \exp \sum_{j=0}^{k} (\beta_n - \delta_{ij})} \qquad x = 0, 1, \ldots, m_i \qquad (3.2.2)$$

The observation $x$ in (3.2.2) is a *count* of the steps person $n$ completes in item $i$. On a dichotomously scored test, $x$ takes the value 1 if item $i$ is answered correctly and 0 otherwise. When several ordered performance levels are identified in an item (e.g., the mathematics item in Figure 3.1a), $x$ is a count of the steps completed. Alternatively, $x$ may be a count of successful attempts at an item or of errors committed while attempting a task. The use of simple counts as its basic data is another distinguishing characteristic of Rasch models. Other models call for *weighted* scores in which some events, successes (or errors), are weighted more than others, and in which the needed weights are inestimable without the introduction of arbitrary constraints.

---

**TABLE 3.2**

**FIVE MEASUREMENT MODELS**

Probability of Completing $x$th step

$$\phi_{nix} = \frac{\pi_{nix}}{\pi_{nix-1} + \pi_{nix}} = \frac{\exp(\beta_n - \delta_{ix})}{1 + \exp(\beta_n - \delta_{ix})} \qquad x = 1, 2, \ldots, m_i$$

Probability of Scoring $x$

$$\pi_{nix} = \frac{\exp \sum_{j=0}^{x} (\beta_n - \delta_{ij})}{\sum_{k=0}^{m_i} \exp \sum_{j=0}^{k} (\beta_n - \delta_{ij})}$$

$\delta_{ix} = \delta_i$ .......................... Dichotomous.

$\delta_{ix} = \delta_{ix}$ ......................... Partial Credit.

$\delta_{ix} = \delta_i + \tau_x$ ...................... Rating Scale.

$\delta_{ix} = \delta_i + \log[x/(m - x + 1)]$ ........ Binomial Trials.

$\delta_{ix} = \delta_i + \log x$ ................. Poisson Counts.

### 3.2.3 Parameters are Separable

From (3.2.2), and with the usual assumption that responses to the $L$ items could be governed by the stipulated response model and so could be conditionally independent of one another, the probability of person $n$ making any particular response vector $(x_{ni})$ on an $L$-item test is

$$P\{(x_{ni});\beta_n,((\delta_{ij}))\} = \prod_{i=1}^{L}\left[\exp\sum_{j=0}^{x_{ni}}(\beta_n-\delta_{ij}) \Big/ \sum_{k=0}^{m_i}\exp\sum_{j=0}^{k}(\beta_n-\delta_{ij})\right]$$

$$= \exp\sum_{i=1}^{L}\sum_{j=0}^{x_{ni}}(\beta_n-\delta_{ij}) / \Psi_n \qquad (3.2.3)$$

$$= \left[\exp(r\beta_n) / \Psi_n\right]\exp(-\sum_{i}^{L}\sum_{j=0}^{x_{ni}}\delta_{ij})$$

where $\Psi_n \equiv \prod_{i=1}^{L}[\sum_{k=0}^{m_i}\exp\sum_{j=0}^{k}(\beta_n-\delta_{ij})]$ and $r = \sum_{i=1}^{L}x_{ni}$.

If the "score" $r_n$ of person $n$ on an $L$-item test is defined as the total count of item steps completed by the person, then the probability of person $n$ making score $r$ is

$$P\{r;\beta_n,((\delta_{ij}))\} = \sum_{(x_{ni})}^{r}\exp\sum_{i}^{L}\sum_{j=0}^{x_{ni}}(\beta_n-\delta_{ij}) / \Psi_n$$

$$= \left[\exp(r\beta_n)/\Psi_n\right]\sum_{(x_{ni})}^{r}\exp(-\sum_{i}^{L}\sum_{j=0}^{x_{ni}}\delta_{ij}) \qquad (3.2.4)$$

where $\sum_{(x_{ni})}^{r}$ denotes the sum over all response vectors $(x_{ni})$ which produce the score $r$.

The conditional probability of response vector $(x_{ni})$ given the score $r$ is obtained by dividing (3.2.3) by (3.2.4)

$$P\{(x_{ni});((\delta_{ij}))|r\} = P\{(x_{ni});\beta_n,((\delta_{ij}))\} / P\{r|\beta_n,((\delta_{ij}))\}$$

$$= \exp(r\beta_n)\exp(-\sum_{i}^{L}\sum_{j=0}^{x_{ni}}\delta_{ij}) / \exp(r\beta_n)\sum_{(x_{ni})}^{r}\exp(-\sum_{i}^{L}\sum_{j=0}^{x_{ni}}\delta_{ij}) \quad (3.2.5)$$

$$= \exp(-\sum_{i}^{L}\sum_{j=0}^{x_{ni}}\delta_{ij}) / \sum_{(x_{ni})}^{r}\exp(-\sum_{i}^{L}\sum_{j=0}^{x_{ni}}\delta_{ij})$$

The significance of (3.2.5) as a basis for establishing a system of measurement resides in the complete absence of the person parameter $\beta_n$. This is a decisive characteristic of Rasch models. By conditioning on the person's score $r$, the person parameter is eliminated from the conditional probability expression. This means that if a person makes a score of $r$ on an $L$-item test, under the Partial Credit model the way in which this score is made is not governed by the person's ability, but depends only on the relative difficulties of the steps in the $L$ items. In other words, a person's score vector $(x_{ni})$ contains no more modelled information about the person's ability $\beta_n$ than we already have in the person's test score $r_n$, which thus becomes a sufficient statistic for $\beta_n$.

The conditional probability of an entire matrix of responses $((x_{ni}))$ given the vector of person test scores $(r_n)$ is

$$P\{((x_{ni}));((\delta_{ij}))\}|(r_n)\} = \prod_{n=1}^{N} \left[ \exp(-\sum_{i} \sum_{j=0}^{x_{ni}} \delta_{ij}) \Big/ \sum_{(x_{ni})}^{r_n} \exp(-\sum_{i} \sum_{j=0}^{x_{ni}} \delta_{ij}) \right]$$

The fact that the person parameters do not appear in this expression means that the item parameters can be estimated independently of the abilities of the persons in the calibrating sample i.e., that the instruments of the measuring system can be calibrated *sui generis* quite separately from the measures of whatever objects are deployed to obtain these calibrations.

Conditioning on the sufficient statistics for the item parameters produces a similar conditional probability expression containing only person parameters. The model probability of observing a particular $N$-person vector of responses $(x_{ni})$ to an item $i$ is

$$P\{(x_{ni});(\beta_n),(\delta_{ij})\} = \prod_{n=1}^{N} \left[ \exp\sum_{j=0}^{x_{ni}} (\beta_n - \delta_{ij}) \Big/ \sum_{k=0}^{m_i} \exp\sum_{j=0}^{k} (\beta_n - \delta_{ij}) \right]$$

$$= \left[ \exp(\sum_{n=1}^{N} x_{ni}\beta_n) \right] \left[ \exp(-\sum_{n=1}^{N} \sum_{j=0}^{x_{ni}} \delta_{ij}) \right] \Big/ \Psi_i \qquad (3.2.6)$$

where $\Psi_i \equiv \prod_{n=1}^{N} [\sum_{k=0}^{m_i} \exp\sum_{j=0}^{k} (\beta_n - \delta_{ij})]$.

The probability of observing some particular vector $(S) = S_{i1}, S_{i2}, \ldots, S_{im}$ for item $i$ is

$$P\{(S);(\beta_n),(\delta_{ij})\} = \left[ \sum_{(x_{ni})}^{(S)} \exp(\sum_{n=1}^{N} x_{ni}\beta_n) \right] \left[ \exp(-\sum_{n=1}^{N} \sum_{j=0}^{x_{ni}} \delta_{ij}) \right] \Big/ \Psi_i \qquad (3.2.7)$$

where $\sum_{(x_{ni})}^{(S)}$ denotes the sum over all response vectors which produce the item count vector $(S)$. Dividing (3.2.6) by (3.2.7) yields the probability of the vector of responses $(x_{ni})$ given $(S)$

$$P\{(x_{ni});(\beta_n)|(S)\} = P\{(x_{ni});(\beta_n),(\delta_{ij})\} \Big/ P\{(S);(\beta_n),(\delta_{ij})\} \qquad (3.2.8)$$

$$= \exp(\sum_{n=1}^{N} x_{ni}\beta_n) \Big/ \sum_{(x_{ni})}^{(S)} \exp(\sum_{n=1}^{N} x_{ni}\beta_n)$$

in which the item step difficulties do not appear. By conditioning on the observed vector of item counts $(S)$, the item parameters have been eliminated. This means that under the Partial Credit model, all the information available in a data matrix about the difficulties of the item steps $((\delta_{ij}))$ is contained in the counts $((S_{ij}))$ of the number of persons completing each step in an item. No further information about the step difficulties can be obtained by keeping track of any other aspect of the performances of individuals.

Equations (3.2.5) and (3.2.8) demonstrate the separability of the parameters in the Partial Credit model. In (3.2.5) the conditional probability of the data $(x_{ni})$ given the person score $r$ is a function of the item parameters *only*. This feature makes it possible to condition person parameters out of the calibration procedure, thereby enabling "sample-free" item calibration.   In (3.2.8) the conditional probability of the data $(x_{ni})$ given the item step scores $S_{i1}$, $S_{i2}$, ..., $S_{im}$ is a function of the person parameters *only*.   This makes it possible to condition the item parameters out of the measurement procedure, thereby enabling "test-free" person measurement.

### 3.2.4 Raw Scores are Sufficient Statistics

A fourth characteristic of Rasch models is that raw person and item scores are minimally sufficient statistics for person and item parameters.   For the five models described in this chapter, the raw score $r_n$ (the total number of steps completed by person $n$) is a sufficient statistic for the person parameter $\beta_n$.   In the Dichotomous model the count $S_{i1}$ is minimally sufficient for $\delta_i$;   in the Partial Credit model the counts $S_{i1}$, $S_{i2}$, ..., $S_{im}$ are jointly sufficient for the item steps $\delta_{i1}$, $\delta_{i2}$, ..., $\delta_{im}$;   in the Rating Scale model, $S_{i+}$ is minimally sufficient for $\delta_i$ and $S_{+1}$, $S_{+2}$, ..., $S_{+m}$ are jointly sufficient for $\tau_1$, $\tau_2$, ..., $\tau_m$, and in the Binomial Trials and Poisson Counts models $S_{i+}$ is minimally sufficient for $\delta_i$.

### 3.3 SUMMARY

The five measurement models described in this chapter and summarized in Table 3.2 have been introduced for five different response formats.   The model used in any particular application will depend on the way in which responses have been recorded and on the user's intentions.   While these five models have appeared more or less independently in the literature, we have seen that all five can be understood as cases of one general model.

This general model is characterized by *separable person and item parameters*.   Parameter separability permits person parameters to be conditioned out of item calibration, enabling sample-free calibration, and item parameters to be conditioned out of person measurement, enabling test-free measurement.

A concomitant of separability is *minimally sufficient statistics* for person and item parameters.   These sufficient statistics are always *counts* of observable events (successes or errors).   This supports the common practice of reporting the number of correct answers as a person's score on an achievement test and the use of "integer scoring" in Likert attitude scales.

To achieve separable person and item parameters, and hence the possibility of objective comparisons, all five measurement models are based on *logistic item operating curves with common slope*.

In Chapter 4 we describe four estimation procedures for this family of measurement models.   In Chapter 5 we describe some statistics for analyzing the fit of data to these models.   In Chapters 6, 7, 8 and 9 we apply the Rating Scale and Partial Credit models to two attitude questionnaires, a school achievement test and a developmental screening test for prekindergarten children.

# 4 ESTIMATION PROCEDURES

## 4.1 INTRODUCTION

Models make ideas about experience explicit. They specify how experience might be simplified so that it can be remembered and managed. We construct measurement models to represent what we think can be the essential process in a measuring procedure. We also construct them so that we can estimate their parameters from observations intended to approximate their government. Parameter estimates are the only realizations of the ideas embodied in measurement models. The procedures by which these estimates are obtained from observations must be generally accessible to implementation, dependable in performance and sufficiently accurate to be useful. The resulting item calibrations and person measures must be qualified with reasonable comments on their inevitable errors, and, since we know that even the most useful models cannot be "true", we must also summarize in some simple ways the extent to which the observations on which each estimate is based follow their modelled expectations.

In this chapter we will describe four estimation procedures: *PROX*, *PAIR*, *CON* and *UCON*, for the family of models described in Chapter 3. These procedures will provide us with estimates and their modelled standard errors. Then in Chapter 5 we will continue with a discussion of how to determine the extent to which a set of observations approximate the expectations of a measurement model.

*PROX* is a procedure simple enough for hand calculation. This procedure approximates the results of more exact but more complicated estimation procedures. Item calibrations and person measures are expressed on a common linear scale and are freed of the location and dispersion of the calibrating sample and the dispersion of the measuring test. The simplifying assumption which enables *PROX* is that the effects of the sample on item calibration and of the test on person measurement can be summarized by means and standard deviations on the variable. This procedure is especially convenient when a computer is not available. It also provides a useful way to illustrate the principles underlying Rasch calibration and measurement.

The second procedure, *PAIR*, is also simple enough to do by hand when the number of items and categories is small, say ten items and three categories. *PAIR* estimates item parameters by considering the items in a questionnaire two at a time. This pairwise approach eliminates the person parameters from the calibration procedure entirely, thereby making full use of the parameter separability in Rasch models. A useful advantage of *PAIR* over other estimation procedures is that it is not disturbed by the incomplete data matrices which result when different persons take different items.

The third procedure, *CON*, takes full advantage of parameter separability by conditioning the person parameters out of the calibration procedure entirely. *CON* makes no assumption about the distribution of persons or items on the variable. The disadvantage of *CON* is the "round-off" error it encounters when there are more than twenty items with multiple response categories.

The fourth procedure, *UCON*, estimates the person parameters simultaneously with the item parameters.  This procedure is an extension of the unconditional procedure developed by Wright and Panchapakesan (1969) and investigated by Wright and Douglas (1977a).  *UCON* does not take full advantage of the separability of the person and item parameters in these models, and the presence of person estimates based on responses to $L$ items in the calibration procedure results in item estimates which must be corrected for a bias of order $L/(L-1)$.  *UCON*, however, does not incur round-off errors, and so, can be used with tests of any length.

In the discussion that follows we will begin in Sections 4.2, 4.3 and 4.4 with a detailed description of the *PROX*, *PAIR* and *UCON* procedures for the Rating Scale model.  Then in Section 4.5 we will outline all four estimation procedures for the more general Partial Credit model.

## 4.2  A SIMPLE PROCEDURE: *PROX*

The advantages of the *PROX* procedure are that it can be done on a hand calculator and that it illustrates most of the principles underlying Rasch calibration and measurement.  All that *PROX* needs for person and item estimation are the column of children scores and the row of activity scores from Figure 2.4b.  *PROX* frees these scores from sample size and test length by division, linearizes them by transforming them to a logit metric, centers these linear score logits to remove the effects of sample level, and then spreads them to remove the effects of test width and sample dispersion.

The *PROX* procedure assumes that the attitudes of the children in this sample and the scale values of these science activities are more or less normally distributed.  This assumption does not make full use of the capacity of Rasch models to calibrate items independently of all of the particulars of the calibrating sample, but it greatly simplifies the calibration of the twenty-five science activities and its results are almost always good enough in practice.  Here are the stages of the *PROX* procedure.

### 4.2.1  Removing Perfect Scores

First, the science data matrix must be edited for children who made perfect scores of 0 or 50 on the questionnaire.  These are children who either liked *all* twenty-five activities or disliked *all* twenty-five activities.  We cannot make a definite estimate of the attitudes of these children because they are beyond the reach of this questionnaire.  Similarly, we cannot estimate a scale value for activities which were liked by *all* seventy-five children or disliked by *all* seventy-five children because these activities are beyond the scope of this sample of children.  Thus we must also edit the data matrix for activities with perfect sample scores of $75 \times 0 = 0$ or $75 \times 2 = 150$.

In this case, only one child (Child *2*, score = 50) must be removed from the calibration.  This reduces each activity score by 2, and so, because there might be an item which only this child liked and all other children disliked, we must check the activities again for zero scores.  Since lowest scoring Activity *5* now has a score of 35, all twenty-four activities can be calibrated from the responses of the remaining seventy-four children.

### 4.2.2 Linearizing Activity Scores

In Chapter 2 we saw that activity scores are not on a linear scale, meaning that a difference of one score point does not have the same meaning throughout the activity score range.   We also saw that this non-linearity could be removed by transforming activity scores to a "logit" metric.

The second stage in *PROX* is to transform each activity score $S_i$ to a proportion $P_i$ of its maximum value ($2 \times 74 = 148$), and then to transform this proportion to a logit scale of "difficulty-to-like" by taking the natural log of $(1 - P_i)/P_i$.   This is done in Table 4.2a, and the resulting

### TABLE 4.2a
### INITIAL *PROX* CALIBRATIONS

$m = 2$, $L = 25$, $N = 74$

| (1) ACTIVITY NUMBER $i$ | (2) ACTIVITY SCORE $S_i$ | (3) PROPORTIONS $P_i$ | (4) $1 - P_i$ | (5) ACTIVITY LOGIT $x_i$ | (6) LOGIT SQUARED $x_i^2$ | (7) INITIAL CALIBRATION $d_i^o$ |
|---|---|---|---|---|---|---|
| 5 | 35 | .24 | .76 | 1.15 | 1.32 | 1.84 |
| 23 | 40 | .27 | .73 | .99 | .98 | 1.68 |
| 20 | 48 | .32 | .68 | .75 | .56 | 1.44 |
| 4 | 50 | .34 | .66 | .66 | .44 | 1.35 |
| 8 | 52 | .35 | .65 | .62 | .38 | 1.31 |
| 7 | 67 | .45 | .55 | .20 | .04 | .89 |
| 9 | 78 | .53 | .47 | −.12 | .01 | .57 |
| 16 | 81 | .55 | .45 | −.20 | .04 | .49 |
| 25 | 83 | .56 | .44 | −.24 | .06 | .45 |
| 3 | 86 | .58 | .42 | −.32 | .10 | .37 |
| 14 | 86 | .58 | .42 | −.32 | .10 | .37 |
| 6 | 89 | .60 | .40 | −.41 | .17 | .28 |
| 17 | 93 | .63 | .37 | −.53 | .28 | .16 |
| 22 | 95 | .64 | .36 | −.58 | .34 | .11 |
| 24 | 105 | .71 | .29 | −.90 | .81 | −.21 |
| 1 | 107 | .72 | .28 | −.94 | .88 | −.25 |
| 15 | 109 | .74 | .26 | −1.05 | 1.10 | −.36 |
| 2 | 114 | .77 | .23 | −1.21 | 1.46 | −.52 |
| 21 | 117 | .79 | .21 | −1.32 | 1.74 | −.63 |
| 11 | 119 | .80 | .20 | −1.39 | 1.93 | −.70 |
| 13 | 125 | .84 | .16 | −1.66 | 2.76 | −.97 |
| 10 | 128 | .86 | .14 | −1.82 | 3.31 | −1.13 |
| 12 | 135 | .91 | .09 | −2.31 | 5.34 | −1.62 |
| 19 | 139 | .94 | .06 | −2.75 | 7.56 | −2.06 |
| 18 | 143 | .97 | .03 | −3.48 | 12.11 | −2.79 |

$mN = 148$          Sum = −17.18          43.82          0.00
Mean =   −.69                    Variance = 1.34

$$P_i = S_i/mN \qquad x. = \sum_i x_i/L \qquad U = (\sum_i x_i^2 - Lx.^2)/(L-1)$$

$$x_i = \log[(1 - P_i)/P_i] \qquad x.^2 = .47 \qquad Lx.^2 = 25(.47) = 11.75$$

$$d_i^o = x_i - x. \qquad\qquad U = (43.82 - 11.75)/24$$

$$= 1.34$$

activity logits are given in Column 5.   (Rather than calculating the proportion $P_i = S_i/mN$, and then the logit $x_i = \log[(1 - P_i)/P_i]$, we could calculate $x_i$ directly as $x_i = \log[(mN - S_i)/S_i]$.   The advantage of working with proportions is that it keeps clear the simple relation between proportions and logits and allows us to use a table of this relation like Table 4.2b.   The advantage of calculating $x_i$ from $S_i$ and $mN$ directly is that the rounding variation produced by passing through $P_i$ is avoided).

### 4.2.3 Removing Sample Level

The activity logits in Column 5 of Table 4.2a are linear in the variable they represent, but they contain the attitude level of the sample of children who produced them.   If a group of children with more positive attitudes had been questioned, the activity scores in Column 2 would have been higher, and so, the activity logits would have been lower.   To remove the effect of sample level, the activity logits are centered by subtracting their own mean ($-.69$ logits).   This locates the origin of the logit scale at the mean of these twenty-five activities,

| | **Explanation of Table 4.2a** | **Notation and Formulae** |
|---|---|---|
| **Column 1** | Lists the activities ordered by score. | $i = 1, L$ |
| **Column 2** | Gives the activity scores reduced by 2 because of the removal of Child *2*. | $S_i$ |
| **Column 3** | Converts activity scores to proportions of their maximum value: $2 \times 74 = 148$. | $P_i = S_i/mN$ |
| **Column 4** | Gives the complement of $P_i$. | $1 - P_i$ |
| **Column 5** | Converts $P_i$ into activity logit $x_i$. This conversion can be read in Table 4.2b. | $x_i = \log[(1 - P_i)/P_i]$ |
| | The activity logits are summed and averaged at the bottom of Col 5. | $x. = \sum_i x_i/L$ |
| **Column 6** | Gives the activity logit squared. | $x_i^2$ |
| | The variance of the activity logits is calculated at the bottom of Col 6. | $U = (\sum_i x_i^2 - Lx.^2)/(L - 1)$ |
| **Column 7** | Centers the activity logits by subtracting their mean. | $d_i^o = x_i - x.$ |

and makes the scale independent of sample level. These centered activity logits are the initial *PROX* calibrations shown in Column 7.

### 4.2.4 Linearizing Children Scores

Initial *PROX* attitude measures for the seventy-four children are obtained by transforming each child's score $r$ to a proportion $P_r$ of its maximum value ($2 \times 25 = 50$) and then transforming this proportion to a logit scale by taking the natural log of $P_r/(1 - P_r)$. These transformed score logits are shown in Column 7 of Table 4.2c. Since they are already centered on the twenty-five science activities, no further centering is called for. Indeed, were we now to center the score logits on this sample of children, we would not only take an unnecessary step, but also spoil the connection we are building between the positions of children and items on the single line of the variable they share. At this point we have centered both item calibrations and the measures they imply at the same place, the center of the test, so that they have a common origin.

### 4.2.5 Removing Sample Dispersion

The initial activity calibrations in Table 4.2a must now be adjusted for sample dispersion. This is because the more dispersed a sample is in attitude, the more the scores they give a particular set of items will be similar, while the more similar a sample is in attitude, the more the scores they give these same items will be dispersed. In order to free the item calibrations

## TABLE 4.2b
### LOGITS FROM PROPORTIONS

| PROPORTION $P$ | LOGIT $\log[P/(1-P)]$ | PROPORTION $P$ | LOGIT $\log[P/(1-P)]$ | PROPORTION $P$ | LOGIT $\log[P/(1-P)]$ | PROPORTION $P$ | LOGIT $\log[P/(1-P)]$ |
|---|---|---|---|---|---|---|---|
| .01 | $-4.60$ | .26 | $-1.05$ | .50 | 0.00 | .75 | 1.10 |
| .02 | $-3.89$ | .27 | $-0.99$ | .51 | 0.04 | .76 | 1.15 |
| .03 | $-3.48$ | .28 | $-0.94$ | .52 | 0.08 | .77 | 1.21 |
| .04 | $-3.18$ | .29 | $-0.90$ | .53 | 0.12 | .78 | 1.27 |
| .05 | $-2.94$ | .30 | $-0.85$ | .54 | 0.16 | .79 | 1.32 |
| .06 | $-2.75$ | .31 | $-0.80$ | .55 | 0.20 | .80 | 1.39 |
| .07 | $-2.59$ | .32 | $-0.75$ | .56 | 0.24 | .81 | 1.45 |
| .08 | $-2.44$ | .33 | $-0.71$ | .57 | 0.28 | .82 | 1.52 |
| .09 | $-2.31$ | .34 | $-0.66$ | .58 | 0.32 | .83 | 1.59 |
| .10 | $-2.20$ | .35 | $-0.62$ | .59 | 0.36 | .84 | 1.66 |
| .11 | $-2.09$ | .36 | $-0.58$ | .60 | 0.41 | .85 | 1.73 |
| .12 | $-1.99$ | .37 | $-0.53$ | .61 | 0.45 | .86 | 1.82 |
| .13 | $-1.90$ | .38 | $-0.49$ | .62 | 0.49 | .87 | 1.90 |
| .14 | $-1.82$ | .39 | $-0.45$ | .63 | 0.53 | .88 | 1.99 |
| .15 | $-1.73$ | .40 | $-0.41$ | .64 | 0.58 | .89 | 2.09 |
| .16 | $-1.66$ | .41 | $-0.36$ | .65 | 0.62 | .90 | 2.20 |
| .17 | $-1.59$ | .42 | $-0.32$ | .66 | 0.66 | .91 | 2.31 |
| .18 | $-1.52$ | .43 | $-0.28$ | .67 | 0.71 | .92 | 2.44 |
| .19 | $-1.45$ | .44 | $-0.24$ | .68 | 0.75 | .93 | 2.59 |
| .20 | $-1.39$ | .45 | $-0.20$ | .69 | 0.80 | .94 | 2.75 |
| .21 | $-1.32$ | .46 | $-0.16$ | .70 | 0.85 | .95 | 2.94 |
| .22 | $-1.27$ | .47 | $-0.12$ | .71 | 0.90 | .96 | 3.18 |
| .23 | $-1.21$ | .48 | $-0.08$ | .72 | 0.94 | .97 | 3.48 |
| .24 | $-1.15$ | .49 | $-0.04$ | .73 | 0.99 | .98 | 3.89 |
| .25 | $-1.10$ | .50 | $-0.00$ | .74 | 1.05 | .99 | 4.60 |

When $\log[(1-P)/P]$ is desired, $\log[(1-P)/P] = -\log[P/(1-P)]$.

from their dependence on sample dispersion we must expand the initial centered item logits by a factor which increases with sample dispersion.   If we are willing to work with the assumption that the sample can be satisfactorily described by a normal distribution, then the expansion factor needed to make this adjustment is

$$Y = [(1 + V/2.89)/(1 - UV/8.35)]^{1/2} = 1.22$$

## TABLE 4.2c
## INITIAL *PROX* MEASURES

$m = 2$, $L = 25$, $N = 74$

| (1)<br>CHILD<br>SCORE<br>$r$ | (2)<br>CHILD<br>COUNT<br>$N_r$ | (3)<br><br>PROPORTION<br>$P_r = r/mL$ | (4)<br>SCORE<br>LOGIT<br>$y_r$ | (5)<br>COUNTED<br>LOGIT<br>$N_r y_r$ | (6)<br>COUNTED<br>LOGIT SQD<br>$N_r y_r^2$ | (7)<br>INITIAL<br>MEASURE<br>$b_r^o = y_r$ |
|---|---|---|---|---|---|---|
| 49 | 1 | .98 | 3.89 | 3.89 | 15.13 | 3.89 |
| 48 | 1 | .96 | 3.18 | 3.18 | 10.11 | 3.18 |
| 47 | 1 | .94 | 2.75 | 2.75 | 7.56 | 2.75 |
| 46 | 1 | .92 | 2.44 | 2.44 | 5.95 | 2.44 |
| 45 | 1 | .90 | 2.20 | 2.20 | 4.84 | 2.20 |
| 44 | 1 | .88 | 1.99 | 1.99 | 3.96 | 1.99 |
| 43 | 2 | .86 | 1.82 | 3.64 | 6.62 | 1.82 |
| 42 | 2 | .84 | 1.66 | 3.32 | 5.51 | 1.66 |
| 41 | 2 | .82 | 1.52 | 3.04 | 4.62 | 1.52 |
| 40 | 3 | .80 | 1.39 | 4.17 | 5.80 | 1.39 |
| 39 | 2 | .78 | 1.27 | 2.54 | 3.23 | 1.27 |
| 38 | 2 | .76 | 1.15 | 2.30 | 2.64 | 1.15 |
| 37 | 2 | .74 | 1.05 | 2.10 | 2.20 | 1.05 |
| 36 | 2 | .72 | .94 | 1.88 | 1.77 | .94 |
| 35 | 3 | .70 | .85 | 2.55 | 2.17 | .85 |
| 34 | 3 | .68 | .75 | 2.25 | 1.69 | .75 |
| 33 | 3 | .66 | .66 | 1.98 | 1.31 | .66 |
| 32 | 3 | .64 | .58 | 1.74 | 1.01 | .58 |
| 31 | 2 | .62 | .49 | .98 | .48 | .49 |
| 30 | 3 | .60 | .41 | 1.23 | .50 | .41 |
| 29 | 3 | .58 | .32 | .96 | .31 | .32 |
| 28 | 5 | .56 | .24 | 1.20 | .29 | .24 |
| 27 | 6 | .54 | .16 | .96 | .15 | .16 |
| 26 | 4 | .52 | .08 | .32 | .03 | .08 |
| 25 | 3 | .50 | .00 | .00 | .00 | .00 |
| 24 | 4 | .48 | − .08 | − .32 | .03 | − .08 |
| 23 | 1 | .46 | − .16 | − .16 | .03 | − .16 |
| 22 |   | .44 | − .24 |   |   | − .24 |
| 21 | 1 | .42 | − .32 | − .32 | .10 | − .32 |
| 20 |   | .40 | − .41 |   |   | − .41 |
| 19 | 2 | .38 | − .49 | − .98 | .48 | − .49 |
| 18 |   | .36 | − .58 |   |   | − .58 |
| 17 | 1 | .34 | − .66 | − .66 | .44 | − .66 |
| 16 | 1 | .32 | − .75 | − .75 | .56 | − .75 |
| 15 |   | .30 | − .85 |   |   | − .85 |
| 14 | 2 | .28 | − .94 | − 1.88 | 1.77 | − .94 |
| 13 |   | .26 | − 1.05 |   |   | − 1.05 |
| 12 | 1 | .24 | − 1.15 | − 1.15 | 1.32 | − 1.15 |

| | | | | | |
|---|---|---|---|---|---|
| $N = 74$ | | | Sum = 47.39 | 92.61 | |
| | | | Mean =   .64 | | Variance = 0.85 |

$P_r = r/mL$        $y. = \sum_r N_r y_r / N$        $V = (\sum_r N_r y_r^2 - N y.^2)/(N-1)$

$y_r = \log[P_r/(1-P_r)]$        $y.^2 = .41$        $N y.^2 = 74(.41) = 30.34$

$b_r^o = y_r$        $V = (92.61 - 30.34)/73$

        $= 0.85$

in which $2.89 = 1.7^2$, $8.35 = 1.7^4$ and 1.7 approximates logits from probits. The initial activity calibrations are expanded to their final values in Column 4 of Table 4.2d.

### 4.2.6 Calculating Errors of Calibration

Approximate standard errors for these *PROX* calibrations can be calculated from

$$SE(d_i) = Y\,[mN/(S_i(mN - S_i))]^{1/2} = Y[1/mNP_i(1 - P_i)]^{1/2} \approx 2.5Y/(mN)^{1/2} \approx .25$$

These standard errors for the twenty-five science activities appear in Column 5 of Table 4.2d.

### 4.2.7 Removing Activity Dispersion

The initial attitude measures must also be adjusted for the dispersion of the science activities. The expansion factor needed for this adjustment is

$$X = [(1 + U/2.89)/(1 - UV/8.35)]^{1/2} = 1.30$$

The initial attitude measures are expanded to their final values in Column 5 of Table 4.2e.

| | **Explanation of Table 4.2c** | **Notation and Formulae** |
|---|---|---|
| **Column 1** | Lists child scores in order. | $r = 1, (mL - 1)$ |
| **Column 2** | Counts the number of children making each score. | $N_r$ |
| **Column 3** | Converts child scores to proportions of their maximum value: $2 \times 25 = 50$. | $P_r = r/mL$ |
| **Column 4** | Converts $P_r$ into a score logit $y_r$. | $y_r = \log[P_r/(1 - P_r)]$ |
| **Column 5** | Multiplies the count by the score logit. | $N_r y_r$ |
| **Column 6** | Multiplies the count by the score logit squared. | $N_r y_r^2$ |
| **Column 7** | Lists the initial attitude measure for each score. | $b_r^o = y_r$ |
| | The sample mean and variance of these attitude measures are calculated at the bottom of Cols 5 and 6. | $y. = \sum_r N_r y_r/N$ <br> $V = (\sum_r N_r y_r^2 - Ny.^2)/(N - 1)$ |

### 4.2.8  Calculating Errors of Measurement

Approximate standard errors for these *PROX* measures can be calculated from

$$SE(b_r) = X\,[mL/(r(mL-r))]^{1/2} = X[1/mLP_r(1-P_r)]^{1/2} \approx 2.5X/(mL)^{1/2} \approx .45$$

These standard errors of measurement appear in Column 6 of Table 4.2e.

## 4.3  A PAIRWISE PROCEDURE: *PAIR*

### 4.3.1  Motivation for *PAIR*

The *PROX* procedure just considered achieves its simple efficiency by assuming that attitudes are normally distributed among persons and items.  The assumption of a normal shape makes it possible to use logit means and variances to estimate the person and item parameters separately.  The decisive characteristic of Rasch models, however, is that they

### TABLE 4.2d
### FINAL *PROX* CALIBRATIONS

$m=2$, $L=25$, $N=74$

| (1) ACTIVITY NUMBER $i$ | (2) INITIAL CALIBRATION $d_i^o$ | (3) SAMPLE SPREAD EXPANSION $Y$ | (4) FINAL CALIBRATION $d_i = Yd_i^o$ | (5) CALIBRATION ERROR $SE(d_i)$ |
|---|---|---|---|---|
| 5 | 1.84 | 1.22 | 2.24 | .24 |
| 23 | 1.68 | 1.22 | 2.05 | .23 |
| 20 | 1.44 | 1.22 | 1.76 | .21 |
| 4 | 1.35 | 1.22 | 1.65 | .21 |
| 8 | 1.31 | 1.22 | 1.60 | .21 |
| 7 | .89 | 1.22 | 1.09 | .20 |
| 9 | .57 | 1.22 | .69 | .20 |
| 16 | .49 | 1.22 | .60 | .20 |
| 25 | .45 | 1.22 | .55 | .20 |
| 3 | .37 | 1.22 | .45 | .20 |
| 14 | .37 | 1.22 | .45 | .20 |
| 6 | .28 | 1.22 | .34 | .20 |
| 17 | .16 | 1.22 | .19 | .21 |
| 22 | .11 | 1.22 | .13 | .21 |
| 24 | −.21 | 1.22 | −.26 | .22 |
| 1 | −.25 | 1.22 | −.30 | .22 |
| 15 | −.36 | 1.22 | −.44 | .23 |
| 2 | −.52 | 1.22 | −.63 | .24 |
| 21 | −.63 | 1.22 | −.77 | .25 |
| 11 | −.70 | 1.22 | −.85 | .25 |
| 13 | −.97 | 1.22 | −1.18 | .28 |
| 10 | −1.13 | 1.22 | −1.38 | .29 |
| 12 | −1.62 | 1.22 | −1.98 | .36 |
| 19 | −2.06 | 1.22 | −2.51 | .42 |
| 18 | −2.79 | 1.22 | −3.40 | .55 |

$$SE(d_i) = Y[mN/S_i(mN-S_i)]^{1/2} = Y[1/mNP_i(1-P_i)]^{1/2}$$

allow the complete separation of parameters whatever their distributions might be.   This is done by rewriting the model in a conditional form in which the unwanted parameters cancel.   A general approach to conditional estimation is developed by Andersen (1973).   A simpler approach is to analyze items two at a time (Rasch 1960, 171–172; Choppin 1968, 1978).   This pairwise approach uses person scores to remove person parameters from the calibration procedure.   For dichotomous items this is done by finding all persons who earn a combined score of one on a particular pair of items and using the distribution of these persons' successes between the two items to estimate the items' difference in difficulty.   After all available pairs are analyzed in this way, the resulting matrix of pairwise differences in difficulty can be reduced by least squares or maximum likelihood to a single set of item calibrations.

## TABLE 4.2e
### FINAL *PROX* MEASURES

$m = 2, L = 25, N = 74$

| (1) CHILD SCORE $r$ | (2) CHILD COUNT $N_r$ | (3) INITIAL MEASURE $b_r^o$ | (4) TEST SPREAD EXPANSION $X$ | (5) FINAL MEASURE $b_r = Xb_r^o$ | (6) MEASUREMENT ERROR $SE(b_r)$ |
|---|---|---|---|---|---|
| 49 | 1 | 3.89 | 1.30 | 5.06 | 1.31 |
| 48 | 1 | 3.18 | 1.30 | 4.13 | .94 |
| 47 | 1 | 2.75 | 1.30 | 3.57 | .78 |
| 46 | 1 | 2.44 | 1.30 | 3.17 | .68 |
| 45 | 1 | 2.20 | 1.30 | 2.86 | .61 |
| 44 | 1 | 1.99 | 1.30 | 2.59 | .56 |
| 43 | 2 | 1.82 | 1.30 | 2.37 | .53 |
| 42 | 2 | 1.66 | 1.30 | 2.16 | .51 |
| 41 | 2 | 1.52 | 1.30 | 1.98 | .48 |
| 40 | 3 | 1.39 | 1.30 | 1.81 | .45 |
| 39 | 2 | 1.27 | 1.30 | 1.65 | .44 |
| 38 | 2 | 1.15 | 1.30 | 1.49 | .43 |
| 37 | 2 | 1.05 | 1.30 | 1.36 | .42 |
| 36 | 2 | .94 | 1.30 | 1.22 | .40 |
| 35 | 3 | .85 | 1.30 | 1.10 | .40 |
| 34 | 3 | .75 | 1.30 | .97 | .39 |
| 33 | 3 | .66 | 1.30 | .86 | .39 |
| 32 | 3 | .58 | 1.30 | .75 | .38 |
| 31 | 2 | .49 | 1.30 | .64 | .38 |
| 30 | 3 | .41 | 1.30 | .53 | .38 |
| 29 | 3 | .32 | 1.30 | .42 | .38 |
| 28 | 5 | .24 | 1.30 | .31 | .36 |
| 27 | 6 | .16 | 1.30 | .21 | .36 |
| 26 | 4 | .08 | 1.30 | .10 | .36 |
| 25 | 3 | .00 | 1.30 | .00 | .36 |
| 24 | 4 | −.08 | 1.30 | −.10 | .36 |
| 23 | 1 | −.16 | 1.30 | −.21 | .36 |
| 22 | | −.24 | 1.30 | −.31 | .36 |
| 21 | 1 | −.32 | 1.30 | −.42 | .38 |
| 20 | | −.41 | 1.30 | −.53 | .38 |
| 19 | 2 | −.49 | 1.30 | −.64 | .38 |
| 18 | | −.58 | 1.30 | −.75 | .38 |
| 17 | 1 | −.66 | 1.30 | −.86 | .39 |
| 16 | 1 | −.75 | 1.30 | −.97 | .39 |
| 15 | | −.85 | 1.30 | −1.10 | .40 |
| 14 | 2 | −.94 | 1.30 | −1.22 | .40 |
| 13 | | −1.05 | 1.30 | −1.36 | .42 |
| 12 | 1 | −1.15 | 1.30 | −1.49 | .43 |

$$SE(b_r) = X[mL/r(mL-r)]^{1/2} = X[1/mLP_r(1-P_r)]^{1/2}$$

This *PAIR* procedure can be generalized to accommodate the Rating Scale and Partial Credit models.   Person parameters are cancelled by grouping persons by their total score on each pair of items and using the distribution of choices within these score groups to estimate the differences in the difficulties of the two items.   The *PAIR* procedure requires no assumptions about the distribution of attitudes because it eliminates the person parameters from the calibration of the items entirely.   A special advantage of *PAIR* is that it can be used to analyze the incomplete data matrices which result when some items are not taken by some persons in the calibration sample.   This is particularly useful when calibrating items into an item bank from data in which different persons take different (but overlapping) test forms.

### 4.3.2 The *PAIR* Procedure

The Rating Scale model defines the probability of person $n$ responding in category $x$ to item $i$ as

$$\pi_{nix} = \frac{\exp \sum_{j=0}^{x_{ni}} [\beta_n - (\delta_i + \tau_j)]}{\sum_{k=0}^{m} \exp \sum_{j=0}^{k} [\beta_n - (\delta_i + \tau_j)]} \qquad (4.3.1)$$

Since the responses to any pair of items $i$ and $j$ are modelled as stochastically independent given their parameters, the probability of person $n$ responding in category $x$ to item $i$ and category $y$ to item $j$ is

$$\pi_{xy} = \pi_{nix} \pi_{njy}$$

and the probability of person $n$ responding in category $y$ to item $i$ and category $x$ to item $j$ is

$$\pi_{yx} = \pi_{niy} \, \pi_{njx}$$

where we have simplified the subscripts of $\pi_{xy}$ and $\pi_{yx}$ by using the first subscript to imply item $i$ and the second to imply item $j$.   The probability of person $n$ responding in category $x$ to either one of these two items and in category $y$ to the other is

$$\pi_{xy} + \pi_{yx}$$

Thus, the conditional probability of person $n$ responding in category $x$ to item $i$ and $y$ to item $j$ given that they respond in category $x$ to one of these two items and category $y$ to the other is

$$\pi_{xy}^* = \frac{\pi_{xy}}{\pi_{xy} + \pi_{yx}} = \frac{\exp[(y - x)\delta_i]}{\exp[(y - x)\delta_i] + \exp[(y - x)\delta_j]} \qquad (4.3.2)$$

This conditional probability contains only the item parameters $\delta_i$ and $\delta_j$.   We see that if person $n$ makes a score of $x + y$ on this pair of items by responding in category $x$ to one of them and category $y$ to the other, then the modelled probability of the response $x$ being made to item $i$ rather than to item $j$ does not depend on the person's attitude $\beta_n$, nor on the "threshold" parameters $\tau_1, \tau_2, \ldots, \tau_m$ but only on the difference between the item difficulties $\delta_i$ and $\delta_j$.

Similarly

$$\pi_{yx}^* = \frac{\pi_{yx}}{\pi_{xy} + \pi_{yx}} = \frac{\exp[(y-x)\delta_j]}{\exp[(y-x)\delta_i] + \exp[(y-x)\delta_j]} \tag{4.3.3}$$

The ratio of these conditional probabilities $\pi_{xy}^*$ and $\pi_{yx}^*$ gives us

$$\pi_{xy}^*/\pi_{yx}^* = \exp[(y-x)(\delta_i - \delta_j)] \tag{4.3.4}$$

This leads to a simple procedure for estimating the difference between $\delta_i$ and $\delta_j$. The conditional probability $\pi_{xy}^*$ can be estimated by $C_{xy}/(C_{xy} + C_{yx})$, where $C_{xy}$ is the number of persons responding in category $x$ to item $i$ and also in category $y$ to item $j$, and $C_{yx}$ is the number of persons responding in category $y$ to item $i$ and category $x$ to item $j$. Similarly, $\pi_{yx}^*$ can be estimated by $C_{yx}/(C_{xy} + C_{yx})$. Thus, $(\delta_i - \delta_j)$ can be estimated by $(\log C_{xy} - \log C_{yx})/(y-x)$. This means that each $(C_{xy}, C_{yx})$ pair provides an estimate of $(\delta_i - \delta_j)$. These frequencies can be collected in a matrix like the one in Figure 4.3a.

This is the data matrix for the *PAIR* procedure. Each entry in the matrix is a count of the number of persons who make an $x$ on item $i$ and a $y$ on item $j$. Only the shaded portions of this matrix contain information about the relative scale values of the $L$ items. Each off-diagonal pair of frequencies in the $(i, j)$th submatrix provides an estimate of $(\delta_i - \delta_j)$  These estimates can be averaged and the resulting estimate $d_{ij}$ stored in a matrix of pairwise differences. Scale value estimates for the items which are centered on the questionnaire can then be obtained from

$$d_i = \sum_{j=1}^{L} d_{ij} / L \qquad\qquad i = 1, L \tag{4.3.5}$$

in which $d_{ii} \equiv 0$ and $d. \equiv 0$.

If some $d_{ij}$ are missing, they can be initialized at zero and improved from temporary values for $d_i$ by setting them equal to $(d_i - d_j)$ at each iteration until subsequent improvements in the $d_i$ become too small to matter.

A maximum likelihood procedure can also be used to calibrate the $L$ items. For this we define the number of persons who make an $x$ on either one of items $i$ and $j$, and a $y$ on the other as

$$N_{xy} = C_{xy} + C_{yx}$$

The probability of these $N_{xy}$ persons being made up of $C_{xy}$ persons who make an $x$ on item $i$ and $C_{yx}$ persons who make the $x$ on item $j$ is

$$\begin{aligned}
\pi_{ijxy} &= \binom{N_{xy}}{C_{xy}} \pi_{xy}^{*C_{xy}} \, \pi_{yx}^{*C_{yx}} \\[2mm]
&= \binom{N_{xy}}{C_{xy}} \frac{\exp[C_{xy}(y-x)\delta_i] \, \exp[C_{yx}(y-x)\delta_j]}{[\exp(y-x)\delta_i + \exp(y-x)\delta_j]^{N_{xy}}}
\end{aligned} \tag{4.3.6}$$

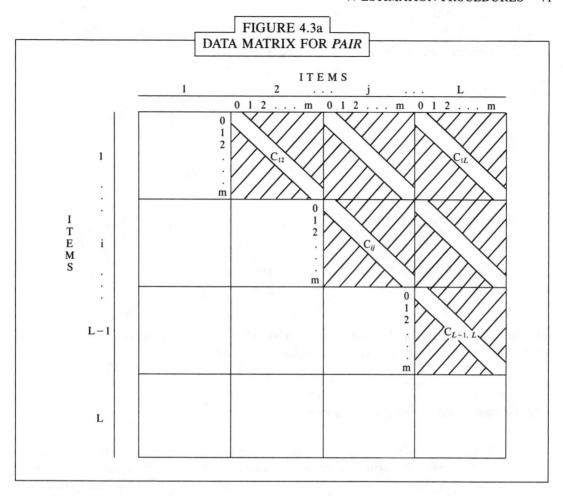

FIGURE 4.3a
DATA MATRIX FOR *PAIR*

If these responses could be considered conditionally independent, then the likelihood of the entire observation matrix would be

$$\Lambda = \prod_{i=1}^{L-1} \prod_{j=i+1}^{L} \prod_{x=0}^{m-1} \prod_{y=x+1}^{m} \pi_{ijxy} \qquad (4.3.7)$$

with log likelihood

$$\lambda = \sum_{i=1}^{L-1} \sum_{j=i+1}^{L} \sum_{x=0}^{m-1} \sum_{y=x+1}^{m} \log \pi_{ijxy}$$

$$= \sum_i \sum_j \sum_x \sum_y \left\{ \log \binom{N_{xy}}{C_{xy}} + (y-x)C_{xy}\delta_i + (y-x)C_{yx}\delta_j \qquad (4.3.8) \right.$$

$$\left. - N_{xy}\log \left[ \exp[(y-x)\delta_i] + \exp[(y-x)\delta_j] \right] \right\}$$

Even though these pairwise responses are not independent over items because responses to any particular item are reused in every comparison of that item with other items, nevertheless, the symmetry of this dependence preserves the utility of pairwise estimates obtained in this way.

Differentiating the log likelihood with respect to $\delta_i$ gives

$$F \;=\; \frac{\partial \lambda}{\partial \delta_i} \;=\; \sum_j \sum_x \sum_y (y-x)C_{xy} \;-\; \sum_j \sum_x \sum_y (y-x)N_{xy}\pi^*_{xy}$$

and

$$F' \;=\; \frac{\partial^2 \lambda}{\partial \delta_i^2} \;=\; -\sum_j \sum_x \sum_y (y-x)^2 \, N_{xy}\pi^*_{xy}(1-\pi^*_{xy})$$

from which the $\delta_i$ can be estimated by

$$d_i^{(t+1)} \;=\; d_i^{(t)} \;-\; \frac{F^{(t)}}{F'^{(t)}} \qquad i=1,L \tag{4.3.9}$$

Unfortunately, the asymptotic error expression $SE(d_i) = [-F']^{-\frac{1}{2}}$ does not apply in this case because the pairwise responses are not independent over items.

### 4.3.3 Comparing *PAIR* and *PROX* Calibrations

The *PAIR* procedure has been used to calibrate the twenty-five science activities from the data matrix in Figure 2.4b. The calibrations obtained are shown in Table 4.3, together with the calibrations from the *PROX* procedure. The two sets of estimates are plotted against each other in Figure 4.3b.

Figure 4.3b shows that for all but three of the twenty-five activities the *PROX* and *PAIR* calibrations are similar enough to be considered equivalent. Even the status of Activity *18* ''Going on a picnic'' which shows a difference of 0.6 logits between *PROX* and *PAIR* is not really objectionable given the large standard error of the *PROX* estimate. But the calibrations of Activities *5* ''Finding old bottles and cans'' and *23* ''Watching a rat'' are clearly inconsistent.

We are already familiar with these two items from our study of the original data matrix in Figure 2.4b. We saw in Chapter 2 that the pattern of responses elicited by these items is inconsistent with the generally orderly structure of these data. These two items do not fit with the other twenty-three activities, and the discrepancies between the *PROX* and *PAIR* attempts to calibrate them brings this out.

## 4.4 AN UNCONDITIONAL PROCEDURE: *UCON*

The third estimation procedure we apply to the science data from Chapter 2, is *UCON*. This unconditional maximum likelihood procedure is based on Wright and Panchapakesan's (1969) estimation algorithm for the Dichotomous model (see Wright and Stone 1979).

## TABLE 4.3
## COMPARING *PROX* AND *PAIR* CALIBRATIONS

$m = 2$, $L = 25$, $N = 74$

| ACTIVITY NUMBER | ACTIVITY CALIBRATION PROX | PAIR | CALIBRATION ERROR PROX | DIFFERENCE PAIR-PROX |
|:---:|:---:|:---:|:---:|:---:|
| 5 | 2.24 | 1.59 | .24 | − .65 |
| 23 | 2.05 | 1.38 | .23 | − .67 |
| 20 | 1.76 | 1.53 | .21 | − .23 |
| 4 | 1.65 | 1.83 | .21 | .18 |
| 8 | 1.60 | 1.60 | .21 | .00 |
| 7 | 1.09 | 1.19 | .20 | .10 |
| 9 | .69 | .82 | .20 | .13 |
| 16 | .60 | .61 | .20 | .01 |
| 25 | .55 | .69 | .20 | .14 |
| 3 | .45 | .62 | .20 | .17 |
| 14 | .45 | .60 | .20 | .15 |
| 6 | .34 | .38 | .20 | .04 |
| 17 | .19 | .30 | .21 | .11 |
| 22 | .13 | .19 | .21 | .06 |
| 24 | − .26 | − .19 | .22 | .07 |
| 1 | − .30 | − .42 | .22 | − .12 |
| 15 | − .44 | − .39 | .23 | .05 |
| 2 | − .63 | − .54 | .24 | .09 |
| 21 | − .77 | − .75 | .25 | .02 |
| 11 | − .85 | − 1.11 | .25 | − .26 |
| 13 | − 1.18 | − 1.00 | .28 | .18 |
| 10 | − 1.38 | − 1.54 | .29 | − .16 |
| 12 | − 1.98 | − 2.31 | .36 | − .33 |
| 19 | − 2.51 | − 2.29 | .42 | .22 |
| 18 | − 3.40 | − 2.77 | .55 | .63 |
| Mean | 0.00 | 0.00 | | .00 |
| S.D. | 1.41 | 1.28 | | .27 |

## 4.4.1 The *UCON* Procedure

We begin with the Rating Scale model which defines the probability of person $n$ responding in category $x$ to item $i$ as

$$\pi_{nix} = \frac{\exp \sum_{j=0}^{x_{ni}} [\beta_n - (\delta_i + \tau_j)]}{\sum_{k=0}^{m} \exp \sum_{j=0}^{k} [\beta_n - (\delta_i + \tau_j)]} \qquad (4.4.1)$$

The likelihood of the $N \times L$ data matrix $((x_{ni}))$ is the continued product of the probability $\pi_{nix}$ over the $N$ persons and $L$ items

$$\Lambda = P\{((x_{ni}));(\beta_n),(\delta_i),(\tau)\} = \prod_{n=1}^{N} \prod_{i=1}^{L} \pi_{nix}$$

$$= \frac{\exp \sum_{n}^{N} \sum_{i}^{L} \sum_{j=0}^{x_{ni}} [\beta_n - (\delta_i + \tau_j)]}{\prod_{n}^{N} \prod_{i}^{L} \left[ \sum_{k=0}^{m} \exp \sum_{j=0}^{k} [\beta_n - (\delta_i + \tau_j)] \right]} \qquad (4.4.2)$$

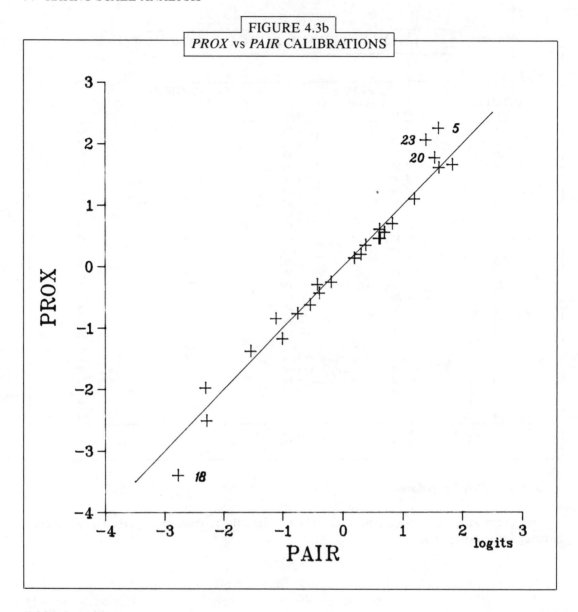

FIGURE 4.3b
*PROX* vs *PAIR* CALIBRATIONS

Taking logarithms

$$\lambda \equiv \log\Lambda = \sum_{n}^{N} \sum_{i}^{L} \sum_{j=0}^{x_{ni}} \beta_n - \sum_{n}^{N} \sum_{i}^{L} \sum_{j=0}^{x_{ni}} \delta_i - \sum_{n}^{N} \sum_{i}^{L} \sum_{j=0}^{x_{ni}} \tau_j$$
$$- \sum_{n}^{N} \sum_{i}^{L} \log\left[\sum_{k=0}^{m} \exp \sum_{j=0}^{k} [\beta_n - (\delta_i + \tau_j)]\right]$$

(4.4.3)

If $\sum_{j=0}^{x_{ni}} \beta_n \equiv x_{ni}\beta_n$, $\sum_{j=0}^{x_{ni}} \delta_i \equiv x_{ni}\delta_i$, $\tau_0 \equiv 0$, $r_n \equiv \sum_{i=1}^{L} x_{ni}$, the score of person $n$ on the $L$-item test, $S_{ij}$ is the number of persons who respond *in or above* category $j$ to item $i$, and $\sum_{n=1}^{N} x_{ni} = \sum_{j=1}^{m} S_{ij} = S_{i+}$, then

$$\sum_{n=1}^{N} \sum_{i=1}^{L} \sum_{j=0}^{x_{ni}} \beta_n = \sum_{n=1}^{N} \sum_{i=1}^{L} x_{ni} \beta_n$$

$$= \sum_{n=1}^{N} r_n \beta_n$$

$$\sum_{n=1}^{N} \sum_{i=1}^{L} \sum_{j=0}^{x_{ni}} \delta_i = \sum_{i=1}^{L} \sum_{n=1}^{N} x_{ni} \delta_i$$

$$= \sum_{i=1}^{L} \sum_{j=1}^{m} S_{ij} \delta_i$$

$$= \sum_{i=1}^{L} S_{i+} \delta_i$$

where $S_{i+}$ is the score of item $i$ on this sample of $N$ persons, and

$$\sum_{n=1}^{N} \sum_{i=1}^{L} \sum_{j=0}^{x_{ni}} \tau_j = \sum_{j=1}^{m} \sum_{i=1}^{L} S_{ij} \tau_j$$

$$= \sum_{j=1}^{m} S_{+j} \tau_j$$

where $S_{+j}$ is the total number of responses (counted over all $N$ persons and all $L$ items) in or above category $j$.

The log likelihood can now be written

$$\lambda = \sum_{n}^{N} r_n \beta_n - \sum_{i}^{L} S_{i+} \delta_i - \sum_{j=1}^{m} S_{+j} \tau_j - \sum_{n}^{N} \sum_{i}^{L} \log \left[ \sum_{k=0}^{m} \exp \sum_{j=0}^{k} [\beta_n - (\delta_i + \tau_j)] \right] \quad (4.4.4)$$

The form of this log likelihood is decisive for the practice of measurement. Person score $r_n$ appears only once in this expression multiplied by its parameter $\beta_n$. Item score $S_{i+}$ appears only once multiplied by its parameter $\delta_i$. Category score $S_{+j}$ appears only once multiplied by its parameter $\tau_j$. This separate pairing of statistics and their associated parameters is what permits the objective comparison of persons, items and thresholds.

In order to define maximum likelihood estimates, the log likelihood is differentiated with respect to each of its parameters. This differentiation is simplified by

$$\frac{\partial \log\left[\sum\limits_{k=0}^{m} \exp \sum\limits_{j=0}^{k}[\beta_n - (\delta_i + \tau_j)]\right]}{\partial \beta_n} \quad = \quad \sum_{k=0}^{m} k\,\pi_{nik}$$

$$\frac{\partial \log\left[\sum\limits_{k=0}^{m} \exp \sum\limits_{j=0}^{k}[\beta_n - (\delta_i + \tau_j)]\right]}{\partial \delta_i} \quad = \quad -\sum_{k=0}^{m} k\,\pi_{nik}$$

$$\frac{\partial \log\left[\sum\limits_{k=0}^{m} \exp \sum\limits_{j=0}^{k}[\beta_n - (\delta_i + \tau_j)]\right]}{\partial \tau_j} \quad = \quad -\sum_{k=j}^{m} \pi_{nik}$$

With these results the first derivatives of $\lambda$ with respect to $\beta_n$, $\delta_i$ and $\tau_j$ are

$$\frac{\partial \lambda}{\partial \beta_n} = r_n - \sum_{i}^{L} \sum_{k=0}^{m} k\,\pi_{nik}$$

$$\frac{\partial \lambda}{\partial \delta_i} = -S_{i+} + \sum_{n}^{N} \sum_{k=0}^{m} k\,\pi_{nik} \qquad (4.4.5)$$

$$\frac{\partial \lambda}{\partial \tau_j} = -S_{+j} + \sum_{n}^{N} \sum_{i}^{L} \sum_{k=j}^{m} \pi_{nik}$$

The expression $\sum\limits_{k=0}^{m} k\pi_{nik}$ is the expected value of $x_{ni}$. When this is summed over items it gives the expected score of person $n$. When summed over persons it gives the expected score of item $i$. The expression $\sum\limits_{k=j}^{m} \pi_{nik}$ is person $n$'s probability of responding *in or above* category $j$ to item $i$. When summed over persons and items it gives the total number of responses expected *in or above* category $j$.

The second derivatives of $\lambda$ with respect to $\beta_n$, $\delta_i$ and $\tau_j$ are

$$\frac{\partial^2 \lambda}{\partial \beta_n^2} = -\sum_{i}^{L}\left[\sum_{k=0}^{m} k^2\pi_{nik} - (\sum_{k=0}^{m} k\pi_{nik})^2\right]$$

$$\frac{\partial^2 \lambda}{\partial \delta_i^2} = -\sum_{n}^{N}\left[\sum_{k=0}^{m} k^2\pi_{nik} - (\sum_{k=0}^{m} k\pi_{nik})^2\right]$$

$$\frac{\partial^2 \lambda}{\partial \tau_j^2} = -\sum_{n}^{N}\sum_{i}^{L}\left[\sum_{k=j}^{m} \pi_{nik} - (\sum_{k=j}^{m} \pi_{nik})^2\right]$$

As a result, the unconditional estimation equations for the Rating Scale model are

$$b_r^{(t+1)} \;=\; b_r^{(t)} \;-\; \frac{r - \sum\limits_i^L \sum\limits_{k=0}^m k\, P_{rik}^{(t)}}{-\sum\limits_i^L \left[ \sum\limits_{k=0}^m k^2 P_{rik}^{(t)} - (\sum\limits_{k=0}^m k P_{rik}^{(t)})^2 \right]} \qquad r = 1,\, M-1$$

$$d_i^{(t+1)} \;=\; d_i^{(t)} \;-\; \frac{-S_{i+} + \sum\limits_r^{M\text{-}1} N_r \sum\limits_{k=0}^m k\, P_{rik}^{(t)}}{-\sum\limits_r^{M\text{-}1} N_r \left[ \sum\limits_{k=0}^m k^2 P_{rik}^{(t)} - (\sum\limits_{k=0}^m k P_{rik}^{(t)})^2 \right]} \qquad i = 1,\, L \qquad (4.4.6)$$

$$h_j^{(t+1)} \;=\; h_j^{(t)} \;-\; \frac{-S_{+j} + \sum\limits_r^{M\text{-}1} N_r \sum\limits_i^L \sum\limits_{k=j}^m P_{rik}^{(t)}}{-\sum\limits_r^{M\text{-}1} N_r \sum\limits_i^L \left[ \sum\limits_{k=j}^m P_{rik}^{(t)} - (\sum\limits_{k=j}^m P_{rik}^{(t)})^2 \right]} \qquad j = 1,\, m$$

where $b_r^{(t)}$ is the estimated ability of a person with score $r$ after $t$ iterations, $d_i^{(t)}$ is the estimated scale value of item $i$ after $t$ iterations, $h_j^{(t)}$ is the estimated value of threshold $j$ after $t$ iterations, $M = mL$, $P_{rik} = \exp\sum\limits_{j=0}^k (b_r - d_i - h_j) / \sum\limits_{g=0}^m \exp\sum\limits_{j=0}^g (b_r - d_i - h_j)$ and $d.$ and $h.$ are reset to zero after each iteration.

Asymptotic standard errors can be estimated from the denominators of the last iteration.

$$\text{SE}(b_r) \;=\; \left[ \sum\limits_i^L [\sum\limits_k^m k^2 P_{rik} - (\sum\limits_k^m k P_{rik})^2] \right]^{-1/2}$$

$$\text{SE}(d_i) \;=\; \left[ \sum\limits_r^{M\text{-}1} N_r [\sum\limits_k^m k^2 P_{rik} - (\sum\limits_k^m k P_{rik})^2] \right]^{-1/2} \qquad (4.4.7)$$

$$\text{SE}(h_j) \;=\; \left[ \sum\limits_r^{M\text{-}1} N_r \sum\limits_i^L [\sum\limits_{k=j}^m P_{rik} - (\sum\limits_{k=j}^m P_{rik})^2] \right]^{-1/2}$$

### 4.4.2 *UCON* Estimates for the Science Data

We have also applied *UCON* to calibrate the twenty-five science activities and to measure the attitudes of the seventy-five children in Figure 2.4b. The results of the *UCON* calibration are shown in Table 4.4a, together with the *PROX* estimates from Section 4.2.5 and the *PAIR* estimates from Section 4.3.3.

***Item Estimates***    The *PROX* and *UCON* item estimates produce the same ordering of the science activities. This is because both procedures use the vector of activity scores at the bottom of Figure 2.4b. The *PAIR* procedure does not use these activity scores, but calibrates the activities by considering them two at a time. The *UCON* estimates are plotted against the *PAIR* estimates in Figure 4.4a.

| | | | | | |
|---|---|---|---|---|---|
| | | TABLE 4.4a | | | |
| | | COMPARING *PROX*, *PAIR* AND *UCON* CALIBRATIONS | | | |

$m = 2$, $L = 25$, $N = 74$

| ACTIVITY NUMBER | PROX | | PAIR | UCON* | |
|---|---|---|---|---|---|
| | $d_i$ | $s_i$ | $d_i$ | $d_i$ | $s_i$ |
| 5 | 2.24 | .24 | 1.59 | 2.28 | .22 |
| 23 | 2.05 | .23 | 1.38 | 2.05 | .21 |
| 20 | 1.76 | .21 | 1.53 | 1.72 | .20 |
| 4 | 1.65 | .21 | 1.83 | 1.64 | .20 |
| 8 | 1.60 | .21 | 1.60 | 1.57 | .19 |
| 7 | 1.09 | .20 | 1.19 | 1.04 | .18 |
| 9 | .69 | .20 | .82 | .66 | .18 |
| 16 | .60 | .20 | .61 | .56 | .18 |
| 25 | .55 | .20 | .69 | .50 | .18 |
| 3 | .45 | .20 | .62 | .39 | .18 |
| 14 | .45 | .20 | .60 | .39 | .18 |
| 6 | .34 | .20 | .38 | .29 | .19 |
| 17 | .19 | .21 | .30 | .15 | .19 |
| 22 | .13 | .21 | .19 | .08 | .19 |
| 24 | − .26 | .22 | − .19 | − .29 | .20 |
| 1 | − .30 | .22 | − .42 | − .37 | .20 |
| 15 | − .44 | .23 | − .39 | − .45 | .20 |
| 2 | − .63 | .24 | − .54 | − .66 | .21 |
| 21 | − .77 | .25 | − .75 | − .80 | .22 |
| 11 | − .85 | .25 | − 1.11 | − .89 | .22 |
| 13 | − 1.18 | .28 | − 1.00 | − 1.21 | .24 |
| 10 | − 1.38 | .29 | − 1.54 | − 1.40 | .25 |
| 12 | − 1.98 | .36 | − 2.31 | − 1.93 | .30 |
| 19 | − 2.51 | .42 | − 2.29 | − 2.35 | .35 |
| 18 | − 3.40 | .55 | − 2.77 | − 3.00 | .46 |
| Mean | 0.00 | | 0.00 | 0.00 | |
| S.D. | 1.41 | | 1.28 | 1.35 | |

*$UCON$ estimates have been adjusted for bias by multiplying by $(L-1)/L = .96$.

When the differences between the *UCON* and *PAIR* estimates are compared with the *UCON* standard errors we see that for most activities the difference is less than a standard error.   While these standard errors cannot provide significance tests because the alternative estimates are based on the same data, they do give us an order of magnitude for judging the differences between procedures.   The only activities with substantially different *UCON* and *PAIR* estimates are activities *5* and *23* for which the differences are more than three standard errors.

When data fit the Rating Scale model we expect these three estimation procedures to produce similar results.   While the *PROX* and *UCON* estimates are very similar, the *PAIR* procedure produces substantially different estimates for Activities *5* and *23*.   This is evidence against the idea that these activities define the same liking for science variable as the others.

***Person Estimates***   *UCON* also provides an estimate of each person's liking for science.   These estimates are shown in Table 4.4b together with the *PROX* estimates from Section 4.2.7.   The two procedures produce identical orderings of the seventy-five children corresponding to their ordering by score on the questionnaire.   The differences between their estimates are shown on the far right of Table 4.4b.   These are largest for high-scoring children and smallest for low-scoring children.   Even for the highest-scoring children, however, the differences are small in comparison to the standard errors of measurement.

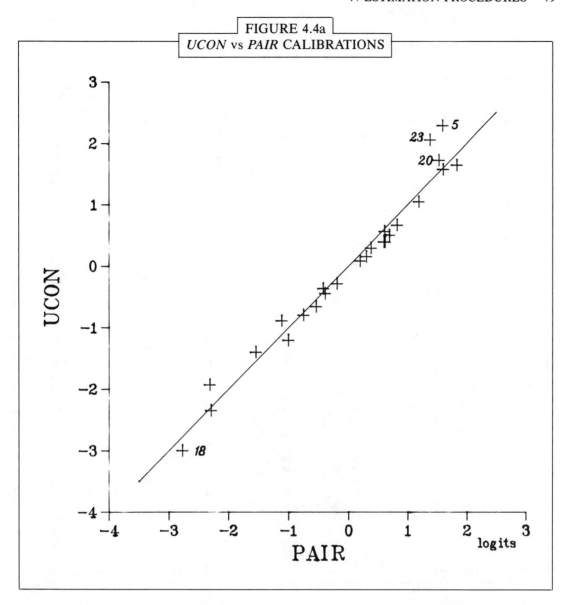

FIGURE 4.4a
*UCON* vs *PAIR* CALIBRATIONS

***Threshold Estimates***    Figure 4.4b shows the category probability curves estimated by *UCON* for the science questionnaire.    The *shape* of these curves is fixed by the threshold estimates $h_1 = -.8$ and $h_2 = +.8$ and is the same for all twenty-five activities.    The *location* of this pattern of curves on the liking for science variable is given by $d_i$ and varies from activity to activity.    In Figure 4.4b, the probability curves are centered on $d_i = +.5$ and so describe the way in which the estimated probabilities of responding "Dislike", "Not Sure/Don't Care" and "Like" vary with attitude for an activity with a scale value estimate $d_i = +.5$ logits.

Category probability curves obtained in this way enable each child's attitude estimate $b_n$ to be interpreted in terms of activities they are expected to like, activities they are expected to be ambivalent about and activities they are expected to dislike.    We will use these expectations in Chapter 5 to investigate unusual response patterns.

| TABLE 4.4b |
| :-: |
| COMPARING *PROX* AND *UCON* MEASURES |

$m = 2$, $L = 25$, $N = 74$

| SCORE | COUNT | PROX | | UCON | | DIFFERENCE |
| :-: | :-: | :-: | :-: | :-: | :-: | :-: |
| $r$ | $N_r$ | $b_r$ | $s$ | $b_r$ | $s_r$ | PROX-UCON |
| 49 | 1 | 5.06 | 1.31 | 4.51 | 1.02 | .55 |
| 48 | 1 | 4.13 | .94 | 3.77 | .74 | .36 |
| 47 | 1 | 3.57 | .78 | 3.31 | .62 | .26 |
| 46 | 1 | 3.17 | .68 | 2.97 | .55 | .20 |
| 45 | 1 | 2.86 | .61 | 2.70 | .50 | .16 |
| 44 | 1 | 2.59 | .56 | 2.47 | .47 | .12 |
| 43 | 2 | 2.37 | .53 | 2.26 | .44 | .11 |
| 42 | 2 | 2.16 | .51 | 2.08 | .42 | .08 |
| 41 | 2 | 1.98 | .48 | 1.91 | .40 | .07 |
| 40 | 3 | 1.81 | .45 | 1.75 | .39 | .06 |
| 39 | 2 | 1.65 | .44 | 1.60 | .38 | .05 |
| 38 | 2 | 1.49 | .43 | 1.46 | .37 | .03 |
| 37 | 2 | 1.36 | .42 | 1.32 | .36 | .04 |
| 36 | 2 | 1.22 | .40 | 1.19 | .36 | .03 |
| 35 | 3 | 1.10 | .40 | 1.07 | .35 | .03 |
| 34 | 3 | .97 | .39 | .95 | .34 | .02 |
| 33 | 3 | .86 | .39 | .83 | .34 | .03 |
| 32 | 3 | .75 | .38 | .72 | .34 | .03 |
| 31 | 2 | .64 | .38 | .61 | .33 | .03 |
| 30 | 3 | .53 | .38 | .50 | .33 | .03 |
| 29 | 3 | .42 | .38 | .39 | .33 | .03 |
| 28 | 5 | .31 | .36 | .28 | .33 | .03 |
| 27 | 6 | .21 | .36 | .18 | .32 | .03 |
| 26 | 4 | .10 | .36 | .07 | .32 | .03 |
| 25 | 3 | .00 | .36 | −.03 | .32 | .03 |
| 24 | 4 | −.10 | .36 | −.14 | .32 | .03 |
| 23 | 1 | −.21 | .36 | −.24 | .32 | .03 |
| 22 | | −.31 | .36 | −.35 | .32 | .04 |
| 21 | 1 | −.42 | .38 | −.45 | .33 | .03 |
| 20 | | −.53 | .38 | −.56 | .33 | .03 |
| 19 | 2 | −.64 | .38 | −.67 | .33 | .03 |
| 18 | | −.75 | .38 | −.78 | .33 | .03 |
| 17 | 1 | −.86 | .39 | −.89 | .34 | .03 |
| 16 | 1 | −.97 | .39 | −1.00 | .34 | .03 |
| 15 | | −1.10 | .40 | −1.12 | .35 | .02 |
| 14 | 2 | −1.22 | .40 | −1.24 | .35 | .02 |
| 13 | | −1.36 | .42 | −1.37 | .36 | .01 |
| 12 | 1 | −1.49 | .43 | −1.50 | .37 | .01 |

## 4.5 ESTIMATION PROCEDURES FOR THE PARTIAL CREDIT MODEL

Our detailed discussion of how to calibrate items and measure persons for the science questionnaire used the Rating Scale model. Now we outline *PROX*, *PAIR*, *CON* and *UCON* procedures for the Partial Credit model.

### 4.5.1 *PROX*

Let

$$x_{ij} = \log[T_{ij-1} / T_{ij}] \qquad i = 1, L \quad j = 1, m_i \qquad (4.5.1)$$

$$y_r = \log[r / (M - r)] \qquad r = 1, M - 1$$

where $T_{ij}$ is the number of persons selecting category $j$ of item $i$, $r$ is a score a person might

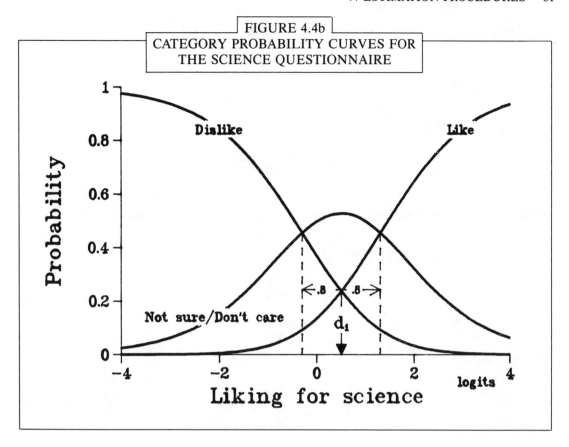

FIGURE 4.4b
CATEGORY PROBABILITY CURVES FOR
THE SCIENCE QUESTIONNAIRE

make and $M = \sum_{i}^{L} m_i$.    When no response is made in category $j$ to item $i$, i.e., $T_{ij} = 0$, then the difficulty of the $j$'th step in item $i$ cannot be estimated, and the scoring of item $i$ must be reduced by not counting the $j$'th step.

The test and sample variances of $x_{ij}$ and $y_r$ are

$$U = \frac{\sum_{i}^{L} \sum_{j}^{m_i} (x_{ij} - x..)^2}{M-1}$$

$$(4.5.2)$$

$$V = \frac{\sum_{r}^{M-1} N_r(y_r - y.)^2}{N-1}$$

where $x.. = \sum_{i}^{L} \sum_{j}^{m_i} x_{ij} / M$, $N_r$ is the number of persons with a score of $r$ and $y. = \sum_{r=1}^{M-1} N_r y_r / N$ is the sample mean.

The consequent factors necessary to remove test width and sample dispersion are

$$X = \left[ \frac{1 + U/2.89}{1 - UV/8.35} \right]^{1/2}$$

$$Y = \left[ \frac{1 + V/2.89}{1 - UV/8.35} \right]^{1/2} \tag{4.5.3}$$

where $2.89 = (1.7)^2$, $8.35 = (1.7)^4$, and division by 1.7 approximates probits from logits.

This yields the *PROX* estimates

$$d_{ij} = Y(x_{ij} - x..)$$

$$b_r = X\, y_r \tag{4.5.4}$$

with standard errors

$$\text{SE}(d_{ij}) = Y \left[ \frac{T_{i,j-1} + T_{ij}}{(T_{i,j-1})(T_{ij})} \right]^{1/2}$$

$$\text{SE}(b_r) = X \left[ \frac{M}{r(M-r)} \right]^{1/2} \tag{4.5.5}$$

### 4.5.2 *PAIR*

The Partial Credit model gives the probability of person $n$ scoring $x$ on item $i$ as

$$\pi_{nix} = \exp(x\beta_n - \sum_{h=0}^{x} \delta_{ih}) / \Psi_{ni} \tag{4.5.6}$$

where $\delta_{i0} \equiv 0$ and $\Psi_{ni}$ is the sum of all numerators.   To develop a *PAIR* procedure for the Partial Credit model we consider the probability of person $n$ scoring $x$ on item $i$ *and* $y$ on a second item $j$.   If we can assume that responses to these two items are stochastically independent given their parameters, then

$$\pi_{nixjy} = \pi_{nix}\, \pi_{njy}$$

$$= \frac{\exp[(x+y)\beta_n - \sum_{h}^{x} \delta_{ih} - \sum_{h}^{y} \delta_{jh}]}{\Psi_{ni}\Psi_{nj}} \tag{4.5.7}$$

Similarly, the probability of person n scoring $w$ on item $i$ and $z$ on item $j$ is

$$\pi_{niwjz} = \pi_{niw}\,\pi_{njz} \tag{4.5.8}$$

$$= \frac{\exp[(w+z)\beta_n - \sum\limits_{h}^{w}\delta_{ih} - \sum\limits_{h}^{z}\delta_{jh}]}{\Psi_{ni}\Psi_{nj}}$$

If we now let $w = x-1$ and $z = y+1$, so that $(w+z) = (x+y)$, then the *conditional* probability of person n responding $(x,y)$ to items $i$ and $j$, given that they respond either $(x,y)$ or $(w,z)$ is

$$\pi^{*}_{ixjy} = \pi_{nixjy} / (\pi_{nixjy} + \pi_{niwjz}) \tag{4.5.9}$$

$$= \frac{\exp(-\sum\limits_{h}^{x}\delta_{ih} - \sum\limits_{h}^{y}\delta_{jh})}{\exp(-\sum\limits_{h}^{x}\delta_{ih} - \sum\limits_{h}^{y}\delta_{jh}) + \exp(-\sum\limits_{h}^{w}\delta_{ih} - \sum\limits_{h}^{z}\delta_{jh})}$$

Similarly

$$\pi^{*}_{iwjz} = \pi_{niwjz} / (\pi_{nixjy} + \pi_{niwjz}) \tag{4.5.10}$$

$$= \frac{\exp(-\sum\limits_{h}^{w}\delta_{ih} - \sum\limits_{h}^{z}\delta_{jh})}{\exp(-\sum\limits_{h}^{x}\delta_{ih} - \sum\limits_{h}^{y}\delta_{jh}) + \exp(-\sum\limits_{h}^{w}\delta_{ih} - \sum\limits_{h}^{z}\delta_{jh})}$$

Notice that the person parameter $\beta_n$ cancels out of these expressions, so that these conditional probabilities are a function of item parameters *only*.

Because $w = x-1$ and $y = z-1$, $\sum\limits_{h}^{x}\delta_{ih} = \sum\limits_{h}^{w}\delta_{ih} + \delta_{ix}$ and $\sum\limits_{h}^{z}\delta_{jh} = \sum\limits_{h}^{y}\delta_{jh} + \delta_{jz}$, so

$$\pi^{*}_{iwjz} / \pi^{*}_{ixjy} = \pi_{niwjz}/\pi_{nixjy} = \exp(\delta_{ix} - \delta_{jz}) \tag{4.5.11}$$

This provides a simple way to estimate the difference between $\delta_{ix}$ and $\delta_{jz}$ because $\pi^{*}_{ixjy}$ can be estimated by

$$n_{ixjy}/(n_{ixjy} + n_{iwjz})$$

and $\pi^{*}_{iwjz}$ can be estimated by

$$n_{iwjz}/(n_{ixjy} + n_{iwjz})$$

where $n_{ixjy}$ is the number of persons responding $(x,y)$, and $n_{iwjz}$ is the number of persons responding (w,z) to items $i$ and $j$.   It follows that

$$\pi^{*}_{iwjz}/\pi^{*}_{ixjy} \approx n_{iwjz}/n_{ixjy}$$

$$\exp(\delta_{ix} - \delta_{jz}) \approx n_{iwjz}/n_{ixjy}$$

$$\delta_{ix} - \delta_{jz} \approx \log n_{iwjz} - \log n_{ixjy}$$

This relation can be used to estimate the differences $d_{ixjz} = \log n_{iwjz} - \log n_{ixjy} \approx \delta_{ix} - \delta_{jz}$ from the counts $n_{ixjz}$.   Then these differences can be used to estimate the item steps

$$d_{ix} = \sum_{j}^{L} \sum_{z}^{m_j} d_{ixjz} / M$$

for which $d.. = 0$.   If some $d_{ixjz}$ are missing, they can be initialized at zero and improved from temporary values for the $d_{ix}$ until subsequent improvements in the $d_{ix}$ become negligible.

A maximum likelihood procedure can also be used.   The probability of $N_{xywz}$ persons being made up of $n_{ixjy}$ persons who respond $(x,y)$, and $n_{iwjz}$ persons who respond $(w,z)$ to items $i$ and $j$ is

$$\pi_{xywz} = \binom{N_{xywz}}{n_{ixjy}} (\pi^*_{ixjy})^{n_{ixjy}} (\pi^*_{iwjz})^{n_{iwjz}}$$

$$= \binom{N_{xywz}}{n_{ixjy}} \frac{\exp\left[ -n_{ixjy}\left( \sum_h^x \delta_{ih} + \sum_h^y \delta_{jh} \right) \right] \exp\left[ -n_{iwjz}\left( \sum_h^w \delta_{ih} + \sum_h^z \delta_{jh} \right) \right]}{\left[ \exp\left( -\sum_h^x \delta_{ih} - \sum_h^y \delta_{jh} \right) + \exp\left( -\sum_h^w \delta_{ih} - \sum_h^z \delta_{jh} \right) \right]^{N_{xywz}}} \tag{4.5.12}$$

If these responses were independent, then the likelihood of the observation matrix would be

$$\Lambda = \prod_{i=1}^{L-1} \prod_{j=i+1}^{L} \prod_{x=1}^{m_i} \prod_{y=0}^{m_j-1} \pi_{xywz}$$

with log likelihood

$$\lambda \equiv \log\Lambda = \sum_i \sum_j \sum_x \sum_y \log \pi_{xywz}$$

$$= \sum_i \sum_j \sum_x \sum_y \left\{ \log\binom{N_{xywz}}{n_{ixjy}} - n_{ixjy}\left( \sum_h^x \delta_{ih} + \sum_h^y \delta_{jh} \right) - n_{iwjz}\left( \sum_h^w \delta_{ih} + \sum_h^z \delta_{jh} \right) \right. \tag{4.5.13}$$

$$\left. - N_{xywz}\log\left[ \exp\left( -\sum_h^x \delta_{ih} - \sum_h^y \delta_{jh} \right) + \exp\left( -\sum_h^w \delta_{ih} - \sum_h^z \delta_{jh} \right) \right] \right\}$$

Even though the pairwise responses are not independent over items because responses to a given item are reused in every comparison of that item with every other item, the symmetry of this dependence preserves the utility of estimators derived as though the pairwise responses were independent.

Differentiating this log likelihood with respect to $\delta_{ix}$ gives

$$F \;=\; \frac{\partial \lambda}{\partial \delta_{ix}} \;=\; -\sum_j \sum_y n_{ixjy} + \sum_j \sum_y N_{xywz}\, \pi_{ixjy}^*$$

$$F' \;=\; \frac{\partial^2 \lambda}{\partial \delta_{ix}^2} \;=\; -\sum_j \sum_y N_{xywz}\, \pi_{ixjy}^* \,(1 - \pi_{ixjy}^*)$$

from which $\delta_{ix}$ can be estimated by

$$d_{ix}^{(t+1)} \;=\; d_{ix}^{(t)} - \frac{F^{(t)}}{F'^{(t)}}$$

Unfortunately, the asymptotic error expression $\mathrm{SE}(d_{ix}) = [-F']^{-1/2}$ does not apply in this case because the pairwise responses are not independent over items.

### 4.5.3 *CON*

A third estimation procedure for the Partial Credit model is the fully conditional procedure *CON*. We begin with the conditional probability of the response vector $(x_i)$ given score $r$

$$P\{(x_i);((\delta_{ij}))|r\} \;=\; \frac{\exp\!\left(-\sum_i^L \sum_{j=0}^{x_i} \delta_{ij}\right)}{\sum_{(x_h)}^{r} \exp\!\left(-\sum_i^L \sum_{j=0}^{x_h} \delta_{ij}\right)} \qquad (4.5.14)$$

where $\delta_{i0} \equiv 0$ and $\sum\limits_{(x_h)}^{r}$ is the sum over all response vectors $(x_h)$ which produce the score $r$.

The conditional probability of responding in category $k$ to item $i$ given score $r$ is

$$\pi_{rik} \;=\; \frac{\exp\!\left(-\sum_{j=0}^{k}\delta_{ij}\right)\sum\limits_{(x_{h\neq i})}^{r\text{-}k}\exp\!\left(-\sum_{h\neq i}^{L}\sum_{j=0}^{x_h}\delta_{hj}\right)}{\sum_{g=0}^{m_i}\left\{\exp\!\left(-\sum_{j=0}^{g}\delta_{ij}\right)\sum\limits_{(x_{h\neq i})}^{r-g}\exp\!\left(-\sum_{h\neq i}^{L}\sum_{j=0}^{x_h}\delta_{hj}\right)\right\}}$$

$$=\; \frac{\exp\!\left(-\sum_{j=0}^{k}\delta_{ij}\right)\gamma_{r\text{-}k,i}}{\sum_{g=0}^{m_i}\exp\!\left(-\sum_{j=0}^{g}\delta_{ij}\right)\gamma_{r\text{-}g,i}} \qquad (4.5.15)$$

$$=\; \frac{\exp\!\left(-\sum_{j=0}^{k}\delta_{ij}\right)\gamma_{r\text{-}k,i}}{\gamma_r}$$

where $\sum\limits_{(x_{h\neq i})}^{r-k}$ is the sum over all response vectors $(x_{h\neq i})$ which *exclude item i* and produce the score $r-k$.

The conditional likelihood over $N$ persons with various scores is

$$\Lambda = \prod_{n}^{N}\left[\exp(-\sum_{i}^{L}\sum_{j=0}^{x_{ni}}\delta_{ij}) \Big/ \gamma_r\right]$$

$$= \exp\left[-\sum_{n}^{N}\sum_{i}^{L}\sum_{j=0}^{x_{ni}}\delta_{ij}\right] \Big/ \prod_{r}^{M-1}(\gamma_r)^{N_r}$$

(4.5.16)

where $M = \sum\limits_{i}^{L}m_i$, $\prod\limits_{n}^{N}\gamma_r = \prod\limits_{r}^{M-1}(\gamma_r)^{N_r}$ and $N_r$ is the number of persons with a particular score $r$. Taking logarithms

$$\lambda \equiv \log\Lambda = -\sum_{j}^{L}\sum_{j=1}^{m_i}S_{ij}\delta_{ij} - \sum_{r}^{M-1}N_r\log\gamma_r$$

(4.5.17)

where $S_{ij}$ is the number of persons responding *in or above* category $j$ to item $i$ so that $\sum\limits_{n}^{N}\sum\limits_{j=0}^{x_{ni}}\delta_{ij} = \sum\limits_{j=1}^{m_i}S_{ij}\delta_{ij}$.

The first derivative of the log likelihood with respect to $\delta_{ij}$ is

$$\frac{\partial\lambda}{\partial\delta_{ij}} = -S_{ij} - \sum_{r}^{M-1}\frac{N_r}{\gamma_r}\left(\frac{\partial\gamma_r}{\partial\delta_{ij}}\right)$$

$$= -S_{ij} + \sum_{r}^{M-1}N_r\sum_{k=j}^{m_i}\pi_{rik}$$

(4.5.18)

This is the estimation equation for $\delta_{ij}$. Notice that $\sum\limits_{k=j}^{m_i}\pi_{rik}$ is the probability of making a score of $j$ or *better* on item $i$ given a score of $r$.

The second derivative is

$$\frac{\partial^2\lambda}{\partial\delta_{ij}^2} = -\sum_{r}^{M-1}N_r\left(\sum_{k=j}^{m_i}\pi_{rik}\right)\left(1-\sum_{k=j}^{m_i}\pi_{rik}\right)$$

(4.5.19)

### 4.5.4 *UCON*

The easiest procedure for estimating the parameters of the Partial Credit model, after *PROX*, is the unconditional maximum likelihood procedure *UCON*. *UCON* produces essentially the same results as *CON*. The likelihood of the data matrix $((x_{ni}))$ is modelled to be the continued product of the unconditional probabilities $\pi_{nix}$ over $n$ and $i$

$$\Lambda = \prod_n^N \prod_i^L \pi_{nix} \tag{4.5.20}$$

$$= \frac{\exp \sum_n^N \sum_i^L \sum_{j=0}^{x_{ni}} (\beta_n - \delta_{ij})}{\prod_n^N \prod_i^L \left[ \sum_{k=0}^{m_i} \exp \sum_{j=0}^{k} (\beta_n - \delta_{ij}) \right]}$$

Taking logarithms

$$\lambda \equiv \log\Lambda = \sum_n^N \sum_i^L x_{ni}\beta_n - \sum_n^N \sum_i^L \sum_{j=1}^{x_{ni}} \delta_{ij} - \sum_n^N \sum_i^L \log \left[ \sum_{k=0}^{m_i} \exp \sum_{j=0}^{k} (\beta_n - \delta_{ij}) \right] \tag{4.5.21}$$

in which $\sum_{j=0}^{x_{ni}} \delta_{ij} = \sum_{j=1}^{x_{ni}} \delta_{ij}$ because $\delta_{i0} \equiv 0$.

To simplify this log likelihood we note that $\sum_{j=1}^{x_{ni}} \delta_{ij}$ is the sum of the difficulties of the steps in item $i$ completed by person $n$. These completed step difficulties can be summed over all $N$ persons to obtain $\sum_n^N \sum_{j=1}^{x_{ni}} \delta_{ij}$, the sum of the difficulties of all steps completed by the sample of $N$ persons. Since $S_{ij}$ is the number of persons completing step $j$ in item $i$, this sum can be rewritten $\sum_n^N \sum_{j=1}^{x_{ni}} \delta_{ij} = \sum_{j=1}^{m_i} S_{ij}\delta_{ij}$.

With this simplification and $\sum_i^L x_{ni} \equiv r_n$ the log likelihood becomes

$$\lambda = \sum_n^N r_n\beta_n - \sum_i^L \sum_{j=1}^{m_i} S_{ij}\delta_{ij} - \sum_n^N \sum_i^L \log \left[ \sum_{k=0}^{m_i} \exp \sum_{j=0}^{k} (\beta_n - \delta_{ij}) \right] \tag{4.5.22}$$

The distinguishing feature of this expression with respect to estimation and measurement is that person score $r_n$ appears only once, multiplied by its parameter $\beta_n$, and item scores ($S_{ij}$) appear only once, multiplied by their parameters ($\delta_{ij}$).

The first and second derivatives of $\lambda$ with respect to $\beta_n$ and $\delta_{ij}$ are simplified by

$$\frac{\partial \log \left[ \sum_{k=0}^{m_i} \exp \sum_{j=0}^{k} (\beta_n - \delta_{ij}) \right]}{\partial \beta_n} = \frac{\sum_{k=0}^{m_i} k \exp \sum_{j=0}^{k} (\beta_n - \delta_{ij})}{\sum_{k=0}^{m_i} \exp \sum_{j=0}^{k} (\beta_n - \delta_{ij})}$$

$$= \sum_{k=0}^{m_i} k \, \pi_{nik}$$

$$= \sum_{k=1}^{m_i} k \, \pi_{nik}$$

and

$$\frac{\partial \log\left[\sum\limits_{k=0}^{m_i} \exp \sum\limits_{h=0}^{k} (\beta_n - \delta_{ih})\right]}{\partial \delta_{ij}} = \frac{-\sum\limits_{k=j}^{m_i} \exp \sum\limits_{h=0}^{k} (\beta_n - \delta_{ih})}{\sum\limits_{k=0}^{m_i} \exp \sum\limits_{h=0}^{k} (\beta_n - \delta_{ih})}$$

$$= -\sum_{k=j}^{m_i} \pi_{nik}$$

in which the difficulty $\delta_{ij}$ of step $j$ appears only in those terms for which $k \geq j$ so that the derivative of $\sum\limits_{k=0}^{m} \delta_{ik}$ with respect to $\delta_{ij}$ truncates the summation from $\sum\limits_{k=0}^{m_i}$ to $\sum\limits_{k=j}^{m_i}$.

With these results the first derivatives of $\lambda$ with respect to $\beta_n$ and $\delta_{ij}$ are

$$\frac{\partial \lambda}{\partial \beta_n} = r_n - \sum_{i}^{L} \sum_{k=1}^{m_i} k\, \pi_{nik} \qquad\qquad n = 1, N$$

$$\frac{\partial \lambda}{\partial \delta_{ij}} = -S_{ij} + \sum_{n}^{N} \sum_{k=j}^{m_i} \pi_{nik} \qquad\qquad i = 1, L \qquad j = 1, m_i$$

(4.5.23)

In the first estimation equation, $\sum\limits_{k=1}^{m_i} k\pi_{nik}$ is the number of steps we expect person $n$ to complete in item $i$. When summed over items this becomes the number of steps person $n$ is expected to complete on the $L$-item test, that is, their expected score.

In the second equation $\sum\limits_{k=j}^{m_i} \pi_{nik}$ is the probability of person $n$ completing *at least j* steps in item $i$. When summed over persons this becomes the number of persons expected to complete *at least j* steps in item $i$, that is, the expected value of $S_{ij}$. This second estimation equation can also be written in terms of the number of persons $T_{ij}$ scoring $j$ on item $i$ $(T_{ij} = S_{ij} - S_{i,j+1})$. This alternative representation may be computationally convenient. The estimation equations for a three-step item, for example, can be written

$$\frac{\partial \lambda}{\partial \delta_{i1}} = (\sum_{n}^{N}\pi_{ni3} - T_{i3}) + (\sum_{n}^{N}\pi_{ni2} - T_{i2}) + (\sum_{n}^{N}\pi_{ni1} - T_{i1}) = 0$$

$$\frac{\partial \lambda}{\partial \delta_{i2}} = (\sum_{n}^{N}\pi_{ni3} - T_{i3}) + (\sum_{n}^{N}\pi_{ni2} - T_{i2}) \qquad\qquad = 0$$

$$\frac{\partial \lambda}{\partial \delta_{i3}} = (\sum_{n}^{N}\pi_{ni3} - T_{i3}) \qquad\qquad\qquad\qquad = 0$$

Solving for $\delta_{i3}$ reduces the estimation equation for $\delta_{i2}$ to $\sum\limits_{n}^{N}\pi_{ni2} = T_{i2}$. Solving this in turn reduces the estimation equation for $\delta_{i1}$ to $\sum\limits_{n}^{N}\pi_{ni1} = T_{i1}$.

The second derivatives of $\lambda$ with respect to $\beta_n$ and $\delta_{ij}$ are

$$\frac{\partial^2 \lambda}{\partial \beta_n^2} = -\sum_i^L \left[ \sum_{k=1}^{m_i} k^2 \pi_{nik} - (\sum_{k=1}^{m_i} k\pi_{nik})^2 \right]$$

$$\frac{\partial^2 \lambda}{\partial \delta_{ij}^2} = -\sum_n^N \left[ \sum_{k=j}^{m_i} \pi_{nik} - (\sum_{k=j}^{m_i} \pi_{nik})^2 \right]$$

(4.5.24)

The *UCON* estimation equations can be improved by

$$b_r^{(t+1)} = b_r^{(t)} - \frac{r - \sum_i^L \sum_{k=1}^{m_i} k \, P_{rik}^{(t)}}{-\sum_i^L \left[ \sum_{k=1}^{m_i} k^2 P_{rik}^{(t)} - (\sum_{k=1}^{m_i} k \, P_{rik}^{(t)})^2 \right]}$$

$$d_{ij}^{(t+1)} = d_{ij}^{(t)} - \frac{-S_{ij} + \sum_r^{M-1} N_r \sum_{k=j}^{m_i} P_{rik}^{(t)}}{-\sum_r^{M-1} N_r \left[ \sum_{k=j}^{m_i} P_{rik}^{(t)} - (\sum_{k=j}^{m_i} P_{rik}^{(t)})^2 \right]}$$

(4.5.25)

where $P_{rik}^{(t)}$ is the estimated probability of a person with a score of $r$ responding in category $k$ to item $i$ after $t$ iterations and $N_r$ is the number of persons with score $r$. The mean step difficulty $d..$ is reset to zero at each iteration to maintain a fixed origin.

Asymptotic standard errors can be estimated from the denominator of the last iteration

$$SE(b_r) = \left[ \sum_i^L (\sum_{k=1}^{m_i} k^2 P_{rik} - (\sum_{k=1}^{m_i} k \, P_{rik})^2) \right]^{-1/2}$$

$$SE(d_{ij}) = \left[ \sum_r^{M-1} N_r (\sum_{k=j}^{m_i} P_{rik} - (\sum_{k=j}^{m_i} P_{rik})^2) \right]^{-1/2}$$

(4.5.26)

In Chapters 6, 7, 8 and 9 we will apply *UCON* for the Rating Scale and Partial Credit models to calibrate items and measure persons on four different instruments. CREDIT, the computer program we use to do this can be obtained from the MESA Psychometric Laboratory, Department of Education, University of Chicago, 5835 Kimbark Avenue, Chicago, 60637.

# 5 VERIFYING VARIABLES AND SUPERVISING MEASURES

## 5.1 INTRODUCTION

The purpose of a measurement model is to extract from suitable data a useful definition of an intended variable and then to measure persons on this variable. The model is constructed to govern our use of data according to the characteristics we require of a measure and to show us, through the exposure of discrepancies between intention and experience, where our efforts to measure are threatened. In Chapter 3 we described five potentially useful measurement models and in Chapter 4 we outlined some procedures for calibrating items and measuring persons according to these models. The questions to which we sought answers were

1) Where is item $i$ located on the variable? (the item's *calibration $d_i$*)
2) How precise is this calibration? (the modelled *error of calibration $s_i$*)
3) Where is person $n$ located on the variable? (the person's *measure $b_n$*)
4) How precise is this measure? (the modelled *error of measurement $s_n$*)

Now we ask

5) How well do responses to item $i$ fit the expectations of the measurement model? (the item's *fit $t_i$*)
6) How well do the responses of person $n$ fit the expectations of the model? (the person's *fit $t_n$*)

We ask these questions because we wish to establish and maintain the validity of our efforts. We want to confirm that the items we construct evoke and define the variable we intend. When we measure a person we want to verify that he has used our items in the way we mean him to. Even the most inspired and disciplined selection and administration of best possible items to appropriate and cooperative persons cannot guarantee the definition of a useful variable nor the successful measurement of a person.

We begin our efforts at quality control by attempting to verify that the items in an instrument are working together to define a recognizable and meaningful variable.

***Have we succeeded in defining a discernible line of increasing intensity?*** This is determined by the extent to which item calibrations are sufficiently spread out to define distinct levels along a variable. Only if items are clearly separated can they identify a direction along which measures can be interpreted.

***Is item placement along this line reasonable?*** The calibration of items places them at points along a possible line. In addition to being sufficiently well separated to define a direction, the items must also be ordered along this line in a way which follows the intentions of the persons who composed them.

***Do the items work together to define a single variable?***    Responses to each item must be examined for their consistency with the idea of a single dimension along which persons have a unique order.    Unless the responses to an item are in general agreement with the ordering of persons implied by the majority of items, the validity of the item is suspect.

A second set of questions examines the extent to which persons are separated along the same line and assesses the validity of individual measures.

***Have we succeeded in separating persons along the line defined by the items?***    Our success in separating persons on a variable depends on the heterogeneity of the group of persons we are measuring.    Although we sometimes work with samples which are rather homogeneous (e.g., graduates of a mastery learning program), most testing situations call for the separation of persons into distinct levels of achievement or attitude.

***Do individual placements on the variable make sense?***    When other information is available about the persons tested, a check can be made on the reasonableness of the measures obtained.    This information may be teachers' judgements of student abilities or performances on other instruments intended to define a related variable.

***How valid is each person's measure?***    Finally, the responses of each person can be examined for their consistency with the idea of a single dimension along which items have a unique order.    Unless the responses of a person are in general agreement with the ordering of items implied by the majority of persons, the validity of the person's measure is suspect.

## 5.2 DEFINING A VARIABLE BY SEPARATING ITEMS

Before we can measure anything, we must mark out the variable along which measures are to be made.    When we measure achievement or attitude, we define the variable in terms of test or questionnaire items.    These items must be sufficiently well separated in difficulty to identify the direction and meaning of the variable.    Our success in defining a line of increasing intensity depends on the extent to which items are separated.    To keep track of this we need some indices which describe the separation of items on a variable in a useful way.

Let the observed variance among item calibrations be $SD_I^2$.    Because each calibration $d_i$ contains error $s_i$, we can improve our estimate of the item variance by adjusting for this calibration error.

**Item Variance**
**Adjusted for** $\qquad\qquad SA_I^2 \;=\; SD_I^2 - MSE_I \qquad\qquad\qquad$ (5.2.1)
**Calibration Error**

where $MSE_I$, the "mean square calibration error", is the mean of the item calibration error variances

**Mean Square Calibration Error**

$$MSE_I = \sum_{i=1}^{L} s_i^2 / L \qquad (5.2.2)$$

If the extent to which the items fail to work together to define a single variable is described by an overall test-to-sample fit mean square $V$, and if $V$ exceeds one, then the test variance could be further adjusted for item inconsistency by

$$SA_I^2 = SD_I^2 - V(MSE_I)$$

However, as $V$ exceeds one, the existence of a variable on which to estimate a variance becomes increasingly clouded. When we encounter a $V$ larger than 1.0 in our work, we concentrate on diagnosing the disturbance and repairing our data rather than on making a second adjustment to $SA_I^2$.

There are three ways the adjusted item standard deviation $SA_I$ can be used to describe the extent to which items are separated in difficulty. First, if we use a root mean square to obtain an average calibration error,

**Root Mean Square Calibration Error**

$$SE_I = (MSE_I)^{1/2}$$

then we can calculate an *item separation* index which gives the item standard deviation in calibration error units

**Item Separation Index**

$$G_I = SA_I / SE_I \qquad (5.2.3)$$

Second, if we define statistically distinct levels of item difficulty as difficulty strata with centers three calibration errors apart, then this separation index $G_I$ can be translated into the number of *item strata* defined by the test

**Number of Item Strata**

$$H_I = (4G_I + 1)/3 \qquad (5.2.4)$$

Finally, we can use the proportion of observed item variance which is not due to estimation error as the *reliability* with which this sample separates these items

**Sample Reliability of Item Separation**

$$R_I = \frac{SA_I^2}{SD_I^2} = 1 - \frac{MSE_I}{SD_I^2} = G_I^2/(1 + G_I^2) \qquad (5.2.5)$$

Table 5.2 shows these calculations for the twenty-five liking-for-science items from Chapter 2. The adjusted test standard deviation $SA_I$ is 5.8 times greater than the root mean square calibration error $SE_I$. This indicates a rather good separation of the twenty-five science activities along the variable which they define. From $H_I$ we see that this questionnaire defines 8.0 statistically distinct attitude strata. Finally, the reliability with which this sample separates these items is .97.

## 5.3 DEVELOPING CONSTRUCT VALIDITY

If the items in a test or questionnaire are sufficiently well separated to define several statistically distinct levels, and hence a direction, we are ready to examine their ordering to see whether it makes sense. The pattern of item calibrations provides a description of the reach and hierarchy of the variable. This pattern can be compared with the intentions of the item writers to see if it confirms their expectations concerning the variable they wanted to construct. To the extent that it does, it affirms the *construct validity* of the variable.

Items which are calibrated at much higher or lower positions on a variable than the item writers intended require investigation. Achievement items which are easier than intended, for example, often contain short-cut solutions not noticed at the time they were written. An item may become harder than expected because of miskeying or the presence of more than one right answer. In an attitude questionnaire, items which are harder to endorse than the constructors intended are usually unintentionally ambiguous. Items which are easier to endorse than expected are often clichés.

In Chapter 2 we asked nine adult judges to order the twenty-five science activities from easiest-to-like to hardest-to-like. Let us compare the nine judges expectations with the ordering of the science activities obtained from the seventy-five children. The *UCON* item scale value estimates are plotted against the judges' placements in Figure 5.3. Figure 5.3 shows that the ordering of the activities based on the responses of the children is in reasonable agreement with the ordering based on the median placements of the judges. The items upon which there was poorest agreement between children and judges are furthest from the diagonal. Activities *8* "Looking in the cracks in sidewalks for small animals", *4* "Watching the

---

**TABLE 5.2**

**SEPARATING THE TWENTY-FIVE
LIKING-FOR-SCIENCE ACTIVITIES**

| | |
|---|---|
| Observed Variance among Items | $SD_I^2 = 1.82$ |
| Mean Square Calibration Error | $MSE_I = \sum_i^L s_i^2 / L = 1.38/25 = .05$ |
| Root Mean Square Calibration Error | $SE_I = (MSE_I)^{1/2} = .23$ |
| Item Variance Adjusted for Calibration Error | $SA_I^2 = SD_I^2 - MSE_I = 1.82 - .05 = 1.77$ |
| Item Standard Deviation | $SA_I = (SA_I^2)^{1/2} = 1.33$ |
| Item Separation Index | $G_I = SA_I / SE_I = 1.33/.23 = 5.8$ |
| Number of Item Strata | $H_I = (4G_I + 1)/3 = (4(5.8) + 1)/3 = 8.0$ |
| Sample Reliability of Item Separation | $R_I = SA_I^2/SD_I^2 = 1.77/1.82 = 0.97$ |

grass change from season to season" and *5* "Finding old bottles and cans" were not liked by the children as much as the judges predicted they would be.   On the other hand, Activities *2* "Reading books on animals", *3* "Reading books on plants", *24* "Finding out what flowers live on" and *9* "Learning the names of weeds" were liked more than predicted.   These adult judges expect children to like junk and dislike learning more than these children say they do.

## 5.4 ANALYZING ITEM FIT

### 5.4.1 Identifying Surprising Responses

In Chapter 2 we inspected the $75 \times 25$ matrix of responses to the science questionnaire (Figure 2.4b) and concluded that responses to at least two of the activities (*5* and *23*) were in poor agreement with responses to the others.   We need fit statistics to describe the extent of

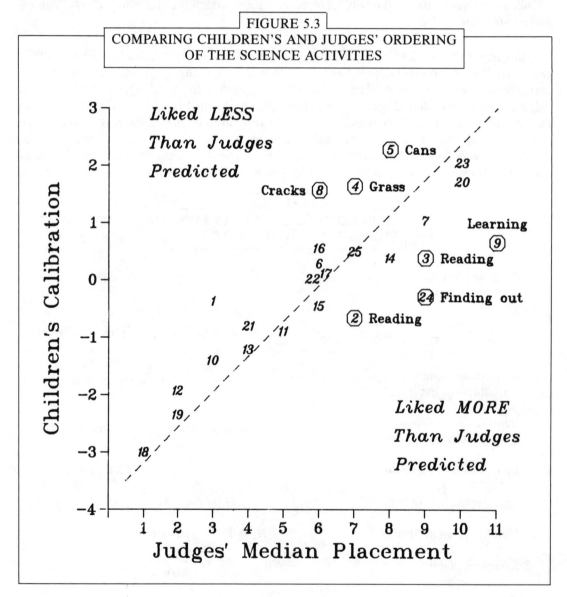

FIGURE 5.3

COMPARING CHILDREN'S AND JUDGES' ORDERING
OF THE SCIENCE ACTIVITIES

such inconsistencies.   Each cell of the science data matrix in Figure 2.4b shows the response of one child to one of the twenty-five science activities.   From Chapter 4 we have a *UCON* attitude measure $b_n$ for each child and a calibration $d_i$ for each statement.   When these estimates are substituted into the Rating Scale model, estimates $P_{ni0}$, $P_{ni1}$ and $P_{ni2}$ of person $n$'s probabilities of scoring 0, 1 and 2 on item $i$ are obtained.

The science data matrix is displayed again in Figure 5.4a.   Now the matrix is divided into three regions.   In the upper left corner of the matrix are person-item encounters for which 2 is the most probable response (i.e., $P_{ni2}$ is the largest of the three probability estimates).   In the middle is a region in which 1 is the most probable response (i.e., $P_{ni1}$ is the largest of the three probability estimates), and in the lower right corner is a region in which 0 is the most probable response (i.e., $P_{ni0}$ is the largest estimate).

Only the most surprising responses are shown in Figure 5.4a.   In the lower right corner of the matrix are the responses of low-scoring children to activities which are hard to like.   Because these activities are hard to like, we expect 0's in this region.   As a result, the 1's and 2's we observe are surprising.   In the upper left of the matrix are the responses of high-scoring children to activities which are easy to like.   Here we expect 2's, and so it is the 1's and 0's which are surprising.

Figure 5.4a provides a pictorial summary of the fit of these data to the Rating Scale model.   Two rows of this matrix contain a number of surprising responses.   These are the response records of Children *71* and *73*.   The last three columns on the right of the matrix also contain a large number of surprising responses.   These are the group's responses to Activities *20* "Watching bugs", *23* "Watching a rat" and *5* "Finding old bottles and cans".   Apart from these two rows and three columns, there is no pattern to the surprising responses.

Some of the responses shown in Figure 5.4a are more surprising than others.   We have circled two of the most improbable responses for closer examination.   Child *71* made a score of 33 on the questionnaire and so obtained an attitude estimate of 0.83 logits.   But this child gave a 0 (Dislike) to Activity *19* "Going to the zoo", which is calibrated at $-2.35$ logits.

Child *71* is estimated to be $b_n - d_i = 0.83 - (-2.35) = +3.18$ logits *above* Activity *19* on the liking for science variable.   We can use the category probability curves in Figure 5.4b to read off this child's estimated probabilities of scoring 0, 1 and 2 on Activity *19*.   At the point $b_n - d_i = +3.18$ in this figure, these probabilities are $P_{ni0} = .00$, $P_{ni1} = .08$ and $P_{ni2} = .92$.   In other words, given our estimate of Child *71*'s position on this attitude variable and the estimated position of Activity *19*, this child is expected to give a 2 (Like) to Activity *19* with probability .92.   Thus in the frame of reference provided by the way most of these twenty-five items were used by most of these seventy-five children, Child *71*'s "Dislike" response is very surprising!

The other circled response was made by Child *12* who scored 17 on the questionnaire and has an attitude estimate of $-.89$ logits.   This child gave a 2 (Like) to Activity *5* "Finding old bottles and cans".   Activity *5* is calibrated at 2.28 logits.   Child *12* is $-.89 - 2.28 = -3.17$ logits *below* Activity *5* on the attitude variable.   From Figure 5.4a Child *12* has an estimated probability of .92 of "Disliking", .08 of responding "Not sure/don't care" and .00 of "Liking" Activity *5*.   Thus Child *12*'s "Like" response to Activity *5* is also very surprising.

Finally, in contrast, consider the response of Child *67* with a score of 29 to Activity *3* "Reading books on plants".   Child *67* and Activity *3* are estimated to be at the same position

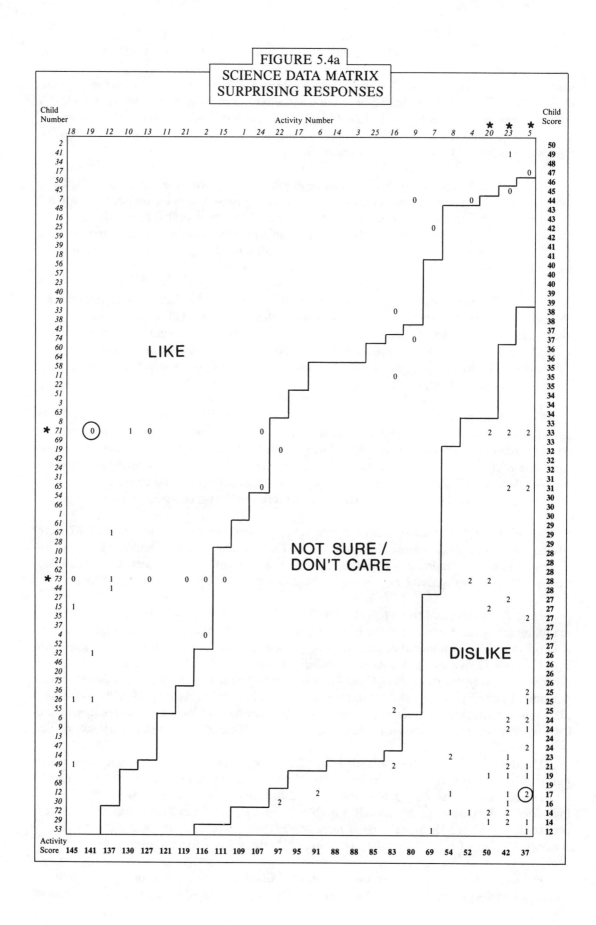

FIGURE 5.4a
SCIENCE DATA MATRIX
SURPRISING RESPONSES

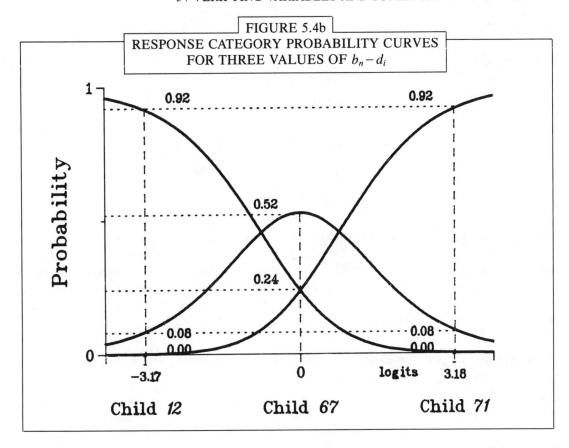

FIGURE 5.4b

RESPONSE CATEGORY PROBABILITY CURVES
FOR THREE VALUES OF $b_n - d_i$

on the attitude to science variable (0.39 logits).   The difference $b_n - d_i = .39 - .39 = .00$, and so, Child 67's probabilities of scoring 0, 1 and 2 on Activity 3 are located at the origin in Figure 5.4b.   Child 67 has a probability of .24 of responding "Dislike", .52 of responding "Not sure/don't care" and .24 of responding "Like" to Activity 3.   Child 67's observed response to this activity was "Not sure/don't care".   This is in accord with the model's expectations for this child.   Because it is not surprising, this response has not been shown in Figure 5.4a.

The Rating Scale model provides an expected value of the response $x_{ni}$ for each person-item encounter in the science data matrix.   This expected value falls between 0 and $m = 2$, and is given by

**Expected value of $x_{ni}$**

$$E_{ni} = \sum_{k=0}^{m} k \, \pi_{nik} \qquad (5.4.1)$$

where $\pi_{nik}$ is person $n$'s modelled probability of responding in category $k$ to item $i$.   The expected values for the three person-item encounters considered above are estimated as

$$E_{71,19} = 0(.00) + 1(.08) + 2(.92) = 1.92$$

$$E_{67,3} = 0(.24) + 1(.52) + 2(.24) = 1.00$$

$$E_{12,5} = 0(.92) + 1(.08) + 2(.00) = 0.08$$

When the expected value $E_{ni}$ is subtracted from the observed response $x_{ni}$, a *score residual* is obtained.

**Score Residual** $y_{ni}$
$$y_{ni} = x_{ni} - E_{ni} \qquad (5.4.2)$$

The score residuals for the three encounters are

$$y_{71,19} = 0 - 1.92 = -1.92$$
$$y_{67,3} = 1 - 1.00 = .00$$
$$y_{12,5} = 2 - 0.08 = +1.92$$

The large negative score residual for Child *71* indicates his surprisingly *low* response to Item *19*. The score residual of zero for Child *67* indicates his *expected* response to Item *3*, and the large positive score residual for Child *12* indicates his surprisingly *high* response to Item *5*. Score residuals can be calculated in this way for every cell of the science data matrix. When data fit the Rating Scale model each score residual has an expected value of zero.

To evaluate the score residual $y_{ni}$ and its square $y_{ni}^2$ we compute the variance of $x_{ni}$

**Variance of** $x_{ni}$
$$W_{ni} = \sum_{k=0}^{m} (k - E_{ni})^2 \, \pi_{nik} \qquad (5.4.3)$$

and its kurtosis

**Kurtosis of** $x_{ni}$
$$C_{ni} = \sum_{k=0}^{m} (k - E_{ni})^4 \, \pi_{nik} \qquad (5.4.4)$$

For the three person-item encounters considered earlier

$$W_{71,19} = (0 - 1.92)^2(.00) + (1 - 1.92)^2(.08) + (2 - 1.92)^2(.92)$$
$$= .00 + .07 + .00 = .07$$
$$W_{67,3} = (0 - 1.00)^2(.24) + (1 - 1.00)^2(.52) + (2 - 1.00)^2(.24)$$
$$= .24 + .00 + .24 = .48$$
$$W_{12,5} = (0 - 0.08)^2(.92) + (1 - 0.08)^2(.08) + (2 - 0.08)^2(.00)$$
$$= .00 + .07 + .00 = .07$$

The variance $W_{ni}$ is largest when the person and item estimates are identical and decreases as person $n$ and item $i$ become further apart.

As $W_{ni}$ is also the variance of score residual $y_{ni}$, this score residual can be standardized by

**Standardized**
**Residual $z_{ni}$**
$$z_{ni} = y_{ni}/W_{ni}^{1/2}$$ (5.4.5)

For the three responses considered earlier

$$
\begin{aligned}
z_{71,19} &= -1.92/(.07)^{1/2} &= -7.11 \\
z_{67,3} &= 0.00/(.48)^{1/2} &= 0.00 \\
z_{12,5} &= +1.92/(.07)^{1/2} &= +7.11
\end{aligned}
$$

The score residuals associated with two of these responses are seven standard deviations away from their expected value of zero. When a standardized residual is calculated for every response in the science data matrix, it is seen that these two responses are the most surprising in the matrix. The responses shown in Figure 5.4a are responses with standardized residuals above $+2$ or below $-2$.

### 5.4.2 Accumulating Item Residuals

Figure 5.4a shows that Child *71*'s score of 0 on Activity *19* is one of only three responses to this item which result in a standardized residual outside plus and minus two. Child *12*'s surprising response to Activity *5*, on the other hand, is one of *fourteen* surprising responses to that activity. The fact that so many of these seventy-five children made unexpected responses to Activity *5* suggests that this activity may not define the same attitude-to-science variable as the majority of these activities do.

One approach to summarizing the fit of an item to a measurement model is to square each of the standardized residuals for that item and average these squared residuals over the $N$ persons

**Unweighted**
**Mean Square**
$$u_i = \sum_{n=1}^{N} z_{ni}^2 / N$$ (5.4.6)

A disadvantage of statistic $u_i$ is that it is rather sensitive to unexpected responses made by persons for whom item $i$ is far too easy or far too difficult. When $u_i$ is used, we may be led to reject an item as misfitting because of just two or three surprising responses made by persons for whom the item was quite inappropriate.

An alternative is to weigh the squared residuals so that responses made by persons for whom the item is remote have less influence on the magnitude of the item fit statistic. A *weighted* mean square can be calculated as

**Weighted**
**Mean Square**
$$
\begin{aligned}
v_i &= \frac{z_{1i}^2 W_{1i} + z_{2i}^2 W_{2i} \ldots + z_{Ni}^2 W_{Ni}}{W_{1i} + W_{2i} \ldots + W_{Ni}} \\[2mm]
&= \sum_{n=1}^{N} z_{ni}^2 W_{ni} / \sum_{n=1}^{N} W_{ni} \\[2mm]
&= \sum_{n=1}^{N} y_{ni}^2 / \sum_{n=1}^{N} W_{ni}
\end{aligned}
$$ (5.4.7)

TABLE 5.4a

## CALCULATING ITEM FIT STATISTICS

Observed Response
$$x_{ni}$$

Expected Mean of $x_{ni}$
$$E_{ni} = \sum_{k=0}^{m_i} k\pi_{nik}$$

$$\pi_{nik} = \exp\sum_{j=0}^{k}(\beta_n - \delta_{ij}) \, / \, \Psi_{ni}$$

Variance of $x_{ni}$
$$W_{ni} = \sum_{k=0}^{m_i} (k - E_{ni})^2 \pi_{nik}$$

$$\Psi_{ni} = \sum_{k=0}^{m_i}\exp\sum_{j=0}^{k}(\beta_n - \delta_{ij})$$

Kurtosis of $x_{ni}$
$$C_{ni} = \sum_{k=0}^{m_i} (k - E_{ni})^4 \pi_{nik}$$

|  | Expectation | Variance |
|---|---|---|
| Score Residual $y_{ni} = X_{ni} - E_{ni}$ | 0 | $W_{ni}$ |
| Standardized Residual $z_{ni} = y_{ni}/W_{ni}^{1/2}$ | 0 | 1 |
| Score Residual Squared $y_{ni}^2 = W_{ni}z_{ni}^2$ | $W_{ni}$ | $C_{ni} - W_{ni}^2$ |
| Standardized Residual Squared $z_{ni}^2$ | 1 | $(C_{ni}/W_{ni}^2) - 1$ |
| Unweighted Mean Square $u_i = \sum_{n=1}^{N} z_{ni}^2/N$ | 1 | $\sum_{n}^{N}(C_{ni}/W_{ni}^2)/N^2 - 1/N$ |
| Weighted Mean Square $v_i = \sum_{n}^{N} W_{ni}z_{ni}^2 \, / \, \sum_{n}^{N} W_{ni}$ | 1 | $q_i^2 = \sum_{n}^{N}(C_{ni} - W_{ni}^2) \, / \, (\sum_{n}^{N} W_{ni})^2$ |
| $= \sum_{n}^{N} y_{ni}^2 \, / \, \sum_{n}^{N} W_{ni}$ | | |
| Standardized Weighted Mean Square $t_i = (v_i^{1/3} - 1)(3/q_i) + (q_i/3)$ | 0 | 1 |

In this statistic each squared residual $z_{ni}^2$ is weighed by its variance $W_{ni}$. Since this variance is smallest for persons furthest from item $i$, the contribution to $v_i$ of their responses is reduced. When data fit the model, the statistic $v_i$ has an approximately mean square distribution with expectation one and variance

**Variance of Weighted Mean Square**
$$q_i^2 = \sum_n^N (C_{ni} - W_{ni}^2) \,/\, (\sum_n^N W_{ni})^2 \qquad (5.4.8)$$

### 5.4.3 Standardizing Mean Squares

To compare values of $v_i$ for different items it is convenient to standardize these mean squares to the statistic

**Item Fit $t$**
$$t_i = (v_i^{1/3} - 1)(3/q_i) + (q_i/3)$$

which, when data fit the model, has a mean near zero and a standard deviation near one. These fit statistics are summarized in Table 5.4a.

### 5.4.4 Estimating Modelled Expectations

These statistics provide a useful approach to analyzing the suitability of data for constructing variables and making measures. Their simple form, however, depends on knowing $\pi_{nik}$. In practice, we do not know $\pi_{nik}$ and must use an estimate $P_{nik}$ based on estimates of the person and item parameters. These estimates usually come from the same data from which the residuals are calculated. This introduces variations in the expectations and variances of the residuals which become conspicuous when the number of items $L$ or persons $N$ are small. For example, the degrees of freedom consumed by the estimation of person abilities and item difficulties reduce the expected value of the mean square by the factor $[(L-1)(N-1)/NL]$.

The departures from expectations and variances based on $\pi_{nik}$ abate as $L$ and $N$ increase. But the rate of abatement depends also on the test spread of item calibrations, the sample spread of person measures and the targeting of test on sample. We have not mastered the statistical details of these effects well enough to provide useful corrections for reducing them. But we have not found this an impediment to practice. The purpose of a model is to help us make sense of data. It is the substantive concomitants of large residuals, rather than the form of their modelled distribution, which are decisive in practice. In the situations we have studied, fit statistics based on $\pi_{nik}$ but using $P_{nik}$ instead have proven entirely satisfactory.

### 5.4.5 Examining Item Misfit

A weighted mean square $v_i$ has been calculated for each of the twenty-five science activities. These mean squares, their expected value and standard errors are shown in Table 5.4b. Each mean square has been standardized to $t_i$, and the activities have been sorted by the values of this standardized fit statistic.

Two activities in Table 5.4b have fit-t values of +5.23 and +5.90. These are 5 "Finding old bottles and cans" and 23 "Watching a rat". In our examination of the science data matrix in Chapter 2 we saw that responses to these two activities were inconsistent with other responses. We also saw that judges had difficulty agreeing on where these two activities belonged on the liking for science variable. In Chapter 4 we saw that the *PROX* and *PAIR* calibration procedures produced substantially different scale value estimates for these two activities. The fit statistics for Activities 5 and 23 in Table 5.4b confirm our earlier suspicions that responses to these two activities do not fit with those to the other twenty-three activities.

There is a school of thought which would interpret this situation to signify the need for a less demanding measurement model—one which might find a way to embrace Items 5 and 23. That is not our approach. The models we work with specify what we mean by measurement. When items do not fit, that signifies to us not the occasion for a looser model, but the need for better items. We are looking for a core of data which can be tried as a basis for measurement because it follows our measurement specifications by conforming to our measurement model.

In Figure 5.4c the fit-t values from Table 5.4b are plotted against the scale value estimates for the twenty-five activities. Most activities have fit-t values between −2 and +2. The three activities with the largest positive fit statistics, 20, 5 and 23, are also the "hardest-to-like" activities with the highest scale values. The activities "Watching bugs", "Finding old

## TABLE 5.4b
### ITEM FIT STATISTICS FOR THE SCIENCE ACTIVITIES

| ACTIVITY NUMBER | SCALE VALUE $d_i$ | ERROR $s_i$ | OBSVD $v_i$ | EXPECTED VALUE | ERROR | FIT $t_i$ |
|---|---|---|---|---|---|---|
| 1 | −.37 | .20 | .51 | 1.00 | .15 | −3.93 |
| 3 | .39 | .18 | .55 | 1.00 | .14 | −3.80 |
| 17 | .15 | .19 | .63 | 1.00 | .14 | −2.98 |
| 11 | −.89 | .22 | .58 | 1.00 | .17 | −2.88 |
| 15 | −.45 | .20 | .73 | 1.00 | .15 | −1.90 |
| 25 | .50 | .18 | .77 | 1.00 | .14 | −1.75 |
| 6 | .29 | .19 | .77 | 1.00 | .14 | −1.73 |
| 12 | −1.93 | .30 | .62 | 1.00 | .25 | −1.70 |
| 14 | .39 | .18 | .79 | 1.00 | .14 | −1.58 |
| 22 | .08 | .19 | .79 | 1.00 | .14 | −1.55 |
| 10 | −1.40 | .25 | .72 | 1.00 | .20 | −1.52 |
| 21 | −.80 | .22 | .79 | 1.00 | .17 | −1.34 |
| 24 | −.29 | .20 | .85 | 1.00 | .15 | −.98 |
| 4 | 1.64 | .20 | .86 | 1.00 | .15 | −.89 |
| 2 | −.66 | .21 | .87 | 1.00 | .16 | −.81 |
| 16 | .56 | .18 | .92 | 1.00 | .14 | −.56 |
| 7 | 1.04 | .18 | .95 | 1.00 | .14 | −.34 |
| 19 | −2.35 | .35 | .96 | 1.00 | .29 | −.04 |
| 8 | 1.57 | .19 | 1.05 | 1.00 | .15 | .41 |
| 13 | −1.21 | .24 | 1.12 | 1.00 | .19 | .70 |
| 18 | −3.00 | .46 | 1.31 | 1.00 | .40 | .84 |
| 9 | .66 | .18 | 1.14 | 1.00 | .14 | .98 |
| 20 | 1.72 | .20 | 1.28 | 1.00 | .15 | 1.71 |
| 5 | 2.28 | .22 | 2.20 | 1.00 | .17 | 5.23 |
| 23 | 2.05 | .21 | 2.31 | 1.00 | .16 | 5.90 |
| Mean | 0.00 | .22 | .96 | | .17 | −.58 |
| S.D. | 1.35 | .06 | .44 | | .06 | 2.33 |

bottles and cans'' and ''Watching a rat'' were intended to demand high levels of liking for science.   They appear, however, to introduce differences among children extraneous to the main line laid out by the other activities.   While most children find these activities hard to like, there are several low scoring children who *like* them.

The poor fit of Activities *20*, *5* and *23* may stem from the stereotype that bugs, rats and cans are unwholesome and to be disposed of.   Perhaps a child's attitude towards these activities depends on the neighborhood in which he lives.   Whatever the explanation, the fact that several low-scoring children responded ''like'' to these three usually disliked activities confounds our efforts to position all twenty-five activities along a single liking-for-science variable.

Two activities in Figure 5.4c have relatively large *negative* fit-t values.   These are Activities *1* ''Watching birds'' and *3* ''Reading books on plants''.   In Chapter 2 we noted that responses to Activity *3* were particularly orderly.   High scoring children liked this activity.

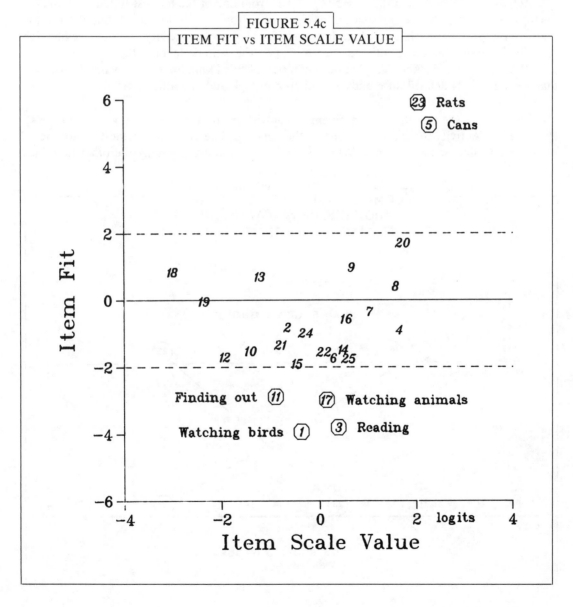

FIGURE 5.4c
ITEM FIT vs ITEM SCALE VALUE

Low scoring children disliked it.   While an orderly pattern of responses is usually considered desirable, when responses to an item are unusually orderly, this inevitably introduces a question as to that item's location among the other items and so clouds the definition of the attitude variable.   To illustrate the ambiguity that can be produced by an excessively orderly pattern of responses we have rescored the twenty-five science activities, first using only children who scored above 35 on the questionnaire and then using only children who scored below 28.   The results of these rescorings are displayed in Figure 5.4d, where the activities are shown in the rank order of their scores.

At the top of Figure 5.4d the twenty-five activities are ordered from easiest-to-like at the left to hardest-to-like at the right according to the responses of the twenty-four children who scored above 35.   At the bottom of Figure 5.4d the twenty-five activities are ordered by the responses of the twenty-six children who scored below 28.

Activity *23* "Watching a rat" ($t = 5.90$) moves from one of the hardest to like activities at the top of Figure 5.4d to one of the easier to like at the bottom.   This documents our observation that several low-scoring children liked this otherwise hard-to-like activity.   Where we position Activity *23* among the other activities depends upon the attitude level of the calibrating sample.   When we include Activity *23* in our definition of this liking-for-science variable, we find that the variable is defined differently by children of high and low attitudes.

But now we see that the same problem arises with Activity *3* "Reading books on plants" ($t = -3.80$).   Activity *3* moves from one of the easier to like activities at the top, to one of the harder to like at the bottom.   Where we position Activity *3* among the other activities

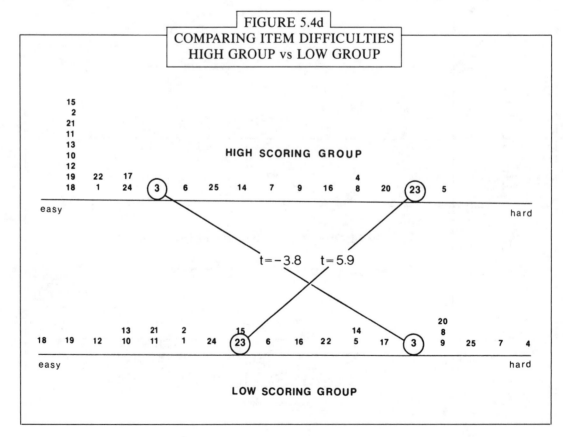

FIGURE 5.4d

COMPARING ITEM DIFFICULTIES
HIGH GROUP vs LOW GROUP

also depends upon the attitude level of the children in the calibrating sample.   Activity *3* also confounds our efforts to construct a single, common liking-for-science variable which maintains a fixed definition over different levels of liking for science.

Activities *23* "Watching a rat" and *3* "Reading books on plants" were considered in Figure 5.4d because of their extreme positive and negative fit statistics.   The contrasting content of these two activities suggests an explanation for their contrasting response patterns.   Opportunities for "Watching a rat" are unlikely in a middle class suburb.   "Reading books on plants" may be rare in urban ghettos.   The failure of Activities *23* and *3* to perform in a way which is consistent with the other activities could be due to their interaction with socio-economic background.

The other activity with a large negative fit-t value is Activity *1* "Watching birds".   The misfit of this activity can be traced to its surprisingly large number of "Not sure/don't care" responses.   The bottom of Figure 2.4b shows that thirty-five children responded "Not sure/don't care" to Activity *1*.   This is unexpectedly high for an activity with a score of 109.   In contrast, only twenty-five children gave a 1 to Activity *15* (raw score = 111), and only twenty-three gave a 1 to Activity *24* (raw score = 107).   A surprising number of "Not sure/don't care" responses can signify that an item is either too bland or too poorly specified.   Watching which birds?   Birds doing what?

## 5.5 IDENTIFYING INDIVIDUAL DIFFERENCES BY SEPARATING PERSONS

We can also ask how well a particular test separates the persons in a particular sample.   While this will depend on the heterogeneity of the sample, the intention of most testing situations is to identify individual differences.   In Chapters 6 and 7, for example, we describe questionnaires which have been constructed to measure college students' attitudes towards drugs and their fear of crime.   These questionnaires were constructed with the intention of identifying individual differences among college students.

The statistics we use to describe the separation of persons on a variable parallel the item separation statistics in Section 5.2.   We begin with the observed variance among children $SD_P^2$ which can be adjusted for the measurement error $s_n$ associated with each measure $b_n$

**Sample Variance
Adjusted for
Measurement Error**
$$SA_P^2 \ = \ SD_P^2 - MSE_P \tag{5.5.1}$$

where $MSE_P$, the "mean square measurement error", is the mean of the person measurement error variances.

**Mean Square
Measurement Error**
$$MSE_P \ = \ \sum_{n=1}^{N} s_n^2 \, / \, N \tag{5.5.2}$$

There are also three ways the adjusted sample standard deviation $SA_P$ can be used to describe the extent to which persons are separated on the variable.   First, if we use a root mean square to obtain an average measurement error

| **Root Mean Square Measurement Error** | $SE_P$ | $=$ | $(MSE_P)^{1/2}$ | |

then we can calculate a *person separation* index which gives the sample standard deviation in standard error units

| **Person Separation Index** | $G_P$ | $=$ | $SA_P / SE_P$ | (5.5.3) |

Second, if we define statistically distinct levels of person ability as ability strata with centers three measurement errors apart, then this separation index can be translated into the number of statistically distinct *person strata* identified by the test

| **Number of Person Strata** | $H_P$ | $=$ | $(4G_P + 1)/3$ | (5.5.4) |

Finally, we can report the proportion of observed sample variance which is not due to measurement error as the *reliability* with which this test separates these persons.

$$\textbf{Test Reliability of Person Separation} \qquad R_P \; = \; \frac{SA_P^2}{SD_P^2} \; = \; 1 - \frac{MSE_P}{SD_P^2} \; = \; G_P^2 / (1 + G_P^2) \qquad (5.5.5)$$

Table 5.5 shows these calculations for the seventy-four children for whom estimates could be made in Figure 2.4b.   The adjusted child standard deviation $SA_P$ is 2.6 times greater than the root mean square error.   This child separation index produces 3.8 statistically distinct child strata.   The test reliability of child separation is .87.

## 5.6 DEVELOPING CONCURRENT VALIDITY

The *content* and *construct* validity of a test or questionnaire can be assessed by examining item fit and comparing the obtained difficulty order of the items with the order anticipated by their authors.   It is also possible to compare the obtained person measures with an anticipated order to assess the *concurrent* validity of these measures.

One approach to establishing the concurrent validity of achievement test scores is to ask teachers to review the test scores made by children in their classes.   This will often be the best way to identify high ability children whose test scores are lower than expected because of illness or test anxiety and low ability children whose test scores are higher than expected because of guessing or cheating.   A second approach is to compare each person's estimate with one or more independent measures of the same person on a similar variable.

A third approach to concurrent validity is to analyze the internal consistency of each person's pattern of responses.   One way this can be done is to partition the items on a test into relevant subsets and then to compare the abilities estimated from performances on these subsets.   Table 5.6 summarizes the performances of a candidate on six booklets of a professional certification examination.   The booklets represent more or less parallel forms.   Ordinarily, candidates' scores on the booklets are summed and certification is based on total scores.   Five of this candidate's six ability estimates are similar (near .45 logits).   But his low score of 29 on the first test booklet gives him an ability estimate of only $-1.54$ logits.   This is inconsistent

## TABLE 5.5
### SEPARATING THE SEVENTY-FOUR CHILDREN WITH THE SCIENCE QUESTIONNAIRE

| | |
|---|---|
| Observed Variance among Children | $SD_P^2 = 1.14$ |
| Mean Square Measurement Error | $MSE_P = \sum_n^N s_n^2 / N = 10.92/74 = .15$ |
| Root Mean Square Measurement Error | $SE_P = (MSE_P)^{1/2} = .38$ |
| Child Variance Adjusted for Measurement Error | $SA_P^2 = SD_P^2 - MSE_P = 1.14 - .15 = .99$ |
| Child Standard Deviation | $SA_P = (SA_P^2)^{1/2} = 1.00$ |
| Child Separation Index | $G_P = SA_P / SE_P = 1.00/.38 = 2.6$ |
| Number of Child Strata | $H_P = (4G_P + 1)/3 = 11.37/3 = 3.8$ |
| Test Reliability of Child Separation | $R_P = SA_P^2 / SD_P^2 = .99/1.14 = .87$ |

## TABLE 5.6
### PERFORMANCES OF ONE CANDIDATE ON SIX PARALLEL TESTS

| TEST BOOKLET | SCORE | ABILITY | ERROR | ABILITY PLOT -2 | -1 | 0 | 1 | 2 | WITHIN FIT-T |
|---|---|---|---|---|---|---|---|---|---|
| 1 | 29 | −1.54 | .23 | --X-- | | | | | 5.8 |
| 2 | 96 | .42 | .18 | | | --X-- | | | .7 |
| 3 | 81 | .45 | .18 | | | --X-- | | | .3 |
| 4 | 82 | .34 | .19 | | | --X-- | | | 1.1 |
| 5 | 90 | .59 | .19 | | | --X-- | | | 1.6 |
| 6 | 74 | .49 | .20 | | | --X-- | | | .3 |

with his ability estimates from the other booklets.   His performance on the items within the first test booklet is also inconsistent (within fit-t = 5.8).

The estimate of −1.54 logits from the first booklet is not supported by the estimates from the other five, nor is it supported by internal consistency within the first booklet.   When this candidate's answer sheets were inspected, his "poor" performance on the first booklet was traced to a damaged answer sheet which had caused the optical scanner to misread his responses to this booklet.   Had this candidate's total test score been reported without comparing his scores on the six booklets or, worse, had his score on the first booklet been used to make a certification decision, he would have been unfairly treated.

## 5.7 ANALYZING PERSON FIT

In Section 5.4 we showed how residuals could be accumulated over persons for an item to obtain a statistic which summarizes the fit of that item to the model. Figure 5.4a shows the most surprising responses to the statements in the liking-for-science questionnaire. These surprising responses sometimes form columns, indicating that responses to particular items are inconsistent. As Figure 5.4a shows, they can also form rows indicating that the inconsistent responses can also be traced to particular children. Residuals can be accumulated over items for each child to obtain a statistic which summarizes the fit of that child to the model.

### 5.7.1 Accumulating Person Residuals

We begin as before by calculating the expected mean $E_{ni}$, variance $W_{ni}$ and kurtosis $C_{ni}$ for each person-item encounter

$$E_{ni} = \sum_{k=0}^{m} k\pi_{nik} \tag{5.7.1}$$

$$W_{ni} = \sum_{k=0}^{m} (k-E_{ni})^2\, \pi_{nik} \tag{5.7.2}$$

$$C_{ni} = \sum_{k=0}^{m} (k-E_{ni})^4\, \pi_{nik} \tag{5.7.3}$$

The expected mean is used to obtain a score residual

$$y_{ni} = x_{ni} - E_{ni} \tag{5.7.4}$$

which when squared and accumulated over items for a child provides the weighted sum of squares

$$\sum_{i=1}^{L} y^2 = \sum_{i=1}^{L} W_{ni}(x_{ni}-E_{ni})^2/W_{ni} = \sum_{i=1}^{L} W_{ni}z_{ni}^2 \tag{5.7.5}$$

and the weighted mean square

$$v_n = \sum_{i=1}^{L} W_{ni}z_{ni}^2 \Big/ \sum_{i=1}^{L} W_{ni} = \sum_{i=1}^{L} y_{ni}^2 \Big/ \sum_{i=1}^{L} W_{ni} \tag{5.7.6}$$

with expectation one and variance

$$q_n^2 = \sum_{i}^{L} (C_{ni} - W_{ni}^2) \Big/ (\sum_{i}^{L} W_{ni})^2 \tag{5.7.7}$$

This weighted mean square can be standardized to

$$t_n = (v_n^{1/3} - 1)(3/q_n) + (q_n/3) \tag{5.7.8}$$

with expectation near zero and variance near one when the model holds.

These statistics parallel the corresponding item fit statistics exactly. The only difference is that now squared residuals are summed over items for a person rather than over persons for an item. Item fit statistics play an important role in the construction and calibration of an instrument. Person fit statistics are useful for assessing the validity of measures made with instruments which have already been established.

Table 5.7 shows the responses and fit statistics of five of the children who took the liking-for-science questionnaire. The table is divided into three panels. The top panel shows two rows for each child. The first row contains the child's responses to the twenty-five science activities ordered from easiest-to-like on the left to hardest-to-like on the right. The second row contains truncated standardized residuals which mark his most surprising responses. These are calculated as

$$z_{ni} = \frac{x_{ni} - E_{ni}}{\sqrt{W_{ni}}} \tag{5.7.9}$$

Standardized residuals inside $\pm 1.0$ which truncate to zero are not shown. A positive residual indicates a surprisingly high score on an item; a negative residual, a surprisingly low score. The middle panel contains each child's score $r$, attitude measure $b$, measurement error $s$, weighted mean square $v$, its error $q$, and standardization $t$.

Child $8$ has an orderly response pattern. He has scored 2's on most of the items for which 2's are expected and 0's on the hardest-to-like activities on the far right. The 0's and 2's in the middle of his response string where 1's are expected are only mildly surprising. His overall response pattern is in good accord with the expectations of the Rating Scale model, and this is reflected in his fit $t$ of .19. Child $71$, on the other hand, with the same total score as Child $8$, has a response pattern which is not in accord with the difficulty ordering of these statements. His scores of 0 and 1 on the far left and 2 on the far right result in large standardized residuals which, when accumulated, result in a fit $t$ of 5.40.

Children $21$, $62$ and $73$ all made scores of 28. The ways in which they made this score, however, are rather different. Child $21$ has an unusually regular pattern of responses—more regular than the Rating Scale model expects for these children responding to these statements. The standardized residuals for this child are all very close to zero, producing the surprisingly low mean square of .29, and fit $t$ of $-3.94$. Child $62$'s pattern is surprising because of the absence of 1's in the region where 1's are most probable. In this middle region, Child $62$'s 0's are unexpectedly low, and his 2's are unexpectedly high. When accumulated, they result in a fit $t$ of 1.87. Finally, Child $73$'s erratic responses, particularly his disliking for very easy-to-like activities, produces a fit $t$ of 5.08.

## TABLE 5.7
## RESPONSE RECORDS AND FIT STATISTICS FOR FIVE CHILDREN

```
CHILD                  RESPONSES TO TWENTY-FIVE ACTIVITIES
NUMBER     EASY-TO-LIKE                                    HARD-TO-LIKE

  8        2 2 2 2 2 2 2 2 2 2 | 2 1 2 0 1 2 0 2 1 0 | 0 0 0 0
                                   1 -1     1 -1 1     -1
           Z       G                                          B R C
 71        2 0 2 1 0 2 2 2 2 0 | 2 2 2 0 0 1 2 0 2 0 | 1 2 2 2
           -7    -1 -4              -2    1 1 -1 -1   1 -1 1 -1   2 2 2

 21        2 2 2 2 2 1 2 1 | 1 1 1 1 1 1 1 1 1 1 1 1 1 1 1 | 1 1 0 0 0

 62        2 2 2 2 2 2 2 2 | 2 2 0 0 2 0 2 2 0 0 2 0 | 0 0 0 0 0
                                1 -1 -1   1 -1 1  1 -1 -1 -1  1 -1
           P
 73        0 2 1 2 0 2 0 0 | 0 2 2 2 1 1 2 1 2 1 2 0 | 1 2 2 0 0
           -7   -2   -2   -2 -2 -2 1  1      1      1    1 -1   2 2
```

| CHILD NUMBER | SCORE r | MEASURE b | ERROR s | MS v | ERROR q | FIT t |
|---|---|---|---|---|---|---|
| 8 | 33 | .83 | .34 | 1.03 | .3 | .19 |
| 71 | 33 | .83 | .34 | 3.16 | .3 | 5.40 |
| 21 | 28 | .28 | .33 | .29 | .3 | − 3.94 |
| 62 | 28 | .28 | .33 | 1.52 | .3 | 1.87 |
| 73 | 28 | .28 | .33 | 2.87 | .3 | 5.08 |

| CHILD NUMBER | SCORE MIN | MAX | DIFF | MEASURE MIN | MAX | DIFF |
|---|---|---|---|---|---|---|
| 8 | 29 | 36 | 9 | .39 | 1.19 | .80 |
| 71 | 21 | 44 | 23 | − .45 | 2.47 | 2.92 |
| 21 | 26 | 30 | 4 | .07 | .50 | .43 |
| 62 | 22 | 34 | 12 | − .35 | .95 | 1.30 |
| 73 | 17 | 39 | 22 | − .89 | 1.60 | 2.49 |

Returning to Child *71*, whose score of 33 puts him near the group mean, we note his surprisingly low scores on some activities and surprisingly high scores on others. This leaves us puzzled about Child *71*'s liking-for-science. We can calculate the higher score Child *71* would have made had his surprisingly *low* responses been, instead, the more positive responses expected of a child with a score of 33. We obtain this *maximum possible score* by changing Child *71*'s 0's and 1's on the left of his response pattern to their most probable value 2 and the 0's in the middle of his pattern to 1's. This gives him a maximum score of 33 + 11 = 44. Similarly, we can calculate the lower score Child *71* would have made had his surprisingly *high* responses been, instead, the less positive responses expected of a child with a score of 33. We obtain this *minimum possible score* by changing Child *71*'s 1's and 2's on the right of his response pattern to their most probable value 0 and the 2's in the middle of his pattern to 1's. This gives him a minimum possible score of 33 − 12 = 21. The score boundaries 21 and 44 embrace a segment of this attitude variable within which we cannot help but be uncertain concerning the standing of Child *71*. We call this segment the "fit box" for Child *71* and we have calculated comparable maximum and minimum possible scores for the other four children in Table 5.7.

Figure 5.7 shows the results of these calculations. On the left of Figure 5.7 the liking-for-science variable is displayed vertically, running from less liking-for-science at the bottom to more liking-for-science at the top.   The attitude estimates for the group of seventy-four children are also shown on the left.   Children *8* and *71* scored 33 on the science questionnaire and have the modelled attitude estimate .83 logits with standard error .34.   Children *21*, *62* and *73* scored 28 and have the modelled estimate .28 logits with standard error .33.   The twenty-five science activities on the right of Figure 5.7 are ordered from easiest-to-like at the bottom to hardest-to-like at the top.   The fit boxes for these five children appear in the middle of Figure 5.7.

Child *71*'s minimum possible score of 21 ($-$.45 logits) and maximum possible score of 44 (2.47 logits) mark the bottom and top of his fit box.   His minimum possible score places him at the ninth percentile among the lowest scoring children.   If we took this as Child *71*'s "true" liking-for-science, then we would conclude that he likes only very easy-to-like activities such as going on a picnic, to a museum and to the zoo.   However, we see in Table 5.7 that Child *71* does not even like going to the zoo.

Child *71*'s maximum possible score places him at the ninety-second percentile among the highest scoring children.   If we took this as Child *71*'s "true" liking-for-science, then we would conclude that he likes even difficult-to-like activities such as talking with friends about plants, watching the same animal move many days and looking in cracks in sidewalks for small animals.   In fact, we see that Child *71* claims to like even more difficult to like activities such as watching bugs and rats and finding old bottles and cans.

Child *71*'s poor fit leads to very different minimum and maximum possible scores and so leaves us confused about his liking for science.   Child *8*, who has the same score as Child *71*, however, has many fewer surprising responses and so has minimum and maximum scores much closer to his obtained score.   The smaller size of his fit box indicates our greater certainty concerning the types of activities Child *8* likes.

Fit boxes for Children *21*, *62* and *73* are also shown in Figure 5.7.   Child *73*'s poor fit results in very different minimum and maximum scores.   His large fit box emphasizes the extent of our confusion over his liking for science.   The very narrow fit box of Child *21* results from his surprisingly orderly pattern of responses.   Notice, however, that his surprisingly low fit statistic of $-3.94$ brings to our attention how noncommittal he has been concerning his liking for science.   Sixteen of his twenty-five responses are "Not sure/Don't care" responses.   When we compare Child *21*'s responses to the ten easiest-to-like activities with those of Child *62* whose performance is more typical of this group of children, we find Child *21* scoring *lower* than Child *62*, 16 to 20 and so seeming to like science *less*.   But when we compare the responses of these two children to the six hardest-to-like activities, we find Child *21* scoring *higher* than Child *62*, 3 to 0 and so seeming to like science *more*!   This contradiction is the consequence of Child *62*'s excessive number of noncommittal responses, the condition signalled by his fit *t* of $-3.94$.

## 5.8 "RELIABILITY" AND "VALIDITY"

Two concepts which have a long history in traditional test theory are "reliability" and "validity".   While these concepts have not played leading parts in our methods for verifying variables and supervising the quality of measures, it is easy to see how they are included in our approach.

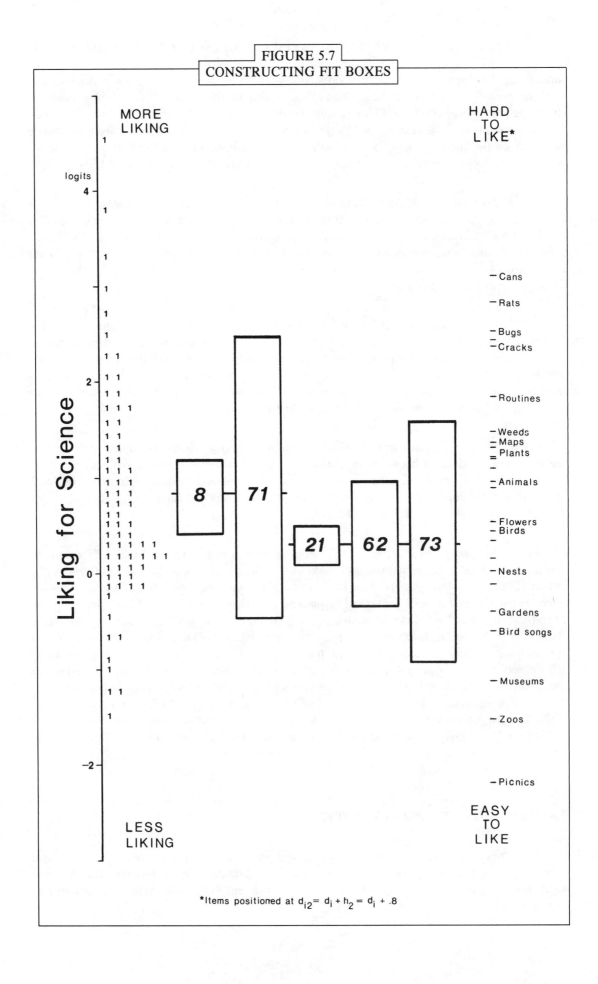

# FIGURE 5.7
## CONSTRUCTING FIT BOXES

*Items positioned at $d_{i2} = d_i + h_2 = d_i + .8$

### 5.8.1 Test "Reliability"

The traditional formulation of test "reliability" can be derived from a "true score" model which assumes that the observed test score of each person can be resolved into two components: an unknowable true score and a random error.   Test reliability is defined as the proportion of a sample's observed score variance $SD^2$ which is due to the sample's true score variance $ST^2$

$$R = ST^2/SD^2 = 1-(SE^2/SD^2)$$

where the observed variance is partitioned into two components $SD^2 = ST^2 + SE^2$, and $SE^2$ is the error variance of the test, averaged over that sample.

The magnitude of the traditional reliability coefficient depends not only on the average test error variance $SE^2$ which is intended to describe how precisely the test measures (i.e., for a given $ST^2$, the greater the precision of measurement, the smaller $SE^2$ and the larger $R$), but also on the sample true score variance $ST^2$ which is intended to describe the "true" ability dispersion of the "true" sample (i.e., for a given $SE^2$, the greater the sample true score variance $ST^2$, the larger $R$).

The observed sample variance $SD^2$ can be calculated directly from the observed measures, but the test error variance $SE^2$ must be derived from a model describing how each score occurs.   The traditional approach to estimating this error variance is to estimate the reliability first.   This is done in various ways, for example, by calculating the correlation between repeated measurements under similar conditions or by correlating split halves or by combining item point biserials.   An average error variance for the test with this particular sample is then estimated as $SD^2(1-R')$ where $R'$ is the estimate of $R$.

In practice, the magnitude of this estimated reliability $R'$ also depends upon a third factor, namely the extent to which the items in the test actually work together to define one variable.   The traditional estimates of $R$ can be thought of as a function of an observed sample variance $SD^2$ and a "working" test error variance $SW^2$:

$$R' = 1 - (SW^2/SD^2)$$

The working error variance has two parts.   The modelled test error variance $SE^2$ is its theoretical basis.   But it is also influenced by the extent to which the items actually fit together in the way they are used by the sample in hand and so are internally consistent.   When item inconsistency is estimated by an overall fit mean square $V$ for the test and sample together and $V > 1$, then the working error variance can be estimated by

$$SW^2 = V(SE^2)$$

so that the estimated reliability becomes

$$R' = 1 - [V(SE^2)/SD^2]$$

Our method deals separately with the three components $V$, $SE$ and $ST$ which are submerged in the traditional test reliability coefficient.   We provide a direct estimate of the modelled test error variance $SE^2$.   This modelled error tells us how precisely we will be able to estimate each person's ability when the items are internally consistent. Unlike the traditional reliability coefficient, $SE$ is not influenced by sample variance or fit and so is not sample specific. It is a sample-free test characteristic of the set of items which make up the test. It estimates how precisely the ability of any person whose response pattern fits can be estimated from their particular score on this test, regardless of any sample to which he may belong.

Unlike the traditional reliability coefficient and the measurement error it implies, this estimate is not an average for the whole test, but is particular to the test score the person actually obtains. This is important because there can be substantial differences in estimation error between extreme and central scores. If the range of scores is $r = 1, M$ where $M = mL$, $m + 1$ is the number of response alternatives and $L$ is the number of items, then approximate boundary values for $SE_r \simeq [M/r(M - r)]^{1/2}$ in logits are

$$SE_1 = SE_{M-1} < 1 + 1/2M$$

and

$$SE_{M/2} > 2/M^{1/2}$$

Thus the precision of measures based on central scores can be $M^{1/2}/2$ greater than the precision of estimates based on extreme scores.

### 5.8.2 Test "Validity"

In traditional test theory a distinction is made between internal and external validity. The usual statistics employed to assess the internal validity of a test are the item point biserials and their accumulation into the test reliability estimate. Since the magnitude of this item statistic depends on the distribution of the sample and in particular on the relationship between the item p-value and the sample spread, it has the disadvantage of being dependent on sample characteristics which need not pertain to validity. When an explicit measurement model is used, the internal validity of a test can be analyzed in terms of the statistical fit of each item to the model in a way that is independent of the sample distribution. To facilitate our item fit analyses, we standardize these mean squares into fit statistics with expected means near zero and expected standard deviations near one. We use the term "valid" to refer to the success of this evaluation of fit. If the fit statistics of an item are acceptable, i.e., near zero, then we say the item calibration is "valid". We also supervise the internal consistency of each person's pattern of performance in the same way and, if the fit statistics for a person's performance are acceptable, say that their measure is "valid".

## 5.9 MAINTAINING VARIABLES BY COMPARING ESTIMATES

When a variable is used with different groups of persons or to measure the same persons on different occasions, it is essential that the identity of the variable be maintained from one occasion to the next. Only if the item calibrations are invariant from group to group and from time to time can meaningful comparisons of person measures be made. To evaluate the invariance of item calibrations we compare centered estimates for the same set of items on different occasions. The simplest case is two occasions.

On the first occasion we obtain a calibration $d_1$ and error $s_1$ for each item $i$ (or item step $ij$). On the second occasion we obtain a second calibration $d_2$ and error $s_2$ for each item. Each of these sets is centered on zero so that their comparison is independent of incidental translation effects. They can be compared by

1) plotting $d_1$ against $d_2$ and evaluating this plot in the context of $s_1$ and $s_2$,

2) computing standardized differences $z = (d_1 - d_2)/(s_1^2 + s_2^2)^{1/2}$ and reviewing their distribution, especially as a function of $d. = (d_1 + d_2)/2$, and

3) correlating $d_1$ and $d_2$ over all $L$ items.

### 5.9.1 Plotting Estimates from Different Occasions

The first approach to comparing item estimates from different calibrating samples, and the one we prefer, is to plot the two sets of estimates against each other. The resulting plot is then examined in the light of expectation, that is, in the light of a confidence band based on the errors of calibration. Figure 5.9 shows how such a confidence band can be constructed. The two estimates $d_1$ and $d_2$ for each item define the point $(d_1, d_2)$ which is marked with an X. The difference $(d_1 - d_2)$ has an estimated standard error $s_{12} = (s_1^2 + s_2^2)^{1/2}$. A confidence band corresponding to $k$ standard errors of this difference can be formed by marking off $k/\sqrt{2}$ error units perpendicular to the identity line on each side of the point $(d., d.)$. These boundary points $C$ and $C'$ are $(d. - ks_{12}/2, \quad d. + ks_{12}/2)$ and $(d. + ks_{12}/2, \quad d. - ks_{12}/2)$.

The amount of confidence is specified by the choice of $k$. When $k = 2$, for example, about 95 percent of the $(d_1, d_2)$ pairs are expected to fall inside the confidence band. If substantially more than 5 percent of them fall outside, that is evidence for a general lack of invariance in the item calibrations. Even when only a few items fall outside the confidence band, we examine those few carefully to see what we can learn from their variation.

### 5.9.2 Analyzing Standardized Differences

The standardized difference between different estimates of the same parameter

$$z = (d_1 - d_2)/(s_1^2 + s_2^2)^{1/2}$$

has an expectation of zero and a variance of one. Trends in these standardized differences can be studied by plotting $z$ against $d$.

### 5.9.3 Analyzing Correlations Between Estimates

The maximum value we can expect the correlation between $d_1$ and $d_2$ to reach is determined by their standard errors $s_1$ and $s_2$ and the variance of their mean. This maximum correlation is

$$R_{max} = 1 - SE^2 / SD^2$$

where

$$SE^2 = \sum_i^L (s_1^2 + s_2^2) / 4L$$

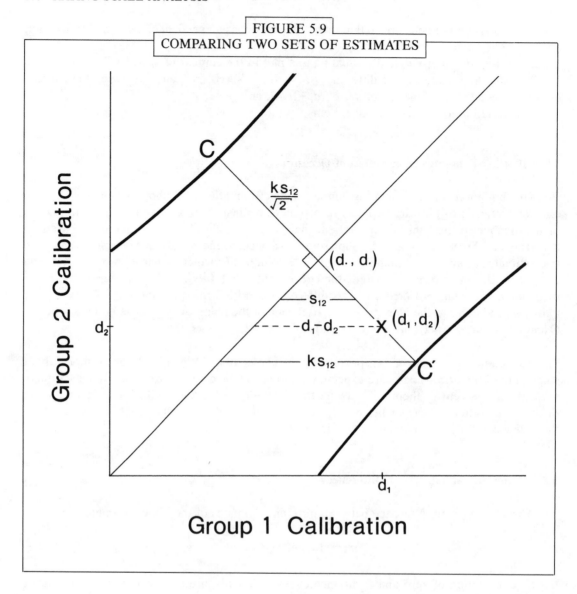

FIGURE 5.9
COMPARING TWO SETS OF ESTIMATES

and, if $d_1$ and $d_2$ have been centered at $\sum\limits^{L} d_1 = \sum\limits^{L} d_2 = 0$,

$$SD^2 = \sum^{L}(d_1 + d_2)^2 / 4(L-1)$$

so that

$$R_{max} = 1 - \left[ (L-1)/L \right]\left[ \sum^{L}(s_1^2 + s_2^2) / \sum^{L}(d_1 + d_2)^2 \right]$$

We can use R. A. Fisher's log transformation for linearizing correlations to compare the *observed* correlation $r_{12}$ between $d_1$ and $d_2$ over the $L$ items in the set with $R_{max}$. The fit statistic

$$t \ = \ \frac{(L-3)^{1/2}}{2} \ \log\left[\frac{(1+r_{12})\,(1-R_{max})}{(1-r_{12})\,(1+R_{max})}\right]$$

has expectation zero and variance one when invariance holds.

This concludes our presentation of method. Chapters 3, 4 and 5 contain the main ideas. But a method cannot be adequately grasped in the abstract. It must be realized in specific applications worked out in enough detail to bring out how the method works in practice. This is the aim of the next four chapters.

In Chapter 6 we use the Rating Scale model to analyze college students attitudes toward drugs. This questionnaire contains a mixture of statements *for* and *against* drugs. We compare students' responses to these two types of statements about drugs and discuss some consequences of including both positively and negatively worded statements in an attitude questionnaire. We also show how the Rating Scale model can be used to expose differences in individual response styles.

In Chapter 7 we analyze a second attitude questionnaire constructed to measure college students' fear of crime. Like the attitude-to-drugs scale, this questionnaire provides a fixed set of response alternatives for use with all nine items. We analyze these data first with the Rating Scale model and then with the Partial Credit model. This gives us an opportunity to compare the similarities and differences between these two approaches.

In Chapter 8 we analyze performances on a school physics test. These performances are scored using an ''answer-until-correct'' format. We begin our analysis with two separate applications of the Dichotomous model, and then show how the same results can be obtained with a single application of the Partial Credit model.

In Chapter 9 we use the Partial Credit model to study performances of infants on a pre-kindergarten screening test and show how the ability variable defined by this test can be understood in terms of the subtasks making up each item.

# 6 ATTITUDE TOWARDS DRUGS

In this chapter we apply our measurement method to measure the attitudes of seventy-five college students towards the use of drugs. These data were collected by Leona Aiken of the Institute for Survey Research, Temple University, Philadelphia. The attitude questionnaire contains twenty statements drawn from the Pennsylvania State University Evaluation Scales (Swisher and Horan, 1973, *87-94*). Ten of these are statements which persons in favor of drug use might be expected to make (Figure 6.0a). The other ten are statements which persons opposed to drug use might be expected to make (Figure 6.0b).

Students were asked to record their agreement or disagreement with each statement in terms of five ordered alternatives. A typical item is

7. I would welcome the opportunity to get high on drugs.

|   |   |   |   |
|---|---|---|---|
| a. | Strongly Agree | d. | Disagree |
| b. | Agree | e. | Strongly Disagree |
| c. | Have No Opinion | | |

We will not analyze the responses to all twenty statements simultaneously. Instead, we will consider the ten positively worded *For* statements and the ten negatively worded *Against* statements separately. Our analysis will show that this separation of *For* and *Against* statements is a necessary step in the identification and definition of this variable.

---

## FIGURE 6.0a
### STATEMENTS *FOR* DRUGS

1. I see nothing wrong with taking an LSD trip.
2. People who make drug legislation should really have personal experience with drugs.
3. I wish I could get hold of some pills to calm me down whenever I get "up tight".
4. All drugs should be made legal and freely available.
5. In spite of what the establishment says, the drug scene is really "where it's at".
6. I admire people who like to get stoned.
7. I would welcome the opportunity to get high on drugs.
8. If people use drugs together, their relationships will be improved.
9. Smoking marijuana is less harmful than drinking alcohol.
10. People who use drugs are more fun to be with than those who don't use drugs.

---

## FIGURE 6.0b
### STATEMENTS *AGAINST* DRUGS

1. Drugs are basically an "unnatural" way to enjoy life.
2. I'd have to be pretty sick before I'd take any drug including an aspirin.
3. Pep pills are a stupid way of keeping alert when there's important work to be done.
4. Students should be told about the harmful side effects of certain drugs.
5. Even if my best friend gave me some hash, I probably wouldn't use it.
6. As a general rule of thumb, most drugs are dangerous and should be used only with medical authorization.
7. Taking any kind of dope is a pretty dumb idea.
8. People who regularly take drugs should not be given positions of responsibility for young children.
9. Experimenting with drugs is dangerous if a person has any psychological problems.
10. Drugs can cause people to say or do things they might later regret.

## 6.1 DATA *FOR* DRUGS

Responses to the ten statements *For* drugs have been scored "Strongly Disagree" (0), "Disagree" (1), "Have No Opinion" (2), "Agree" (3) and "Strongly Agree" (4). The responses of the seventy-five students to these ten statements are shown in Table 6.1. The entries in each row of this score matrix have been summed to obtain an attitude score for each student. The minimum score a person can make on these ten statements is $10 \times 0 = 0$. The maximum is $10 \times 4 = 40$. The seventy-five students have been sorted by score so that students with the highest scores are at the top of the table. A high score is obtained by strongly agreeing with most of these statements *For* drugs, and reflects a favorable attitude toward drug use. In contrast, the low scoring students at the bottom of Table 6.1 strongly disagree with most of these statements, and are therefore less in favor of drug use.

The entries in the columns have also been summed to obtain a score for each statement, and the statements have been sorted by score. Statements with high scores are statements with which these students were more inclined to agree. These are on the left of Table 6.1. Statements with low scores are harder to agree with. They are on the right.

At the top left of Table 6.1 are responses of students most in favor of drugs to the statements with which it is easiest to agree. In this corner we expect agreement (4's and 3's). At the bottom right of Table 6.1 are responses of students least in favor of drugs to the statements with which it is hardest to agree. In this corner we expect disagreement (0's and 1's).

The person scores order the students on the basis of their agreement or disagreement with these ten statements. But this order has meaning only if the ten statements join together to define a single dimension—that is, only if these statements are consistent with one another in their ordering of the seventy-five students.

Responses to Statement 6 "I admire people who like to get stoned", are in good accord with the person score ordering. Students with scores above 13 tend to respond "have no opinion" (2) to Statement 6; students with scores between 8 and 13 tend to respond "disagree" (1), and students with scores below 8 tend to respond "strongly disagree" (0).

## TABLE 6.1
### DATA *FOR* DRUGS

STATEMENTS *FOR* DRUGS

| PERSON NUMBER | EASY TO AGREE 9 | 2 | 8 | 7 | 1 | 3 | 6 | 5 | 10 | HARD TO AGREE 4 | PERSON SCORE |
|---|---|---|---|---|---|---|---|---|---|---|---|
| 51 | 4 | 4 | 4 | 4 | 1 | 3 | 2 | 3 | 4 | 4 | 33 |
| 47 | 3 | 4 | 2 | 3 | 3 | 1 | 2 | 2 | 2 | 3 | 25 |
| 68 | 3 | 4 | 3 | 3 | 3 | 3 | 2 | 1 | 0 | 3 | 25 |
| 67 | 4 | 4 | 2 | 3 | 2 | 3 | 2 | 1 | 2 | 0 | 23 |
| 49 | 4 | 1 | 2 | 2 | 3 | 3 | 2 | 2 | 2 | 2 | 23 |
| 77 | 4 | 1 | 2 | 2 | 1 | 2 | 1 | 3 | 2 | 3 | 21 |
| 25 | 3 | 1 | 1 | 3 | 3 | 3 | 2 | 2 | 1 | 1 | 20 |
| 78 | 3 | 3 | 3 | 1 | 3 | 1 | 1 | 1 | 3 | 1 | 20 |
| 60 | 3 | 4 | 0 | 4 | 2 | 3 | 1 | 1 | 0 | 1 | 19 |
| 76 | 1 | 3 | 3 | 1 | 3 | 2 | 2 | 1 | 3 | 0 | 19 |
| 66 | 3 | 3 | 1 | 3 | 2 | 3 | 2 | 1 | 1 | 0 | 19 |
| 57 | 4 | 2 | 2 | 2 | 0 | 3 | 2 | 2 | 0 | 2 | 19 |
| 91 | 4 | 3 | 2 | 2 | 3 | 0 | 3 | 1 | 1 | 0 | 19 |
| 52 | 3 | 1 | 3 | 3 | 0 | 1 | 2 | 1 | 3 | 1 | 18 |
| 72 | 1 | 4 | 4 | 1 | 1 | 1 | 1 | 2 | 2 | 1 | 18 |
| 74 | 3 | 3 | 1 | 3 | 3 | 0 | 2 | 0 | 1 | 1 | 17 |
| 53 | 4 | 4 | 1 | 1 | 2 | 1 | 1 | 1 | 0 | 1 | 16 |
| 61 | 4 | 2 | 3 | 1 | 1 | 0 | 2 | 1 | 2 | 0 | 16 |
| 62 | 3 | 1 | 2 | 2 | 2 | 1 | 2 | 2 | 1 | 0 | 16 |
| 94 | 3 | 2 | 2 | 3 | 1 | 1 | 1 | 1 | 1 | 1 | 16 |
| 9 | 4 | 0 | 1 | 2 | 4 | 1 | 2 | 1 | 0 | 0 | 15 |
| 56 | 1 | 3 | 1 | 2 | 2 | 0 | 2 | 1 | 2 | 1 | 15 |
| 27 | 3 | 1 | 2 | 1 | 1 | 3 | 0 | 1 | 2 | 1 | 15 |
| 28 | 4 | 0 | 2 | 3 | 0 | 0 | 0 | 1 | 2 | 3 | 15 |
| 70 | 3 | 3 | 1 | 1 | 0 | 1 | 1 | 1 | 1 | 3 | 15 |
| 33 | 4 | 4 | 0 | 0 | 1 | 0 | 2 | 4 | 0 | 0 | 15 |
| 85 | 3 | 4 | 1 | 1 | 0 | 0 | 2 | 1 | 1 | 1 | 14 |
| 81 | 4 | 1 | 1 | 2 | 0 | 1 | 2 | 1 | 0 | 1 | 13 |
| 50 | 3 | 3 | 1 | 2 | 0 | 0 | 0 | 1 | 2 | 1 | 13 |
| 87 | 3 | 1 | 1 | 0 | 3 | 1 | 1 | 1 | 1 | 1 | 13 |
| 10 | 3 | 4 | 1 | 0 | 1 | 0 | 0 | 3 | 1 | 0 | 13 |
| 93 | 4 | 3 | 0 | 2 | 0 | 1 | 1 | 1 | 1 | 0 | 13 |
| 22 | 3 | 3 | 1 | 1 | 1 | 0 | 1 | 1 | 1 | 1 | 13 |
| 1 | 2 | 3 | 1 | 1 | 1 | 2 | 0 | 1 | 1 | 0 | 12 |
| 34 | 4 | 4 | 1 | 0 | 0 | 3 | 0 | 0 | 0 | 0 | 12 |
| 90 | 2 | 2 | 1 | 0 | 0 | 3 | 0 | 0 | 0 | 4 | 12 |
| 5 | 4 | 3 | 3 | 1 | 0 | 0 | 1 | 0 | 0 | 0 | 12 |
| 92 | 2 | 2 | 1 | 0 | 0 | 0 | 1 | 3 | 3 | 0 | 12 |
| 31 | 2 | 1 | 1 | 1 | 4 | 0 | 0 | 0 | 3 | 0 | 12 |
| 54 | 3 | 2 | 1 | 1 | 1 | 0 | 1 | 1 | 1 | 1 | 12 |
| 69 | 3 | 1 | 1 | 1 | 1 | 1 | 1 | 1 | 1 | 0 | 11 |
| 63 | 3 | 1 | 1 | 0 | 3 | 0 | 1 | 1 | 0 | 1 | 11 |
| 8 | 3 | 3 | 0 | 1 | 0 | 0 | 1 | 0 | 0 | 3 | 11 |
| 73 | 3 | 0 | 2 | 1 | 3 | 0 | 1 | 0 | 1 | 0 | 11 |
| 96 | 4 | 0 | 1 | 2 | 0 | 1 | 1 | 1 | 1 | 0 | 11 |
| 86 | 3 | 2 | 2 | 0 | 0 | 0 | 0 | 1 | 1 | 1 | 10 |
| 58 | 4 | 1 | 2 | 1 | 0 | 0 | 1 | 1 | 0 | 0 | 10 |
| 45 | 3 | 3 | 1 | 2 | 0 | 1 | 0 | 0 | 0 | 0 | 10 |
| 23 | 1 | 2 | 3 | 2 | 1 | 1 | 0 | 0 | 0 | 0 | 10 |
| 79 | 3 | 1 | 3 | 0 | 0 | 1 | 0 | 0 | 1 | 0 | 9 |
| 83 | 0 | 3 | 4 | 0 | 1 | 0 | 0 | 0 | 0 | 1 | 9 |
| 84 | 2 | 1 | 2 | 2 | 0 | 0 | 1 | 1 | 0 | 0 | 9 |
| 2 | 1 | 1 | 1 | 1 | 0 | 1 | 1 | 1 | 1 | 0 | 8 |
| 95 | 2 | 1 | 0 | 0 | 0 | 0 | 1 | 3 | 1 | 0 | 8 |
| 89 | 2 | 1 | 1 | 1 | 1 | 0 | 1 | 0 | 1 | 0 | 8 |
| 3 | 3 | 4 | 0 | 0 | 0 | 0 | 0 | 0 | 0 | 0 | 7 |
| 64 | 3 | 4 | 0 | 0 | 0 | 0 | 0 | 0 | 0 | 0 | 7 |
| 75 | 1 | 2 | 2 | 0 | 0 | 1 | 0 | 0 | 0 | 0 | 6 |
| 24 | 1 | 3 | 0 | 0 | 0 | 0 | 1 | 0 | 1 | 0 | 6 |
| 7 | 1 | 3 | 0 | 0 | 1 | 1 | 0 | 0 | 0 | 0 | 6 |
| 59 | 2 | 0 | 1 | 0 | 3 | 0 | 0 | 0 | 0 | 0 | 6 |
| 29 | 3 | 0 | 0 | 0 | 0 | 3 | 0 | 0 | 0 | 0 | 6 |
| 26 | 4 | 0 | 0 | 0 | 0 | 0 | 1 | 0 | 0 | 1 | 6 |
| 82 | 2 | 4 | 0 | 0 | 0 | 0 | 0 | 0 | 0 | 0 | 6 |
| 48 | 3 | 3 | 0 | 0 | 0 | 0 | 0 | 0 | 0 | 0 | 6 |
| 55 | 3 | 2 | 0 | 0 | 0 | 1 | 0 | 0 | 0 | 0 | 6 |
| 32 | 3 | 1 | 1 | 0 | 0 | 1 | 0 | 0 | 0 | 0 | 6 |
| 88 | 1 | 4 | 0 | 0 | 0 | 0 | 0 | 0 | 0 | 0 | 5 |
| 11 | 3 | 0 | 0 | 0 | 0 | 1 | 0 | 0 | 1 | 0 | 5 |
| 6 | 2 | 1 | 0 | 0 | 0 | 1 | 0 | 0 | 0 | 1 | 5 |
| 65 | 0 | 4 | 0 | 0 | 0 | 0 | 0 | 0 | 0 | 0 | 4 |
| 46 | 0 | 4 | 0 | 0 | 0 | 0 | 0 | 0 | 0 | 0 | 4 |
| 4 | 1 | 1 | 0 | 0 | 0 | 1 | 0 | 1 | 0 | 0 | 4 |
| 71 | 3 | 0 | 0 | 0 | 0 | 0 | 0 | 0 | 0 | 0 | 3 |
| 80 | 2 | 0 | 0 | 0 | 0 | 0 | 0 | 0 | 0 | 0 | 2 |
| Statement Score | 203 | 162 | 93 | 82 | 72 | 67 | 64 | 63 | 63 | 51 | |

TABLE 6.2
DATA *AGAINST* DRUGS

STATEMENTS *AGAINST* DRUGS

| PERSON NUMBER | EASY TO AGREE 4 | 10 | 9 | 6 | 1 | 3 | 8 | 7 | 5 | HARD TO AGREE 2 | PERSON SCORE |
|---|---|---|---|---|---|---|---|---|---|---|---|
| 7 | 4 | 4 | 4 | 4 | 4 | 4 | 4 | 4 | 4 | 4 | 40 |
| 80 | 4 | 4 | 4 | 4 | 3 | 4 | 4 | 4 | 4 | 4 | 39 |
| 75 | 4 | 4 | 4 | 4 | 4 | 3 | 4 | 4 | 4 | 3 | 38 |
| 64 | 4 | 4 | 4 | 4 | 4 | 3 | 4 | 4 | 4 | 3 | 38 |
| 83 | 4 | 4 | 3 | 4 | 4 | 4 | 4 | 4 | 4 | 3 | 38 |
| 72 | 4 | 3 | 3 | 4 | 4 | 3 | 4 | 4 | 4 | 4 | 37 |
| 4 | 3 | 4 | 4 | 4 | 4 | 3 | 4 | 4 | 4 | 3 | 37 |
| 46 | 4 | 4 | 4 | 4 | 4 | 0 | 4 | 4 | 4 | 4 | 36 |
| 59 | 4 | 3 | 4 | 4 | 3 | 4 | 4 | 4 | 4 | 2 | 36 |
| 3 | 4 | 4 | 4 | 4 | 4 | 4 | 4 | 4 | 4 | 0 | 36 |
| 65 | 4 | 4 | 4 | 0 | 4 | 4 | 4 | 4 | 4 | 4 | 36 |
| 88 | 4 | 3 | 4 | 3 | 4 | 4 | 3 | 3 | 4 | 4 | 36 |
| 50 | 4 | 3 | 3 | 3 | 4 | 4 | 4 | 4 | 2 | 4 | 35 |
| 82 | 4 | 4 | 0 | 4 | 4 | 4 | 4 | 4 | 4 | 3 | 35 |
| 92 | 4 | 3 | 1 | 4 | 4 | 4 | 4 | 3 | 4 | 4 | 35 |
| 2 | 4 | 4 | 4 | 4 | 2 | 2 | 4 | 4 | 2 | 4 | 34 |
| 86 | 4 | 4 | 4 | 4 | 3 | 3 | 3 | 3 | 4 | 1 | 33 |
| 87 | 4 | 3 | 4 | 3 | 3 | 4 | 2 | 3 | 4 | 3 | 33 |
| 5 | 4 | 4 | 4 | 4 | 4 | 4 | 4 | 3 | 1 | 1 | 33 |
| 11 | 4 | 3 | 4 | 3 | 4 | 4 | 4 | 3 | 3 | 1 | 33 |
| 96 | 4 | 3 | 4 | 4 | 4 | 2 | 4 | 3 | 4 | 1 | 33 |
| 10 | 4 | 4 | 4 | 0 | 3 | 3 | 4 | 4 | 3 | 3 | 32 |
| 48 | 4 | 2 | 4 | 4 | 4 | 4 | 3 | 3 | 1 | 3 | 32 |
| 58 | 4 | 4 | 4 | 3 | 3 | 4 | 4 | 3 | 1 | 1 | 31 |
| 22 | 4 | 3 | 3 | 3 | 3 | 3 | 3 | 3 | 3 | 3 | 31 |
| 6 | 4 | 3 | 2 | 3 | 4 | 3 | 2 | 4 | 3 | 3 | 31 |
| 95 | 4 | 3 | 3 | 3 | 4 | 1 | 3 | 2 | 4 | 4 | 31 |
| 79 | 4 | 4 | 4 | 4 | 2 | 1 | 3 | 4 | 4 | 1 | 31 |
| 33 | 4 | 4 | 4 | 4 | 4 | 4 | 2 | 0 | 4 | 0 | 30 |
| 24 | 4 | 0 | 0 | 4 | 4 | 3 | 4 | 4 | 4 | 3 | 30 |
| 71 | 4 | 3 | 4 | 4 | 4 | 1 | 3 | 3 | 4 | 0 | 30 |
| 69 | 4 | 3 | 3 | 3 | 3 | 3 | 3 | 3 | 3 | 1 | 29 |
| 85 | 3 | 3 | 3 | 3 | 3 | 3 | 3 | 3 | 1 | 4 | 29 |
| 81 | 4 | 4 | 3 | 3 | 4 | 1 | 4 | 1 | 1 | 3 | 28 |
| 90 | 4 | 3 | 4 | 4 | 0 | 3 | 0 | 4 | 4 | 1 | 27 |
| 54 | 4 | 3 | 2 | 3 | 2 | 1 | 3 | 2 | 3 | 4 | 27 |
| 84 | 4 | 4 | 2 | 4 | 3 | 2 | 4 | 0 | 1 | 3 | 27 |
| 55 | 4 | 4 | 4 | 4 | 3 | 1 | 1 | 1 | 4 | 1 | 27 |
| 70 | 3 | 3 | 3 | 3 | 3 | 1 | 1 | 3 | 3 | 3 | 26 |
| 32 | 4 | 4 | 3 | 4 | 2 | 1 | 0 | 3 | 4 | 1 | 26 |
| 60 | 4 | 3 | 4 | 3 | 1 | 1 | 3 | 3 | 0 | 4 | 26 |
| 1 | 3 | 3 | 4 | 3 | 3 | 1 | 4 | 2 | 1 | 2 | 26 |
| 94 | 3 | 3 | 3 | 3 | 3 | 3 | 1 | 3 | 3 | 1 | 26 |
| 26 | 0 | 4 | 4 | 3 | 1 | 3 | 4 | 3 | 3 | 1 | 26 |
| 27 | 3 | 2 | 3 | 3 | 3 | 3 | 2 | 3 | 3 | 1 | 26 |
| 45 | 4 | 3 | 3 | 3 | 3 | 1 | 4 | 1 | 1 | 1 | 24 |
| 34 | 4 | 0 | 0 | 4 | 4 | 3 | 0 | 4 | 0 | 4 | 23 |
| 91 | 4 | 3 | 2 | 3 | 3 | 4 | 2 | 1 | 0 | 1 | 23 |
| 53 | 4 | 4 | 3 | 3 | 1 | 3 | 1 | 2 | 2 | 0 | 23 |
| 57 | 4 | 4 | 4 | 2 | 2 | 0 | 2 | 4 | 0 | 0 | 22 |
| 76 | 3 | 3 | 1 | 1 | 2 | 1 | 3 | 3 | 3 | 2 | 22 |
| 23 | 4 | 4 | 3 | 3 | 3 | 1 | 0 | 1 | 3 | 0 | 22 |
| 52 | 3 | 3 | 3 | 3 | 1 | 3 | 4 | 1 | 0 | 0 | 21 |
| 28 | 4 | 3 | 4 | 3 | 1 | 3 | 2 | 1 | 0 | 0 | 21 |
| 73 | 4 | 3 | 3 | 1 | 3 | 4 | 0 | 1 | 1 | 1 | 21 |
| 9 | 4 | 4 | 0 | 1 | 4 | 1 | 0 | 2 | 1 | 3 | 20 |
| 25 | 4 | 3 | 3 | 3 | 1 | 3 | 1 | 1 | 1 | 0 | 20 |
| 93 | 3 | 3 | 3 | 1 | 1 | 1 | 3 | 1 | 4 | 0 | 20 |
| 62 | 4 | 3 | 3 | 0 | 1 | 3 | 2 | 2 | 0 | 1 | 19 |
| 47 | 4 | 3 | 3 | 1 | 1 | 3 | 2 | 1 | 1 | 0 | 19 |
| 77 | 0 | 4 | 3 | 2 | 3 | 1 | 3 | 2 | 0 | 1 | 19 |
| 56 | 4 | 3 | 3 | 2 | 3 | 1 | 1 | 1 | 0 | 1 | 19 |
| 8 | 4 | 0 | 0 | 0 | 3 | 4 | 0 | 1 | 3 | 4 | 19 |
| 78 | 3 | 3 | 3 | 1 | 3 | 1 | 1 | 1 | 1 | 1 | 18 |
| 51 | 4 | 4 | 4 | 3 | 0 | 1 | 1 | 1 | 0 | 0 | 18 |
| 67 | 3 | 2 | 2 | 3 | 3 | 1 | 1 | 1 | 1 | 1 | 18 |
| 66 | 3 | 3 | 2 | 2 | 3 | 1 | 2 | 1 | 0 | 0 | 17 |
| 89 | 3 | 3 | 2 | 1 | 3 | 2 | 2 | 1 | 0 | 0 | 17 |
| 31 | 0 | 1 | 0 | 4 | 4 | 4 | 1 | 3 | 0 | 0 | 17 |
| 49 | 3 | 3 | 3 | 3 | 1 | 1 | 1 | 1 | 0 | 0 | 16 |
| 63 | 0 | 3 | 3 | 1 | 1 | 1 | 1 | 1 | 4 | 1 | 16 |
| 68 | 4 | 3 | 3 | 1 | 1 | 1 | 1 | 1 | 1 | 0 | 16 |
| 61 | 4 | 1 | 4 | 1 | 1 | 2 | 0 | 1 | 0 | 0 | 14 |
| 74 | 3 | 3 | 2 | 1 | 1 | 3 | 0 | 0 | 0 | 0 | 13 |
| 29 | 0 | 0 | 0 | 4 | 4 | 0 | 0 | 0 | 0 | 1 | 9 |
| Statement Score | 265 | 234 | 223 | 215 | 212 | 184 | 184 | 183 | 168 | 134 | |

Responses to Statement *2*, "People who make drug legislation should really have personal experience with drugs", are less orderly. Ten students scoring 13 or more either "disagree" (1) or "strongly disagree" (0) with this statement, while eleven students scoring 10 or less either "agree" (3) or "strongly agree" (4). In other words, this statement fails to provide attitude information which is consistent with the information implied by the other nine statements in the questionnaire. When students are ordered on the basis of their responses to Statement *2*, the resulting order is different from the person score order. This leads us to suspect that Statement *2* is not defining the same drug attitude variable as the other statements.

Statement *2* is the only statement involving "legislation", and the "personal experience" to which it refers could be bad as well as good. The disorderliness of the responses to Statement *2* might lead us to delete it from the questionnaire were it not the only statement near its particular level of difficulty. Instead we will retain Statement *2*, for now, because it can help us to "see" the general range of the variable defined by these ten statements. When we have an opportunity to improve our definition of this drug attitude variable, we can try to replace Statement *2* with two or three statements which are equally easy to agree with, but less ambiguous.

The statement scores order the ten statements from those with which it is relatively easy to agree to those with which it is relatively hard to agree. We can examine rows of responses to these statements for consistency with this difficulty ordering. Consider, for example, the response vector of Person *94* with a score of 16. This person has scored 3's and 2's on the statements easy to agree with, but 1's on the statements hard to agree with. His pattern of responses is in good accord with the statement score ordering.

The responses of Person *90* with a score of 12, on the other hand, are in poor accord with the ordering of statement scores. This is because of the surprising responses this person made to Statements *3* and *4*. Given the difficulty of agreeing with these statements, this person should have strongly disagreed (0) with both of them. This would have given Person *90* a score of 5 and placed him near the bottom of the table. In fact, he agreed (3) and strongly agreed (4) with these two statements, resulting in a score of 12, and leading to confusion in our minds as to where this person should be located among the other seventy-four persons. We are forced to conclude that we have not yet measured the attitude of Person *90* successfully. Since his pattern of responses is so chaotic, we could improve our calibration of these statements slightly by dropping this person from the calibration sample. If we wish to know Person *90*'s attitude, we will have to test him again.

The attitude variable defined by these statements *For* drugs can be seen by examining the ordering of the statements by score. Statement *9*, with a score of 203, is easy to agree with

*9.* Smoking marijuana is less harmful than drinking alcohol.

A person does not have to be much in favor of drug use to agree with this. Statement *2*, with a score of 162, is somewhat harder to agree with

*2.* People who make drug legislation should really have personal experience with drugs.

Still harder to agree with is Statement *8*, with a score of 93

*8.* If people use drugs together their relationships will be improved.

Finally, Statement *4*, with a score of 51, describes an attitude very much in favor of drugs

    *4.*   All drugs should be made legal and freely available.

The statement scores at the bottom of Table 6.1 represent points on the drug attitude variable.   To become fully useful,however, these scores still need to be transformed into calibrations on an interval scale and freed from the particular attitudes of the persons in the sample.

## 6.2 DATA *AGAINST* DRUGS

Responses to the ten statements *Against* drugs are displayed in Table 6.2.   Once again, "strongly agree" has been scored 4 and "strongly disagree" 0, and persons and statements have been ordered by score.   This scoring points the *Against* variable in the opposite direction from the *For* variable.

The first difference we notice between Tables 6.1 and 6.2 is in the frequency with which 0's and 4's occur.   In Table 6.2 many more persons "strongly agree" (4) with these statements opposing drugs, and very few "strongly disagree" (0).   Person *7* at the top of Table 6.2 strongly agreed with all ten statements opposing drug use to make a score of 40.   He is as much against drugs as this *Against* scale can record.   (If the *For* and *Against* attitude scales define the same variable, we expect persons at the top of Table 6.2 who are most against drugs to be least for drugs and so to appear at the bottom of Table 6.1.   We will investigate the extent of agreement between the *For* and *Against* scales presently).

We can examine the columns of the data matrix in Table 6.2 to see if any statements digress from the common variable defined by the majority of statements.   In this case, responses to nine of the ten statements seem in good accord with the person score order.   Responses to Statement *7*, however, may be too orderly to be consistent with the other items.

Not all rows of responses are orderly, however.   While the responses of some persons, like Person *69* with a score of 29 and Person *78* with a score of 18, are in good agreement with the statement score ordering, the responses of others, like Person *34* with a score of 23, bear almost no relationship to the statement score order.   This makes Person *34*'s score of dubious validity as an indicator of his drug attitude and his response pattern useless for statement calibration.

## 6.3 *FOR* DRUGS VARIABLE

Table 6.3 lays out the *For* drugs variable.   Our psychometric method has transformed the person and statement scores into measures and calibrations in logits.   This logit scale is on the left of the table and runs from +1.4 logits to −2.6 logits.   The distribution of persons on the *For* drugs variable appears under the heading "Persons Tested".   Persons toward the top of Table 6.3 are more in favor of drug use than persons toward the bottom.   One person appears to be considerably more in favor of drug use than the others.   From Table 6.1 we see that this is Person *51* who had a score of 33 on the *For* drugs scale.

On the right of Table 6.3 eight of the ten statements *For* drugs are positioned at their calibrations on the attitude variable.   The four statements discussed earlier are circled.   The

| TABLE 6.3 |
| FOR DRUGS VARIABLE |

| ATTITUDE SCALE IN LOGITS | PERSONS TESTED | | EXPECTED PERCENT AGREEMENT WITH STATEMENTS | | | | STATEMENTS DEFINING THE FOR DRUGS VARIABLE |
|---|---|---|---|---|---|---|---|
| | STATS | PLOT | 9 | 2 | 8 | 4 | |
| MORE FOR | | | | | | | STRONG STATEMENTS FOR |
| — | | X | | | | | |
| +1 | | | | | | | |
| — | | | | | | | |
| — | M + 2S | | 97 | 92 | 74 | 42 | ④ All drugs should be made legal and freely available. |
| — | | XX | | | | | 10. People who use drugs are more fun to be with. |
| — | | XX | | | | | 3. I wish I could get hold of some pills to calm me down. |
| — | | | | | | | 1. I see nothing wrong with taking an LSD trip. |
| — | | X | | | | | 7. I would welcome the opportunity to get high on drugs. |
| 0 | | XX | | | | | |
| | M + S | XXXXX | 89 | 78 | 42 | 14 | ⑧ If people use drugs together, their relationships will be improved. |
| — | | XXX | | | | | |
| | | XXXX | | | | | |
| — | | XXXXXX | | | | | |
| | | X | | | | | |
| — | | XXXXXX | | | | | |
| | | XXXXXXX | | | | | |
| — | M | XXXXX | 70 | 48 | 14 | 03 | |
| −1 | | XXXX | | | | | ② People who make drug legislation should really have personal experience with drugs. |
| | | XXX | | | | | |
| — | | XXX | | | | | |
| — | | XX | | | | | ⑨ Smoking marijuana is less harmful than drinking alcohol. |
| | M − S | XXXXXXXXXX | 38 | 17 | 03 | 00 | |
| — | | XXX | | | | | |
| −2 | | XXX | | | | | |
| — | M − 2S | | 09 | 03 | 00 | 00 | |
| | | X | | | | | |
| — | | | | | | | |
| — | | X | | | | | |
| LESS FOR | | | | | | | WEAK STATEMENTS FOR |

content and construct validity of the *For* drugs variable can be judged from the texts and the ordering of these eight statements.

The middle panel of Table 6.3 provides a content interpretation of measures on this variable. This interpretation is couched in terms of expected agreement (choosing either "agree" or "strongly agree") in response to statements like 9, 2, 8 and 4. Persons located at the mean *M* of the sample distribution, for example, are expected to agree or strongly agree with statements as weak as 9, 70 percent of the time. Statement 2 is somewhat stronger. Persons estimated to be at position *M* on the attitude variable are expected to agree with statements like 2 only 48 percent of the time. Statements 8 and 4 are stronger still, and persons at position *M* are expected to agree with statements as strong as these only 14 and 3 percent of the time.

Persons more in favor of drug use are more likely to agree with all four statements.   Persons less in favor of drug use are less likely to agree.   In fact, the two persons at the bottom of Table 6.3, who are estimated to be least in favor of drugs, can be expected to agree with statements like 8 and 4 less than one percent of the time.

Most of the statements favoring drug use are positioned between $M + S$ and $M + 2S$ on the variable.   This means that most of these students found these statements difficult to endorse.   Our capacity to measure the attitudes of these students would be improved if we could compose some new statements favoring drug use with which it was easier to agree.

## 6.4 *AGAINST* DRUGS VARIABLE

Results of the analysis of the ten statements *against* drugs are shown in Table 6.4.   Person measures and statement calibrations are in logits and persons near the top of Table 6.4 are more *against* drugs than persons near the bottom.

Eight of the ten statements *against* drugs are shown on the right of this table.   Statement 4 is easiest to agree with.   A person does not have to be much against drugs to agree that students should be told about the harmful side effects of drugs.   Statement 2 "I'd have to be pretty sick before I'd take any drug, including an aspirin", is at the other extreme.   It is the statement hardest to agree with.   A person has to be strongly against drugs before he agrees with this extreme statement.

The four circled statements can be used to interpret the attitude measures.   A person located at the mean $M$ of the sample distribution can be expected to agree with weak statements like 4 about 96 percent of the time.   He will be less likely to agree with stronger statements like 10 and 3, but can be expected to agree even with statements as strong as 2 about 34 percent of the time.

The person at the bottom of Table 6.4 who is least against drugs (from Table 6.2, this is Person 29, with a score of 9) can be expected to agree with statements like 4 about 55 percent of the time, but will agree with strong statements like 2 less than 2 percent of the time.

## 6.5 RESULTS OF THE ANALYSES

The variable maps in Tables 6.3 and 6.4 were constructed from output produced by the computer program we used to analyze the *For* and *Against* statements.   The statistics for the *For* drugs statements are displayed in Table 6.5a.   These statistics appear twice, rank ordered by scale value and by fit.   The estimated difficulties of the statements appear under the heading Scale Value in each panel of the table.   In the left panel, the statements are ordered so that those easiest to agree with are at the bottom, and those hardest to agree with are at the top.

The right panel orders the statements by fit.   The statement at the top of the Fit column is 6.   In Table 6.1 we noted that responses to this statement were in almost perfect accord with the person score ordering.   As we saw in Chapter 5, the consequence of this near perfect ordering is that the statement does not maintain its position with respect to the other nine statements.   It is one of the easiest statements to agree with for the high scoring persons, but one of the hardest to agree with for the low scorers.   This makes its participation in the

| TABLE 6.4 |
| --- |
| *AGAINST* DRUGS VARIABLE |

| ATTITUDE SCALE IN LOGITS | PERSONS TESTED | | EXPECTED PERCENT AGREEMENT WITH STATEMENTS | | | | STATEMENTS DEFINING THE *AGAINST* DRUGS VARIABLE |
| --- | --- | --- | --- | --- | --- | --- | --- |
| | STATS | PLOT | 4 | 10 | 3 | 2 | |
| MORE *AGAINST* | | | | | | | STRONG STATEMENTS *AGAINST* |
| +3 | | | | | | | |
| — | | X | | | | | |
| — | | | | | | | |
| — | | | | | | | |
| — | | | | | | | |
| | | XXX | | | | | |
| +2 | | | | | | | |
| — | | | | | | | |
| | M + 2S | XX | 99 | 99 | 96 | 90 | |
| — | | | | | | | |
| — | | XXXXX | | | | | |
| — | | XXX | | | | | |
| | M + S | X | 98 | 96 | 89 | 70 | |
| +1 | | XXXXX | | | | | |
| | | XX | | | | | |
| — | | XXXXX | | | | | |
| | | XXX | | | | | ②  I'd have to be pretty sick before I'd take any drug including an aspirin. |
| — | | XX | | | | | |
| | M | X | 96 | 89 | 65 | 34 | |
| — | | XXXXXXX | | | | | 5. Even if my best friend gave me some hash I probably wouldn't use it. |
| | | XXX | | | | | ③  Pep pills are a stupid way of keeping alert. |
| — | | XXXX | | | | | 8. People who regularly take drugs should not be given |
| | | XXXXXX | | | | | positions of responsibility for young children. |
| 0 | | XXX | | | | | 1. Drugs are basically an "unnatural" way to enjoy life. |
| | M − S | XXXXXXXX | 86 | 65 | 28 | 09 | 9. Experimenting with drugs is dangerous if a person |
| — | | XXXXXX | | | | | has any psychological problems. |
| | | | | | | | ⑩  Drugs can cause people to do or say things |
| — | | XX | | | | | they might later regret. |
| — | | | | | | | |
| | M − 2S | | 59 | 28 | 07 | 02 | |
| — | | X | | | | | ④  Students should be told about the harmful |
| −1 | | | | | | | side effects of certain drugs. |
| — | | | | | | | |
| — | | | | | | | |
| LESS *AGAINST* | | | | | | | WEAK STATEMENTS *AGAINST* |

definition of this attitude variable ambiguous.   The statement at the bottom of the Fit column is *2*.   We saw in Table 6.1 that responses to this statement were least in accord with the ordering of the persons by the other statements.

The statistics for the *Against* statements are shown in Table 6.5b.   The scale values in this table were used to position these statements on the variable in Table 6.4.   None of these statements has a large positive fit value.   This is consistent with our earlier observation that none of the statements in Table 6.2 produced an unusual ordering of persons.   Statement 7, however, at the top of the Fit column with a value of $-3.86$, has responses which, as we noted,

### TABLE 6.5a
### *FOR* DRUGS STATISTICS

| SCALE VALUE ORDER | | | | FIT ORDER | | | | | |
|---|---|---|---|---|---|---|---|---|---|
| ITEM NAME | SCALE VALUE | ERROR | FIT t | ITEM NAME | SCALE VALUE | ERROR | WEIGHTED v | s | FIT t |
| 4 | 0.59 | 0.14 | 0.67 | 6 | 0.36 | 0.13 | 0.46 | 0.18 | −3.81 |
| 5 | 0.37 | 0.13 | −1.45 | 7 | 0.09 | 0.12 | 0.65 | 0.16 | −2.43 |
| 10 | 0.37 | 0.13 | −0.97 | 5 | 0.37 | 0.13 | 0.75 | 0.18 | −1.45 |
| 6 | 0.36 | 0.13 | −3.81 | 8 | −0.06 | 0.12 | 0.84 | 0.15 | −1.08 |
| 3 | 0.31 | 0.13 | 0.19 | 10 | 0.37 | 0.13 | 0.83 | 0.18 | −0.97 |
| 1 | 0.23 | 0.13 | 1.70 | 9 | −1.38 | 0.12 | 1.02 | 0.16 | 0.17 |
| 7 | 0.09 | 0.12 | −2.43 | 3 | 0.31 | 0.13 | 1.02 | 0.17 | 0.19 |
| 8 | −0.06 | 0.12 | −1.08 | 4 | 0.59 | 0.14 | 1.12 | 0.20 | 0.67 |
| 2 | −0.87 | 0.11 | 4.83 | 1 | 0.23 | 0.13 | 1.30 | 0.17 | 1.70 |
| 9 | −1.38 | 0.12 | 0.17 | 2 | −0.87 | 0.11 | 1.87 | 0.15 | 4.83 |
| Mean | 0.00 | | −0.22 | | 0.00 | | 0.99 | 0.17 | −0.22 |
| S.D. | 0.62 | | 2.38 | | 0.62 | | 0.40 | 0.02 | 2.38 |

### TABLE 6.5b
### *AGAINST* DRUGS STATISTICS

| SCALE VALUE ORDER | | | | FIT ORDER | | | | | |
|---|---|---|---|---|---|---|---|---|---|
| ITEM NAME | SCALE VALUE | ERROR | FIT t | ITEM NAME | SCALE VALUE | ERROR | WEIGHTED v | s | FIT t |
| 2 | 0.69 | 0.10 | 0.85 | 7 | 0.21 | 0.10 | 0.54 | 0.14 | −3.86 |
| 5 | 0.36 | 0.10 | 0.21 | 8 | 0.20 | 0.10 | 0.76 | 0.14 | −1.81 |
| 7 | 0.21 | 0.10 | −3.86 | 1 | −0.09 | 0.10 | 0.84 | 0.15 | −1.06 |
| 3 | 0.20 | 0.10 | 0.11 | 10 | −0.35 | 0.11 | 0.83 | 0.18 | −0.95 |
| 8 | 0.20 | 0.10 | −1.81 | 6 | −0.12 | 0.11 | 0.90 | 0.15 | −0.61 |
| 1 | −0.09 | 0.10 | −1.06 | 3 | 0.20 | 0.10 | 1.01 | 0.14 | 0.11 |
| 6 | −0.12 | 0.11 | −0.61 | 5 | 0.36 | 0.10 | 1.02 | 0.14 | 0.21 |
| 9 | −0.21 | 0.11 | 0.92 | 2 | 0.69 | 0.10 | 1.13 | 0.15 | 0.85 |
| 10 | −0.35 | 0.11 | −0.95 | 9 | −0.21 | 0.11 | 1.15 | 0.16 | 0.92 |
| 4 | −0.92 | 0.16 | 1.94 | 4 | −0.90 | 0.16 | 1.61 | 0.28 | 1.94 |
| Mean | −0.00 | | −0.43 | | −0.00 | | 0.98 | 0.16 | −0.43 |
| S.D. | 0.42 | | 1.64 | | 0.42 | | 0.29 | 0.04 | 1.64 |

are in an agreement with the score ordering of the persons which may be too good to be useful.   Statement *7* shifts its standing among the other statements from the easiest to agree with for the high scoring persons to one of the hardest to agree with for the low scoring persons.   This shift spoils the participation of Statement *7* in a general definition of an attitude against drugs variable.

The statement scale values from the output in Tables 6.5a and 6.5b were used to position the *For* and *Against* statements along the attitude variable on the right of Tables 6.3 and 6.4.   The person plots on the left of Tables 6.3 and 6.4 were also constructed from computer output showing the distribution of attitude estimates for this sample of students.   Finally, the expected percent agreement levels in the middle of Tables 6.3 and 6.4 were read from the category probability curves shown in Figures 6.5a and 6.5b.

Figure 6.5a shows the way in which the estimated probabilities of strongly disagreeing, disagreeing, having no opinion, agreeing and strongly agreeing with statements on the *For* drugs scale vary with attitude.  There is a different curve in this picture for each response category.  These five curves show that the probability of strongly disagreeing decreases, and the probability of strongly agreeing increases as attitudes become more favorable to drugs.  The probabilities for the middle three categories increase to a maximum and then decrease.

The probability curves in Figure 6.5a are centered on the scale value $d_2 = -.9$ logits of *For* drugs Statement *2*, and so, can be used to read off the estimated probability of any person selecting any one of the five responses to this statement *For* drugs.  To see how this works suppose that we wanted to estimate the probability of a person with a score of 29 on the *For* drugs scale "agreeing" with Statement *2*.  A person with a score of 29 has an attitude estimate *b* of $-.1$ logits.  To find this person's estimated probability of "agreeing" with Statement *2*, we find $-.1$ logits on the horizontal axis and look for the height of the "agree" curve at this point.  As it turns out, the probability at this point is .44, the maximum of the "agree" curve.  Since the "agree" curve is the highest curve at $-.1$ logits, we can also see that "agree" is the most likely response a person with a score of 29 will make to Statement *2*.

We have used the category probability curves in Figure 6.5a to read off the estimated probabilities of selecting each response to Statement *2* for each of five attitude levels $M+2S$, $M+S$, $M$, $M-S$, and $M-2S$.  These estimated probabilities are shown in Table 6.5c.

From Table 6.5c it can be seen that a person at attitude level $M+2S$ has a probability of .37 of agreeing, and a probability of .55 of strongly agreeing with Statement *2*.  This means that a person at this attitude level is expected to either agree or strongly agree with statements like *2* $37+55=92$ percent of the time.  This expectation has been used to provide the content

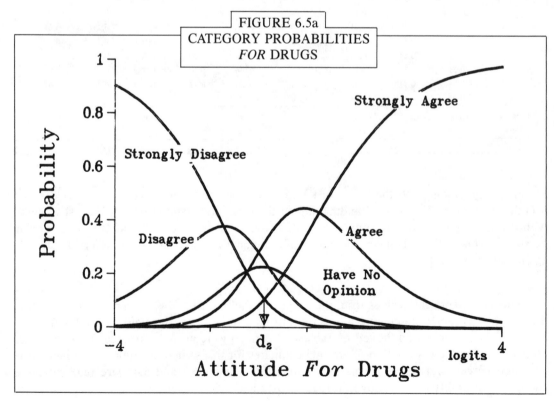

FIGURE 6.5a
CATEGORY PROBABILITIES
*FOR* DRUGS

| | | | TABLE 6.5c | | | | |
|---|---|---|---|---|---|---|---|
| | | | RESPONSE PROBABILITIES AT FIVE ATTITUDE LEVELS (*FOR* DRUGS STATEMENT 2) | | | | |
| ATTITUDE ESTIMATE | | | RESPONSE CATEGORY | | | | |
| LEVEL | SCORE | LOGITS | Strongly Disagree | Disagree | Have No Opinion | Agree | Strongly Agree |
| M + 2S | 34 | .6 | .00 | .01 | .07 | .37 | **(.55)** |
| M + S | 29 | − .1 | .01 | .07 | .14 | **(.44)** | .34 |
| M | 21 | − .8 | .07 | .23 | **(.22)** | .35 | .13 |
| M − S | 13 | − 1.5 | .28 | **(.37)** | .18 | .14 | .03 |
| M − 2S | 3 | − 2.2 | **(.54)** | .34 | .09 | .03 | .00 |

interpretation of the variable shown in Table 6.3.   Similarly, persons at attitude level $M + S$ are expected to either agree or strongly agree with statements like 2 $44 + 34 = 78$ percent of the time; persons at level $M$, $35 + 13 = 48$ percent of the time; persons at $M - S$, $14 + 3 = 17$ percent of the time, and persons at level $M - 2S$, $3 + 0 = 3$ percent of the time.

In Figure 6.5a the response category probability curves are centered on Statement 2's scale value $d_2 = - .9$ logits.   To read off the response probabilities for other statements *For* drugs, we need only move this shared pattern of curves to other positions on the *For* drugs variable.   The response probabilities for Statement 4, for example, are obtained by moving the curves in Figure 6.5a further to the right and centering them on Statement 4's scale value $d_4 = + .6$ logits.

Figure 6.5b shows the pattern of probability curves shared by the *Against* statements.   Here, the *Against* curves are centered on the scale value of Statement 1, and so, can be used to read off the probability of any student making any particular response to Statement 1 on the *Against* scale.   In both Figure 6.5a and Figure 6.5b the "have no opinion" curve is less prominent than the other curves.   This indicates that on these two scales the "have no opinion" response was a relatively unattractive alternative for these students.

## 6.6 COMPARING *FOR* AND *AGAINST* STATEMENTS

The ten statements for drugs and the ten statements against drugs were constructed to define one drug attitude variable.   But by analyzing the *For* and *Against* statements separately, we have obtained two drug attitude estimates for each student.   If the *For* and *Against* statements define the same variable, as intended, persons who make high scores on the *For* statements should make low scores on the *Against* statements.   Whether responses to these two sets of statements can be combined and analyzed simultaneously to obtain a single attitude estimate for a student depends upon whether they are providing similar information about this student's attitude towards drug use.

Measures from the *For* and *Against* scales are plotted against each other in Figure 6.6.   The majority of the points in this plot do lie near the line which identifies "for" as the opposite of "against".   This indicates that the two sets of statements are providing similar information about the attitudes of the majority of students.   It is consistent with our expectation that a

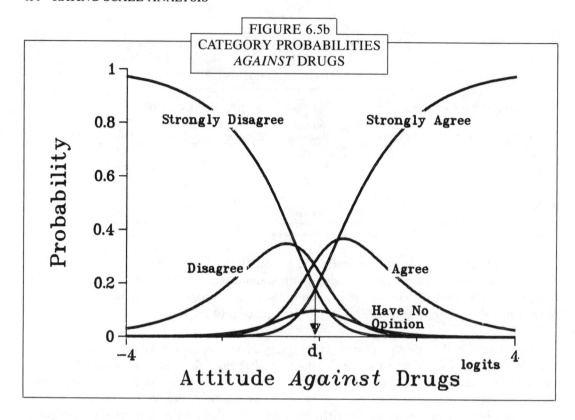

FIGURE 6.5b
CATEGORY PROBABILITIES
*AGAINST* DRUGS

person who is more for drugs should also be less against them.    But several students lie some distance from this "inverse" identity line.    These are students whose responses to the statements on the *For* and *Against* scales are substantially inconsistent.

The student farthest from the identity line is Person *29*.    From the demographic information accompanying her responses we know that she is a thirty-four year old white female.    Her responses place her to the left of all the other students in Figure 6.6 meaning that she is estimated to be the student least *against* drugs.    But her location towards the bottom of Figure 6.6 shows that she is also one of the students least *for* drugs.    This combination of attitudes is puzzling.

Person *29*'s responses to the ten statements on the *For* drugs scale are

$$3\ 0\ 0\ 0\ 0\ 3\ 0\ 0\ 0\ 0$$

where we have ordered the statements by difficulty, with the statement most difficult to agree with on the right.    She strongly disagrees (0) with all statements in favor of drugs except Statements *3* and *9*, and thus makes the low score of 6, implying a strong opposition to drugs.    But her responses to the ten statements *Against* drugs are

$$0\ 0\ 0\ 4\ 4\ 0\ 0\ 0\ 0\ 1$$

where the statements are again ordered by difficulty.    So she also strongly disagrees with most of these statements!

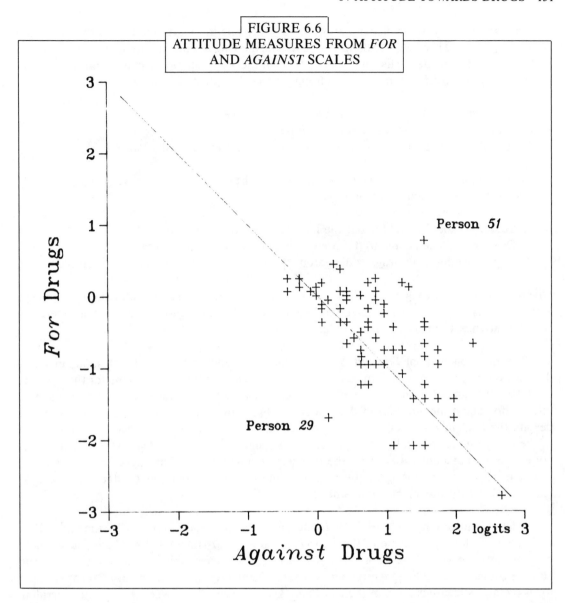

FIGURE 6.6
ATTITUDE MEASURES FROM *FOR*
AND *AGAINST* SCALES

Not only do these two scales give inconsistent information about this woman's attitude, but her responses within each scale show inconsistencies. She disagrees with eight of the ten statements *for* drugs. This would normally indicate a high level of opposition to drug use. However, she agrees with difficult Statement *3* "I wish I could get hold of some pills to calm me down whenever I get up tight". This answer is inconsistent with her other responses and results in a fit statistic for her responses to the *For* scale of +1.50.

Her responses to the statements on the *Against* scale are even more inconsistent and result in a fit of +2.59. In particular, she "strongly agrees" with Statement *6* "As a general rule of thumb, most drugs are dangerous and should be used only with medical authorization". But "strongly disagrees" with Statement *9* "Experimenting with drugs is dangerous if a person has any psychological problems". Person *29*'s negative set against sixteen of these twenty statements interferes with our attempt to measure her attitude towards drugs.

Person *51* is also some distance from the identity line in Figure 6.6, but on the other side of the diagonal. This suggests that Person *51* is displaying a tendency to agree with both *For* and *Against* statements. His high score of 33 on the *For* statements makes him the person estimated to be most for drugs. He "strongly agrees" with statements like

4. All drugs should be made legal and freely available.
10. People who use drugs are more fun to be with.
5. In spite of what the establishment says, the drug scene is really "where it's at".

He is not, however, estimated to be least against drugs. This is because he also "strongly agrees" with *Against* statements like

4. Students should be told about the harmful side effects of certain drugs.
10. Drugs can cause people to do or say things they might later regret.
9. Experimenting with drugs is dangerous if a person has any psychological problems.

Given Person *51*'s strong stance in favor of drugs on the *For* statements, these responses *Against* drugs are surprising. Person *51*'s tendency to agree regardless of content interferes with our attempt to measure his attitude.

The decision to pool *For* and *Against* statements and to analyze them simultaneously depends on the extent to which the use of the response alternatives is the same for the two sets of statements, and also on the extent to which the two sets of statements provide consistent information about the attitudes of the students. From Figures 6.5a and 6.5b we can see that despite the tendency for students to make greater use of the extreme categories and less use of the middle noncommittal category when responding to statements *Against* drugs, the categories are used in similar ways with the two sets of statements. This suggests that it may be useful to reverse the scoring of the response alternatives for one set of statements and to analyze all twenty statements simultaneously.

That simplification will work well enough for most of these seventy-five students. But, as Figure 6.6 shows, for some of them the *For* and *Against* statements produce substantially different attitude estimates. For these persons it is not reasonable to attempt a single drug attitude estimate by pooling their responses to the *For* and *Against* statements. What is called for is a diagnostic comparison of their *For* and *Against* measures to see whether an overriding response set has interfered with their sensitivity to statement content and spoiled our attempt to measure them.

In general we do not recommend pooling *For* and *Against* statements. Whether *For* and *Against* statements should be included in a questionnaire depends on whether the intended attitude variable needs both kinds of statements to be adequately represented, and whether problems with response set such as those illustrated by persons *29* and *51* in Figure 6.6 are expected and need to be detected.

## 6.7 PERSON DIAGNOSIS

Table 6.7 shows the responses of eight students to all of the statements in the *For* and *Against* scales. Responses to the *For* and *Against* statements are shown separately. The statements in each set are ordered by difficulty, with the statements easiest to agree with on the left and the ones hardest to agree with on the right.  The frequency with which each of the response categories was chosen, the person score, attitude measure and standard error associated with this measure are also shown.  These eight persons have been selected because they typify the response patterns encountered in these questionnaire data.

The first person in Table 6.7, Person *74*, is included because his responses are reasonably consistent with the statement difficulty ordering.  Person *74* agreed with the weaker statements and disagreed with the stronger in both the *For* and *Against* scales.  This consistency produces fit statistics in the Person Fit column of $-0.46$ and $-0.86$ which are close to their expected value of 0 and reflect the orderliness of this person's responses.

On the far right of the table is the standardized difference between the *For* and *Against* attitude estimates.  This statistic shows the extent to which Person *74*'s responses to the *For* and *Against* statements point to a single drug attitude estimate.  In this case, the agreement is relatively good.

Person *31*, however, has not made an orderly pattern of responses to either the *For* or the *Against* statements.  The 4 and 3 in his pattern of responses to the *For* statements are inconsistent with the rest of his behavior.  This produces a fit of $+1.95$.  His responses to the *Against* statements are even more disorderly and produce the even more extreme fit value of $+3.05$.  An examination of all twenty responses made by Person *31* shows him to have disagreed and strongly disagreed with thirteen of the statements over both scales. This produces the large standardized difference of $-2.2$.  This person's responses to the attitude questionnaire are erratic and we must conclude that we have failed to measure his attitude towards drugs.

Person *29* was identified in Figure 6.6 as a person who disagreed with a surprising number of statements on *both* scales.  From the frequencies of category choice we see that sixteen of this woman's twenty responses were either "disagree" or "strongly disagree", even though ten of these twenty statements are for drugs, and ten are against.  Her negative response set prevents us from combining her responses to the *For* and *Against* statements to obtain a meaningful attitude estimate.  This is reflected in her very high standardized difference of $-4.4$ and in her negative attitude estimates ($-1.55$ and $-0.77$) on both the *For* and *Against* scales.

Person *65*, identified from his large positive fit statistics ($+2.35$ and $+2.15$), is another interesting case.  The unusual nature of this man's responses can be seen from the frequencies with which he has used the extreme response categories.  On ten of the statements he has strongly disagreed and on ten he has strongly agreed.  We might describe this man as an "extremist".  His responses are reasonably consistent (he is clearly against drugs), but he has used only the extreme response categories to express his attitude, ignoring the middle three.

The next three persons, *67*, *69* and *78*, all have relatively large negative person fit statistics on both the *For* and *Against* scales.  Their standardized differences are small, indicating reasonably good agreement between these two scales.  However, these three persons all show a reluctance to commit themselves to extreme responses.  In this they are the opposite of Person *65* (the "extremist").  Person *67* is particularly noncommittal.  He uses the "have no opinion" response six times.  Persons *69* and *78* have resisted the "have no opinion" response,

## TABLE 6.7
### DIAGNOSING RESPONSE PATTERNS

| PERSON | STATEMENTS (Ordered by Difficulty) FOR | AGAINST | FREQUENCIES OF CATEGORY CHOICE 0 | 1 | 2 | 3 | 4 | PERSON SCORE F | A | PERSON MEASURE F | A | MEASURE ERROR F | A | PERSON FIT F | A | COMPARISONS OF FOR AND AGAINST DIFF* | ERROR | STZD DIFF |
|---|---|---|---|---|---|---|---|---|---|---|---|---|---|---|---|---|---|---|
| 74 | 3313302011 | 3321130000 | 6 | 5 | 2 | 7 | 0 | 17 | 13 | −.24 | −.44 | .29 | .27 | −.46 | −.86 | −.68 | .40 | −1.7 |
| 31 | 2111400030 | 0104441300 | 8 | 5 | 1 | 2 | 4 | 12 | 17 | −.73 | −.18 | .33 | .25 | 1.95 | 3.05 | −.91 | .41 | −2.2 |
| 29 | 3000030000 | 0004400001 | 15 | 1 | 0 | 2 | 2 | 6 | 9 | −1.55 | −.77 | .42 | .31 | 1.50 | 2.59 | −2.32 | .52 | −4.4 |
| 65 | 0400000000 | 4440444444 | 10 | 0 | 0 | 0 | 10 | 4 | 36 | −1.97 | 1.44 | .50 | .47 | 2.35 | 2.15 | −.53 | .69 | −.8 |
| 67 | 442323120 | 3223311111 | 1 | 6 | 6 | 5 | 2 | 23 | 18 | .25 | −.12 | .29 | .25 | −1.67 | −3.69 | .13 | .38 | .3 |
| 69 | 3111111110 | 4333333331 | 1 | 9 | 0 | 9 | 1 | 11 | 29 | −.84 | .59 | .34 | .28 | −2.21 | −3.32 | −.25 | .44 | −.6 |
| 78 | 3331311131 | 3331311111 | 0 | 11 | 0 | 9 | 0 | 20 | 18 | .01 | −.12 | .29 | .25 | −1.45 | −3.29 | −.11 | .38 | −.3 |
| 51 | 4444132344 | 4443011100 | 3 | 4 | 1 | 3 | 9 | 33 | 18 | 1.32 | −.12 | .40 | .25 | .93 | −.37 | 1.20 | .47 | 2.5 |

* DIFF = F − (−A) = F + A where (−A) orients A to correlate positively with F.

but they have been reluctant to say that they feel strongly about any of these statements.    We might describe these three persons as "conservatives".

Finally, Table 6.7 gives the responses of the other person identified in Figure 6.6.    Person *51*'s set to "agree" with the statements whatever their content has produced a standardized difference of +2.5.    Twelve of his twenty responses were either "agree" or "strongly agree".

## 6.8 DISCUSSION

This drug attitude questionnaire differs from the science questionnaire in that five rather than three response alternatives were provided, and both positively and negatively worded statements about drugs were used.

The practice of including both *For* and *Against* statements in attitude questionnaires stems from a concern over individual differences in response style.    The observation that not all persons use response alternatives in the same way was first made in psychophysics experiments.    Angell (1907), for example, reported differences in the way respondents used the alternatives *Clearly Louder, Louder, Like, Softer, Clearly Softer* when comparing sounds.

> Some individuals are more prone to express judgments of *Like* than others, and this difference corresponds to the difference between deliberate and impulsive temperaments.    (Angell 1907, *254*)

Similar tendencies, including the tendency for some persons to respond "True" rather than "False" and "Agree" rather than "Disagree", were observed in educational achievement tests and attitude questionnaires.    This led Cronbach (1946, 1950) to recommend "reducing the five-choice pattern of the Likert-type scale to a two-choice judgment", and

> In view of the overwhelming evidence that many common item forms invite response sets, and in view of the probability that these sets interfere with accurate measurement, it will rarely be wise to build new tests around item forms such as "Agree—Undecided—Disagree". (Cronbach 1950, *29*)

It has become popular in attitude measurement to construct questionnaires with equal numbers of positively and negatively worded statements.    This is done in the hope that tendencies to favor "Agree" or "Disagree" will "balance out" so that the effects on attitude measures of differences in response style will be eliminated.    The behavior studied in this chapter shows that this balancing does not work.    It is necessary to establish that responses to *For* and *Against* statements each provide consistent information about a person's attitude before combining them to obtain a single attitude measure for that person.    Rather than using *For* and *Against* statements to "balance out" differences in response style, we use them to *expose* persons with unusual response tendencies.    When persons show such tendencies it may be impossible to combine their responses to these two types of statements to obtain one interpretable attitude measure for them.

Individual differences in response style can interfere with our efforts to infer a single position for each person on one line of increasing opposition to drugs.    Nevertheless, we do not recommend reducing this five-point Likert scale to a two-choice Disagree/Agree format.   The increased precision of measurement made possible by the five-point format justifies its use in this questionnaire.   The opportunity to distinguish between Person *65* who used only the most extreme alternatives and Person *78* who did not express a strong opinion on any statement is an additional reason to prefer the five-point format over two alternatives.

# 7  FEAR OF CRIME

So far we have used only one of the five measurement models in Chapter 3 to construct a "Liking-for-Science" variable (Chapters 4 and 5) and an "Attitude-to-Drugs" variable (Chapter 6).  In this chapter we analyze responses to a third attitude questionnaire developed to measure college students' fear of neighborhood crime.  We analyze these data twice, first with the Rating Scale model and then with the Partial Credit model.  This gives us an opportunity to compare these two approaches to the analysis of ordered category data.

## 7.1  A FEAR OF CRIME VARIABLE

The Evaluation Institute at the Westinghouse National Issues Center in Evanston, Illinois developed a nine-item questionnaire to measure college students' fear of crime.*  The nine items are shown in Figure 7.1.  Three items ask students how *concerned* they are about being burgled, robbed or harmed.  Another three ask students how *likely* they think it is that they will be victims of these crimes, and the remaining three ask students how *afraid* they are of these crimes.

There are two bases on which to anticipate the difficulty order of these nine items.  Certainly the threat of being HARMED is more frightening than the threat of being ROBBED, and it would seem likely that being robbed is in turn more frightening than being BURGLED.  Among the three states of fear, believing a crime is *likely* would seem to represent a higher state of fear than being *afraid*, and being afraid certainly represents a higher state of fear than merely being *concerned*.  It is more difficult, however, to anticipate how these three crimes and these three states of fear will combine to define a fear-of-crime variable.  Which represents a greater fear of crime—being *concerned* about being harmed, or believing that you are *likely* to be burgled?

As in the Liking-for-Science and Attitude-to-Drugs scales, a fixed set of response alternatives ("Not at All", "Not Too", "Pretty" and "Very") is used with every item in the questionnaire.  A typical item is

8. How *afraid* are you that someone will BREAK INTO your house or apartment when no one is home?

> Very ................... 3
> Pretty ................. 2
> Not too ............... 1
> Not at All ............. 0

A maximum score of $9 \times 3 = 27$ is made for responding "Very" to all nine items on the questionnaire, and a minimum score of $9 \times 0 = 0$, for responding "Not at All" to every item.  The data come from 202 Chicago college students.

* We are grateful to Terry Baumer for the opportunity to study these data.

| FIGURE 7.1 |
| A FEAR OF CRIME QUESTIONNAIRE |

*CR* 1. When you are walking alone in your neighborhood at night, how *concerned* are you that someone will TAKE SOMETHING from you by force or threat?

*CB* 2. How *concerned* are you that someone will BREAK INTO your house or apartment when no one is at home?

*CH* 3. When you are walking alone in your neighborhood at night, how *concerned* are you that someone will HARM YOU?

*LR* 4. When you are walking alone in your neighborhood at night, how *likely* is it that someone will TAKE SOMETHING from you on the street by force or threat?

*LH* 5. When you are walking alone in your neighborhood at night, how *likely* is it that someone will HARM YOU on the street?

*LB* 6. During the course of a year, how *likely* is it that someone will BREAK INTO your house or apartment when no one is home?

*AR* 7. When you are walking alone in your neighborhood at night, how *afraid* are you that someone will TAKE SOMETHING from you by force or threat?

*AB* 8. How *afraid* are you that someone will BREAK INTO your house or apartment when no one is home?

*AH* 9. When you are walking alone in your neighborhood at night, how *afraid* are you that someone will HARM YOU?

## 7.2  RESULTS OF RATING SCALE ANALYSIS

Table 7.2 shows the *UCON* item statistics from the Rating Scale analysis.  The items appear twice in this table, in scale value order and fit order.  The item which defines the highest level of fear on this questionnaire, because it has the most positive scale value estimate, is Item *5* "When you are walking alone in your neighborhood at night, how *likely* is it that someone will HARM YOU on the street?".  This implies that only a student with a relatively high fear of crime will believe that he is *likely* to be harmed.  The item which defines the lowest level of fear on this questionnaire, because it has the most negative scale value estimate, is Item *2* "How *concerned* are you that someone will BREAK INTO your house or apartment when no one is at home?"  This implies that a student does not have to be much afraid of crime to be *concerned* about being burgled.

The item fit statistics in Table 7.2 range from $-3.83$ for Item *4* to $+2.64$ for Item *2*.  Three items, *4*, *5* and *7*, have rather large negative misfit statistics.  The two items with the most positive misfit statistics, Items *6* and *2*, are both concerned with burglary.  The mean ($-.52$) and standard deviation ($2.37$) of these nine fit values are somewhat off their expected values of zero and one.  Whether this much departure from expectation has any practical implications requires further investigation.

Even though the fit of these items to the Rating Scale model may not seem particularly good, the item separation and reliability indices show that the nine items are reasonably well separated in difficulty, and an examination of their difficulty order shows them to be sensibly ordered, with the three *concerned* items defining the lowest levels of fear, and the three *likely* items defining the highest.  This is one of the orders we anticipated, and the rating scale

## TABLE 7.2
## ITEM STATISTICS FROM RATING SCALE ANALYSIS

| SCALE VALUE ORDER | | | | FIT ORDER | | | | | |
|---|---|---|---|---|---|---|---|---|---|
| ITEM NAME | SCALE VALUE | ERROR | FIT $t_i$ | ITEM NAME | SCALE VALUE | ERROR | WEIGHTED $v_i$ | $s_i$ | FIT $t_i$ |
| LH 5 | 0.79 | 0.17 | −3.64 | LR 4 | 0.62 | 0.17 | 0.62 | 0.12 | −3.83 |
| LR 4 | 0.62 | 0.17 | −3.83 | LH 5 | 0.79 | 0.17 | 0.63 | 0.12 | −3.64 |
| LB 6 | 0.31 | 0.16 | 1.94 | AR 7 | 0.28 | 0.16 | 0.73 | 0.11 | −2.64 |
| AR 7 | 0.28 | 0.16 | −2.64 | AH 9 | 0.19 | 0.16 | 0.92 | 0.11 | −0.70 |
| AH 9 | 0.19 | 0.16 | −0.70 | AB 8 | −0.15 | 0.16 | 1.01 | 0.11 | 0.09 |
| AB 8 | −0.15 | 0.16 | 0.09 | CR 1 | −0.43 | 0.15 | 1.04 | 0.11 | 0.45 |
| CR 1 | −0.43 | 0.15 | 0.45 | CH 3 | −0.51 | 0.15 | 1.11 | 0.11 | 1.01 |
| CH 3 | −0.51 | 0.15 | 1.01 | LB 6 | 0.31 | 0.16 | 1.23 | 0.11 | 1.94 |
| CB 2 | −1.10 | 0.15 | 2.64 | CB 2 | −1.10 | 0.15 | 1.29 | 0.10 | 2.64 |
| Mean | 0.00 | 0.16 | −0.52 | | | | 0.95 | 0.11 | −0.52 |
| S.D. | 0.60 | 0.01 | 2.37 | | | | 0.25 | 0.00 | 2.37 |

Adjusted Test S.D. = .58    Error RMS = .17    Item Separation = .58/.17 = 3.4
Sample Reliability of Item Separation = $3.4^2/(1+3.4^2)$ = .92
Sample Size = 201    Mean = −1.46    Unadjusted S.D. = 2.30
Adjusted Sample S.D. = 2.16    Error RMS = .80    Person Separation = 2.16/.80 = 2.7
Test Reliability of Person Separation = $2.7^2/(1+2.7^2)$ = .88

## FIGURE 7.2a
## RESPONSE CATEGORY PROBABILITY CURVES FOR THE FEAR-OF-CRIME QUESTIONNAIRE

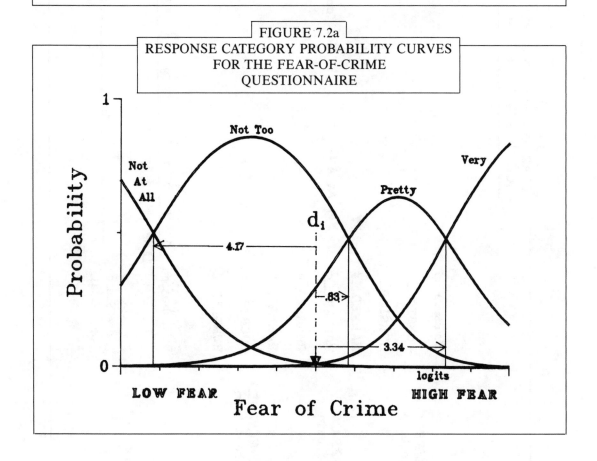

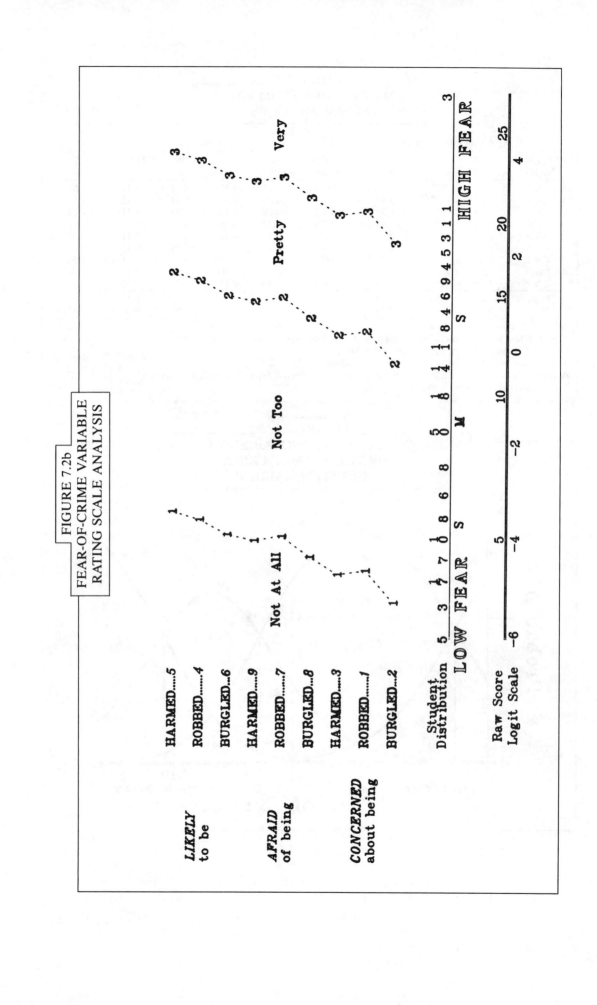

FIGURE 7.2b
FEAR-OF-CRIME VARIABLE
RATING SCALE ANALYSIS

analysis shows that this "state of fear" order dominates these nine items.  Our second order of crimes, from burgled through robbed to harmed is born out only when combined with the most serious state of fear, *likely*.  This sensible arrangement of the items suggests that in spite of the somewhat disappointing fit values, we may be able to build a useful fear-of-crime variable from these data and encourages us to continue.

The rating scale analysis also provides three "threshold" estimates which define four category probability curves for these fear-of-crime items.  These curves, displayed in Figure 7.2a, show that only students with attitude estimates more than 4.17 logits below the scale value $d_i$ of an item are likely to respond "Not at All" to that item.  For students with estimates between $d_i - 4.17$ and $d_i + .83$ the most probable response is "Not Too"; for students with estimates between $d_i + .83$ and $d_i + 3.34$, the most probable response is "Pretty", and only students estimated to be more than 3.34 logits above the scale value of an item are likely to respond "Very" to that item.

The Rating Scale analysis of these fear-of-crime data is summarized in Figure 7.2b.  The variable is laid out at the bottom of Figure 7.2b running from low fear on the left to high fear on the right.  It is marked off in logits and in the corresponding raw scores.

The student distribution at the bottom of Figure 7.2b shows that student estimates range from $-6.12$ logits (raw score = 1) for the five students on the far left to $+5.31$ logits (raw score = 26) for the three students on the far right.  When the number of students in a score group exceeds nine, the count is printed vertically (e.g., there are seventeen students with an estimate of $-4.81$ logits, ten with an estimate of $-3.93$ logits).

The body of Figure 7.2b shows the difficulties of the three steps from "Not at All" to "Very" for each item.  These step estimates have been calculated from the scale value estimates in Table 7.2 and the threshold estimates $h_1 = -4.17$, $h_2 = +.83$ and $h_3 = +3.34$ in Figure 7.2a.  The first step in each item is from "Not at All" to "Not Too".  The estimated difficulty of this step, $d_{i1} = d_i + h_1 = d_i - 4.17$ is labelled '1'.  Students to the right of $d_{i1}$ are more likely to respond "Not Too" than "Not at All" to item $i$.  The second step up this ladder of increasing fear is from "Not Too" to "Pretty".  The estimated difficulty of this second step, $d_{i2} = d_i + h_2 = d_i + .83$, is labelled '2'.  Students to the right of $d_{i2}$ are more likely to respond "Pretty" than "Not Too" to item $i$.  Finally, the third step from "Pretty" to "Very", with estimated difficulty $d_{i3} = d_i + h_3 = d_i + 3.34$, is labelled '3'.  Students to the right of $d_{i3}$ are more likely to respond "Very" than "Pretty" to item $i$.  To facilitate the integration of our analysis with our prior expectations we show these nine items in the *concerned-afraid-likely* and BURGLED-ROBBED-HARMED orders which we anticipated.

Figure 7.2b can be used to read off any student's most probable response to any of these nine items, and so, provides a detailed interpretation for every score on this questionnaire.  The seven students with an estimate of $-4.35$ logits (raw score = 4), for example, are expected to respond "Not at All" to the six questions at the top of Figure 7.2b which ask how *likely* they believe it is that they will be robbed, harmed or burgled, and how *afraid* they are of these crimes.  But because they are to the right of the first step in Items *1*, *3* and *2*, we expect them to respond "Not Too" to these three questions which ask how *concerned* they are about being victims of these crimes.  Similarly, the eight students with an estimate of $+.49$ logits (raw score = 13) are expected to respond "Not Too" to the six questions at the top of Figure 7.2b.  But because they are to the right of the second step in Items *1*, *3* and *2*, we expect them to respond "Pretty" to the three questions which ask how *concerned* they are about being burgled, robbed or harmed.

The repeated pattern in Figure 7.2b exposes the basic structure of a rating scale analysis. Under the Rating Scale model, the pattern of step difficulties (labelled '1', '2' and '3' in Figure 7.2b) is dictated by the threshold estimates $h_1$, $h_2$ and $h_3$ estimated *once* for all nine items (Figure 7.2a). The only modelled difference between items is the difference in location $d_i$ of this fixed pattern.

In this analysis we have placed each item's location $d_i$ at the mean of its three step estimates. This follows from imposing the constraint $h. = 0$ on the three threshold estimates. We could, however, have chosen some other constraint on $h_1$, $h_2$ and $h_3$. The alternative constraint $h_1 = 0$, for example, would have placed $d_i$ at the first step '1' in each item. Because the choice of the necessary constraint on the threshold estimates, and hence the definition of item "location" $d_i$, is arbitrary, and because this choice does not influence the item step estimates or the interpretation of the variable, there is no point in showing the item scale values $d_i$ of Table 7.2 in Figure 7.2b.

## 7.3 RESULTS OF PARTIAL CREDIT ANALYSIS

The Partial Credit analysis of these fear-of-crime data differs from the Rating Scale analysis only in that it estimates the steps in each item separately without requiring that the pattern of step difficulties be the same for each item. These estimates $d_{i1}$, $d_{i2}$ and $d_{i3}$, their standard errors $s_{i1}$, $s_{i2}$ and $s_{i3}$, and the fit of each item to the Partial Credit model are shown in Table 7.3a.

TABLE 7.3a

ITEM STATISTICS FROM PARTIAL CREDIT ANALYSIS

| ITEM NAME | ITEM STEP ESTIMATES | | | STANDARD ERRORS | | | ITEM FIT | | |
|---|---|---|---|---|---|---|---|---|---|
| | $d_{i1}$ | $d_{i2}$ | $d_{i3}$ | $s_{i1}$ | $s_{i2}$ | $s_{i3}$ | $v_i$ | $s_i$ | $t_i$ |
| LH 5 | −3.41 | 1.57 | 5.16 | .23 | .27 | .96 | 0.66 | .11 | −3.54 |
| LR 4 | −3.65 | 1.52 | 4.43 | .23 | .27 | .86 | 0.65 | .11 | −3.49 |
| LB 6 | −4.12 | 1.44 | 3.44 | .25 | .27 | .65 | 1.26 | .12 | 2.11 |
| AH 9 | −3.53 | 0.67 | 3.09 | .23 | .24 | .52 | 0.78 | .11 | −2.12 |
| AR 7 | −3.69 | 1.05 | 2.98 | .24 | .25 | .52 | 0.65 | .11 | −3.49 |
| AB 8 | −4.52 | 0.85 | 3.04 | .27 | .24 | .52 | 1.03 | .11 | 0.29 |
| CH 3 | −4.02 | −0.08 | 2.54 | .25 | .21 | .40 | 0.96 | .10 | −0.38 |
| CR 1 | −3.80 | −0.04 | 2.40 | .24 | .22 | .39 | 0.82 | .10 | −1.86 |
| CB 2 | −5.49 | −0.31 | 2.45 | .33 | .21 | .38 | 1.32 | .11 | 2.84 |
| Mean | | 0.00 | | | 0.36 | | 0.90 | .11 | −1.07 |
| S.D. | | 3.18 | | | 0.20 | | 0.26 | .01 | 2.43 |

Adjusted Test S.D. = 3.15    Error RMS = .42    Step Separation = 3.15/.42 = 7.6
Sample Reliability of Step Separation = $7.6^2/(1 + 7.6^2)$ = .98
Sample Size = 201    Mean = −1.47    Unadjusted S.D. = 2.24
Adjusted Sample S.D. = 2.10    Error RMS = .78    Person Separation = 2.10/.78 = 2.7
Test Reliability of Person Separation = $2.7^2/(1 + 2.7^2)$ = .88

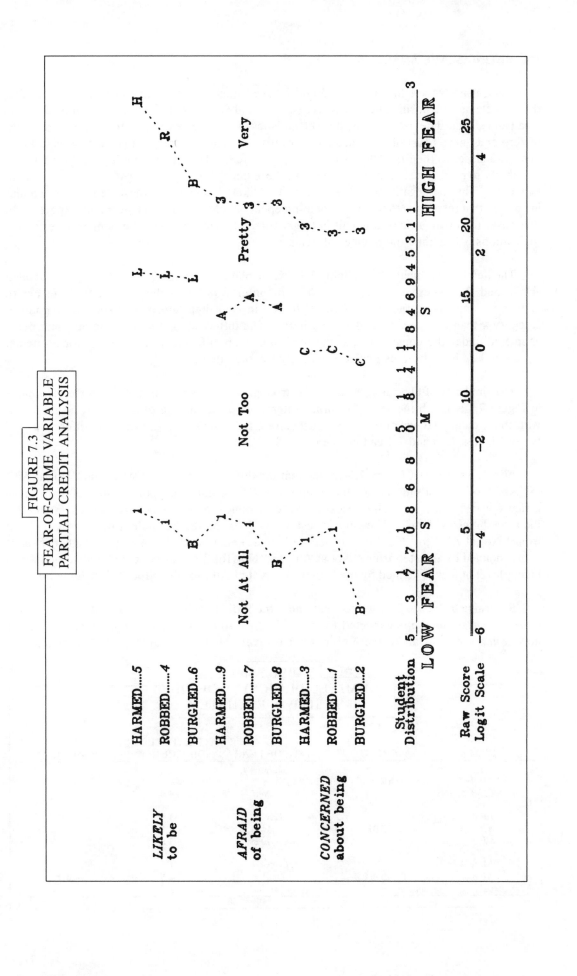

FIGURE 7.3
FEAR-OF-CRIME VARIABLE
PARTIAL CREDIT ANALYSIS

Once again we see that Items *4, 5* and *7* have rather large negative fit statistics, and that the three items with positive fit statistics (Items *2, 6* and *8*) all refer to fear of being burgled.   The mean and standard deviation of the item fit statistics are still somewhat off their expected values of zero and one.   Most of the items have negative fit values, implying that responses to these items are closer to their modelled values than expected.   This might be mistaken to mean that our ability to predict a student's responses to these items from his total test score is better than expected.   But the negative fit statistics are more likely to mean that these items are so similar in content that responses to them are not as independent of each other as the model expects.   In that case, the error of measurement is *larger* than expected because the number of effective replications is less than the number of items.

The item step estimates from Table 7.3a are displayed in Figure 7.3 where they are labelled '1', '2' and '3'.   These estimates have the same interpretation as the step estimates in Figure 7.2b, i.e., students to the right of the $k$'th step in each item are more likely to respond in category $k$ than in category $k-1$ to that item.   The difference is that now, rather than being estimated under the constraint that the pattern of step difficulties be the *same* for all items, $d_{i1}$, $d_{i2}$ and $d_{i3}$ have been estimated separately for each item.

The similarity of Figures 7.2b and 7.3 is striking.   The fact that the pattern of step estimates in Figure 7.3 is much the same for all nine items supports the use of the Rating Scale model with these data.   However, on closer inspection, three small but informative differences between Figures 7.2b and 7.3 can be seen.

First, on the left of Figure 7.3 we see that the difficulty of the first step from "Not at All" to "Not Too" depends more upon the seriousness of the crime than upon the state of fear.   This is laid out in Table 7.3b.   The easiest items to respond "Not Too" to are Items *2, 8* and *6*— the three burglary items.   The very lowest level of fear on this variable is defined by the step from "Not at All" to "Not Too" *concerned* about being burgled.   A slightly higher level of fear is defined by the step from "Not at All" to "Not Too" *afraid* of being burgled, and a still higher level of fear is defined by the step from "Not at All" to "Not Too" *likely* to be burgled.

Returning to Figure 7.2b we see that under the Rating Scale analysis, a student who scores 4 on this questionnaire is expected to respond "Not Too" to only the three items which ask how *concerned* he is about these crimes.   However, when the item steps are estimated sep-

TABLE 7.3b

## ESTIMATED DIFFICULTY OF THE FIRST STEP IN EACH ITEM

| ITEM | CRIME | STATE OF FEAR | FIRST STEP DIFFICULTY | CRIME MEAN |
|------|-------|---------------|-----------------------|------------|
| LH 5 | | *likely* | −3.4 | |
| AH 9 | HARMED | *afraid* | −3.5 | −3.7 |
| CH 3 | | *concerned* | −4.0 | |
| LR 4 | | *likely* | −3.6 | |
| AR 7 | ROBBED | *afraid* | −3.7 | −3.7 |
| CR 1 | | *concerned* | −3.8 | |
| LB 6 | | *likely* | −4.1 | |
| AB 8 | BURGLED | *afraid* | −4.5 | −4.7 |
| CB 2 | | *concerned* | −5.5 | |

arately, as in Figure 7.3, a student who scores 4 is expected to respond "Not Too" to the three burglary items.   By removing the Rating Scale constraint we have detected a fine structure to this fear-of-crime variable which was smoothed out by the Rating Scale analysis.   At the low end of the variable the dominance of logical orders is reversed.   Here it is the most prevalent and least serious crime *burglary* which takes precedence over state of fear.

Figure 7.3 also shows that the difficulty of the second step from "Not Too" to "Pretty" in each of these items is determined not so much by the seriousness of the crime as by the state of fear described in the item (i.e., *concerned*, *afraid* or *likely*).   These students found it easier to say that they were "Pretty" *concerned* than to say that they were "Pretty" *afraid*, or that the crime was "Pretty" *likely*, regardless of the crime.

Finally, it is the third steps in *likely* Items 6, 4 and 5 which define the high end of this variable.   To take these steps, a student must believe that he is "Very" *likely* to be burgled, robbed and even harmed.   At the most fearful end of the variable it is again the seriousness of the crime which shapes the variable rather than the state of fear.

The Partial Credit analysis brings out a subtle but meaningful interaction between seriousness of crime and state of fear.   At the extremes of high and low fear, it is the seriousness of the crime which dominates.   But in the middle region of the variable, where most of these students are estimated to be, it is the state of fear which rules.

## 7.4   COMPARING SCALE AND CREDIT ANALYSES

### 7.4.1   Comparing Step Estimates

We have used both the Rating Scale and Partial Credit models to analyze the fear-of-crime data.   To compare these analyses, we display the differences between the SCALE and CREDIT item step estimates in Figure 7.4a.   The arrows show the displacement of CREDIT step estimates in Figure 7.3 from the corresponding SCALE estimates in Figure 7.2b.

For some items, like burglary Items 2, 6 and 8, the match between the SCALE and CREDIT step estimates is very good.   For others, like Items 1, 3 and 9, the match is not as good.   The largest difference between the SCALE and CREDIT estimates in Figure 7.4a is for the third step in Item 5.   The SCALE estimate for this step is $d_5 + h_3 = .79 + 3.34 = 4.13$ logits.   The CREDIT estimate is $d_{53} = 5.16$ logits, making the difference $5.16 - 4.13 = 1.03$ logits.   This step, however, is very difficult for these students to take, and so, has a large CREDIT calibration error ($s_{53} = 0.96$ logits).   When considered in terms of its estimation error, this difference represents only $1.03/.96 = 1.07$ standard error units.

Each of the differences shown in Figure 7.4a has been divided by the corresponding CREDIT calibration error for that step.   The resulting standardized differences are shown in Table 7.4a.   These standardized differences have been accumulated to give a statistic which summarizes the match of the SCALE step estimates for each item to the CREDIT estimates for that item.   If we use SCALE estimates $d_i$ and $h_j$ to define the CREDIT parameters $\delta_{ij} = d_i + h_j$, then the statistic on the right of Table 7.4a should have a mean near zero and a standard deviation near one.   Table 7.4b shows how this statistic is calculated.

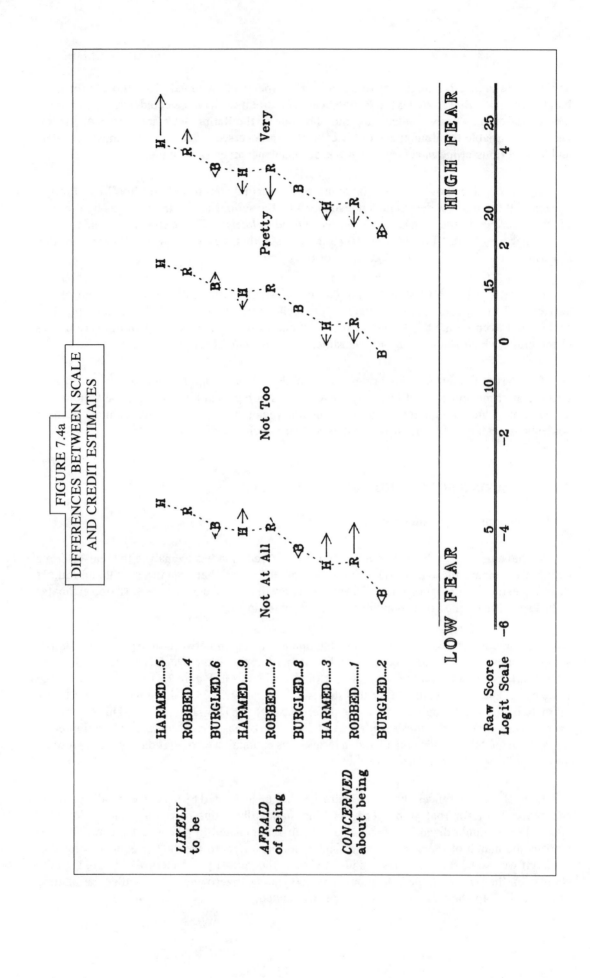

FIGURE 7.4a
DIFFERENCES BETWEEN SCALE
AND CREDIT ESTIMATES

| | TABLE 7.4a | | | |
| :---: | :---: | :---: | :---: | :---: |
| | EXAMINING THE MATCH BETWEEN SCALE AND CREDIT STEP ESTIMATES | | | |

| ITEM NAME | STANDARDIZED DIFFERENCES | | | MATCH |
| :---: | :---: | :---: | :---: | :---: |
| | $z_{i1}$ | $z_{i2}$ | $z_{i3}$ | $t$ |
| LH 5 | −.13 | −.19 | 1.07 | −.69 |
| LR 4 | −.41 | .27 | .55 | −1.32 |
| LB 6 | −1.01 | 1.14 | −.31 | .03 |
| AH 9 | 1.93 | −1.47 | −.84 | 1.37 |
| AR 7 | .84 | −.24 | −1.23 | −.05 |
| AB 8 | −.75 | .71 | −.29 | −.73 |
| CH 3 | 2.66 | −1.85 | −.71 | 2.27 |
| CR 1 | 3.27 | −2.04 | −1.33 | 3.10 |
| CB 2 | −.68 | −.22 | .55 | −1.03 |
| Mean | | −0.03 | | .33 |
| S.D. | | 1.56 | | 1.27 |

Formulation of $z$ and $t$ explained in Table 7.4b

The statistics in Table 7.4a confirm what we have already noted in our comparison of Figures 7.2b and 7.3—the Rating Scale and Partial Credit analyses of these data produce very similar item estimates. The items for which the SCALE-CREDIT match is poorest are Items *1, 3* and *9*. The dominance of state of fear over seriousness of crime which characterizes the SCALE analysis, however, is found to hold only for the central step from "Not Too" to "Pretty". The CREDIT analysis brings out that at the lowest and highest levels of fear, the seriousness of the crime counts more than the state of fear.

### 7.4.2  Comparing Item Fit Statistics

The SCALE analysis provides three step estimates $d_i + h_1$, $d_i + h_2$ and $d_i + h_3$ for each item on this fear-of-crime questionnaire. When these item estimates and a student estimate are substituted in the model, an expected score $E_{ni} = \sum_{k=0}^{m} kP_{nik}$ can be estimated for each of the nine items for each of the 202 students. The comparison of each student's observed score $x_{ni}$ with this estimate of their expected score $E_{ni}$ forms the basis for testing the fit of an item (or student) to the Rating Scale model. The item fit statistics in Table 7.2 show that these nine items do not fit the Rating Scale model as well we might like. Three items (*5, 4* and *7*) have large negative fit statistics, and Item *2* has a large positive fit statistic.

The fit of an item to the Partial Credit model can be similarly evaluated by substituting the step estimates $d_{i1}$, $d_{i2}$ and $d_{i3}$ into the model and re-estimating each student's expected score accordingly. Table 7.3a shows the fit of the nine items to the Partial Credit model.

Removing the Rating Scale constraint on the item step estimates and estimating each of the twenty-seven item steps separately reduces the squared differences between observations $x_{ni}$ and estimated expectations $E_{ni}$. For some items the difference between SCALE and CREDIT step estimates is so small that there is very little difference between their SCALE and CREDIT fit statistics. Other items like *1, 3* and *9* which have somewhat different step estimates under these two analyses have lower fit mean squares for the CREDIT analysis.

**TABLE 7.4b**

**SCALE-CREDIT MATCH**

Step parameters "defined" by SCALE estimates $\qquad$ $\delta_{ij} \equiv d_i + h_j$

CREDIT Step Estimate $\qquad d_{ij} \qquad\qquad$ Error $s_{ij}$

Difference $\qquad d_{ij} - \delta_{ij}$

Standardized Difference $\qquad z_{ij} = (d_{ij} - \delta_{ij}) \,/\, s_{ij}$

Mean Square Match $\qquad v_i = \sum_{j=1}^{m} z_{ij}^2 \,/\, m \qquad\qquad$ df $= m$

Standardized Match $\qquad t_i = (v_i^{1/3} - 1)\, 3/q \; + \; q/3 \qquad q = \sqrt{2/m}$

Item 5

$$\delta_{51} \equiv .79 - 4.17 = -3.38$$
$$\delta_{52} \equiv .79 + 0.83 = +1.62$$
$$\delta_{53} \equiv .79 + 3.34 = +4.13$$

$$d_{51} = -3.41 \qquad s_{51} = .23$$
$$d_{52} = \;\;\; 1.57 \qquad s_{52} = .27$$
$$d_{53} = \;\;\; 5.16 \qquad s_{53} = .96$$

$$z_{51} = (-3.41 + 3.38) \,/\, .23 = -.13$$
$$z_{52} = \;\;\;(1.57 - 1.62) \,/\, .27 = -.19$$
$$z_{53} = \;\;\;(5.16 - 4.13) \,/\, .96 = \;\;1.07$$

$$v_5 \;=\; \frac{(-.13)^2 + (-.19)^2 + (1.07)^2}{3} \;=\; \frac{1.20}{3} \;=\; .40$$

$$t_5 \;=\; (.40^{1/3} - 1)3.67 \; + \; .27 \;=\; -.69 \qquad q = \sqrt{2/3} = .82$$

The item fit statistics from the SCALE and CREDIT analyses are plotted against each other in Figure 7.4b. The five items along the identity line have very similar SCALE and CREDIT step estimates and hence very similar fit statistics under the two analyses. Items 1, 3, 9 and possibly 7, on the other hand, have rather different fit statistics under the SCALE and CREDIT analyses, and so, lie some distance from the identity line in Figure 7.4b. For these items the fit mean squares are substantially reduced, making their fit-t's more negative when the Rating Scale constraint is removed and the steps in these items are estimated directly.

An interesting consequence of this change in the fit of Items 1, 3 and 9 is the separation of the burglary items 2, 6 and 8 from the assault and robbery items. When the item steps are estimated individually, the fit statistics for the three burglary items are positive, and the fit statistics for the six assault and robbery items are negative. This suggests that the burglary items may not define quite the same fear-of-crime variable as the other six items.

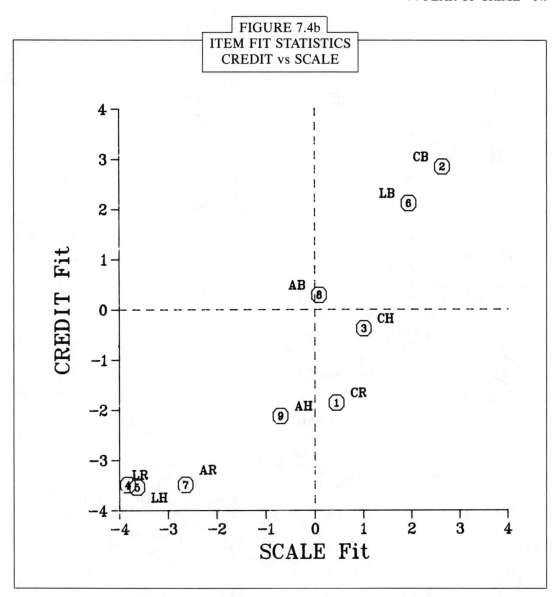

FIGURE 7.4b
ITEM FIT STATISTICS
CREDIT vs SCALE

We could also compare the SCALE and CREDIT fit statistics for each item to see whether they are significantly different.   One way to do this is to begin with the weighted mean squares from the two analyses.

$$\text{From SCALE} \qquad u_i \;=\; \sum_{n=1}^{N}(x_{ni}-E_{Sni})^2 \,/\, \sum_{n=1}^{N} W_{Sni}$$

$$\text{From CREDIT} \qquad v_i \;=\; \sum_{n=1}^{N}(x_{ni}-E_{Cni})^2 \,/\, \sum_{n=1}^{N} W_{Cni}$$

If person and item parameters were known so that $E$ and $W$ were exact, then $NLu_i$ and $NLv_i$ would each be $\chi^2_{NL}$. Since the parameters must be estimated, the $NL$ degrees of freedom reduce to $f = N(L-1) - (m+L-2)$ for $NLu_i$ and $g = N(L-1) - (mL-1)$ for $NLv_i$.

## TABLE 7.4c
### REDUCTION IN RESIDUALS FROM SCALE TO CREDIT

| ITEM NAME $i$ | SCALE MN SQ $u_i$ | CREDIT MN SQ $v_i$ | DIFFERENCE $u_i - v_i$ | REDUCTION IN RESIDUALS MN SQ $r_i$ | FIT $t_i$ |
|---|---|---|---|---|---|
| LH 5 | .63 | .66 | * | | |
| LR 4 | .62 | .65 | * | | |
| LB 6 | 1.23 | 1.26 | * | | |
| AH 9 | .92 | .78 | .14 | 1.64 | 1.6 |
| AR 7 | .73 | .65 | .08 | 0.96 | 0.0 |
| AB 8 | 1.01 | 1.03 | * | | |
| CH 3 | 1.11 | .96 | .15 | 1.77 | 1.9 |
| CR 1 | 1.04 | .82 | .22 | 2.53 | 3.2 |
| CB 2 | 1.29 | 1.32 | * | | |
| Mean | .95 | .90 | | | |
| S.D. | .25 | .26 | | | |

$r = (fu - gv)/L(f-g) = (1598u - 1582v)/144$      $f = N(L-1) - (m+L-2) = 1598$

$s = [2/(L-1)(m-1)]^{1/2} = (1/8)^{1/2} = .35$      $g = N(L-1) - (mL-1) = 1582$

$t = (r^{1/3} - 1)(3/s) + (s/3) = 8.49(r^{1/3} - 1) + .12$      $f - g = (m-1)(L-1) = 26$

$u = \sum(x - E_S)^2 / \sum W_S$      $v = \sum(x - E_C)^2 / \sum W_C$

Although $\sum(x - E_S)^2 > \sum(x - E_C)^2$, when $\sum W_S < \sum W_C$, then $u < v$ is possible.

## TABLE 7.4d
### COMPARING SCALE AND CREDIT FIT ANALYSES

| ITEM NAME | SCALE FIT $t_S$ | CREDIT FIT $t_C$ | DIFFERENCE $t_S - t_C$ | STEP MATCH $t_m$ | RESIDUAL REDUCTION $t_r$ |
|---|---|---|---|---|---|
| LH 5 | −3.6 | −3.5 | −0.1 | −0.7 | |
| LR 4 | −3.8 | −3.5 | −0.3 | −1.3 | |
| LB 6 | 1.9 | 2.1 | −0.2 | 0.0 | |
| AH 9 | −0.7 | −2.1 | 1.4 | 1.4 | 1.6 |
| AR 7 | −2.6 | −3.5 | 0.9 | 0.0 | 0.0 |
| AB 8 | 0.1 | 0.3 | −0.2 | −0.7 | |
| CH 3 | 1.0 | −0.4 | 1.4 | 2.3 | 1.9 |
| CR 1 | 0.4 | −1.9 | 2.3 | 3.1 | 3.2 |
| CB 2 | 2.6 | 2.8 | −0.2 | −1.0 | |
| Mean | −0.5 | −1.1 | 0.6 | 0.3 | |
| S.D. | 2.4 | 2.4 | 1.0 | 1.6 | |
| Source | Table 7.2 | Table 7.3a | | Table 7.4a | Table 7.4c |

A fit statistic for the improvement of CREDIT over SCALE for any item $i$ can be calculated from the mean square

$$r_i = (fu_i - gv_i)/L(f - g)$$

with variance

$$s_i^2 = 2 / (m-1)(L-1)$$

and standardization

$$t_i = (r_i^{1/3} - 1)(3/s_i) + (s_i/3)$$

The results of these SCALE-CREDIT fit comparisons are shown in Table 7.4c. A mean square $r$ and its standardization $t$ are shown for Items $1$, $3$, $7$ and $9$—the four items below the identity line in Figure 7.4b. These statistics show that the only item for which there is a clear improvement in fit from the SCALE to the CREDIT analysis is Item $1$ (concerned about being robbed), although Items $3$ and $9$ come close.

Another very simple approach is to use the differences between the SCALE and CREDIT item fit $t$'s. We have done this in Table 7.4d where we also compare the results of all three approaches to gauging the extent to which the CREDIT analysis is an improvement over the SCALE analysis. Table 7.4d shows that, for these data, the three approaches lead to identical conclusions. The fit of Item $1$ "Concerned about being robbed" is clearly improved by the CREDIT analysis. The improvements in Items $3$ "Concerned about being harmed" and Item $9$ "Afraid of being harmed" are marginal. The fit of the other six items is not significantly improved.


## 7.5  DISCUSSION

When we offer the same set of ordered response alternatives with every item in a questionnaire, we expect that the relative difficulties of the steps within each item will not vary much from item to item. This expectation is implemented in the Rating Scale model which estimates *one* pattern of item steps for every item in the questionnaire (Figure 7.2b).

Whether or not an item fits the Rating Scale model depends in part on how closely this common pattern of step estimates matches the estimates that would have been obtained had they been estimated with the Partial Credit model (Figure 7.3). The match between the SCALE and CREDIT step estimates seems good enough to support the use of the Rating Scale model with this questionnaire.

The Partial Credit analysis, however, does expose a fine structure in the fear-of-crime variable. This fine structure is lost in the Rating Scale analysis which underestimates the difficulty of the first step and overestimates the difficulty of the second and third steps in Items $1$, $3$ and $9$. While these differences are small, they make sense and so provide additional insight into the nature of this variable.

# 8   KNOWLEDGE OF PHYSICS

In this chapter we apply our measurement method to build a knowledge-of-physics variable from performances on a school achievement test.   We will analyze these data first using the Dichotomous model and then the Partial Credit model.   This will give us an opportunity to compare the results of these alternative approaches.

The physics data were collected by the National Foundation for Educational Research in England and Wales using an "answer-until-correct" scoring format.*   This format gives each student immediate feedback telling him whether his first choice on a multiple-choice question is right or wrong.   If his *first* choice is correct, the student receives full credit for that question and goes on to the next.   If incorrect, he is allowed a second attempt.   A correct answer on the *second* attempt earns partial credit.   But if the second choice is also incorrect, then the student receives no credit for the question.   A typical question on this thirty-item physics test is shown in Figure 8.0.   The correct answer is alternative *A*.

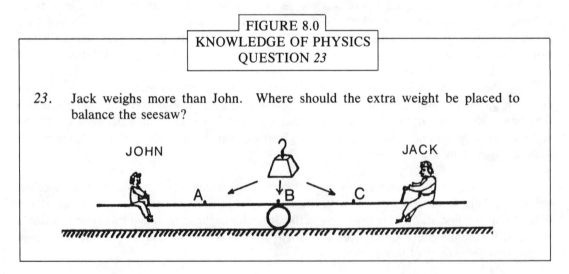

FIGURE 8.0
KNOWLEDGE OF PHYSICS
QUESTION *23*

*23.*   Jack weighs more than John.   Where should the extra weight be placed to balance the seesaw?

JOHN                                                    JACK

A          B          C

Twenty-one of the 321 students who took this item gave alternative *A* as their *third* choice.   These twenty-one students thought that both *B* and *C* were better positions for the weight than *A*.   They received no credit, and earned a score of 0 on this item.

Another forty-two students gave alternative *A* as their *second* choice.   These students first chose either *B* or *C* as a better position for the weight than *A*.   Because they were able to give the correct answer on their second attempt, these forty-two students earned a score of 1 on the item.   The remaining 258 students gave alternative *A* as their *first* choice, and so, earned the maximum score of 2.

* We are grateful to Bruce Choppin, Andy Stillman and Christopher Whetton for making these data available to us.

This scoring format defines three ordered performance levels

| Right | Right | Right |
|-------|-------|-------|
| Third | Second | First |
| Try | Try | Try |
| **0** | **1** | **2** |

In this chapter we will use performances scored in this way to build a knowledge-of-physics variable and to measure the physics knowledge of 321 students.

## 8.1 ANSWER-UNTIL-CORRECT SCORING

Answer-until-correct (AUC) scoring originated with the Troyer-Angell punchboard.   This was a cardboard answer sheet upon which students recorded their answers by punching out perforated circles corresponding to the options they chose.   If the correct option was chosen, a red dot was exposed and the student moved on to the next question.   If no dot appeared, then the student had the opportunity to re-read the question and try again.   A student's score on each item (in this case counting failure rather than success) was the number of circles he had to remove to expose the red dot (Jones and Sawyer 1949).

Paper answer sheets have also been used with answer-until-correct scoring.   Students record their answer to each question either by scratching the surface from a shield corresponding to the option they have chosen, or by marking the answer sheet with a special pen.   If the option chosen is correct, a ☑ is exposed.   If it is incorrect, an ☒ appears.

When a test is taken interactively at a computer terminal, still more detailed feedback can be provided.   Incorrect responses can be used to diagnose misconceptions and gaps in a student's knowledge, to alert the student to the need for remedial work and to offer items of more appropriate difficulty.

Performances on multiple-choice questions are usually scored dichotomously, depending on whether or not the correct answer is selected in one attempt.   Under AUC scoring, however, performances can be scored into several ordered performance levels.   This raises the possibility, when students' knowledge is incomplete, of making more precise estimates of ability from these more detailed records of performance.

## 8.2 ANALYZING PERFORMANCES DICHOTOMOUSLY

We begin our analyses by scoring performances on the thirty items dichotomously.   The two ways to dichotomize the original three-category data are shown in Table 8.2a.   The first of these scoring schemes (001) corresponds to the usual right/wrong scoring of performances and gives no credit for getting an item correct on a second try.   The second (011) scheme gives full credit for getting an item correct in two tries, but does not give additional credit for getting an item correct on the *first* try.

Table 8.2b shows the number of students succeeding in one, two and three attempts at each of these thirty physics items.   (Fifteen of the items allow for *five* attempts.   To simplify

## TABLE 8.2a
## RESCORING THE PHYSICS DATA

|  | RIGHT THIRD TRY | RIGHT SECOND TRY | RIGHT FIRST TRY |
|---|---|---|---|
| Original Scoring | 0 | 1 | 2 |
| Right First Try (001) | 0 | 0 | 1 |
| Right in Two Tries (011) | 0 | 1 | 1 |

## TABLE 8.2b
## ITEM SCORE VECTORS

| N = 321 | (0) | (1) | (2) |
|---|---|---|---|
| ITEM NAME | RIGHT THIRD TRY | RIGHT SECOND TRY | RIGHT FIRST TRY |
| 1 | 12 | 29 | 280 |
| 2 | 152 | 77 | 92 |
| 3 | 70 | 51 | 200 |
| 4 | 103 | 75 | 143 |
| 5 | 102 | 62 | 157 |
| 6 | 40 | 67 | 214 |
| 7 | 146 | 36 | 139 |
| 8 | 79 | 73 | 169 |
| 9 | 117 | 58 | 146 |
| 10 | 143 | 58 | 120 |
| 11 | 52 | 24 | 245 |
| 12 | 87 | 64 | 170 |
| 13 | 118 | 90 | 113 |
| 14 | 68 | 62 | 191 |
| 15 | 177 | 81 | 63 |
| 16 | 41 | 75 | 205 |
| 17 | 71 | 104 | 146 |
| 18 | 35 | 59 | 227 |
| 19 | 11 | 112 | 198 |
| 20 | 46 | 43 | 232 |
| 21 | 57 | 80 | 184 |
| 22 | 31 | 72 | 218 |
| 23 | 21 | 42 | 258 |
| 24 | 81 | 102 | 138 |
| 25 | 108 | 107 | 106 |
| 26 | 36 | 77 | 208 |
| 27 | 47 | 69 | 205 |
| 28 | 36 | 70 | 215 |
| 29 | 123 | 105 | 93 |
| 30 | 144 | 92 | 85 |
| Totals | 2354 | 2116 | 5160 |

TABLE 8.2c
ITEM STATISTICS
SCORING (001)

| ITEM NAME | DIFFICULTY $d$ | ERROR $s$ | FIT MS | SE | FIT $t$ |
|---|---|---|---|---|---|
| 1 | −1.91 | .17 | 1.04 | .12 | .36 |
| 2 | 1.20 | .13 | .98 | .06 | −.30 |
| 3 | −.38 | .12 | 1.01 | .05 | .29 |
| 4 | .42 | .12 | .89 | .04 | −2.63 |
| 5 | .23 | .12 | 1.10 | .04 | 2.28 |
| 6 | −.60 | .13 | 1.10 | .05 | 1.84 |
| 7 | .48 | .12 | .83 | .04 | −4.13 |
| 8 | .06 | .12 | .98 | .04 | −.59 |
| 9 | .38 | .12 | .89 | .04 | −2.68 |
| 10 | .76 | .12 | 1.10 | .05 | 2.04 |
| 11 | −1.12 | .14 | .93 | .07 | −1.03 |
| 12 | .04 | .12 | 1.02 | .04 | .39 |
| 13 | .86 | .13 | 1.06 | .05 | 1.11 |
| 14 | −.25 | .12 | 1.10 | .04 | 2.17 |
| 15 | 1.75 | .15 | 1.07 | .09 | .78 |
| 16 | −.46 | .12 | .86 | .05 | −3.01 |
| 17 | .38 | .12 | 1.02 | .04 | .48 |
| 18 | −.80 | .13 | .90 | .06 | −1.71 |
| 19 | −.35 | .12 | .99 | .05 | −.20 |
| 20 | −.89 | .13 | .90 | .06 | −1.74 |
| 21 | −.15 | .12 | 1.10 | .04 | 2.37 |
| 22 | −.66 | .13 | 1.04 | .05 | .76 |
| 23 | −1.37 | .15 | .90 | .08 | −1.23 |
| 24 | .49 | .12 | .98 | .04 | −.46 |
| 25 | .97 | .13 | .98 | .05 | −.32 |
| 26 | −.50 | .12 | .97 | .05 | −.67 |
| 27 | −.46 | .12 | .85 | .05 | −3.22 |
| 28 | −.61 | .13 | .96 | .05 | −.80 |
| 29 | 1.18 | .13 | 1.11 | .06 | 1.75 |
| 30 | 1.32 | .14 | 1.25 | .07 | 3.54 |
| Mean | .00 | .13 | 1.00 | .05 | −.15 |
| S.D. | .86 | .01 | .10 | .02 | 1.88 |

Adjusted Test S.D. = .85     Error RMS = .13     Item Separation = .85/.13 = 6.4
Sample Reliability of Item Separation = $6.4^2/(1+6.4^2)$ = .98
Sample Size = 321     Mean = .19     Unadjusted S.D. = .85
Adjusted S.D. = .74     Error RMS = .43     Person Separation = .74/.43 = 1.7
Test Reliability of Person Separation = $1.7^2/(1+1.7^2)$ = .74

this analysis we have scored performances on these items into only three categories by giving students who took three, four or five attempts at an item the lowest score 0). Columns (1) and (2) of Table 8.2b are needed for the partial credit (012) analysis of these data. For the (001) analysis, only the counts in Column (2) are needed. For the (011) analysis the required counts are obtained by adding column (1) to column (2). We will investigate all three scoring schemes.

## 8.2.1 Right First Try (001)

Under the first dichotomous scoring scheme a student scores 1 if he is successful on his *first* try and zero otherwise. We have analyzed these rescored data using Rasch's Dichotomous model. The results of the item calibration are shown in Table 8.2c

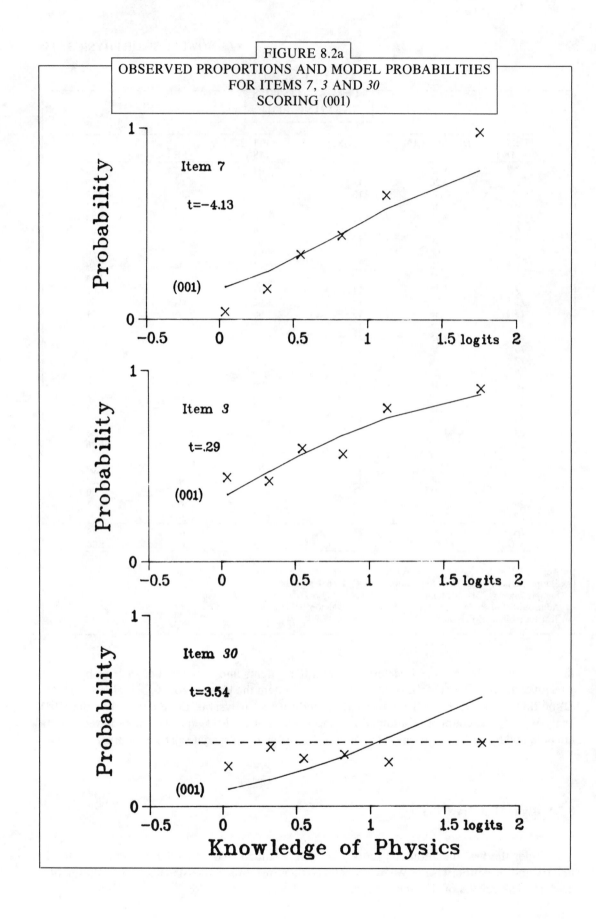

FIGURE 8.2a
OBSERVED PROPORTIONS AND MODEL PROBABILITIES
FOR ITEMS 7, 3 AND 30
SCORING (001)

FIGURE 8.2b
ITEMS *7, 3* AND *30*

*7.* A block of iron weighs 40 newtons at room Temperature. When it is heated until it is red hot it gets bigger. How much will it weigh when red hot?

    A) 39 newtons   B) 40 newtons   C) 40.5 newtons   D) 41 newtons
    E) 42 newtons.

*3.* Where can a jet plane not fly?

    A) Over deep water.
    B) Over high mountains.
    C) Over mountains on the moon.
    D) Very low.
    E) 8 miles above the earth.

*30.*

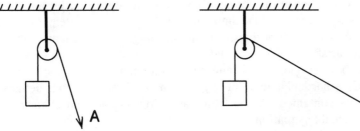

Two men try to lift the same weight by pulling in different directions. Which requires more effort? If both the same put B.

Table 8.2c shows that the thirty physics items are reasonably well separated in difficulty. The easiest is Item *1* with a difficulty estimate of $-1.91$ logits. The hardest is Item *15* with a difficulty estimate of $+1.75$ logits. The test standard deviation after adjusting for calibration error is .85, or 6.4 times the error root mean square.

The item fit statistics on the right of Table 8.2c have a mean of $-.15$ and a standard deviation of 1.88, and so, are somewhat more dispersed than modelled. Only one item (Item *30*, $t = 3.54$), however, has a fit statistic greater than $+3.0$. This is the last item on the test and, if time was a factor for some students, may have been spoiled by last minute guessing. Three items (*7, 16* and *27*) have fit statistics below $-3.0$.

To explore the fit of these items to the Dichotomous model, we have divided the 321 students into six ability strata and calculated the proportion of students in each of these strata getting each item correct on the first try. These proportions and their corresponding model probabilities are plotted in Figure 8.2a for Item *7* with the most negative fit statistic, Item *30* with the most positive fit statistic, and Item *3* with a fit statistic near zero. The text of these items is in Figure 8.2b.

Figure 8.2a shows that the negative fit statistic for Item *7* is the result of too few low ability students and too many high ability students getting the item correct.   Item *7* is based on the common laboratory demonstration that a block of iron "gets bigger" when heated.   By providing three alternatives which are greater than the correct answer, 40 newtons, and only one which is less, Item *7* invites students to associate an increase in size with an increase in weight.   It seems that more low ability students were seduced by this distraction than is consistent with their performances on the other items.   This causes Item *7* to look more difficult for the group as a whole than it would have had we considered only high-scoring students.

The misfit picture for Item *7* is typical of items which offer especially seductive distractors, require special knowledge, involve a common misconception, or for which the correct answer is particularly counter-intuitive.   The problem with including items like Item *7* in a test dominated by items which do not function the same way is that the misfitting items disorganize the definition of the variable.   The relative location of Item *7* on the knowledge-of-physics variable marked out by the majority of these items is not fixed.   It depends on the ability level of the students in the calibrating sample.   When Item *7* is calibrated by high ability students, it is estimated to be relatively easy.   But when it is calibrated by low ability students, some of whom fall for the common, but in this case irrelevant, experience that bigger is heavier, it is estimated to be relatively difficult.   This ambiguity in the position of Item *7* among the other items prevents Item *7* from contributing to a sample-free (i.e., invariant) definition of this knowledge-of-physics variable.   Since its relative position depends on the knowledge level of the students in the calibrating sample, we cannot give it a fixed position among the other items unless we first specify a particular level of student knowledge.   But that defines a variable which is different in its content definition from sample to sample and even from person to person—hardly an acceptable situation.

The observed proportions of students answering Item *3* correctly on the first try are close to their model probabilities.   This item fits the Dichotomous model well, and is included as background for the performance of misfitting Items *7* and *30*.

The misfit picture for Item *30* at the bottom of Figure 8.2a shows that the positive fit statistic for this item is the result of too many low ability students and too few high ability students getting the item correct.   The broken line drawn horizontally through this picture shows the probability of getting Item *30* correct by random guessing (.33).   As Item *30* is the last item on the test, it seems likely that some responses to it are spoiled by last minute guessing.   This hypothesis could be tested by moving Item *30* nearer to the beginning of the test or by increasing the time available for test completion.

Figure 8.2c shows the location of these thirty items on the knowledge-of-physics variable when performances are scored (001).   The variable runs vertically up the middle of Figure 8.2c.   The most difficult items, defining high levels of knowledge, are towards the top.   On the far right are the item scores (number of students getting each item correct).   Easy Item *1* was answered correctly by 280 students.   Difficult Item *15* was answered correctly by only sixty-three.   On the left is the distribution of ability estimates.   We see that these items are well centered on this sample.   Finally, on the far left are the scores made by these 321 students.   Three students had only five items correct on their first attempt.   Two students had twenty-eight items correct.

## FIGURE 8.2c
## MAP OF PHYSICS VARIABLE SCORING (001)

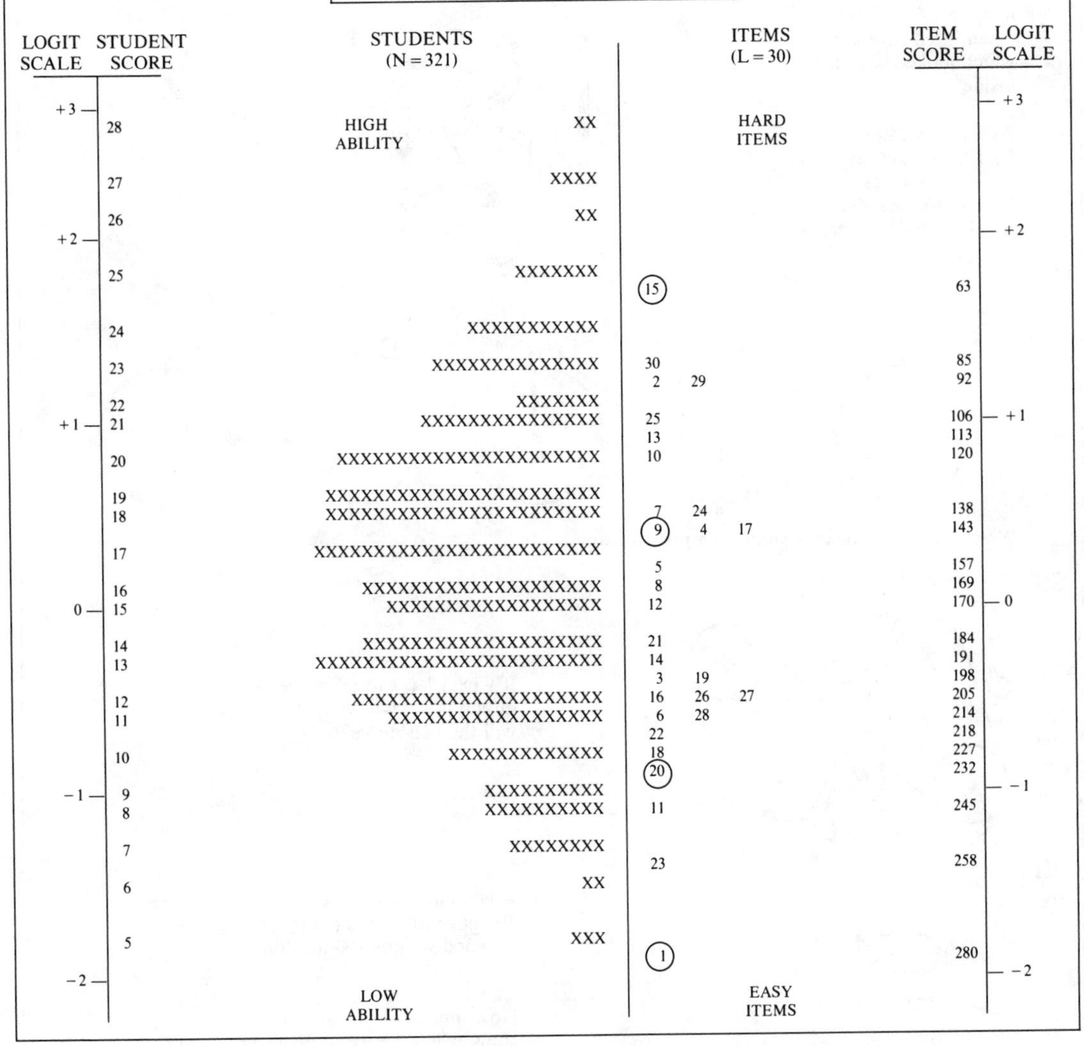

| LOGIT SCALE | STUDENT SCORE | STUDENTS (N = 321) | | ITEMS (L = 30) | | ITEM SCORE | LOGIT SCALE |
|---|---|---|---|---|---|---|---|
| +3 | 28 | HIGH ABILITY | XX | HARD ITEMS | | | +3 |
| | 27 | | XXXX | | | | |
| | 26 | | XX | | | | |
| +2 | | | | | | | +2 |
| | 25 | | XXXXXXX | 15 | | 63 | |
| | 24 | | XXXXXXXXXX | | | | |
| | 23 | | XXXXXXXXXXXXX | 30 | | 85 | |
| | | | | 2    29 | | 92 | |
| | 22 | | XXXXXXX | | | | |
| +1 | 21 | | XXXXXXXXXXXX | 25 | | 106 | +1 |
| | | | | 13 | | 113 | |
| | 20 | | XXXXXXXXXXXXXXXXXXX | 10 | | 120 | |
| | 19 | | XXXXXXXXXXXXXXXXXXXXXX | | | | |
| | 18 | | XXXXXXXXXXXXXXXXXXXXX | 7    24 | | 138 | |
| | | | | 9    4    17 | | 143 | |
| | 17 | | XXXXXXXXXXXXXXXXXXXXX | 5 | | 157 | |
| | 16 | | XXXXXXXXXXXXXXXXXX | 8 | | 169 | |
| 0 | 15 | | XXXXXXXXXXXXXXXXX | 12 | | 170 | 0 |
| | 14 | | XXXXXXXXXXXXXXXXX | 21 | | 184 | |
| | 13 | | XXXXXXXXXXXXXXXXXXXXXX | 14 | | 191 | |
| | | | | 3    19 | | 198 | |
| | 12 | | XXXXXXXXXXXXXXXXX | 16    26    27 | | 205 | |
| | 11 | | XXXXXXXXXXXXXXXX | 6    28 | | 214 | |
| | | | | 22 | | 218 | |
| | 10 | | XXXXXXXXXXXXX | 18 | | 227 | |
| | | | | | | 232 | |
| -1 | 9 | | XXXXXXXXX | 20 | | | -1 |
| | 8 | | XXXXXXXXX | 11 | | 245 | |
| | 7 | | XXXXXXX | | | | |
| | 6 | | XX | 23 | | 258 | |
| | 5 | | XXX | | | | |
| | | | | 1 | | 280 | |
| -2 | | LOW ABILITY | | EASY ITEMS | | | -2 |

Four of the items in Figure 8.2c are circled.   These items, shown in Figure 8.2d, mark out four successive levels of knowledge on this knowledge-of-physics variable.   Item *1* is the easiest.   To answer this item, a student need only know that the weight of two objects when combined is the sum of their individual weights.   Item *1* defines the lowest level of knowledge on this variable.

Item *20* is somewhat more difficult.   It requires the student to visualize the movement of the belt in the figure.   Item *9* is still harder.   To answer Item *9*, a student must understand the relation between the minute and hour hand of a clock.   Finally, the highest level of knowledge is defined by Item *15*.   To answer this item a student must understand the implications of a "3 amps" fuse and know which of the five appliances draws the most electricity.

FIGURE 8.2d
ITEMS *1, 20, 9* AND *15*
SCORING (001)

*15.* Which one of the following items would not work when fitted with a plug which looked like this inside?

A) Electric radio
B) Electric kettle
C) Electric clock
D) Electric blanket
E) Household electric light bulb

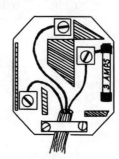
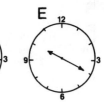

*9.*

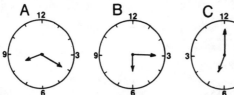

Which of these clocks is showing a possible time?

*20.*

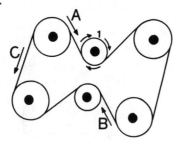

If wheel 1 is turned in the direction shown, which way will the belt move?

*1.*

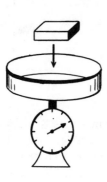

A bowl and water weigh 200 newtons and a piece of wood weighs 100 newtons.

How much will the scales show when the wood floats in the water?

A) 100 newtons  B) 200 newtons  C) 300 newtons  D) 400 newtons  E) 500 newtons.

### 8.2.2 Right in Two Tries (011)

The second dichotomous scoring scheme assigns a score of 1 for getting an item correct on either the first *or* second try, and a score of 0 if the correct answer is not given in two attempts.   The results of this analysis are shown in Table 8.2d.

Giving *two* opportunities to provide the correct answer to an item makes the item easier.   However, in our analyses we center item difficulties at zero during their calibration.   The consequence is that instead of every item appearing easier in the (011) analysis as we know it must be, this greater easiness appears as a higher ability estimate for every person.   Under the (001) scoring, the 321 students have a mean ability of .19 logits and a standard deviation of .85.   Under the (011) scoring they have a mean ability of 1.45 logits and a standard deviation of .87.   If we make the almost inarguable assumption that these data measure the same physics

| | TABLE 8.2d | | | | |
| | ITEM STATISTICS | | | | |
| | SCORING (011) | | | | |

| ITEM NAME | DIFFICULTY $d$ | ERROR $s$ | FIT MS | SE | FIT $t$ |
|---|---|---|---|---|---|
| 1 | −3.24 | .30 | .99 | .26 | .05 |
| 2 | .05 | .12 | .96 | .04 | −.99 |
| 3 | −1.23 | .14 | 1.01 | .07 | .23 |
| 4 | −.67 | .13 | .96 | .05 | −.82 |
| 5 | −.68 | .13 | 1.03 | .05 | .60 |
| 6 | −1.94 | .17 | .97 | .12 | −.17 |
| 7 | −.03 | .12 | .87 | .04 | −3.51 |
| 8 | −1.07 | .14 | .94 | .07 | −.86 |
| 9 | −.45 | .12 | .87 | .04 | −3.07 |
| 10 | −.08 | .12 | 1.09 | .04 | 2.21 |
| 11 | −1.62 | .16 | .97 | .10 | −.30 |
| 12 | −.93 | .13 | .95 | .06 | −.87 |
| 13 | −.44 | .12 | 1.00 | .04 | −.10 |
| 14 | −1.27 | .14 | 1.00 | .08 | .07 |
| 15 | .40 | .12 | 1.19 | .04 | 4.15 |
| 16 | −1.91 | .17 | .90 | .12 | −.81 |
| 17 | −1.21 | .14 | 1.04 | .07 | .63 |
| 18 | −2.09 | .18 | .99 | .13 | −.02 |
| 19 | −3.33 | .31 | .97 | .28 | −.02 |
| 20 | −1.77 | .17 | .96 | .11 | −.37 |
| 21 | −1.50 | .15 | 1.05 | .09 | .53 |
| 22 | −2.23 | .19 | 1.02 | .14 | .16 |
| 23 | −2.66 | .23 | .95 | .19 | −.19 |
| 24 | −1.03 | .14 | 1.05 | .06 | .83 |
| 25 | −.59 | .13 | .99 | .05 | −.24 |
| 26 | −2.06 | .18 | .96 | .13 | −.27 |
| 27 | −1.74 | .16 | .95 | .10 | −.49 |
| 28 | −2.06 | .18 | .99 | .13 | −.06 |
| 29 | −.36 | .12 | 1.18 | .04 | 4.10 |
| 30 | −.06 | .12 | 1.16 | .04 | 3.83 |
| Mean | −1.26 | .16 | 1.00 | .09 | .14 |
| S.D. | .96 | .05 | .08 | .06 | 1.67 |

Adjusted Test S.D. = .95    Error RMS = .17    Item Separation = .95/.17 = 5.6
Sample Reliability of Item Separation = $5.6^2/(1+5.6^2)$ = .97
Sample Size = 321    Mean = .19    Unadjusted S.D. = .87
Adjusted Sample S.D. = .70    Error RMS = .52    Person Separation = .70/.52 = 1.3
Test Reliability of Person Separation = $1.3^2/(1+1.3^2)$ = .63

ability whether scored (001), (011) or (012), then we can attribute this apparent difference in ability to the difference caused by scoring (011) rather than (001). Thus the effect of giving *two* opportunities to provide the correct answer is, on the average, to decrease the difficulty of an item by $1.45 - .19 = 1.26$ logits. In order to compare these two sets of difficulty estimates we have adjusted the person and item estimates from the (011) analysis by $-1.26$ logits so that they are centered on the results of the (001) analysis.

The fit statistics on the right of Table 8.2d show that, once again, Item *7* has the most negative fit value. Item *30*, which had the most positive fit statistic in the (001) analysis, has a fit-t of $+3.83$. But now two other items, *15* and *29*, also have large positive fit values. Item *29* is the next to last item on the test, and so, if time was a factor, may also have suffered from some guessing. The poor fit of Item *15* is more puzzling. This item was shown in Figure 8.2d. The correct answer is alternative *B*—Electric kettle. Item *15* is estimated to be the most difficult item on the test by both the (001) and (011) analyses. However, while it fits reasonably well ($t = .78$) when scored (001), it fits poorly ($t = 4.15$) when scored (011).

To examine these misfits more closely, we have plotted the proportions of students succeeding on the first attempt and the proportions succeeding in two attempts for Items *3*, *30* and *15* in Figure 8.2e. The lower curve in each picture describes the model probability of getting that item correct on the *first* try. The upper curve shows the model probability of getting the item correct in *two* tries. For Item *3* at the top of Figure 8.2e, the match between the observed proportions and model probabilities is good for both the (001) and (011) analyses. As a result, both fit statistics for this item are close to their expected value of zero.

For Item *30* in the middle of Figure 8.2e, the match between observation and expectation is poor for both analyses. As a result, both fit statistics for this item are large and positive. The misfit picture for Item *15* is at the bottom of Figure 8.2e. The proportions of students getting this item correct on the *first* try match the model probabilities reasonably well. There is some tendency for low ability students to do better than expected on the first try and for high ability students to do worse than expected, and this has produced the fit statistic of .78. However, the upper (011) curve shows that when *two* attempts at Item *15* are allowed, this tendency becomes even more marked.

A surprising number of low ability students have succeeded on their second attempt at Item *15*. For the lowest ability group we expect 6 percent of students to succeed on their first attempt, and 24 percent to succeed in two attempts. In other words, we expect $(24 - 6)/(100 - 6) = 19$ percent of the students who missed on their first attempt to be successful on their second. Actually, $(39 - 8)/(100 - 8) = 34$ percent of these low ability students who missed were successful on their second try. On the other hand, students in the highest ability group have been *less* successful than expected on their second attempt at Item *15*. For these high ability students we expect $(77 - 48)/(100 - 48) = 55$ percent of students who miss on their first attempt to be successful on their second. Actually, only $(62 - 43)/(100 - 43) = 33$ percent of these students were successful.

The alternatives in Item *15* fall into two categories which are quite distinct, if recognized. Only the electric kettle draws a heavy current. If a student sees this, then the item is easy. But if he does not, then his answer must necessarily deteriorate into a random guess. Thus a plausible explanation for the misfit of second attempts at Item *15* is that most students who failed this item on their first attempt *guessed* on their second. The pair of curves

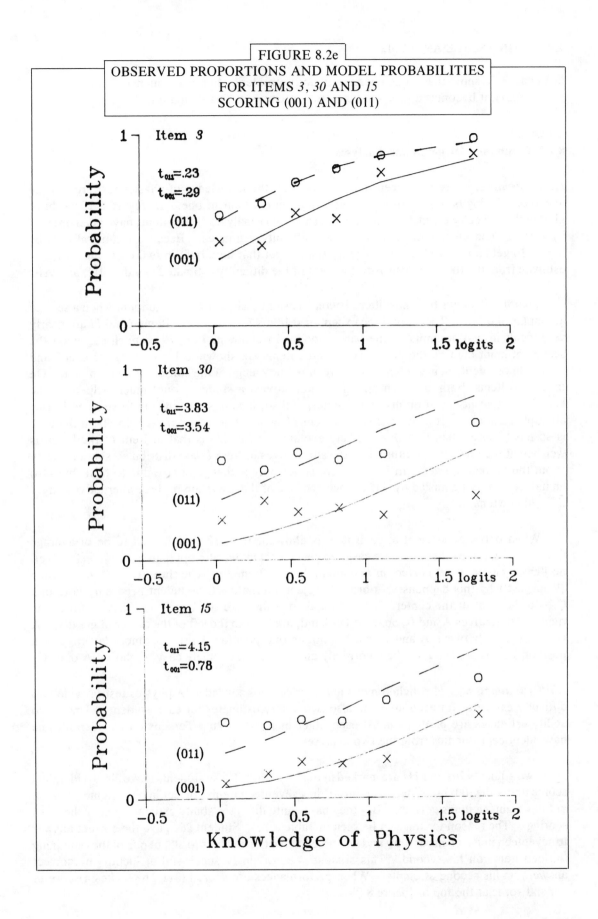

FIGURE 8.2e
OBSERVED PROPORTIONS AND MODEL PROBABILITIES
FOR ITEMS 3, 30 AND 15
SCORING (001) AND (011)

in Figure 8.2e show that while guessing is not a problem when performances on Item *15* are scored (001), it becomes a problem when two attempts at this item are allowed.


### 8.2.3  Comparing Dichotomous Analyses

***Item Estimates.***   We have seen that the items on the knowledge-of-physics test are, on the average, 1.26 logits easier to answer in two attempts than in one.   In Figure 8.2f we have plotted the difficulty estimates from the (001) and (011) analyses.   The items have been ordered by sorting them on the means of their two difficulty estimates.   Because it must always be harder to get an item right on the *first* try than to get that item right in two tries, the difficulty estimate from the (001) analysis is to the right of the difficulty estimate from the (011) analysis.

Figure 8.2f shows that most items become easier by about the same amount when a second attempt is allowed.   There are three exceptions: Items *7, 11* and *19*.   Items *7* and *11* are nearly as difficult in two attempts as they are in one.   In contrast, Item *19* is much easier on the second attempt than on the first.   These three items are shown in Figure 8.2g.   Items *7* and *11* are almost identical in content.   Both require knowledge of the conservation of matter.   On these two items, both of which offer five alternatives, a student is not much helped by the knowledge that he failed on his first attempt, and so, is almost as unlikely to succeed in two attempts as in one.   It is interesting that Item *11*, which follows Item *7* so closely in the test, is so much easier than Item *7*.   A likely explanation for this is that in Item *11* the block is weighed at the *same* temperature, and the alternatives in Item *11* are distributed symmetrically about the correct answer.   In Item *7* there is not only a change in size due to heat, but also an inducement to be misled by this change because of the provision of three alternatives larger than 40 newtons.

When only one attempt at each item is allowed, Item *19* is estimated to be of average difficulty.   Twelve other items are easier to get correct in *one* attempt than Item *19*.   However, no item is easier to get correct in *two* attempts than Item *19*.   The three alternatives of Item *19* suggest why this happens.   In order to reject alternative C a student need only note that C is to the right of the center of gravity, and so, will make the bus more likely to tip to the right.   Alternatives A and B, on the other hand, are both to the left of the center of gravity.   A correct choice between A and B requires noting that position A provides more leverage than position B.   Thus, should B be incorrectly chosen, it is extremely easy to choose A over C.

***Ability Estimates.***   The dichotomous analyses of the knowledge-of-physics test provide two difficulty estimates for each item and also two ability estimates for each student.   These two ability estimates are plotted against each other in Figure 8.2h.   Persons on the identity line have identical estimates from the two analyses.

Two students *201* and *211* are marked in Figure 8.2h.   These students make almost identical scores under the (001) scoring.   Person *201* has seventeen items correct in one attempt. Person *211* has eighteen items correct.   But they have quite different ability estimates under the (011) scoring.   The reason for this can be seen in Table 8.2e.   Student *201* gave the correct answer to seventeen items on his first try and was able to give the answers to all but one of the remaining thirteen items on his second.   This student is surprisingly successful at identifying correct answers on his second attempts.   When performances are scored (011), he makes a score of 29, and so, is at the top of Figure 8.2h.

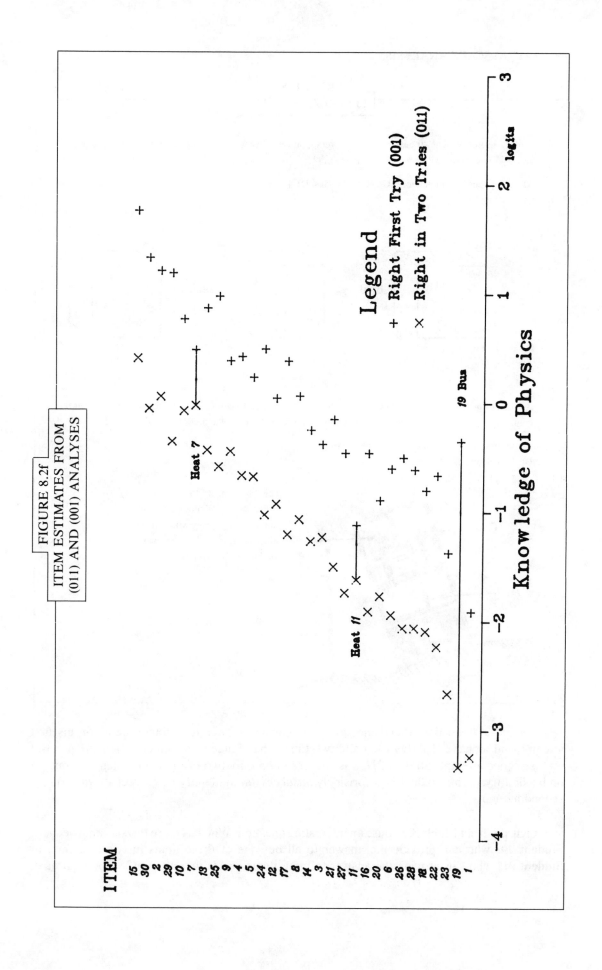

FIGURE 8.2f
ITEM ESTIMATES FROM
(011) AND (001) ANALYSES

FIGURE 8.2g
ITEMS *7, 11* AND *19*

7. A block of iron weighs 40 newtons at room temperature.   When it is heated until it is red hot it gets bigger.   How much will it weight when red hot?

A) 39 newtons B) 40 newtons C) 40.5 newtons D) 41 newtons
E) 42 newtons

*11.*

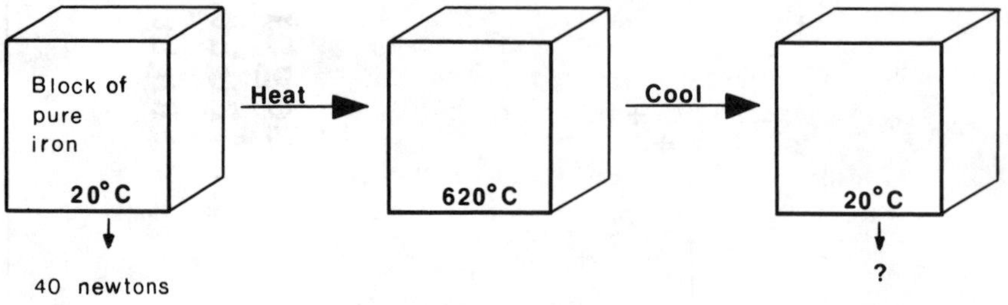

Block of
pure
iron
20°C

Heat →

620°C

Cool →

20°C

?

40 newtons

A block of pure iron weighs 40 newtons at 20°C.   It is heated to 620°C in vacuum and then allowed to cool.   If it expanded when being heated, how much does it weigh when cool?

A) 38 newtons B) 39 newtons C) 40 newtons
D) 41 newtons E) 42 newtons.

*19.*

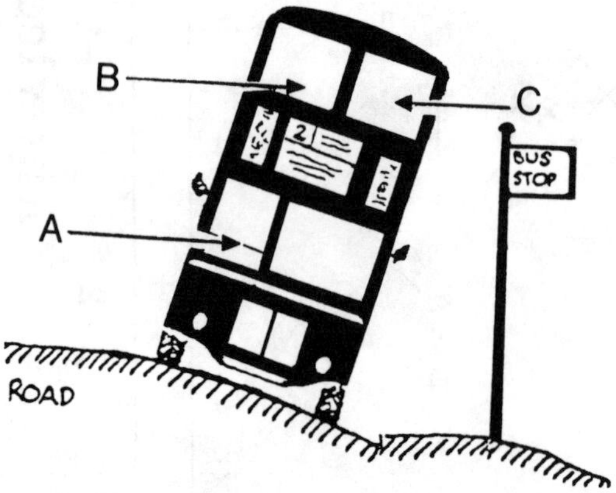

This bus appears to be very nearly falling over.   Where on the bus should a large man with a heavy suitcase sit if he does not want the bus to fall over?

Student *211*, on the other hand, gave the correct answer to eighteen items on his first attempt, and so, has a slightly higher ability estimate than Student *201* under (001) scoring.   But on his second attempt, Student *211* was successful on only two of the twelve items he missed on his first try.   This student is surprisingly *unsuccessful* in identifying correct answers on his second attempts.

Figure 8.2h and Table 8.2e raise an interesting question: Who has more physics knowledge— Student *201* who can provide the answer to all but one of these items in two attempts, or Student *211* who can provide the answer to more items on his *first* attempt?   The records of

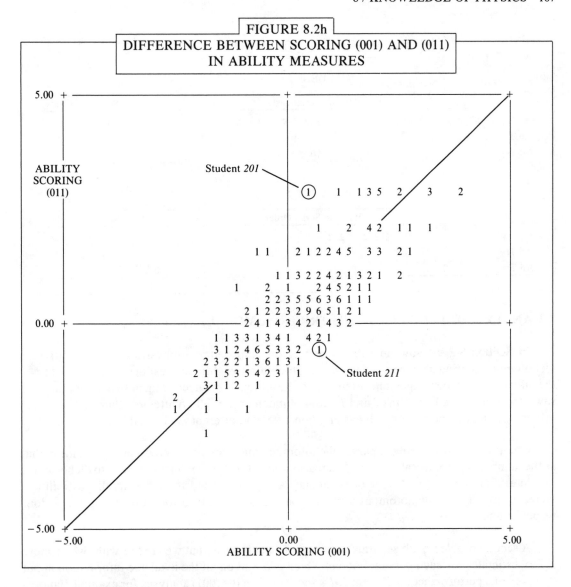

FIGURE 8.2h
DIFFERENCE BETWEEN SCORING (001) AND (011)
IN ABILITY MEASURES

these two students resemble records we encountered in our analyses of the attitude-to-science and attitude-to-drugs questionnaires where we found some persons with unusual tendencies to respond in the middle category and others with unusual tendencies to give extreme responses.

In attitude questionnaires, this observation is usually attributed to an interaction between the "ambiguity" of the middle response category and the assertiveness of the individual.   Here we see the same response pattern in a different context.   This kind of difference among individuals is possible whenever more than two categories of response are possible.   The implications for measurement, however, are the same.   The different success rates of Persons 201 and 211 on their second attempts represent a difference among individuals which we have not modelled.   This difference interferes with our attempt to represent the abilities of Persons 201 and 211 as two points on the same line of increasing knowledge.

**TABLE 8.2e**

**PERFORMANCES OF STUDENTS *201* AND *211***

STUDENT *201*

| | Items in Serial Order | Score | Ability |
|---|---|---|---|
| 1st Try | 2  2    2 2 2    2 2    2      2    2    2 2 2 2      2 2 | 17 | .30 |
| 2nd Try | 1    1 1          1      1    1      1    1            1 1        1 1 | 29 | 2.48 |
| 3rd Try |                                0 | | |

STUDENT *211*

| | Items in Serial Order | Score | Ability |
|---|---|---|---|
| 1st Try | 2   2    2 2 2    2 2 2    2 2    2    2      2 2 2 2    2    2 | 18 | .46 |
| 2nd Try |                                          1    1 | 20 | − .48 |
| 3rd Try | 0   0      0        0      0          0          0        0  0 | | |

## 8.3 ANALYZING PERFORMANCES TRICHOTOMOUSLY (012)

In Section 8.2 we saw how, by analyzing the knowledge-of-physics data with different dichotomous scoring schemes, we were able to obtain two difficulty estimates for each item—the difficulty of succeeding in one attempt and the difficulty of succeeding in two attempts. We saw that some items like Items *7* and *11* are not much easier in two attempts than in one, while others like Item *19* become much easier when a second attempt is allowed.

One problem with using separate dichotomous analyses of ordered category data is that as the number of response alternatives increases above three, the number of ways to dichotomize the data, and hence the number of secondary analyses needed to complete all possibilities, increases rapidly. A dichotomous approach becomes impractical for more than three or four response alternatives.

A second problem with separate dichotomous analyses is that we are left with two or more ability estimates for each person, none of which is based on all the available information about that person's performance. Student *201*'s score of 17 in the (001) analysis, for example, ignores the fact that he was able to answer another twelve items on his second attempt. Student *211*'s score of 20 in the (011) analysis ignores the fact that he had eighteen of these twenty items correct on his *first* try.

We will now use the Partial Credit model to analyze the knowledge-of-physics data scored (012). The advantages of this approach are that it requires only *one* analysis and provides only *one* ability estimate for each student based on all available information about that student's performance. We will see that the partial credit approach is capable of exposing most, if not all, of the data features which we discovered in our detailed comparisons of the two dichotomous analyses.

### 8.3.1 Estimating Item Difficulties

The item statistics from the partial credit analysis of the knowledge-of-physics data are

TABLE 8.3a
ITEM STATISTICS
SCORING (012)

| ITEM NAME | STEP ESTIMATES | | ERRORS | | FIT MS | SE | FIT $t_i$ |
|---|---|---|---|---|---|---|---|
| | $d_{i1}$ | $d_{i2}$ | $s_{i1}$ | $s_{i2}$ | | | |
| 1 | − .64 | − 1.75 | .30 | .17 | 1.01 | .16 | .10 |
| 2 | 1.10 | .53 | .12 | .13 | .99 | .05 | − .15 |
| 3 | .62 | − .78 | .14 | .12 | 1.01 | .06 | .20 |
| 4 | .68 | − .01 | .13 | .12 | .92 | .05 | − 1.64 |
| 5 | .84 | − .30 | .13 | .12 | 1.09 | .05 | 1.81 |
| 6 | − .22 | − .61 | .18 | .12 | 1.03 | .08 | .42 |
| 7 | 1.76 | − .66 | .12 | .12 | .84 | .05 | − 3.50 |
| 8 | .41 | − .24 | .14 | .12 | .95 | .06 | − .99 |
| 9 | 1.06 | − .28 | .12 | .12 | .85 | .05 | − 3.14 |
| 10 | 1.29 | − .04 | .12 | .13 | 1.15 | .05 | 2.89 |
| 11 | 1.02 | − 1.75 | .16 | .14 | .94 | .08 | − .66 |
| 12 | .64 | − .37 | .13 | .12 | .99 | .05 | − .21 |
| 13 | .66 | .43 | .12 | .13 | 1.04 | .05 | .85 |
| 14 | .40 | − .54 | .14 | .12 | 1.06 | .06 | 1.00 |
| 15 | 1.24 | 1.00 | .12 | .15 | 1.16 | .06 | 2.41 |
| 16 | − .30 | − .46 | .17 | .12 | .86 | .07 | − 1.98 |
| 17 | − .02 | .26 | .14 | .12 | 1.04 | .06 | .70 |
| 18 | − .24 | − .81 | .19 | .13 | .93 | .09 | − .80 |
| 19 | − 1.97 | − .05 | .31 | .12 | .95 | .08 | − .66 |
| 20 | .34 | − 1.13 | .17 | .13 | .92 | .08 | − 1.00 |
| 21 | − .02 | − .26 | .15 | .12 | 1.09 | .06 | 1.37 |
| 22 | − .54 | − .57 | .19 | .12 | 1.02 | .08 | .29 |
| 23 | − .43 | − 1.29 | .23 | .15 | .91 | .12 | − .78 |
| 24 | .14 | .31 | .14 | .12 | 1.01 | .05 | .17 |
| 25 | .41 | .66 | .12 | .13 | .99 | .05 | − .14 |
| 26 | − .45 | − .45 | .18 | .12 | .95 | .08 | − .69 |
| 27 | − .08 | − .53 | .16 | .12 | .88 | .07 | − 1.79 |
| 28 | − .37 | − .58 | .18 | .12 | .96 | .08 | − .52 |
| 29 | .57 | .79 | .12 | .13 | 1.19 | .05 | 3.25 |
| 30 | .87 | .78 | .12 | .14 | 1.28 | .06 | 4.61 |
| Mean | .00 | | .14 | | 1.00 | .07 | .05 |
| S.D. | .78 | | .04 | | .10 | .02 | 1.77 |

Adjusted Test S.D. = .76    Error RMS = .15    Step Separation = .76/.15 = 5.1
Sample Reliability of Step Separation = $5.1^2/(1+5.1^2)$ = .96
Sample Size = 321    Mean = .53    Unadjusted S.D. = .54
Adjusted Sample S.D. = .47    Error RMS = .26    Person Separation = .54/.47 = 1.8
Test Reliability of Person Separation = $1.8^2/(1+1.8^2)$ = .76

shown in Table 8.3a.   This analysis provides two step estimates $d_{i1}$ and $d_{i2}$ for each item.   On the far right of Table 8.3a the fit of each item to the Partial Credit model is summarized in an item fit statistic $t_i$.

The item step estimates in Table 8.3a define three category probability curves for each item in the knowledge-of-physics test.   The probability curves for Item *1* are shown at the top of Figure 8.3a.   These curves describe the estimated probabilities of succeeding on the *first*, *second* and *third* tries at Item *1*.   The item step estimates $d_{i1} = -.64$ and $d_{i2} = -1.75$ are located at the intersections of these curves.

In our dichotomous analyses of performances on Item *1* we considered first the difficulty of getting Item *1* correct in *one* try, and then the difficulty of getting Item *1* correct in *two* tries.   This pair of difficulties can also be inferred from the results of the (012) analysis.   To show how this is done, we have redrawn the category '2' curve (Right-First-Try) at the bottom of Figure 8.3a.   The $p = 0.5$ intercept of this ogive provides an estimate $g_{i2}$ of the difficulty of getting Item *1* correct on the *first* try.   To obtain a second ogive which describes the probability

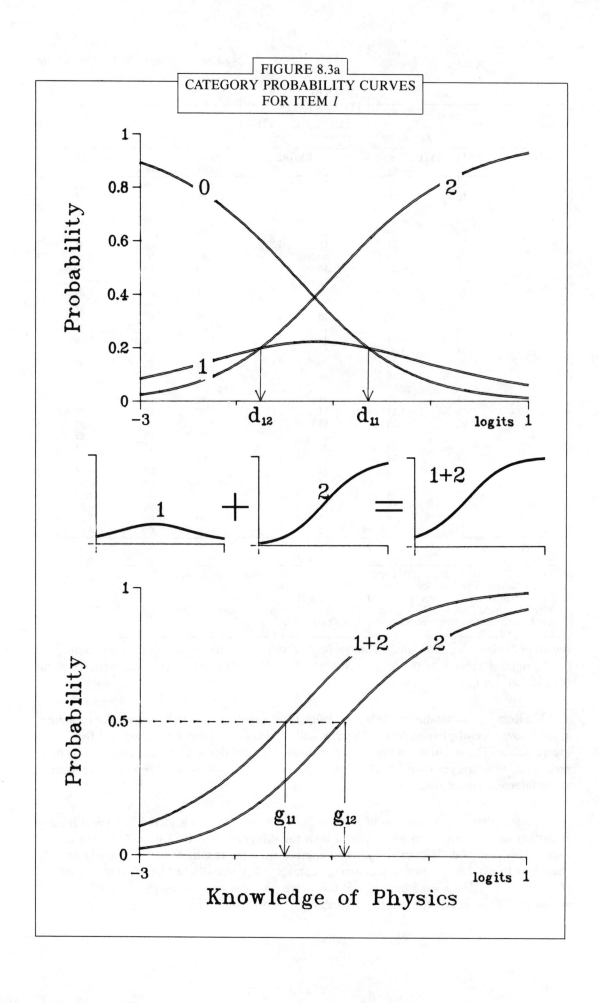

FIGURE 8.3a
CATEGORY PROBABILITY CURVES
FOR ITEM *1*

Knowledge of Physics

of succeeding on either the first *or* second try at Item *1* we have summed the curves for categories '1' and '2'. This is shown in the middle of Figure 8.3a. The resulting cumulative ogive is also shown at the bottom of Figure 8.3a. Its $p = 0.5$ intercept provides an estimate $g_{i1}$ of the difficulty of getting Item *1* correct in *two* tries which we can compare with our estimate from the (011) analysis.

Figure 8.3a brings out a fundamental feature of the Rasch approach to analyzing ordered response category data. Thurstone began his approach to analyzing rating scale data with the bottom picture in Figure 8.3a and modelled the probability of scoring *k or better* on item *i* in terms of the locations of these cumulative ogives. This is also the approach taken by Samejima (1969). Her Graded Response model is written in terms of the ordered item parameters defined by the $p = 0.5$ intercepts at the bottom of Figure 8.3a. When the model is written in these parameters rather than in item steps, however, the person and item parameters in the model *cannot be separated*. This means that the Thurstone-Samejima Graded Response model does *not* belong to the class of models developed in Chapter 3 which enable objective measurement.

The Partial Credit model begins with a simple logistic expression for the probability of completing each step in an item, that is, the probability of scoring 1 rather than 0, 2 rather than 1, and so on. It is these "step" difficulties which then define the intersections of the response category probability curves shown at the top of Figure 8.3a. While this approach does not model the *g* statistics directly, the cumulative ogives shown at the bottom of Figure 8.3a are easy to construct from the curves at the top. The *g* statistics can then be found at the $p = 0.5$ intercept of these cumulative ogives. Item estimates $g_{i1}$ and $g_{i2}$ have been obtained in this way for each of the thirty physics items. These estimates are plotted in Figure 8.3b where the items are sorted by the mean of $g_{i1}$ and $g_{i2}$.

The item estimates displayed in Figure 8.3b are almost identical in pattern to the corresponding estimates obtained from the separate dichotomous analyses of these data (Figure 8.2f). The equivalence of Figures 8.2f and 8.3b shows that the (012) analysis of these data provides the same definition of this knowledge-of-physics variable as the two dichotomous analyses. The thirty items are ordered identically in Figures 8.2f and 8.3b, and in both pictures Items *11*, *7* and *19* are distinguished by their unusual difficulty patterns.

### 8.3.2 Analyzing Item Fit

We have established that the item information obtained from two separate dichotomous analyses of the knowledge-of-physics data can be recovered from an analysis of the (012) data. Our next job is to analyze the fit of these thirty items to the Partial Credit model.

To facilitate the comparison of item fits in the (001), (011) and (012) analyses, we have plotted all ninety fit statistics in Figure 8.3c. The item with the most negative misfit in all three analyses is Item *7* on the left of Figure 8.3c. The other item with a consistently negative misfit is Item *9*. The items with the most positive misfit on the right of Figure 8.3c are Items *29* and *30*, the last two items on the test. We have marked the shift for Item *15*, from fitting reasonably well in the (001) analysis, to fitting poorly in the (011) analysis. Item *29* behaves in the same way.

Figure 8.3d shows that the item fits from the dichotomous analyses appear in the (012) analysis as their average. Items *27*, *16* and *4*, for example, have fit values near $-3$ when

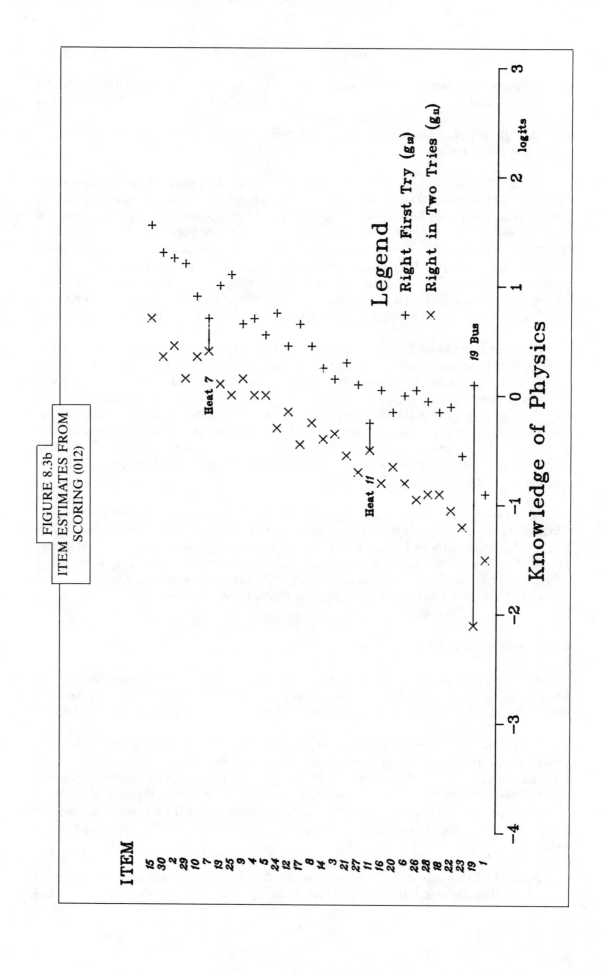

FIGURE 8.3b
ITEM ESTIMATES FROM
SCORING (012)

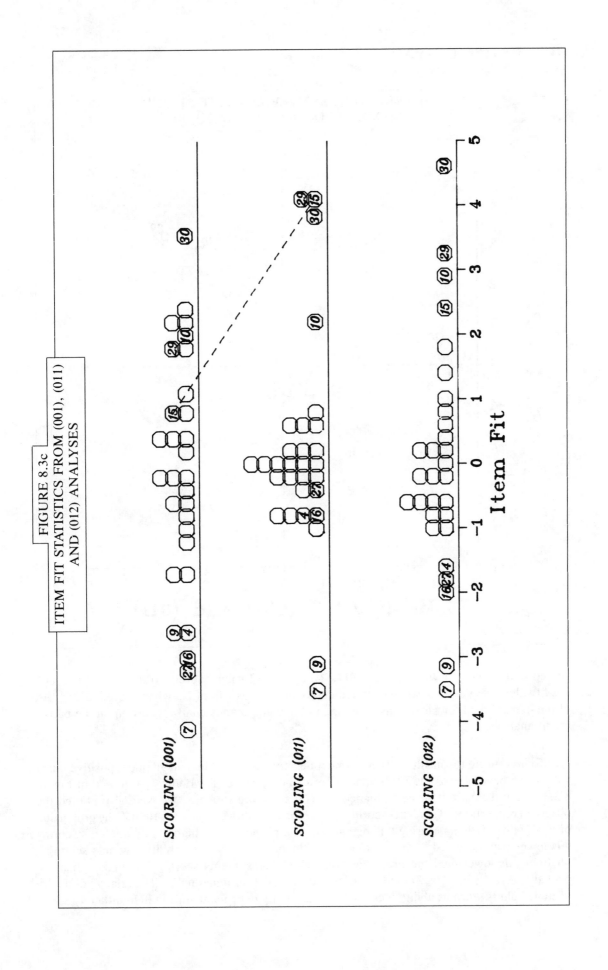

FIGURE 8.3c
ITEM FIT STATISTICS FROM (001), (011)
AND (012) ANALYSES

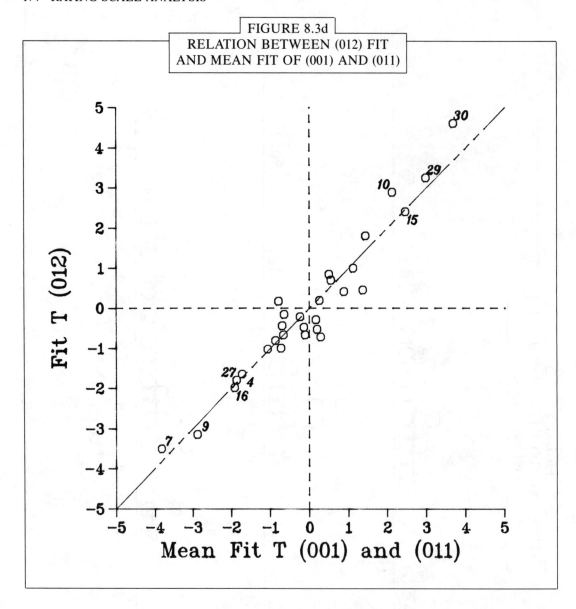

FIGURE 8.3d
RELATION BETWEEN (012) FIT
AND MEAN FIT OF (001) AND (011)

scored (001), near −1 when scored (011), and near −2 when scored (012).  Item *15*, which has fit values of .8 and 4.2 when scored dichotomously, has a fit of 2.5 when scored (012).  All of the items tagged for further investigation in the dichotomous analyses turn up in the partial credit analysis.

To investigate the misfit of Items *7* (most negative misfit value) and *30* (most positive misfit value), we have plotted the (012) analysis probability curves for Items *7, 3* and *30* in Figure 8.3e.  Only the curves for performance levels 0 and 2 are shown.  We have also plotted the observed proportions of students scoring 0 and 2 for six ability strata.  On Item *7*, the proportion of low ability students scoring 0 is higher, and the proportion of high ability students scoring 0 is lower than expected.  At the same time, the proportion of low ability students scoring 2 on Item *7* is lower, and the proportion of high ability students scoring 2 is higher than expected.  As a result, Item *7* could be described as "too discriminating".  The relative difficulty of Item *7* shifts *down* as ability increases.  This ability dependent shift in item difficulty spoils

FIGURE 8.3e
OBSERVED PROPORTIONS AND MODEL PROBABILITIES
FOR ITEMS 7, 3 AND 30
(012) ANALYSIS

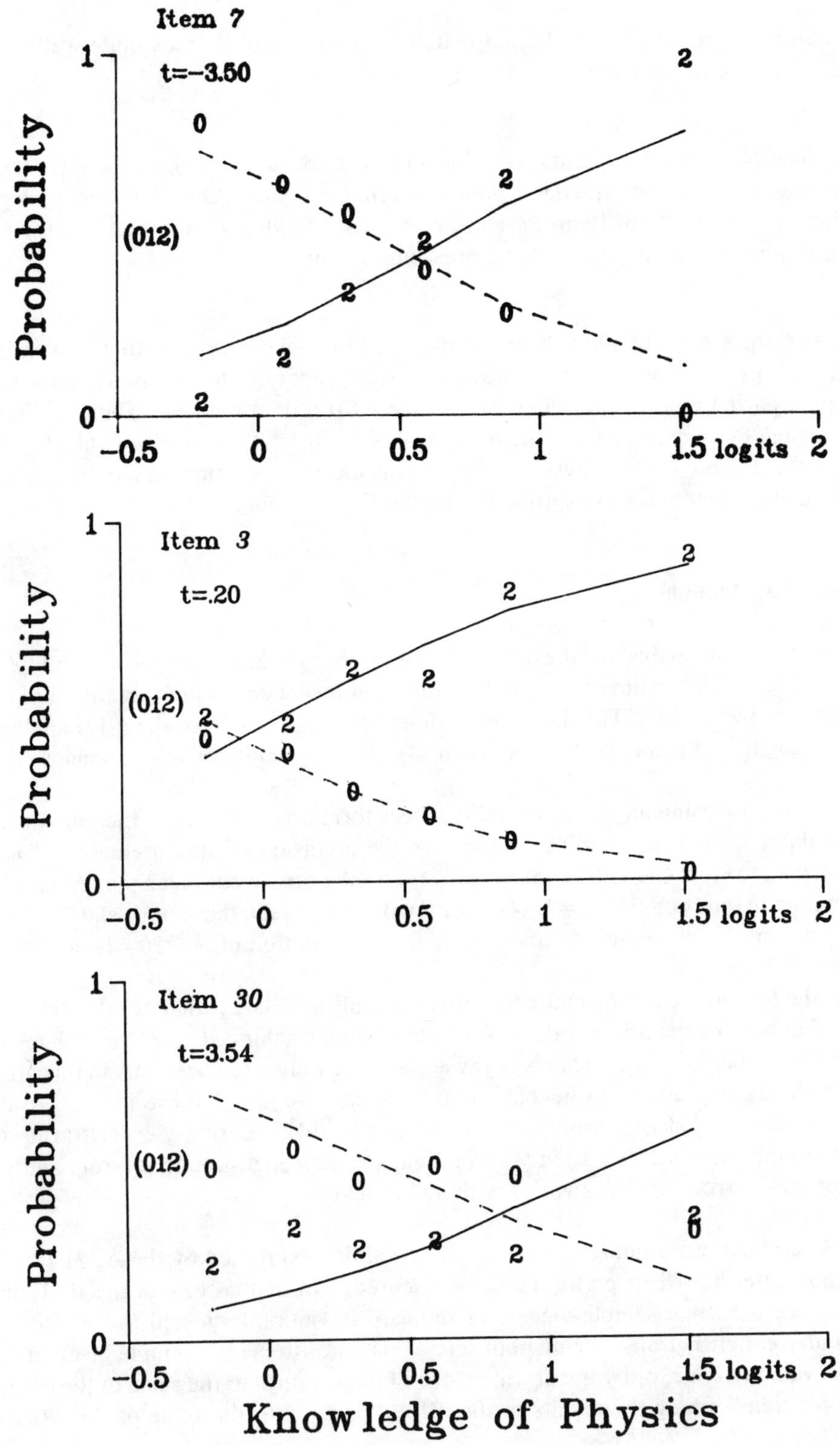

the invariance of item calibration.   The $-3.50$ fit of Item 7 tells us that the way Item 7 measures knowledge of physics is not the same as the way a knowledge-of-physics variable is marked out by the twenty-four items which fit together to provide its general definition.

The observed proportions for Item 3 match the model probabilities quite well.   This has produced a fit close to the expected value of zero.

On Item 30, low ability students score higher than expected and high ability students score lower.   Item 30 could be described as "poorly discriminating".   As we have noted, a plausible explanation for the misfits of Items 30 and 29, the last two items on the test, is the presence of some last minute guessing by students pressed for time.

Figures 8.3b, 8.3c, 8.3d and 8.3e show that everything we were able to discover about the functioning of these knowledge-of-physics items from separate dichotomous analyses is also exposed by a partial credit analysis of the complete (012) data matrix.   The cumulative item difficulty estimates calculated from the (012) analysis (Figure 8.3b) are equivalent to the estimates from the dichotomous analyses, and the items identified as misfitting in the dichotomous analyses are also identified as misfitting the Partial Credit model.

### 8.3.3 Estimating Abilities

The partial credit analysis of these knowledge-of-physics data provides *one* ability estimate for each student.   This estimate is based on the total test score, which, in this sample, takes values between 18 and 57.   The distribution of ability estimates from the (012) analysis has a mean of .53 logits and a standard deviation of .47 after adjusting for measurement error.

One reason for using an Answer-Until-Correct format is to increase the amount of information available from a test, and so, to improve the precision of measurement.   The sample standard deviation from the (001) analysis is .74, and the error root mean square is .43.   This gives a separation index of $.74/.43 = 1.74$.   For the (012) analysis, the sample standard deviation and error root mean square are .47 and .26, giving a separation of $.47/.26 = 1.77$.

While the person separation index for the (012) analysis is larger than for the (001) analysis, indicating that better separation of these students has been achieved, the overall improvement for the whole sample is small.   This is because there are only a few students in this group who are of sufficiently low ability to benefit from a second attempt at these items.   In order to compare the information gathering power of (001) and (012) scoring we must bring the two scorings onto the same scale.   Then we can compare their measurement errors and see how the ratio of these error variances varies with ability level.

We will do this by assuming that the physics abilities expressed by these 321 students are the same no matter how their performances are scored.   In that case, scorings (001) and (012) should produce the same sample mean and standard deviation (adjusted for error).   We can apply this idea either by transforming both sets of statistics to meet a sample mean of zero and standard deviation of one, or by transforming one of the scorings to the scale of the other.   The equations for transforming the results of the (012) scoring onto the scale of the (001) scoring are

$$b'' = 1.58b' - 0.65$$
$$s'' = 1.58s'$$

where $b'$ and $s'$ are the measure and its error given by the (012) analysis, and $b''$ and $s''$ are these estimates expressed on the scale laid out by the (001) analysis.

Figure 8.3f shows how measurement error varies with ability for the (001) and (012) analyses. At abilities above the sample mean, $M$, the measurement errors $s$ and $s''$ are very similar. At abilities below the sample mean, measurement error is smaller for (012) scoring than for (001) scoring. The relative efficiency of (012) over (001) scoring, $E = (s/s'')^2$, is plotted below the measurement error curves. Two standard deviations below the sample mean, marked $W$, the relative efficiency of (012) scoring is 1.5. This means that for students at this ability level, fifteen items scored (001) are needed to obtain the information provided by ten items scored (012).

### 8.3.4 Diagnosing Person Fit

Table 8.3b shows the fit statistics for six of the 321 students. Students *22* and *26* are included because they have the largest positive misfits in the (012) analysis. These two low-

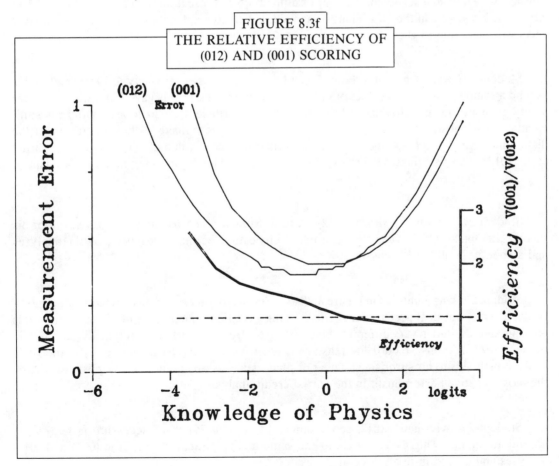

FIGURE 8.3f
THE RELATIVE EFFICIENCY OF
(012) AND (001) SCORING

| TABLE 8.3b |
| :---: |
| ABILITY ESTIMATES AND FIT STATISTICS FOR SIX STUDENTS |

| STUDENT | SCORE | | | RIGHT SECOND TRY | ABILITY | | | | FIT | | |
| :---: | :---: | :---: | :---: | :---: | :---: | :---: | :---: | :---: | :---: | :---: | :---: |
| | 001 | 011 | 012 | | 001 | 011[1] | Mean[2] | 012[3] | 001 | 011 | 012 |
| 22 | 14 | 22 | 36 | 8 | −.15 | −.09 | −.12 | −.13 | 2.94 | 1.71 | 2.60 |
| 26 | 11 | 21 | 32 | 10 | −.62 | −.29 | −.46 | −.48 | 2.79 | 1.97 | 2.35 |
| 211 | 18 | 20 | 38 | 2 | .46 | −.48 | −.01 | .05 | −.41 | −.20 | 1.13 |
| 243 | 15 | 22 | 37 | 7 | .00 | −.09 | −.04 | −.05 | .10 | −.33 | −.08 |
| 201 | 17 | 29 | 46 | 12 | .30 | 2.48 | 1.39 | .84 | −.97 | .14 | −2.58 |
| 237 | 21 | 26 | 47 | 5 | .95 | .89 | .92 | .95 | .55 | .25 | .60 |

[1] Transformed to (001) scale using $b' = 1.06b - 1.36$ where $1.06 = .74/.70$ and $-1.36 = 0.19 - (1.06)(1.46)$
[2] Mean of (001) and (011) ability estimates
[3] Transformed to (001) scale using $b' = 1.58b - 0.65$ where $1.58 = .74/.47$ and $-0.65 = 0.19 - (1.58)(0.53)$

The formula for common person scale equating is

$$b' = (s'/s)b + [m' - (s'/s)m]$$

in which $m$ and $m'$ are sample means and $s$ and $s'$ are sample standard deviations adjusted for measurement error.

scoring students had a surprising number of difficult items correct on their first try, and so, had large positive misfits in the (001) analysis as well. A likely explanation is that their surprising successes were due to guessing.

Student *211* was identified in Figure 8.2h because he was surprisingly *unsuccessful* on his second attempts—only two correct out of twelve second tries. This gave him rather different ability estimates in the (001) and (011) analyses. Nevertheless, his response pattern is sufficiently consistent with the difficulty order of the thirty items to make his fit statistics under the dichotomous analyses (−.4 and −.2) close to their expected value of zero. Only the partial credit (012) analysis brings out his slightly unusual behavior by marking him with a misfit of 1.1.

Student *243* who had a similar (012) score to Student *211* was successful on seven of his second attempts. This gave him comparable ability estimates under the (001) and (011) analyses and a good fit in all three analyses.

Student *201* was identified in Figure 8.2h as surprisingly *successful* on his second attempts—twelve correct out of thirteen second tries. This gave him a high score of 29 under the (011) analysis and resulted in very different ability estimates from the (001) and (011) analyses. While Student *201*'s response record fits reasonably well when analyzed dichotomously, the (012) analysis responds to his surprising number of successful second attempts with a misfit of −2.58, the most negative person misfit in the partial credit analysis.

Student *237* who had a (012) score similar to Student *201* was successful on five of his second attempts. This gave him about the same ability estimates under the (001) and (011) analyses and a good fit in all three analyses.

## 8.4 DISCUSSION

By comparing dichotomous and partial credit analyses of the same data, we have seen that the information obtained by applying the Partial Credit model encompasses the results of separate dichotomous analyses. A single partial credit analysis provides the same definition of the knowledge-of-physics variable as the (001) and (011) analyses combined. When each item's pair of difficulty estimates are averaged, and the thirty items are sorted by these averages, the partial credit and dichotomous analyses provide identical item orderings. Items 7 and 11 are identified as not much easier in two attempts than in one. Item 19 is identified as much easier when a second attempt is allowed.

The partial credit and dichotomous approaches also yield equivalent information about the extent to which these thirty items define a single knowledge-of-physics variable. Items 7 and 9 are identified as "too discriminating" to be positioned unambiguously among the twenty-four best-fitting items. Where these two items stand among the others depends upon the abilities of the students in the calibrating sample. Items 29 and 30, the last items in the test, were also identified as misfitting by both models. It seems likely that last minute guessing spoiled performances on these items.

A disadvantage of the dichotomous approach to multiple response category data is that it requires several separate analyses which must then be compared. A single partial credit analysis yields the same information about item position and fit. An even bigger disadvantage of the dichotomous approach is that it yields several estimates of ability for each person, none of which encompasses their full performance. A partial credit analysis uses all the available information to provide *one* ability estimate for each person. Further, by testing the fit of individuals to the Partial Credit model it is possible to identify not only persons whose performances are inconsistent with the difficulty ordering of the items, but also persons who are surprisingly successful or surprisingly unsuccessful on their second attempts.

Finally, the comparison of measurement errors shows that while dichotomous (001) and answer-until-correct (012) scoring do about equally well among those of high ability who usually succeed on their first try, a partial credit analysis of answer-until-correct scoring is slightly more precise among those of average ability and far more precise among the least able.

# 9   PERFORMANCE OF INFANTS

In this chapter we use our measurement method to analyze performances on some simple cognitive and psychomotor tasks constructed to identify learning problems among prekindergarten children. This screening test (*DIAL*, **D**evelopmental **I**ndicators for the **A**ssessment of **L**earning) was developed by Mardell and Goldenberg (1972, 1975). The *DIAL* users' manual provides a detailed description of four performance levels for each item. In Item *2*, for example, each child is asked to copy a three-block tower, a three-block bridge and a six-block pyramid, in that order. Each new structure is attempted only after the preceding ones have been completed. The four levels of performance on Item *2* are shown in Figure 9.0.

The first step in Item *2* is to score a 1 rather than a 0 by completing a three-block tower. If the tower is completed, the child may try a three-block bridge in an attempt to score a 2 rather than a 1. If the child completes both the tower and the bridge, then he may try a six-block pyramid in an attempt to score a 3 rather than a 2.

We will use the Partial Credit model to analyze performances on fourteen items from the "Fine Motor" and "Cognitive" sections of the *DIAL* test. Our objective will be to construct one ability variable from these items and to measure the abilities of prekindergarten children along this variable. The data are from five-hundred children between two-and-a-half and five-and-a-half years of age observed in Northbrook, Illinois in 1978 under the supervision of Mardell and Goldenberg.*

## 9.1 DEFINING THE ABILITY VARIABLE

The partial credit analysis of these data provides three step estimates $d_{i1}$, $d_{i2}$ and $d_{i3}$ for each item on the *DIAL* test. These estimates, which govern the probability of scoring 1 rather than 0, 2 rather than 1, and 3 rather than 2 on each item, are shown in Table 9.1a together with their calibration errors and a statistic summarizing the fit of each item to the Partial Credit model.

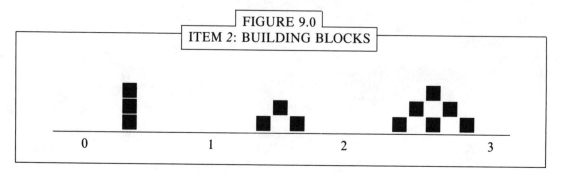

**FIGURE 9.0**
**ITEM *2*: BUILDING BLOCKS**

0        1        2        3

* We are grateful to Carol Mardell and Dorothea Goldenberg for the opportunity to study these data.

TABLE 9.1a

## ITEM STATISTICS FOR *DIAL* SCREENING TEST

| ITEM NAME | STEP ESTIMATES | | | ESTIMATION ERRORS | | | FIT |
|---|---|---|---|---|---|---|---|
| | $d_{i1}$ | $d_{i2}$ | $d_{i3}$ | $s_{i1}$ | $s_{i2}$ | $s_{i3}$ | $t_i$ |
| 1 | −1.33 | −1.28 | −1.03 | .55 | .35 | .18 | −0.21 |
| 2 | −.91 | −.93 | 1.29 | .35 | .21 | .11 | −2.02 |
| 3 | −.91 | .98 | .21 | .26 | .17 | .13 | .48 |
| 4 | −2.25 | 1.21 | 3.47 | .35 | .12 | .12 | −4.81 |
| 5 | −1.34 | 1.72 | 3.40 | .24 | .15 | .12 | −5.28 |
| 6 | 1.81 | 1.07 | 1.46 | .15 | .15 | .12 | 3.79 |
| 7 | .32 | .86 | 2.21 | .18 | .14 | .11 | 1.71 |
| 8 | .58 | .63 | −.49 | .22 | .19 | .15 | −.37 |
| 9 | −1.76 | −.09 | .19 | .41 | .20 | .13 | 1.38 |
| 10 | −2.50 | −.85 | 2.28 | .55 | .19 | .11 | −1.27 |
| 11 | −1.49 | −.83 | 2.66 | .38 | .18 | .11 | 3.33 |
| 12 | −2.20 | −1.33 | −.48 | .67 | .32 | .15 | 1.67 |
| 13 | −2.25 | −1.80 | 1.66 | .65 | .27 | .11 | −.60 |
| 14 | −.54 | −2.11 | .74 | .43 | .30 | .12 | .88 |
| Mean | 0.00 | | | .24 | | | −.10 |
| S.D. | 1.61 | | | .15 | | | 2.65 |

Adjusted Test S.D. = 1.58    Error RMS = .28    Step Separation = 1.58/.28 = 5.5
Sample Reliability of Step Separation = $5.5^2/(1 + 5.5^2)$ = .97
Sample Size = 500    Mean = 2.21    Unadjusted S.D. = 1.43    Adjusted S.D. = 1.30
Error RMS = .60    Person Separation = 1.30/.60 = 2.2
Test Reliability of Person Separation = $2.2^2/(1 + 2.2^2)$ = .82

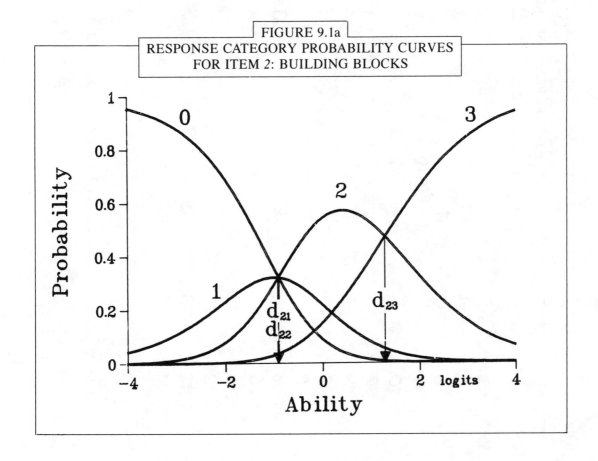

FIGURE 9.1a

## RESPONSE CATEGORY PROBABILITY CURVES FOR ITEM *2*: BUILDING BLOCKS

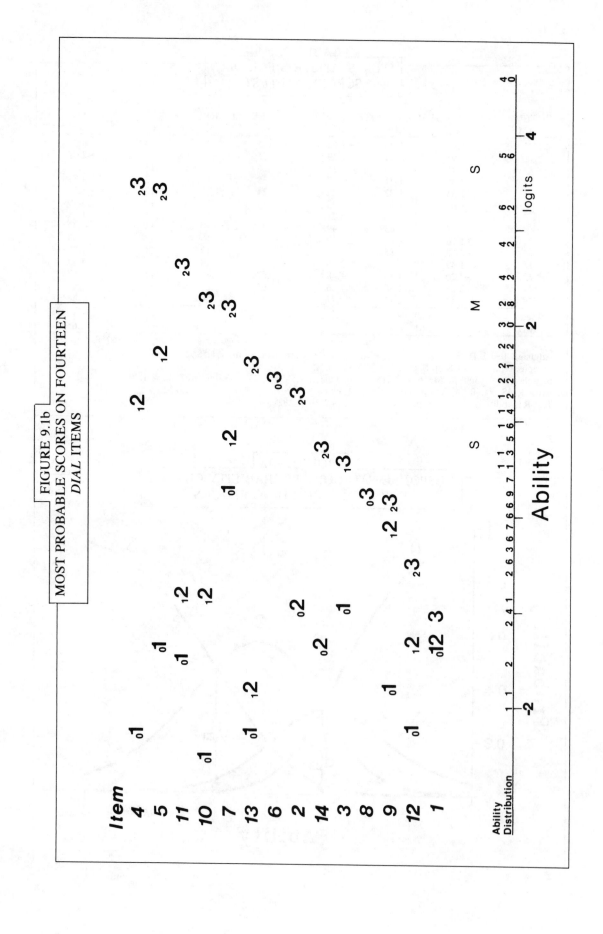

FIGURE 9.1b
MOST PROBABLE SCORES ON FOURTEEN
*DIAL* ITEMS

The three step estimates for each item define a unique set of probability curves for the four performance levels in that item.    Figure 9.1a shows the curves defined by the three step estimates for Item *2* "Building Blocks."    The estimates $d_{21} = -.91$, $d_{22} = -.93$ and $d_{23} = 1.29$ are located at the intersections of successive category probability curves.    These curves show that for children with estimates below $-.92$ logits, the most probable score on Item *2* is a 0.    Children with ability estimates below $-.92$ logits will most likely not even complete the three-block tower.    Children with estimates between $-.92$ logits and 1.29 logits will most probably complete both the three-block tower *and* the three-block bridge to score 2 on Item *2*, and children with ability estimates greater than 1.29 logits will most probably complete all three structures to score 3.    We have used the estimated probability curves for each of these fourteen items to construct Figure 9.1b.

Figure 9.1b shows regions of "most probable score" for each of the fourteen items.    The most probable score on Item *4* "Copying Shapes," for example, is 0 for children with ability estimates to the left of the '1' in the top row of this picture (i.e., for children with estimates below $d_{41} = -2.25$ logits), 1 for children with ability estimates between '1' and '2' ($d_{42} = 1.21$ logits), 2 for children with estimates between '2' and '3' ($d_{43} = 3.47$ logits), and 3 for children with ability estimates to the right of '3'.

The fourteen items have been sorted so that the item easiest to complete for a score of 3 (Item *1*) is at the bottom of Figure 9.1b, and the item hardest to complete (Item *4*) is at the top.    The estimated abilities of the five-hundred children are shown at the bottom of Figure 9.1b.    Most of these items are easy for this group of children to complete.    A child one standard deviation, marked *S*, below the sample mean, for example, is expected to complete the six easiest-to-complete items at the bottom of Figure 9.1b, but to score less than the maximum score of 3 on the other eight items.    A child at the sample mean *M* is expected to complete all but the five hardest-to-complete items, and a child one standard deviation *S* above the mean is expected to complete all fourteen items.

Figure 9.1b shows that some items like *4*, *5*, *11* and *10* cover a wide range of the ability variable defined by these items.    It is relatively easy to complete the first step in each of these four items to score 1.    It is more difficult to complete the second step to score 2, and still more difficult to complete the third step to score 3.    As a result, while low ability children have a good chance of succeeding on the *first* step in these items and scoring 1, only high ability children are likely to *complete* Items *4*, *5*, *11* and *10* to make a score of 3.

Other items cover a much smaller range of the variable.    In Item *1*, for example, there is a very small ability range in which a 1 or a 2 is the most probable score.    Children with ability estimates below $-1.33$ logits will most probably score 0 on Item *1*, while children with estimates above $-1.03$ logits will most probably complete all three steps and score 3.

These differences among items, and hence the ability variable that they define, can be understood by examining the details of the scoring schemes for individual items.    We will study the role the item subtasks play in defining this ability variable by examining the scoring schemes for Items *2*, *4*, *10*, *1* and *8*.

### 9.1.1 Examining Item Subtasks

*Item 2*: **"Building Blocks".** The three subtasks in Item *2* are shown in Figure 9.0. The category probability curves for Item *2* in Figure 9.1a show that the completion of only the first step in this item is a relatively improbable event. Even for children at $-.92$ logits, near the peak of the 1 curve, the probability of completing only one step is less than one third. This is because the first two steps in Item *2* are about equally difficult. A child with a good chance of completing the three-block tower also has a good chance of completing the three block bridge. Because the third step is significantly more difficult than the first two, however, it takes significantly more ability to succeed on this third step. The combined effect of an easy second step and a hard third step makes a score of 0 or 2 more likely than a score of 1 on Item *2*. Figure 9.1a shows that the first two step estimates $d_{21}$ and $d_{22}$ are well to the left of the sample mean $M$, indicating that the first two steps in Item *2* are relatively easy for these children.

*Item 4*: **"Copying Shapes"** In Item *4* each child is shown four shapes: a circle, a cross, a square and a triangle, and asked to copy each shape with a pencil. Three points can be earned on each shape, giving a maximum of twelve points for the item. The four levels of performance are

**Performance Level**

| | 0 | | 1 | | 2 | | 3 |
|---|---|---|---|---|---|---|---|
| | | +1 point | | +5 points | | +4 points | |
| Total Points Needed | 0 | ⟶ | 1 | ⟶ | 6 | ⟶ | 10 |

The DIAL instructions for scoring performances on each shape are shown in Figure 9.1c. A child who makes "no response" to a shape earns no points. One point is earned for simply marking the paper (e.g., scribbling). Two points are earned for a rough, but recognizable copy of the shape, and three points are earned for an accurate copy.

When the points earned on all four shapes are summed and converted to scores of 0 to 3, we see that to score 1 on Item *4* a child needs only *one* point. This can be earned by marking the paper *once* in response to any of the four shapes. This is an extremely easy first step, and should be failed only by children who do not cooperate. To score 2 on Item *4* a child must earn at least six points. This requires three points (accuracy) on at least one shape, or two points (recognizability) on at least two shapes, and so, defines a much higher level of functioning than scribbling. Finally, to score 3 on Item *4* a child must earn at least ten points, e.g., three points (accuracy) on two shapes and two points (recognizability) on two shapes. This requires a relatively high degree of coordination, and defines a rather high level of functioning.

The probability curves for Item *4* are shown in Figure 9.1d. These curves are different from the curves for Item *2* (Figure 9.1a) in that there is now a wide range of abilities for which 1 is the most probable score. In Item *2* the first two steps are about equally easy, and so, the probability of completing *only* the first step in Item *2* is never high. In Item *4*, however, the first step is very easy and the second step is relatively hard. For children with estimates between $d_{41} = -2.25$ logits and $d_{42} = +1.21$ logits, the most probable outcome on Item *4* is the completion of only the *first* step.

We can use Items *2* and *4* to begin to lay out the variable we are trying to construct. In Figure 9.1e we summarize what we have learned about this variable from Items *2* and *4*. The

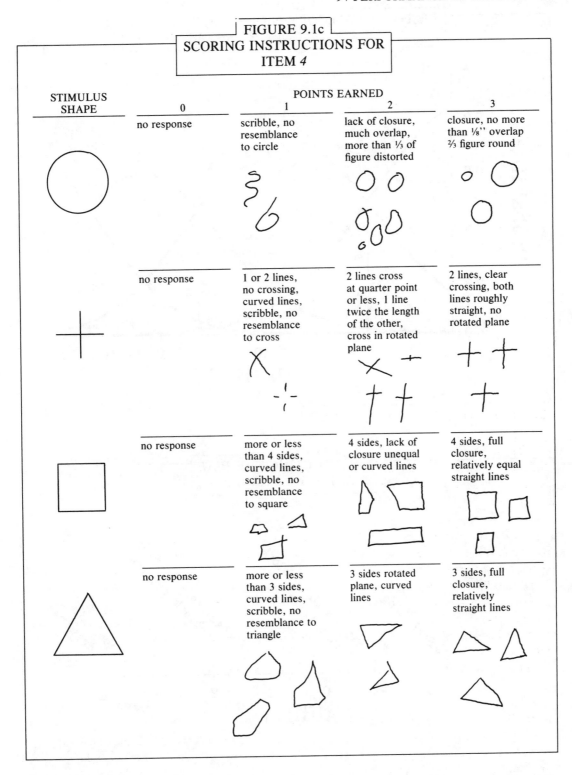

FIGURE 9.1c
SCORING INSTRUCTIONS FOR
ITEM *4*

step estimates for these two items divide the ability continuum into five regions.   Children with estimates above $-2.25$ logits, but below $-.92$ logits, will most probably score 1 on Item *4* (make some attempt at copying at least one shape), but 0 on Item *2* (fail simple three block structures).   Children with abilities between $-.92$ logits and 1.21 logits will most probably score 2 on Item *2* (build simple three-block structures like the tower and the bridge).   Children

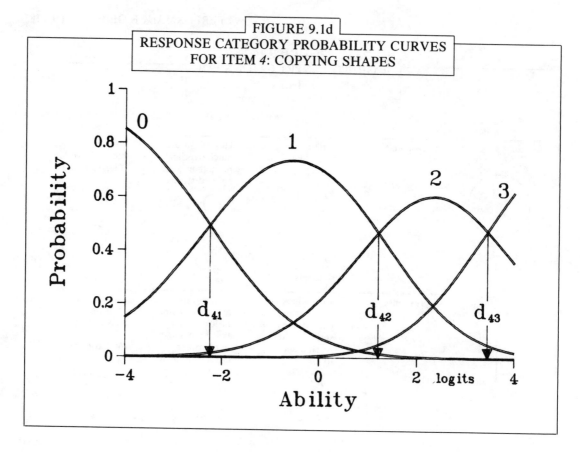

FIGURE 9.1d
RESPONSE CATEGORY PROBABILITY CURVES
FOR ITEM *4*: COPYING SHAPES

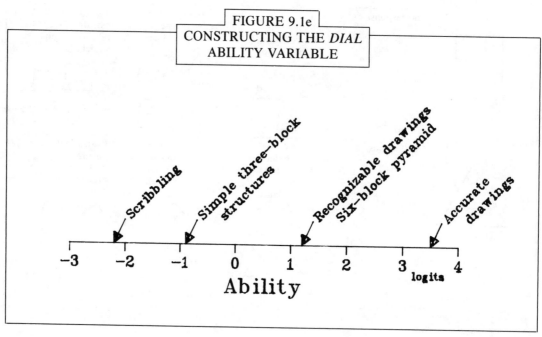

FIGURE 9.1e
CONSTRUCTING THE *DIAL*
ABILITY VARIABLE

with estimates between 1.21 logits and 3.47 logits will most probably score 2 on Item *4* (draw rough but recognizable copies of simple shapes), and 3 on Item *2* (build six-block structures like the pyramid), while children with estimates above 3.47 logits will most probably score 3 on both items (make accurate copies of simple shapes).

**Item 10: "Counting".**   In Item *10* each child is asked to count to eight and then to take one, three and five blocks from a pile of blocks.   The highest number the child counts to (maximum = 8), and the highest number of blocks taken from the pile (maximum = 5) are added to give a maximum of thirteen points on Item *10*.   The four performance levels are

|  | **Performance Level** | | | |
|---|---|---|---|---|
|  | **0** | **1** | **2** | **3** |
| Total Points Needed | 0 —— +1 point ——→ 1 | | —— +4 points ——→ 5 | —— +8 points ——→ 13 |

To score 1 on Item *10* a child needs only one point.   This can be earned either by saying the word "one", or by taking one block from the pile when asked.   This should be a very easy first step.   The second step is to earn four more points to make a total of five.   A child can score 2 on Item *10* by counting to "four" and taking one block from the pile.   The third step is to earn all eight remaining points.   A child scores 3 on Item *10* by counting to "eight" and taking one, three and five blocks from the pile when asked.

The estimated difficulties of the steps in Item *10* are $d_{10,1} = -2.50$, $d_{10,2} = -.85$ and $d_{10,3} = 2.28$.   The category probability curves they define are given in Figure 9.1f.   These curves show that children with ability estimates greater than $-2.50$ logits will most probably score 1 on Item *10*.   Children with estimates greater than $-.85$ logits will most probably score 2, and children with estimates greater than 2.28 logits will most probably score 3.

Once again we see that because the first step in Item *10* is so easy and the third step so hard, there is a wide range of abilities for which a 1 or a 2 is the most probable score.   However, the first two steps in Item *10* are very easy for these children.   Only the harder third step with its difficulty near the sample mean is effective in differentiating among the abilities of this group of children.

**Item 1: "Matching Shapes".**   In Item *1* each child is provided with the ten shapes

and asked to match each shape to a shape on a design.   The shapes are handed to the child in the above order, and the item ends if the child fails to match three consecutive shapes.

The four levels of performance are

|  | **Performance Level** | | | |
|---|---|---|---|---|
|  | **0** | **1** | **2** | **3** |
| Total Number of Shapes Matched | 0 —— +1 shape ——→ 1 | | —— +3 shapes ——→ 4 | —— +4 shapes ——→ 8 |

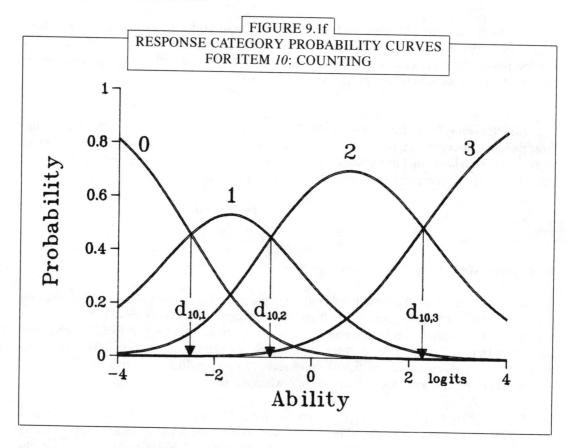

FIGURE 9.1f
RESPONSE CATEGORY PROBABILITY CURVES
FOR ITEM *10*: COUNTING

The first step is completed as soon as the child matches one shape.   The second step is to match another three shapes, and the third step is to match four more shapes to make a total of at least eight.

The step estimates for Item *1* are $d_{11} = -1.33$, $d_{12} = -1.28$ and $d_{13} = -1.03$.   When examined in the light of their standard errors, these three estimates are not significantly different from each other.   This implies that a child with a good chance of completing the first step in this item also has a good chance of completing the second and third steps.

Because the three steps in Item *1* are about equally difficult, the matching of only one shape (performance level 1), and the matching of only four shapes (performance level 2) are relatively improbable events.   This can be seen in Figure 9.1g.   According to the category probability curves for this item, children with abilities below $-1.33$ logits will most likely make a 0 (i.e., not match even one shape), while children with abilities above $-1.21$ logits will probably make a 3 (i.e., match eight or more shapes).   The positions of *M* and *S* show that all three steps in Item *1* are easy for the children in this group.

***Item 8*: "Sorting Blocks".**   In Item *8* each child is given a pile of twenty-four blocks and asked to arrange the blocks into six squares, each of a different color.   One point is awarded for identifying and grouping four blocks of the same color.   An additional point is awarded if the four blocks are arranged in a square.   Since six squares are possible, this gives a maximum of twelve points on the item.

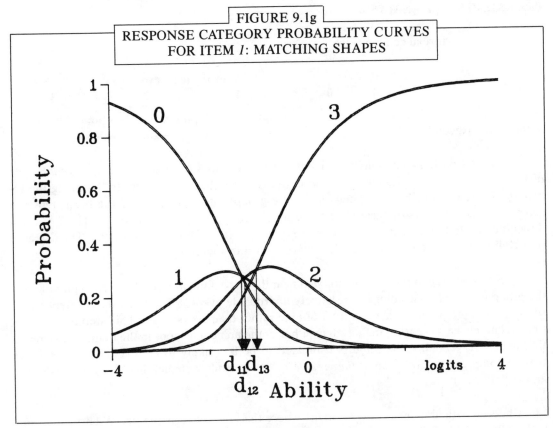

FIGURE 9.1g
RESPONSE CATEGORY PROBABILITY CURVES
FOR ITEM *1*: MATCHING SHAPES

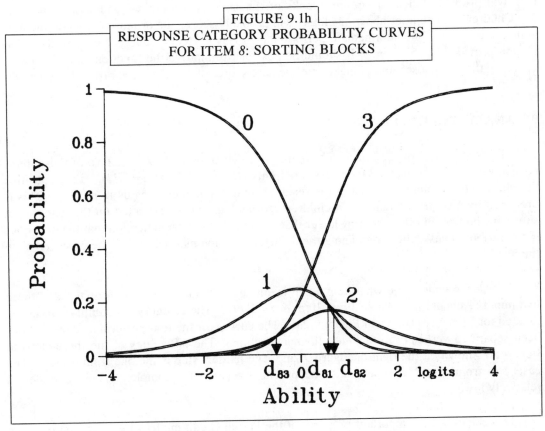

FIGURE 9.1h
RESPONSE CATEGORY PROBABILITY CURVES
FOR ITEM *8*: SORTING BLOCKS

The four performance levels are

|  | **Performance Level** | | | |
|---|---|---|---|---|
|  | **0** | **1** | **2** | **3** |
| Total Points Needed | | | | |

$$0 \xrightarrow{\text{+1 point}} 1 \xrightarrow{\text{+5 points}} 6 \xrightarrow{\text{+3 points}} 9$$

To score 1 on Item *8* a child must identify any four blocks of the same color from the pile of twenty-four blocks. The second step is to score another five points (by grouping the remaining five colors, or by arranging some color groups into squares), and the third step is to score three more points (by arranging three more color groups into squares). The estimated difficulties of the three steps in this item are $d_{81} = .58$, $d_{82} = .63$ and $d_{83} = -.49$. The category probability curves these difficulties define are shown in Figure 9.1h.

The second step in this item is not significantly more difficult than the first, signifying that the grouping of only one color is a relatively improbable event. The third step in Item *8* is to score three more points to make a total of nine rather than six points. This step is estimated to be relatively easy—easier, in fact, than either of the preceding steps in the item. This means that under the model, every child is estimated to be less likely to complete the second step than to complete the third step, *if they reach it*. As a result, completing only two steps is also an unlikely event.

Children with abilities below .24 logits where the '0' curve crosses the '3' curve in Figure 9.1h will probably fail to group any blocks of the same color, and so, will score 0 on Item *8*. Children with abilities above .24 logits will probably score nine or more points on the item and so make a 3. The intermediate performance levels in Item *8* add very little to the information provided by this item. It should be possible to improve the functioning of Item *8* by changing the scoring scheme to make intermediate scores of 1 and 2 more probable outcomes.

## 9.2 ANALYZING ITEM FIT

The fit statistics for the fourteen *DIAL* items are given in Table 9.1a. Two of these items have fit values greater than +3.0. These are Items *6* ($t = 3.79$) and *11* ($t = 3.33$). Large positive fit values indicate more variation in the residuals than the model leads us to expect. This is produced by a surprising number of children scoring higher than expected on the item, and a surprising number of others scoring lower than expected. It is an indication that the item does not contribute consistently to defining the ability dimension marked out by the other items on the test.

In order to understand what item misfit means we will analyze the performances of these five hundred children on worst fitting Item *6* ($t = 3.79$). The category probability curves estimated for Item *6* are shown in Figure 9.2a. The curves for the four performance levels have been separated vertically to facilitate their inspection. The difficulties of the three steps in Item *6* are shown on the right of Figure 9.2a. The hardest step is the one from 0 to 1. The easiest is from 1 to 2. As a result, the probability curve for completing only one step is relatively low.

This brings out an important property of the Partial Credit model—the observed ordering of step difficulties need not resemble in any way the designed order of the response categories (0, 1, 2, 3). The horizontal *ordering* of the category probability curves in Figure 9.2a is fixed

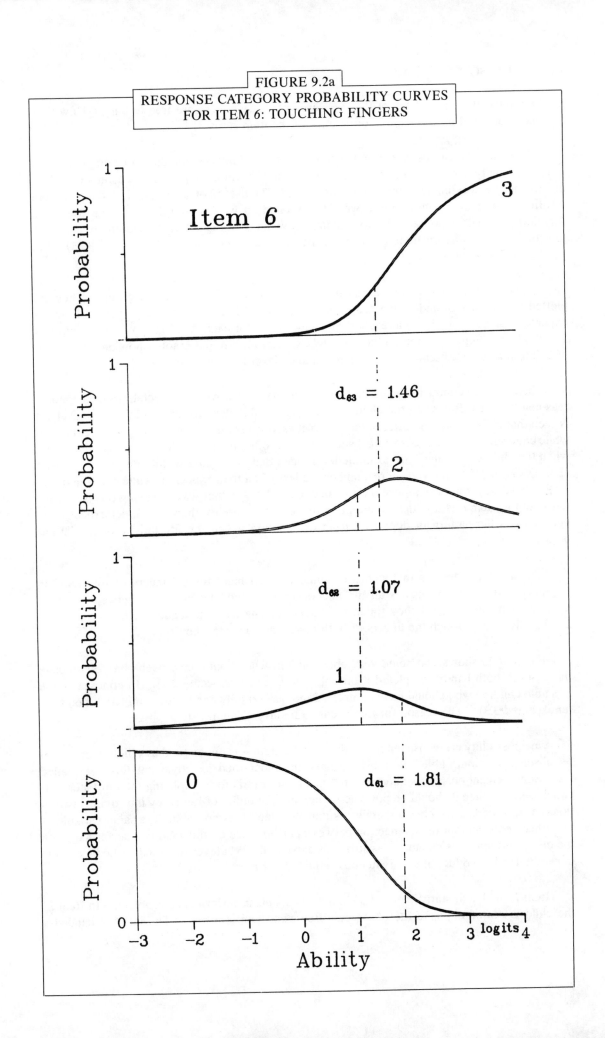

FIGURE 9.2a
RESPONSE CATEGORY PROBABILITY CURVES
FOR ITEM 6: TOUCHING FINGERS

by the model. But the *heights* of these ordered category curves are free to vary. How they vary is determined by the relative difficulties of the item steps.

We can use the curves in Figure 9.2a to read off any child's estimated probability of scoring 0, 1, 2 or 3 on Item 6. A child who scores 35 on the test, for example, has an estimated ability of 2.02 logits and estimated probabilities of .08, .11, .29 and .52 of scoring 0, 1, 2 and 3 on Item 6. In this particular sample there were thirty children who scored 35. We can use these sample-free category probabilities to calculate how many of these thirty children are expected to score 0, 1, 2 and 3 on Item 6. These expected frequencies are $30(.08) = 2.4$, $30(.11) = 3.3$, $30(.29) = 8.7$ and $30(.52) = 15.6$.

Expected frequencies have been calculated in this way for each score group. They are plotted in Figure 9.2b and connected by straight lines. These frequency polygons show the expected number of children at each performance level for each score group of this sample of 500 children. Superimposed on these model expectations are bar graphs showing the number of children actually observed at each performance level for each score group.

The observed counts in Figure 9.2b appear to match the overall expectations of the model reasonably well. But when the children scoring 3 on this item are examined more closely, it is seen that children with abilities *below* 1.5 logits score 3 somewhat more often than expected, while children *above* 1.5 logits score 3 somewhat less often than expected. On the other hand, when the children scoring 2 are examined, it is seen that among these children, it is those with abilities *below* 1.5 logits who score 2 somewhat less often than expected, while children *above* 1.5 logits score 2 somewhat more often than expected. Another way of saying this is that the third step in Item 6 is *less discriminating* with respect to ability than the model expects it to be. This is the pattern of departure from expectation which the fit statistic of $+3.79$ has detected.

The task in Item 6 is to touch the thumb of each hand to the fingers of that hand in sequence. If the child touches all the fingers on one hand, but not in sequence, then they make a 1 on the item. If they touch the fingers of one hand in sequence, then they score 2. Finally, if they touch the fingers of both hands in sequence, they score 3.

Figure 9.2b shows that some very able children who should have been able to complete this task on both hands completed it on only one hand (unexpected 2's). In contrast, some less able children who should have completed the task on only one hand, completed it on both (unexpected 3's). The reason for this needs to be investigated.

One possibility is inconsistencies in the way this item was understood by children or scored by observers. Some able children may have misunderstood exactly what this item called for. Some lenient observers may have relaxed their criteria for completing the third step. If either were so, then it should be possible to increase the utility of Item 6 by improving instructions to observers. Another possibility is that this item does not define the same variable as the other items, so that the connection between performance on this task and performance on the other thirteen tasks cannot be as strong as expected. Whatever the reason, the fit statistic of $+3.79$ for Item 6 identifies this item as requiring scrutiny.

Item *11* with a fit statistic of $+3.33$ manifests a similar performance problem. In Item *11* the child is seated opposite the observer. Between them is a box. The child is handed a

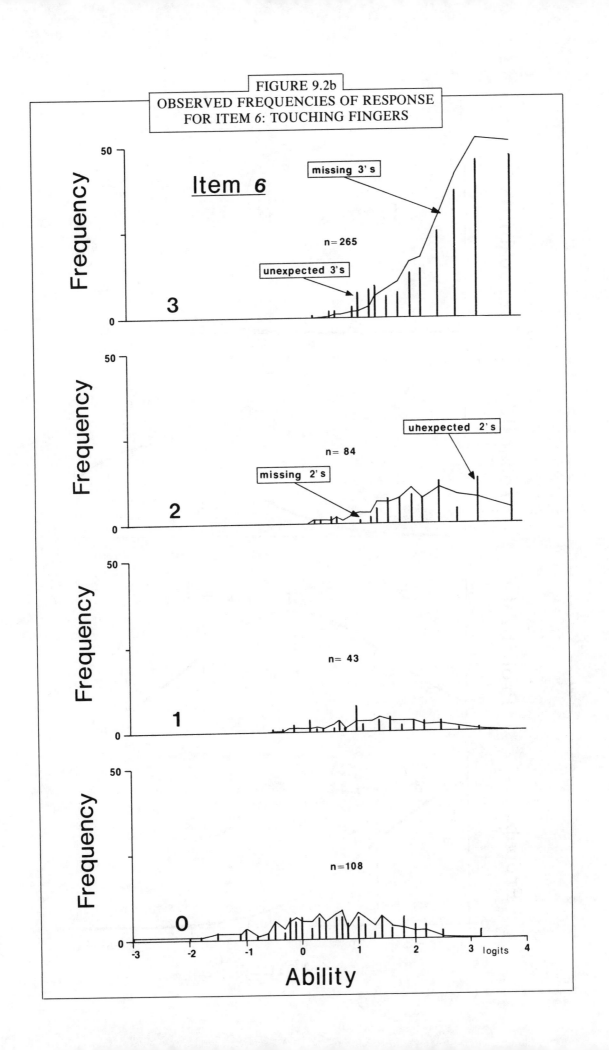

FIGURE 9.2b
OBSERVED FREQUENCIES OF RESPONSE
FOR ITEM 6: TOUCHING FINGERS

Item 6

missing 3's

n = 265

unexpected 3's

3

uhexpected 2's

n = 84

missing 2's

2

n = 43

1

n = 108

0

-3    -2    -1    0    1    2    3  logits  4

Ability

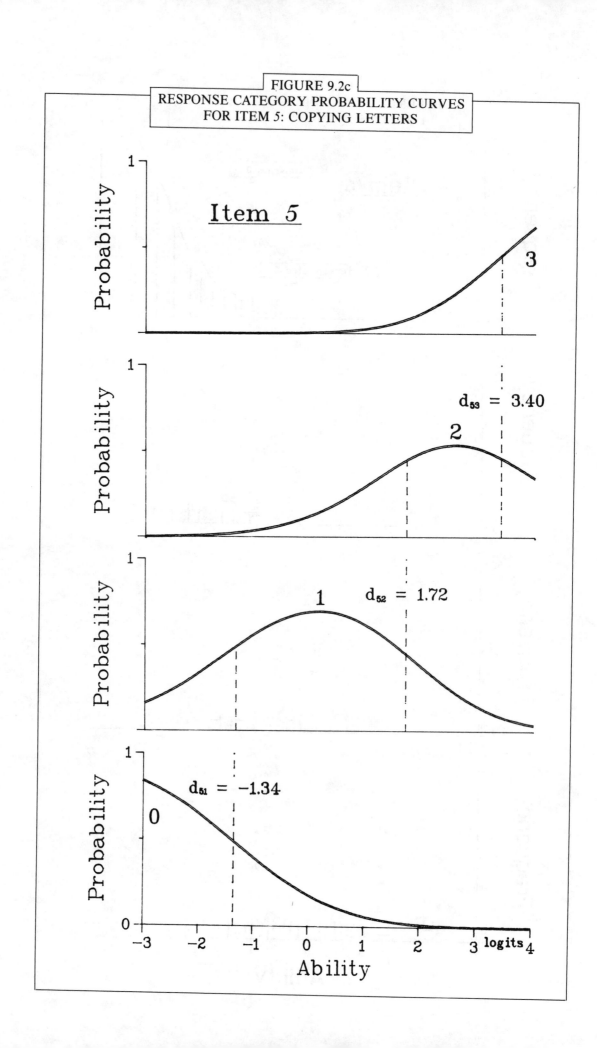

FIGURE 9.2c
RESPONSE CATEGORY PROBABILITY CURVES
FOR ITEM 5: COPYING LETTERS

Item 5

3

$d_{53} = 3.40$

2

$d_{52} = 1.72$

1

$d_{51} = -1.34$

0

Ability

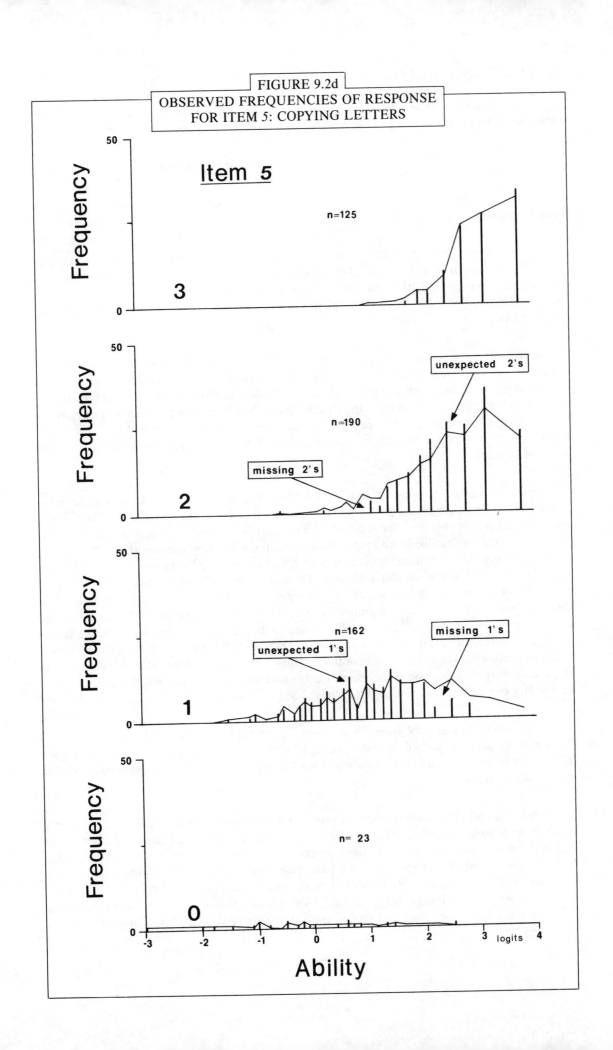

FIGURE 9.2d
OBSERVED FREQUENCIES OF RESPONSE
FOR ITEM 5: COPYING LETTERS

block and is asked to place it *on, under, next to, in front of* and *in back of* the box. The four performance levels are defined by the number of instructions correctly followed

<br>

|  | **Performance Level** | | | |
|---|---|---|---|---|
|  | **0** | **1** | **2** | **3** |

Total Instructions Followed

$$0 \xrightarrow{\ +1\ } 1 \xrightarrow{\ +2\ } 3 \xrightarrow{\ +2\ } 5$$

Of the 500 children, 456 correctly followed at least three instructions, and so, completed the first two steps in Item *11*. But of these 456 children, only 208 correctly followed all five instructions. As a result, the first two steps in Item *11* are estimated to be relatively easy $(d_{11,1} = -1.49, d_{11,2} = -.83)$, and the third step is estimated to be relatively difficult $(d_{11,3} = 2.66)$.

A possible explanation for the misfit of Item *11* is confusion over which side of the box is the "front" and which is the "back". The DIAL manual requires that the block be placed in front of the box from the child's perspective. But older children may realize that the "front" of the box from their perspective is the "back" from the observer's perspective and position the block from the observer's perspective instead. Being older and better able to appreciate the perspectives of others may count against children taking Item *11* and thus account for the misfit of this item.

Two items of the DIAL test, Item *4* $(t = -4.81)$ and Item *5* $(t = -5.28)$ have large negative fit statistics. The category probability curves for Item *5* are shown in Figure 9.2c. First, notice the differences between these curves and the curves for Item *6* in Figure 9.2a. Extreme scores of 0 or 3 are less likely on Item *5* than on Item *6* for every point on the ability continuum. At the same time, in-between scores of 1 and 2 are more likely on Item *5*. This can be understood in terms of the step difficulties for these items. The first step in Item *5* is very easy ($-1.34$ logits) making a score of 0 on this item unlikely except at very low ability levels. The third step in Item *5* is very difficult ($+3.40$ logits) making a score of 3 unlikely except at very high levels of ability. The easy first step and difficult third step in Item *5* make scores of 1 and 2 more likely on Item *5* than on Item *6*. Figures 9.2a and 9.2c show that while there is no connection between the ordering of the response categories and the difficulties of the item steps in the Partial Credit model, there is a direct connection between the heights of the category probability curves and the relative difficulties of the item steps.

Once again, the category probability curves can be used to obtain the number of children in each score group expected to make scores of 0, 1, 2 and 3. These are shown in Figure 9.2d. The numbers of children actually making these scores have been superimposed on the model expectations.

When the 190 children who made a score of 2 on Item *5* are examined it is seen that children with ability estimates above 1.50 logits scored 2 more often than expected, while children with estimates below 1.50 logits scored 2 less often than expected. On the other hand, when the 162 children who scored 1 are examined it is seen that children with ability estimates above 1.50 logits scored 1 less often than expected while children below 1.50 logits scored 1 more often than expected. Another way of saying this is that the second step in Item *5* is *more discriminating* than the model expects. This is the pattern of departures from expectation which the fit statistic of $t = -5.28$ has detected.   It is opposite to the pattern we observed for step 3 in Item 6.

The tasks in Items 4 and 5 are very similar.   In Item 4 each child is asked to copy four shapes, a circle, a cross, a square and a triangle, and in Item 5, to copy four letters E, N, D and S.   The scoring systems for the two items are identical.   If a child makes no attempt at any of the letters in Item 5 they score 0.   If they scribble on any one of the four attempts, they make a 1.   This means that the first step in Item 5 is taken as soon as the child marks the paper.

The second step in Item 5 is estimated to be much more difficult than the first.   To make a 2 on Item 5 two of the child's attempts must resemble the letters being copied.   The third step is estimated to be even more difficult than the second.   To make a 3, two attempts must resemble the letters being copied, and the other two letters must be reasonably well-formed.

Figure 9.2d shows that the misfit of Item 5 is due to more high ability children than expected completing the second step in the item (unexpected 2's), and more low ability children than expected failing the second item step (unexpected 1's).   This could be the result of inconsistencies in the way observers recorded performances on this item.   If so, then it should be possible to control these irregularities by improving the instructions for Items 4 and 5.   Another possibiltiy is that some of the older and generally more able children in this sample have been recently taught the copying skills needed for success on Items 4 and 5.   This would give them an advantage on these items which went beyond their general level of development.   If this were found to be the case, the measuring performance of this screening test could be improved by replacing Items 4 and 5 with items less contaminated by the effects of recent training.

## 9.3 DIAGNOSING MISFITTING RECORDS

We can also examine the performances of children for misfit.   The five children with the largest misfit values are shown in Table 9.3.   The responses of these children are displayed on

## TABLE 9.3
### DIAGNOSING PERSON MISFIT

| CHILD NUMBER | ABILITY $b_n$ | ERROR $s_n$ | FIT $t_n$ | RESPONSES IN ITEM SEQUENCE ORDER | | | | | | | | | | | | | |
|---|---|---|---|---|---|---|---|---|---|---|---|---|---|---|---|---|---|
| 60 | 1.12 | .39 | 3.78 | 3 | 0* | 0* | 0* | 3* | 3 | 2 | 3 | 2 | 3 | 3 | 3 | 3 | 2 |
| 105 | 1.28 | .40 | 3.41 | 3 | 3 | 0* | 1 | 2 | 3 | 2 | 3 | 3 | 3 | 3 | 2* | 3 | 0* |
| 324 | 2.53 | .55 | 3.31 | 3 | 3 | 0* | 3 | 3 | 3 | 1* | 3 | 3 | 3 | 3 | 3 | 3 | 3 |
| 149 | 3.26 | .67 | 3.30 | 3 | 3 | 3 | 3 | 3 | 0* | 3 | 3 | 3 | 3 | 3 | 3 | 3 | 3 |
| 297 | 3.26 | .67 | 3.30 | 3 | 3 | 3 | 3 | 3 | 0* | 3 | 3 | 3 | 3 | 3 | 3 | 3 | 3 |

$$* \mid x_{ni} - E_{ni} \mid / W_{ni}^{1/2} > 2$$

the right of the table, and the scores identified as most surprising are marked with asterisks. Child *60* with an estimated ability of 1.12 logits, for example, made a 3 on Item *1*. This means they matched at least eight shapes to the design in the "Matching Shapes" item. This is not surprising for a child of this ability. But their scores of 0 on the next three items are very surprising. These three 0's mean that they did not complete even the three-block tower in Item *2*, that they did not take even the first step in Item *3* "Cutting Paper" and that they did not even mark the paper in Item *4* "Copying Shapes."

These are surprisingly poor performances for a child of this ability. They become even more surprising when we note that this child then made a perfect score of 3 on Item *5*, "Copying Letters." A child who can complete all three steps in Item *5* should certainly be able to complete all three steps on the easier "Copying Shapes" item. This leads us to be suspicious of this child's performance record. It seems probable that these surprising 0's are missing data or misrecordings that do not represent this child's ability. Whatever the reason, it is doubtful that this child's measure of 1.12 logits is a valid indication of his ability.

The records for the other four children in this table show similar anomalies. Children *149* and *297* would have made perfect scores on this test had it not been for Item *6*, upon which they both scored 0. These two children appear in the bottom right corner of Figure 9.2b. From Figure 9.2a it can be seen that the estimated probability of a child of ability 3.26 logits scoring 0 on Item *6* is very close to zero.

Before we can accept the ability estimates of these five children we must uncover the source of their improbable response patterns and evaluate the diagnostic significance of their unexpected lapses. If they are due to scoring, recording or typing errors, then the ability estimates can be recalculated without the misinformation of these erroneous scores. If they are due to actual lapses in the children's performance, then the implications of these particular lapses must be included in the final evaluation of each child.

# REFERENCES

Allport, F.H. and Hartman, D.A. Measurement and motivation of atypical opinion in a certain group. *American Political Science Review*, 1925, *19*, 735-760.

Andersen, E.B. Asymptotic properties of conditional maximum likelihood estimators. *Journal of the Royal Statistical Society B*, 1970, *32*, 283-301.

Andersen, E.B. The numerical solution of a set of conditional estimation equations. *Journal of the Royal Statistical Society*, 1972, *34*, 42-54.

Andersen, E.B. Conditional inference for multiple choice questionnaires. *British Journal of Mathematical and Statistical Psychology*, 1973, *26*, 31-44.

Andersen, E.B. Sufficient statistics and latent trait models. *Psychometrika*, 1977a, *42*, 69-81.

Andersen, E.B. The logistic model for m answer categories. In W.E. Kempf and B.H. Repp *Mathematical Models for Social Psychology*, Vienna: Hans Huber, 1977b.

Andrich, D. A binomial latent trait model for the study of Likert-style attitude questionnaires. *British Journal of Mathematical and Statistical Psychology*, 1978a, *31*,84-98.

Andrich, D. A rating formulation for ordered response categories. *Psychometrika*, 1978b, *43*, 561-573.

Andrich, D. Scaling attitude items constructed and scored in the Likert tradition. *Educational and Psychological Measurement*, 1978c, *38*, 665-680.

Andrich, D. Application of a psychometric rating model to ordered categories which are scored with successive integers. *Applied Psychological Measurement*, 1978d, *2*, 581-594.

Andrich, D. A model for contingency tables having an ordered response classification. *Biometrics*, 1979, *35*, 403-415.

Andrich, D. Using latent trait measurement models to analyse attitudinal data: A synthesis of viewpoints. In *Proceedings of the Invitational Conference on the Improvement of Measurement in Education and Psychology*, Australian Council for Educational Research, Melbourne, 1980.

Angell, F. On judgements of "like" in discrimination experiments. *American Journal of Psychology*, 1907, *18*, 253-260.

Barndorff-Nielsen, O. *Information and Exponential Families*. New York: John Wiley and Sons, 1978.

Birnbaum, A. Some latent trait models and their use in inferring an examinee's ability. In F. Lord and M. Novick, *Statistical Theories of Mental Test Scores*. Reading: Mass. Addison-Wesley, 1968.

Bock, R.D. Estimating item parameters and latent ability when responses are scored in two or more nominal categories. *Psychometrika*, 1972, *37*, 29-51.

Brogden, H. E. The Rasch model, the law of comparative judgment and additive conjoint measurement. *Psychometrika*, 1977, *42*, 631-634.

Choppin, B.H. An item bank using sample-free calibration. *Nature*, 1968, *219*, 870-872.

Choppin, B.H. *Item Banking and the Monitoring of Achievement*. Slough: National Foundation for Educational Research, 1978.

Cohen, L. Approximate expressions for parameter estimates in the Rasch model. *British Journal of Mathematical and Statistical Psychology*, 1979, *32*, 113-120.

Cronbach, L.J. Response sets and test validity. *Educational and Psychological Measurement*, 1946, *6*, 475-494.

Cronbach, L.J. Further evidence on response sets and test design. *Educational and Psychological Measurement*, 1950, *10*, 3-31.

Douglas, G.A. Conditional maximum-likelihood estimation for a multiplicative binomial response model. *British Journal of Mathematical and Statistical Psychology*, 1978, *31*, 73-83.

Douglas, G.A. Conditional inference in a generic Rasch model. In *Proceedings of the Invitational Conference on the Improvement of Measurement in Education and Psychology*, Australian Council for Educational Research, Melbourne, 1980.

Edwards, A.L. *Techniques of Attitude Scale Construction*, New York: Appleton-Century-Crofts, 1957.

Edwards, A.L. and Thurstone, L.L. An internal consistency check for scale values determined by the method of successive intervals. *Psychometrika*, 1952, *17*, 169-180.

Fisher, R.A. Two new properties of mathematical likelihood. *Proceedings of the Royal Society, A*, 1934, *144*, 285-307.

Gustafsson, J.E. Testing and obtaining fit of data to the Rasch model. *British Journal of Mathematical and Statistical Psychology*, 1980, *33*, 205-233.

Guttman, L. The basis for scalogram analysis. In Stouffer et. al. *Measurement and Prediction*, New York, Wiley, 1950.

Haberman, S. Maximum likelihood estimates in exponential response models. *The Annals of Statistics*, 1977, *5*, 815-841.

Jones, H.L., and Sawyer, M.O. New evaluation instrument. *Journal of Educational Research*, 1949, *42*, 381-385.

Likert, R. A technique for the measurement of attitudes. *Archives of Psychology*, 1932, No. 140.

Luce R.D. and Tukey J.W. Simultaneous conjoint measurement: A new type of fundamental measurement. *Journal of Mathematical Psychology*, 1964, *1*, 1-27.

Lumsden, J. Person reliability. *Applied Psychological Measurement*, 1977, *4*, 477-482.

Mardell, C. and Goldenberg, D.S. *DIAL: Developmental Indicators for the Assessment of Learning*. Highland Park, Ill.: DIAL Inc., 1972.

Mardell, C. and Goldenberg, D.S. For prekindergarten screening information: DIAL. *Journal of Learning Disabilities*, 1975, *8*, 140-147.

Masters, G.N. A Rasch model for rating scales. Doctoral dissertation, University of Chicago, 1980.

Masters, G.N. A Rasch model for partial credit scoring. *Psychometrika*, in press.

Masters, G.N. and Wright, B.D. A model for partial credit scoring. *Research Memorandum No. 31*, MESA Psychometric Laboratory, Department of Education, University of Chicago, 1981.

Perline, R., Wright, B.D. and Wainer, H. The Rasch model as additive conjoint measurement. *Applied Psychological Measurement*, 1979, *3*, 237-256.

Rasch, G. *Probabilistic Models for Some Intelligence and Attainment Tests*. Copenhagen: Danmarks Paedogogiske Institut, 1960 (Chicago: University of Chicago Press, 1980).

Rasch, G. On general laws and the meaning of measurement in psychology. *Proceedings of the Fourth Berkeley Symposium on Mathematical Statistics and Probability*, 1961, 321-333.

Rasch, G. A mathematical theory of objectivity and its consequences for model construction. In *Report from the European Meeting on Statistics, Econometrics and Management Sciences*, Amsterdam, 1968.

Rasch, G. Objektivitet i samfundsvidenskaberne et metodeproblem. Paper presented at the University of Copenhagen, 1972 (mimeo).

Rasch, G. On specific objectivity: An attempt at formalizing the request for generality and validity of scientific statements. *Danish Yearbook of Philosophy*, 1977, *14*, 58-94.

Samejima, F. Estimation of latent ability using a response pattern of graded scores. *Psychometrika, Monograph Supplement No.17*, 1969.

Swisher, J. and Horan, J. Pennsylvania State University evaluation scales. In L.A. Abrams, E.F. Garfield and J.D. Swisher *Accountability in Drug Education: A Model for Evaluation*, Washington, D.C., The Drug Abuse Council, 1973.

Thurstone, L.L. Attitudes can be measured. *American Journal of Sociology*, 1928a, *33*, 529-554.

Thurstone, L.L. The measurement of opinion. *Journal of Abnormal and Social Psychology*, 1928b, *22*, 415-430.

Thurstone, L. L. Measurement of social attitudes. *Journal of Abnormal and Social Psychology*, 1931, *26*, 249-269.

Thurstone, L.L. The measurement of values. *Psychological Review*, 1954, *61*, 47-58.

Thurstone, L.L. and Chave, E.J. *The Measurement of Attitude*. Chicago: University of Chicago Press, 1929.

Wright, B.D. Solving measurement problems with the Rasch model. *Journal of Educational Measurement*, 1977, *14*, 97-116.

Wright, B.D. Afterword in G. Rasch *Probabilistic Models for Some Intelligence and Attainment Tests*. Chicago: University of Chicago Press, 1980.

Wright, B.D. and Douglas, G.A. Conditional versus unconditional procedures for sample-free item analysis. *Educational and Psychological Measurement*, 1977a, *37*, 47-60.

Wright, B.D. and Douglas, G.A. Best procedures for sample-free item analysis. *Applied Psychological Measurement*, 1977b, *1*, 281-294.

Wright, B.D. and Masters, G.N. The measurement of knowledge and attitude. *Research Memorandum No. 30*, MESA Psychometric Laboratory, Department of Education, University of Chicago, 1981.

Wright, B.D. and Panchapakesan, N. A procedure for sample-free item analysis. *Educational and Psychological Measurement*, 1969, *29*, 23-48.

Wright, B.D. and Stone, M.H. *Best Test Design*. Chicago: MESA Press, 1979.

# INDEX

Ability β, *b*
    infant performance   180–198
    physics knowledge   152–179
Additive conjoint measurement   4, 7–8
Additivity   6–10
Ancillarity   6–7
Andrich, David   vi, 38, 49, 51, 199
Answer–until–correct   152–154
Attitude β, *b*   2
    crime fear   137–151
    drugs *for* and *against*   118–136
    science liking   11–32, 61–67, 72, 77
Assessment of performance   180–198

Binomial Trials
    format   50
    model   50–52, 54–59

Calibration δ, *d*   1, 24, 34, 63–65, 69–70, 73–77, 80–89, 90–94
    crime fear   140, 143, 146
    drugs *against*   126, 127
    drugs *for*   124, 127
    errors *s*   66–67, 77, 82, 89
    infant performance   181, 182, 186
    physics knowledge   155, 159, 161, 165, 169, 172
    science liking   62, 67, 73, 78, 102
    validity   91
Cancellation axiom   4, 8
Category boundaries   44–48, 171
Category probability curves   40, 44–45, 47, 55, 81, 97, 128, 130, 139, 156, 163, 170, 175, 181, 186, 188, 189, 191, 194
Choppin, Bruce   vii, 68, 152, 199
*CON* Conditional maximum likelihood   60, 85–86
Concurrent validity   91, 106–111
Conjoint measurement   4, 7–8
Construct validity   vi, 12–15, 90–94, 105
Content validity   vi, 12–15, 91, 94–105
Control lines for identity plots   114–115
Counting steps   3, 5–6, 9–10, 43–48, 50–52, 56, 59
CREDIT computer program   vii, 89
Crime fear   137–151
    calibration   139, 142
    map   140, 143, 146

    questionnaire   138
    response format   137

Data matrices
    drugs *against*   121
    drugs *for*   120
    science liking   18
Developmental assessment   180–198
Diagnosing misfit   108–111, 132–135, 177–178, 197–198
DIAL Developmental Indicators for the Assessment of Learning   180–198
Dichotomous
    analyses   153–167
    format   15–16, 23–24, 38
    model   38–40, 54–59
    scoring   23–27, 153–155
Difficulty δ, *d*   63–65, 69–70, 73–77, 80–94, 155, 159, 161, 165, 169, 172, 181, 182, 186
Discrimination   55, 59, 103–105, 158, 174–176, 179, 192–197
Douglas, Graham   vii, 61, 85, 200
Drugs *for* and *against*   118–136
    calibrations   127
    data matrices   120–121
    maps   124, 126
    questionnaires   118, 119
    response format   118

Efficiency of Partial Credit over Dichotomous   176–179
Errors of calibration and measurement *s*   66–67, 77, 82, 89
Estimation methods   vi, 4, 6–8, 60–89
    *CON*   vi, 60, 85–86
    *PAIR*   vi, 60, 67–72, 82–85
    *PROX*   vi, 60–68, 80–82, 84–85, 89
    *UCON*   vi, 60, 73–80, 86–89
Estimation sufficient   4, 6–8, 59, 75
Expansion factors *X* and *Y*   65–68, 82

Fear of Crime   137–151
Fit   vi, 5, 15, 19–23, 60, 72, 74, 78–79, 90–117
    analysis   90–117
    boxes   110–112
    diagnosing misfit   108–111, 132–135, 177–178, 197–198

item fit  vi, 15, 19–21, 90–91, 94–105, 127, 139, 142, 149–151, 155–164, 169, 171–175, 181, 190–197
mean square $u$, $v$  99–101, 108–109
person fit  vi, 19–23, 31, 90–91, 94–99, 109–111, 132–135, 164–168,176–178, 197–198
residual  98, 108
Fit statistics for a response
    expectation $E$  97, 108
    kurtosis $C$  98, 108
    score residual $y$  98, 108
    standardized residual $z$  99, 109
    variance $W$  98, 108
Fit statistics for a set of responses
    standardized mean square $t$  101, 109
    unweighted mean square $u$  99
    weighted mean square $v$  99–101, 108–109

Graded response model  44–48, 171
Guessing  157–158, 162, 178–179
Guttman scale  4, 19–22

Incomplete data  60, 67–69
Independence  3–4, 6
Infant performance  180–198
Inferential separation  4, 6–7
Invariance  5, 114–117
Item $\delta$, $d$  77
    calibration $d$  63–65, 69–70, 73–77
    construction  3, 184–190
    discrimination  55–59, 103–105, 158, 174–176, 179, 192–197
    error $s$  66–67, 77
    fit $t$  vi, 19–21, 90–91, 94–105, 127, 139, 142, 149–151, 155–164, 169,171–175, 181, 190–197
    operating curve  36, 39, 43, 49, 170
    scale value $d$  102, 127, 139, 155, 161
    separation index $G_I$  92–93, 139, 155, 161
    score S  18, 25–27, 29–30, 36, 154
    steps  3, 5, 39–48, 50–51, 169–171
    step values $d$  142, 169, 181
    strata $H_I$  92–93
    validity  91, 99–105

Judgements of science activities  12–16, 93–94

Knowledge of physics  152–179

Levels  44–48, 171
Linearity and linearizing  2–3, 6–10, 27–37, 61–64

Logits and logistic ogives  6, 10, 28–31, 33–36, 42, 51, 54–55, 59, 64

Map
    crime fear  140, 143, 146
    drugs against  126
    drugs for  124
    infant performance  182, 186
    physics knowledge  159, 165, 172
Mean square residual
    weighted $v$  99–101, 108–109
    unweighted $u$  99
Measurement $\beta$, $b$  1–3, 34, 66–69, 78, 80, 82, 89, 90, 102, 105–108
    attitude  118–151
    crime fear  140, 143, 146
    errors  67–68, 77, 80, 82, 89
    infant performance  182
    knowledge  152–179
    models  v, 3–4, 6–7, 38–59, 102
    performance  180–198
    physics knowledge  159
    requirements  v, 2–4, 7–8, 17–19
    science liking  65, 68
    validity  91
Model  v, 3–4, 6, 7, 38–59, 60, 102
    Binomial Trials  50–52, 54–59
    Dichotomous  38–40, 54–59
    distinguishing properties  54–59
    Partial Credit  40–48, 54–59
    Poisson Counts  52–59
    probability  4
    Rating Scale  48–49, 54–59

Negatively worded statements  129–132
Neutral response alternative  16–17, 129, 133–135
Nonlinearity of scores  27–28, 31–34, 61–64
Normal approximation PROX  61–69, 80–82, 84–85, 89
    Cohen, L.  199
    example  61–65
    vs. PAIR  72–74, 78, 80
    vs. UCON  77–80

Objectivity  1, 6, 59, 68–70, 75, 83, 87
    specific  6–8
Observation  60
    constructing  3
    formats  11–12, 15–17, 40–41, 48, 50, 52, 118, 137, 152–154, 180, 184–190
    modelling  3
Order  2–5, 9, 17, 19
Origin  2, 6, 9, 34, 61–62, 142

PAIR Pairwise calibration  60, 67–72, 82–85

vs. *PROX* 72–74, 78, 80
vs. *UCON* 77–80
Pairwise difference 9
Panchapakesan, Nargis 61, 72
Parameter separability vi, 4, 6, 8, 47–48, 57–59, 68–70, 75, 83, 87, 171
Parameters 1, 4, 6, 60
Partial Credit 3, 40–48, 80–89
    analysis 142–145, 168–176, 180–198
    CREDIT computer program vii, 89
    format 40–41, 152–154, 180
    model 40–48, 54–59
    vs. Dichotomous 176–179
    vs. Rating Scale 145–151
Performance assessment 180–198
Person β, *b*
    ability *b* 159, 164–168, 176–178
    attitude *b* 11–32, 61–65, 72, 77, 118–135, 137–151
    diagnosis 109–111, 132–135, 177–178, 197–198
    fit *t* 19–23, 90–91, 94–99, 109–111, 132–135, 164–168, 176–178, 197–198
    guessing 157–158, 162, 178–179
    measurement *b* 68, 77–78, 82, 89
    score *r* 18, 20, 22, 24–26, 31–33, 35
    separation index $G_P$ 105–107, 139, 142, 155, 161, 169, 181
    strata $H_P$ 106–107
Physics knowledge 152–179
    calibration 155, 161, 169
    map 159, 165, 172
    response format 152–154
Poisson Counts
    format 52
    model 52–59
*PROX* Normal approximation 61–68, 80–82, 84–85, 89
    example 61–65
    vs. *PAIR* 72–74, 78, 80
    vs. *UCON* 77–80

Quality control vi, 90–117
Questionnaires
    crime fear 138
    drugs *against* 119
    drugs *for* 118
    science liking 13

Rasch, Georg vi, 4, 6, 38, 46, 51, 52, 60, 67–68, 171, 200–201
Rasch model 6–10, 38–59
    distinguishing properties 54–59
Rating Scale vi
    analyses 123–129, 138–142
    format 48, 118, 137

model 48–49, 54–59
    vs. Partial Credit 145–151
    SCALE subroutine in CREDIT computer program vii, 89
Reliability 90–92, 105–106, 111–114
Repeated Trials 50–59
Residual
    score *y* 98, 108
    standardized *z* 99, 109
Response
    category probability curves 40, 44–45, 47, 55, 81, 97, 128, 130, 139, 156, 163, 170, 175, 181, 186, 188, 189, 191, 194
    expectation E 97, 108
    Kurtosis C 98, 108
    pattern 129–132, 134, 164, 168, 178, 197–198
    probabilties 129
    set vi, 129–136
    style 23, 135–136
    surprising 19–23, 91, 94–99, 109–111, 132–135, 171–178, 190–198
    validity 91
    variance W 98, 108
Response format 11–12, 15–17
    binomial trials 50
    dichotomous 23–24, 38
    partial credit 40–41, 152–154, 180, 184–190
    poisson counts 52
    rating scale 48, 118, 137

Samejima, F. 44, 171, 201
Sample
    reliability of item separation $R_I$ 92–93, 155, 161, 169, 181
    strata $H_P$ 106–107, 155, 161, 169, 181
    variance adjusted 105, 155, 161, 169, 181
Sample–free item calibration 4–8, 15, 34, 57–59, 63–66
SCALE subroutine in CREDIT computer program vii, 89
Science liking 11–32, 61–67, 72, 77
    calibrations 62, 67, 73, 78, 102
    data matrix 18
    judgements of 12–16, 93–94
    questionnaire 13
    response format 11–12, 15–17, 23–24
Scores and scoring 2, 23–27, 30, 32–36, 42–44, 59, 154, 176–179
Scoring format 11–12, 15–17, 48, 118, 137, 152–154, 180, 184–190
Separability vi, 4, 6, 8, 47–48, 57–59, 68–70, 75, 83, 87, 171

Separating   vi
    items   90–93
    parameters   vi, 4, 6, 8, 47–48, 57–59,
        68–70, 75, 83, 87, 171
    persons   91, 105–106
Standardized mean square $t$   101, 109
Standardized residual $z$   99, 109
Standard errors of calibration and
    measurement $s$   66–67, 77, 82, 89
Step δ, $d$   3, 5, 39–48, 50, 51, 169–171
    calibration $d$   80–94
    discrimation   158, 174–176, 179,
        192–197
    error $s$   82, 89
    scale value $d$   142, 169, 181
    separation index G   142, 169, 181
Sufficiency   4, 6–8, 59, 75
Surprising responses   19–23, 94–99,
    109–111, 132–135, 171–178, 190–198

Test
    reliability of person separation $R_P$
        106–107, 113–114, 155, 161, 169, 181
    strata $H_I$   92–93, 155, 161, 169, 181
    variance adjusted   91–93, 155, 161,
        169, 181
Test–free person measurement   4–8, 34,
    57–59, 66
Tests
    infant performance   184–190
    physics knowledge   152, 157, 159–160,
        166
Thresholds τ, $h$   48–49, 56, 73–77, 79, 81,
    128–130, 135–136, 139–142

Thurstone, L.L.   2, 5, 12–15, 44, 171, 201

UCON Unconditional maximum likelihood
    estimation   60, 72–80, 86–89
        vs. PROX and PAIR   77–80
Unidimensionality   v, 2–3, 8
Unit   1–3, 6–10, 28–37
Unweighted mean square $u$   99

Validity   106, 111, 114
    concurrent   91, 106–111
    concomitant   vi
    construct   vi, 12–15, 90–94, 105
    content   vi, 12–15, 91, 94–105
    item   91, 94–105
    response   19–23, 91, 94–99, 109–111,
        132–135, 171–178, 190–198
    test   114
Variable
    construct validity   vi, 12–16, 90–94
    constructing   v–vi, 1
    content validity   vi, 12–15, 91, 94–105
    defining   vi, 1, 5, 12–15, 24–27, 90–105,
        121–129, 138–147, 158–160, 180–190
    inventing   1
    maintaining   114–117
    unidimensional   v, 2–3, 8
    verifying   90–117

Weighted mean square $v$   99–101, 108–109

$X$ Test spread expansion factor   66, 82
$Y$ Sample spread expansion factor   65, 82

Zero   2, 6, 9, 34, 61–62, 142

# NOTATION

**MODEL**

| | | |
|---|---|---|
| probability | $\pi_{nik}$ | Model probability of Person $n$ responding in category $k$ to Item $i$ |
| | $P_{nik}$ | Estimated probability of Person $n$ responding in category $k$ to Item $i$ |
| | $P_{rik}$ | Estimated probability of a person with test score $r$ responding in category $k$ to Item $i$ |
| person | $\beta_n$ | Ability/attitude of Person $n$ |
| | $b_n$ | Estimated ability/attitude of Person $n$ |
| | $b_r$ | Estimated ability/attitude of a person with score $r$ |
| | $s_n$ | Measurement error |
| item step | $\delta_{ij}$ | Difficulty of $j$'th step in Item $i$ |
| | $d_{ij}$ | Estimated difficulty of $j$'th step in Item $i$ |
| | $s_{ij}$ | Calibration error |
| item | $\delta_i$ | Scale value of item $i$ |
| | $d_i$ | Estimated scale value of Item $i$ |
| | $s_i$ | Calibration error |
| threshold | $\tau_j$ | Response threshold $j$ |
| | $h_j$ | Estimated response threshold $j$ |
| | $s_j$ | Calibration error |

**DATA**

| | |
|---|---|
| $x_{ni}$ | Response of Person $n$ to Item $i$ |
| $m_i$ | Number of steps in Item $i$ |
| $m$ | Number of thresholds in response format |
| $r_n$ | Test score of Person $n$ |
| $T_{ij}$ | Number of persons responding in category $j$ of Item $i$ |
| $S_{ij}$ | Number of persons responding *in or above* category $j$ of Item $i$ |
| $S_{i+}$ | Sample score of Item $i$ |
| $S_{+j}$ | Sample score of category $j$ |
| $L$ | Number of items |
| $M$ | Number of points on test |
| $N$ | Number of persons |
| $N_r$ | Number of persons with score $r$ |